The
FATE
of
AFRICA

▲▲▲▲▲▲▲▲▲▲▲▲▲▲▲▲Trial
by Fire

Jeremy Harding

SIMON & SCHUSTER
New York • London • Toronto
Sydney • Tokyo • Singapore

SIMON & SCHUSTER
Simon & Schuster Building
Rockefeller Center
1230 Avenue of the Americas
New York, New York 10020

Copyright © 1993 by Jeremy Harding
This is a revised edition of Small Wars, Small Mercies,
originally published in Great Britain
in 1993 by Penguin Books Ltd.
All rights reserved
including the right of reproduction
in whole or in part in any form.
SIMON & SCHUSTER and colophon are
registered trademarks of Simon & Schuster Inc.
Designed by Edith Fowler
Manufactured in the United States of America

10 9 8 7 6 5 4 3 2 1

Library of Congress Cataloging-in-Publication Data

Harding, Jeremy.
  The fate of Africa : trial by fire / Jeremy Harding.
    p. cm.
  Includes bibliographical references and index.
  1. Africa—Politics and government—1960–
  2. Africa—History—Autonomy and indepen-
  dence movements. 3. Insurgency—Africa—
  History—20th century. 4. Africa—History,
  Military. I. Title.
  DT30.5.H36 1993
  960–dc20   93–8287 CIP

ISBN: 0-671-72359-6

Some of the material in this book has appeared, in dif-
ferent format, in articles by the author for African
Concord, Africa Report, The Financial Times,
Gemini News Service, Granta, GQ, The
Guardian (London), The London Review of
Books, and The Weekly Mail (Johannesburg).

ACKNOWLEDGMENTS

▲▲▲▲▲▲▲▲▲▲▲▲

This book is heavily indebted, except for errors of fact or judgment, which are mine. Above all, I must thank Ewan Smith and Mary-Kay Wilmers for making sense of the manuscript in the first place. I would also like to thank my editors at Simon & Schuster, Alice Mayhew and Eric Steel. Scrutiny and guidance came from Tony Lacey, my English publisher, and from Gill Coleridge, my agent. Yaba Badoe and John Lanchester also cast an improving eye on the text.

Then there are the editors, radio producers, and filmmakers who kept me in Africa: Michael Holman and J. D. F. Jones at *The Financial Times;* Marcelino Komba and Adotey Bing, formerly at *Africa Journal;* Dallas Galvin at Translation Productions; Fidel Odum at *African Concord;* Sammy Okomilo, formerly at Africa Newsfile; Tariq Ali, Darcus Howe, and Maurice Hatton for Bandung Productions; Derek Ingram and Dan Nelson at Gemini News Service; Margaret A. Novicki at *Africa Report;* Michel Proust, formerly at the BBC French African Service; Jean-Victor Nkolo and Robin White at the BBC African Service; Andrew Snell at BBC Television; Adam Low, also formerly at the BBC; Toni Strasburg and Adrian Pennink for Channel Four Television; Bill Buford and Tim Adams at *Granta;* Angus MacKinnon at *Granta* and now *GQ;* Mary-Kay Wilmers and Karl Miller at *The London Review of Books;* Anton Harber at *The Weekly Mail* (Johannesburg); and Patrick Smith, now at Africa Confidential.

I would like to acknowledge the help of many journalists: In Mozambique, Fernando Gonçalves, António Gumende, Gil Lauriciano, Rachel Waterhouse, Karl Maier, and Paul Fauvet; in South Africa, Kenneth Manona, the late Nat Diseko, Julian Borger, Mike Wooldridge, Howard Barrel, Eddie Koch, and Rian Malan; in Western Sahara, Rizu Hamid, Angela Cobbina, John Howe, and Nelson Smith; elsewhere in Africa, Simon Bright, Ahmed Said Hassan, Katia Iorola, Bob Jobbins and the late Godwin Matatu. Advice and assistance have also come from many individuals, neither journalists nor publishers, among them Osei Kofi, Senai Kifleyesus, Joaquim Segurado, Chip Lyons, Claire Gerhard, Iain Levine, Roger Naumann, James Firebrace, Margie Robertson, Jim Wilson, Ilse Fischer, and Par and Kari Alvim.

Thanks are also due to the guides I was assigned by liberation movements, or by chance. Throughout this book I refer to them as minders, a term that more adequately describes the guardians to whom one is both captive and companion in many parts of Africa: givers and takers away of access in a world through which there is no routine passage.

CONTENTS

NAMES OF PLACES
AND PEOPLE

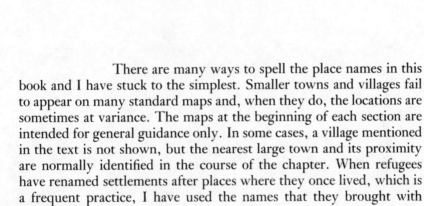

There are many ways to spell the place names in this book and I have stuck to the simplest. Smaller towns and villages fail to appear on many standard maps and, when they do, the locations are sometimes at variance. The maps at the beginning of each section are intended for general guidance only. In some cases, a village mentioned in the text is not shown, but the nearest large town and its proximity are normally identified in the course of the chapter. When refugees have renamed settlements after places where they once lived, which is a frequent practice, I have used the names that they brought with them.

Many names of people have been changed, usually by request. Transliterations of Tigrinya and Amharic names are a matter of personal taste. They are given as people wrote them down; so are transliterations from Arabic.

I also know, and so do you, that in the past, as well as in the present, there have been many anonymous heroic actions among us. But not everything we have done has been heroic.

Sembène Ousmane, White Genesis

You cannot expect from me a full account of my journey. I fail to mention many interesting or celebrated things, because they have made only a slight impression on me. I wish to remain free and to describe solely that which strikes me forcibly.

Marquis de Custine

INTRODUCTION

▲▲▲▲▲▲▲▲

At any given time in Africa, there are several areas of conflict that we might expect to read about in the news, or see on television. No sooner does one war come to an end than another seems to take its place, sometimes in the same country, sometimes in a neighboring state. Between 1960 and the time of writing not a day has passed without fighting in some part of the Horn of Africa. When peace was signed in Angola in 1991, the country had been at war for thirty years; by 1993 fighting had resumed. Some wars, like the one in Sudan, have deep ethnic and religious roots and threaten to end in genocide or partition but never, quite simply, to end. Minor skirmishes in border areas, more serious outbursts of interethnic bloodshed and even quite large wars fought with armor and air power are almost institutions on the continent. One of the most familiar images of political expression is the young man, or even the child, carrying an assault rifle.

Until the mid-1980s, Uganda was the epitome of African war: perplexing to an outsider, apparently fruitless, apparently insoluble; then came Mozambique, Liberia, Somalia. There is almost always a model of this kind that rises out of Africa to throw a shadow at the margins of our consciousness. Around it stands an array of lesser conflicts, or ones to which we pay less attention—often for historical reasons, or because they do not coincide with the news values of the day. Chad, Western Sahara, Senegal, Angola, Burundi, Djibouti and large parts of Ethiopia were among the places where conflict flared up, or merely simmered, in the 1980s.

This book is not a survey of war in Africa. It deals with six countries plagued by armed conflict and the problems that come with it: displacement, alienation, the spread of hunger and poverty, and the rise of a culture of violence. In each case, one superpower and sometimes both contributed to the intractability of these problems by putting their geostrategic interests above the welfare of ordinary Africans. All six countries—or strictly speaking, territories, since there are those that are not fully recognized as states—are also places in which national liberation was still an issue in the closing stages of the Cold War.

By national liberation I mean the struggle for fully independent African nations, free of colonial, imperial or white minority rule—an ideal that gathered momentum after the Second World War and, following the success of armed resistance in Algeria, led many movements to take up arms during the 1960s in pursuit of their ambitions. The first objective of national liberation—self-determination—should have been achieved many years ago, but in two countries, Mozambique and Angola, independence was merely the signal for a new and far more serious challenge to national liberation than colonial rule. Still other liberation movements remained under arms in conflicts deadlocked by the Cold War. How this deadlock was broken at the end of the 1980s and why the "new world order" of the 1990s gives no indemnity against more fragmentary kinds of violence are subjects that take up much of this book.

There is also material about military campaigns that have influenced the course of things in the various countries I write about. Unless you are a general or a medical orderly, war looks much the same from one part of Africa to the next. It is determined by factors beyond the field—which may be a front line or a blank stretch of bush or an impoverished township—yet it takes on a life of its own. Gunfire and bombardment are only the most obvious affirmations of this life: they are the finery that war puts on for formal occasions, vesting itself with a frightening authority. But it goes about its routine business of disabling civilian culture with less ceremony and more diligence. In Africa, or the parts of Africa I know, this process of attrition, which can occur far from any front or battlefield, shows war in its element.

As they move from place to place reporting on the effects of conflict in an enormous continent, journalists are often obliged to repeat themselves. But the places about which we say the same things are in fact quite different—or at least, they were, before the mantle of war fell across them. I have tried not to repeat myself too much here. I have also focused on a small number of conflicts—Angola, Namibia, Western Sahara, South Africa, Mozambique and Eritrea—in the belief that it is better to return to a place, with the aim of discovering more, than to stay on the move retelling the same story in a string of different territories.

In most of the countries where I worked at the end of the 1980s, the chances of peace seemed better than fair, which also influenced my decision to go back to four of them after 1990. I wanted to celebrate the peace along with the new decade. By 1993, however, the majority were still hovering in limbo. Whether one calls it war or peace is a matter of judgment, not of hope. In a continent where violence has for many years been the norm, hope turns swiftly to illusion. It is rash to expect too much in Africa, but the constant downward adjustment of one's expectations is dangerous too, for it leads to false economies in the realm of principle, notably on issues of human and political rights, which war and bad government have already pared to the bone.

Each chapter tells the story of a single country—and by no means all of that. What I have set down is determined by the places I was able to get to, the length of time I could spend in them and the people I met. As a rule, the further I strayed from a capital city the more material I would find. I often suspected that this principle was a good one and, over the last three years, I have tried to stay away from the offices of ministers and dignitaries in the belief that it is more important to hear from men and women who have no portfolios to defend. With the exception of Namibia, which I visited only once, each of the chapters is based on two journeys, sometimes three, in the country concerned.

In retracing my steps, I also found myself going back over the past of these countries, in hope of understanding the origins of their turmoil. But I worked as a journalist in Africa, not a historian, and made my fitful living from the present, with very few column inches to spare for anything that was not news. I often wondered how a reader would make sense of my reports without the same background that I had scratched together in order to write them. Rather than ask the same question again here, I have written at length about the origins of conflict in each country. I hope that readers will find it helpful next time they see a report about one of the countries concerned. But they should be warned: there are few archives in Africa and even fewer touchstones. History is transmitted by word of mouth and, with so much of the continent under arms, the past becomes a ground of endless contention and reinterpretation. In this respect, Africa is no different from our own continents—but the stakes are higher.

When I set out on the journeys described in this book, I shared to a large extent in the belief that peace would fill the vacuum left by the withdrawal of the superpowers. I was certainly more gullible than many other journalists I knew, though not on this point: the view that the superpowers were adding to Africa's woes with bad policies, enforced by client governments propped up by weapons and credit, was common enough. I worked for half a dozen editors, mostly in London and Lagos, and sometimes with documentary film crews. Late in the day, I wanted to report on the unfinished business of national liberation in Africa.

Gradually I made my way to Eritrea, Western Sahara, Mozambique, Angola, Namibia and the townships of South Africa, where wars against white minority rule, superpower coercion and African imperialism—the annexation of a former colony by a neighboring state—were still in progress. In setting out, my sympathies lay with movements like the African National Congress, rather than their adversaries. To most of my editors, I was embarking on assignments to report on "small wars" that deserved coverage of a judicious kind and we were able to make common cause.

The phrase "small wars" has often been used to describe conflicts in Africa. And there are standards by which they may indeed be small. Poverty and sickness have a firm hold in countries where unrest and political violence are familiar, but not war as such. The difficulty of getting by in any number of African states is so severe that, in order to continue at all, most human activity is thrown onto a kind of war footing. Many states remain damaged by debt, which is a serious contender with war and famine for its pound of flesh. In 1985, a year of somber "negative imagery" in Africa, the continent's debt repayments were roughly double what it received in emergency aid for the famines. With indebtedness to the IMF comes "structural adjustment," the package of reforms that forces debtor nations to devalue their currencies and cut back on minimal public provision, typically in health, education and food subsidies. The cuts made by indebted African regimes in order to "adjust" during the 1980s were reckoned by UNICEF, the United Nations Children's Fund, to have cost the lives of a million children over the decade. Such estimates in Africa can be deeply misleading, but there is a core of truth here: that the entanglement with lending institutions—a decision taken by political elites in Africa, not by the governed—has had much the same effect on the poor as armed conflict and epidemic disease.

In their own right, however, the wars of the 1980s were not so trifling. It is true, compared to the two world wars, they did not claim drastic numbers of lives; nor was there the same intensity of destruction, but they were spread over many more years and visited ruin on millions of civilians, especially in Angola, Mozambique and Eritrea. There was incremental ruin too in the land, on which most people depended. In covering "small wars," I was looking largely at their effects on civilian life, which were immense. In the end, it is these things that matter. In Africa, war tends to impose three extremely serious conditions on those who are caught in it. The first is idleness, which takes hold like a wasting disease as people can no longer graze their livestock or tend their fields. The second is congestion: they seek refuge, or are forcibly resettled, in sanctuaries, often cities, where they are turned from subsistence farmers into a dispossessed underclass. The third is dependency: they grow reliant on appeals by their governments to foreign donors. In places where war has gone on for a decade or more, this is often the only function that a government is able to fulfill with any competence. By then, the pattern of crisis is already defined as food producers abandon food production and swell the cities to which they should be selling their surplus. It only needs a drought or a military offensive for thousands of people to be thrown from absolute poverty into a state of grave short-term risk.

A good deal of foreign journalism in Africa has to do with human suffering, beating a familiar path to refugee camps, feeding centers, hospitals and mass funerals. Most reporters are uncomfortable with these tours of purgatory, even if they serve a purpose, but it is wrong to shrink from writing about what one has seen. Seeing is not the whole business of believing, however, and the belief that there may be something more than an interminable epic of despair in Africa is important. If war brings out the worst in governments and nations, it is not the way with all their citizens. There is another story in "war-torn" Africa, of people contriving to live beyond the wars, or in spite of them, in a rarefied universe of small mercies—mercies that might well have been greater, were it not for the scale of the adversity in which they flourish.

National liberation was supposed to do away with the bulk of African adversity, yet where the small wars continued into the 1980s, it was obvious that history had miscarried fearfully. By 1990, the old liberation struggles, or the ones that lingered on, faced a challenge to the very concept of the nation state that held their hopes in place. The first aim of liberation had been to win independence for the territories carved out by the colonial powers in the 1880s: unsatisfactory though they were, colonial boundaries would form the basis of the newly sovereign states, whose members, irrespective of language or ethnic origins, would become "nationals." It was in many ways a transitional program: the larger dream was of unity beyond colonial borders and, by the early 1960s, of a global democracy, based on a range of Marxisms, most of them qualified or adapted.

The pan-African vision fell drastically short of realization. Many of the national liberation movements, and the newly independent states, were racked by ethnic divisions. Some exponents of the armed struggle would refine their idea of citizenship to exclude their enemies: the Pan-Africanist Congress wanted South Africa for the Africans, not whites; in Angola, Jonas Savimbi and UNITA wanted control of Angola by pure blacks, Ovimbundu preferably, rather than people of mixed descent. On the whole, the larger idea of nationhood prevailed, along with the belief that it was rash to tamper with colonial boundaries.

It is an irony, but perhaps no coincidence, that the ANC was unbanned and made ready to negotiate a nonracial democratic South Africa at a time when the very idea of multi-ethnic, unitary states fell into disrepute in eastern Europe and the Soviet republics. In many ways it was the republican ideal of nationhood—broad and inclusive—that Mandela bore through the gates of Victor Verster prison on February 11, 1990, into a world that had called that very proposition into question. He greeted the crowds and television cameras "in the name of peace, democracy and freedom for all," intent on the grand themes that had informed the modern nations of Europe. Namibia's independence, a few weeks later, was one of the last tributes to those themes in Africa. The other took place in Eritrea. For thirty years the Eritreans had fought for the idea that nine ethnic groups, defined by the old colonial borders, amounted to a nation. As they celebrated in Asmara, Somalia was tearing itself apart a few hundred miles to the south. In its hour of victory, Eritrea too was like an elder stepping from the shadows of a long confinement, only to discover that the light of day was dimmer.

Most of these journeys were made after Mandela's release, at the end of a period in which national liberation had been the prevailing idea. I wanted to record what had happened to people in the closing stages of the liberation wars and also to describe what some of these places were like, how they looked and felt, in a period of change. I have also said a good deal about earlier visits, when the older adversarial structures were still in place. I have done so especially in the case of Angola, where the South African withdrawal from Cuito Cuanavale was a turning point in the region. Angola's obsession with the past runs very deep, which is one reason why an outsider can feel puzzled and hostile. I have not tried to hide my own reactions. I have set down a lengthy version of events between 1961 and 1976, a period that holds the country captive to this day. Without some sense of those years, which will still be a source of controversy to Angolans after the century is out, it is hard to grasp why Jonas Savimbi should be so mistrusted, or why his first response to his party's defeat in the elections of 1992 was to retire to the central highlands while his fighters went on the rampage.

National liberation gave a moral language to the disputes in Africa and, whether one agreed with it or not, it was part of its business to simplify the issues. Colonialism and minority rule stood on one side, the cause of political and human rights ("communism" in Cold War vocabulary) on the other. The heroic period of liberation is over but the legacy persists. Legitimate grievance and the right to bear arms are as easily invoked by the new, freelance warrior in Africa as they were by the national movements. And they are desirable assets in the de-regulated markets of armed struggle, which thrive on cheap weaponry from exhausted or disbanded Cold War armies. In the right hands, the gun confers absolute legitimacy, while grievance is left to take care of itself.

There is a danger, certainly, that the opportunity which arose for peace in 1990—the era of the "new world disorder" as it has become known—cannot be grasped with sufficient confidence, and that the old wars of position, fought with money from Washington or armor from Moscow, will begin to look like "good old wars," whose fronts followed the clean moral contours of the African freedom struggle. That they were muddled and cruel, and needlessly protracted by the superpowers, will be glossed over. That would be as dangerous as forgetting that they had been fought at all.

"Anybody can imagine war," wrote the journalist Martha Gellhorn, "there is nothing arcane about it. It happens to people one by one"—which is a useful way to hear them out. I hope that people and places will speak for themselves; that they can make themselves heard above the massive rhetorical clash of the Cold War, whose echo still rings in the ears of millions of Africans. The sounds of armed conflict are easy to record, and are easily heard; but we must listen more attentively to know what its survivors have to say, and what has become of them.

GABON

CONGO

Brazzaville

Kinshasa
(ex Leopoldville)

ZAÏRE
(formerly Belgian Congo)

Cabinda

Quimbele

UÍGE

Luanda • Caxito

Catete

ATLANTIC
OCEAN

ANGOLA

Luena

Lumbala
Kaquengue

Lobito

Huambo

Benguela

Kuito (Bié)

MOXICO

Cangamba

Lumbala
N'guimbo

Menongue

Lubango

Cuito Cuanavale

ZAMBIA

CUANDO CUBANGO

Mavinga

Cunene river

Xangongo

NAMIBIA

BOTSWANA

Jamba (Savimbi's base area 1976–92)

Benguela railway

0   km   400

0   miles   200

1

ANGOLA

▲▲▲▲▲

A train
climbing from a difficult African vale
creaking and creaking
slow and absurd

It shrills and shrills . . .

Many lives
have drenched the land
where the rails lie
crushed under the weight of the engine
and the din of the third class . . .

Slow absurd and cruel
the African train . . .

Agostinho Neto, *African Train*

Nothing is lost in history, and every action, every policy, finds
its adequate reward in later events, not, to be sure, in the
moral, but in the political sense.

Franz Borkenau, *The Spanish Cockpit*

Angola was a hidden country for most of the
1980s. Even at the hottest part of the day, it could evoke a northern
winter. Color and tone were subdued, as they would be under a lamina
of frost; people seemed swathed in a copious, insulating privacy. Angola's unseasonal disorder was war. By the mid-1980s, this ample
quadrant of southern Africa, nearly half a million square miles, was
scored with military fronts and patched with no-go areas. Unlike many
of the wars on the continent, the Angolan conflict had a formal aspect,

with large deployments of troops on both sides and regular campaigns in which the government tried to flush out the rebels in the south.

It was one of the hardest countries in Africa to report from. Day and night in the capital, Luanda, you heard the war effort in the air above you, as planes ferried troops and supplies from one place to another; and it was a fact of life on the streets, where there were so many amputees or enlisted men. Every other form of life seemed on the verge of exhaustion; only the war blazed on. If conflict was the most palpable thing about Angola, it had to be reported. But to say anything about it, one needed a clearer view of it, from beyond Lu-anda, and this was not easy: the government was slow to let most journalists see what was happening in the rest of the country. All movement in the provinces was strictly controlled; the chances of an enterprising dash from Luanda without proper papers and a minder were nil. And if permission and facilities were granted for a journey outside the capital, there was no guarantee that the war would disclose anything more than its own monotonous logic.

I did get away from Luanda in 1988 and south to the fronts. Traveling by helicopter to a town at the center of the fighting, I found myself gazing down from a height of sixty meters at a column of military matériel that ran for well over a mile: armored cars, tanks, trucks with mounted machine guns, mortars and towed artillery; a few miles further south, even more equipment was deployed. I knew the extent of the Soviet commitment in Angola as a set of figures on paper, but I only grasped it properly at that moment. I would see nothing comparable until nearly three years later, traveling in northern Eritrea, where a similarly large array of Russian armor lay in twisted ruins, running back from the neck of a narrow mountain pass. The amount of weaponry that Moscow had dispensed to African regimes was daunting.

The war in Angola was a lavish show of strength by the providers on each side. The Soviet Union made plenty of heavy equipment and up-to-date air power available to the government. Cuba dispatched thousands of troops. The "free world" (apartheid generously included) gave the rebels training and high-technology weapons; South Africa fought alongside them. The build-up of forces behind two separate ideas of the subcontinent—capitalist or collectivist, pro- or anti-apartheid—turned the country into a moral testing ground; and be-cause Angola had been forced to argue the case with firepower, the news from the fronts became a convenient way of judging how things stood with the dispute.

During the heaviest phases of the fighting, there were a dozen other conflicts in Africa, but few had the moral weight of the Angolan war. From the outset, in the mid-1970s, Angola was an object of international liberal sympathy and ferocious conservative energy. A cause that set a belligerent Henry Kissinger on one side and a lyrical Gabriel García Márquez on the other was unusual in Africa. Thousands of miles away, it was easy to identify the issues at stake, or to imagine that one could. In degree at least, Angola inflamed the same kinds of passions among observers as the war in Southeast Asia and, once the main liberation movement took power in 1975, striking analogies were drawn with the beleaguered Spanish Republic of the 1930s. South Africa's support for the rebels was compared to that of the Axis for the Spanish Fascists. By its own reckoning, somewhat more modest, the MPLA government stood for the right of Angolans to throw off the legacy of Portuguese colonialism and determine their own future. Anyone who opposed them could be accused of hostility toward the fundamental ideals of postcolonial society, not merely in Angola but throughout Africa.

Reporting from Angola was partisan. Many who were flown in from South Africa to see the rebel UNITA stronghold in the south came away with unstinting praise for its commander, Jonas Savimbi, urging continued support from Washington for his "anticommunist" crusade. Others who went in with the government tended to play down the inability of the ruling party to provide for those areas of the country that were firmly in its control. The government did not set much store by public relations. It treated the rank and file of sympathetic reporters with Spartan contempt. Maddening though it could be, there was something impressive about its reluctance to lift a finger on behalf of the press. It had the war against South Africa to fight and seemed to regard this as its best bona fide.

If the Cold War reduced Angola's troubles to a set of stark moral issues, apartheid's involvement made the picture clearer still. After independence, the government of Angola could claim that its citizens were suffering for its own principled opposition to apartheid. It gave bases and material support to the ANC and the liberation movement of Namibia, which was fighting against South African rule in its own country. In return, Angola bore the brunt of Pretoria's anger. The United States stood with South Africa and the rebels; Moscow and Havana with the government of Angola. By 1988 Castro had fifty thousand Cubans fighting for the government. In Havana, amid deepening unpopularity, he argued the case for a just war against apartheid.

By 1988 he claimed to have won it, at the town of Cuito Cuanavale in southern Angola, where the government and the Cubans had held off a large South African force and their Angolan rebel allies for nine months, finally forcing South Africa out of Angola. The truth was probably more nuanced. Perestroika and the end of high Soviet expenditure in Africa had much to do with it. So did sanctions against South Africa, especially the UN arms embargo; these were effective precisely because it cost Pretoria so much to break them. The Reagan administration wished to bury its policy of "constructive engagement" with honor rather than ignominy, and leaned on South Africa to come to terms with the Angolan government. Even so, there was some justification for Fidel's vanity: the South African army did not withdraw from Angola because it was bored, or had better things to do, but because it had failed to make headway against superior numbers and better air power. The end of the argument between apartheid and its regional opponents had been reached and the time had come for something quite new.

I went back to Angola in 1990 to try and tell the story of that new thing. The Cubans were leaving, the Soviet Union was on its way, but the country was still at war. The fighting was fierce and UNITA— Savimbi's movement—was wreaking havoc in the north. This time I was not allowed to the fronts, partly I think because the government was losing ground; partly too, because it could no longer be bothered to organize journeys of that kind. Now that the Cold War was over— and in Africa it ended with the South African withdrawal from Cuito Cuanavale—the mysterious Angolan winter was lifting; there were signs of life beyond conflict: the parallel markets, or *candongas*, where all types of informal transaction, big or small, took place, were thriving; debate was freer, but there was still an immense preoccupation with the past—with the same recriminations that the rival liberation movements had hurled at each other for twenty or thirty years. Within a year, graffiti began appearing in Luanda: "MPLA robbers, UNITA murderers." If the country's future lay with either, there was little to look forward to.

Anger in the present, apprehension about the future: these left the past intact as a powerful force. For many who fought the liberation war against Portugal, the 1960s and 1970s were a period of elation and sacrifice, redeeming a litany of failures, then and afterward; for others, they provide the necessary clues to Angola's difficulties. Long explanations of the past are common in Angola; they are ventured with an intensity that convinced me of the need to set down at least one version. It is the story of liberation in Africa writ large, with an undue share of the bitterness, bloodletting and rivalry that are excised from more summary accounts of the anticolonial struggle and the Cold War era. It is better, I think, to forge a path through the tangle of factions and acronyms than to duck away toward some well-worn generality that fails to explain the defeats that this country has suffered. Angola is an African labyrinth. Going in is difficult enough for an outsider, but for Angolans, it is harder still to find a way out.

Jonas Savimbi and the government signed a comprehensive peace in 1991 and the ceasefire held, with a few violations, for a year and a half. It was time to reckon up the damage. The government claimed that half a million Angolans had died in the conflict. Tens of thousands more had lost limbs on land mines. To defray its own expenses in Angola, the South African Defence Force had slaughtered elephant and run ivory out of the country in large quantities. Savimbi had also topped up his budget with ivory and hardwoods. Fidel's most dependable commander in the field, Division General Arnaldo Ochoa Sánchez, had traded sugar and soft currency for dollars on the *candongas;* he also confessed to obtaining diamonds and ivory in Angola and was accused of involvement in the Colombian drug trade. He was executed in 1989.

Throughout the war the Angolan government had kept a running total of the costs; now they were able to draw a line under the figures: 500,000 dead and two million displaced. There is no way whatever to gauge their accuracy. The government also reckoned that Angola had sustained $30 billion worth of lost production and damage to its infrastructure: roads, railways, lost aircraft, bridges, housing, industrial plant and the like. The Russian federation, meanwhile, was refusing to waive the debt due to the former Soviet Union for its steady contribution to the war effort: Boris Yeltsin wanted $350 million out of Angola's exchequer. There were hidden damages too, of a kind that come with all conflict in Africa: the disruption of small-scale agriculture, on which millions depended, and the rapid flight of rural people from the land. Many youngsters born to peasant families had grown up on the streets of the cities, with a dwindling memory of the countryside. To rectify such a dangerous imbalance could take years.

The project, moreover, presupposed real peace. I was in Mozambique when the Angolan ceasefire was signed and a date set for elections. I watched from South Africa in late 1992 as the ruling party won the legislative ballot and Jonas Savimbi returned to the gun. By 1993 Angola was back at war. Savimbi had never been a democrat; simply a man of many guises. He had courage and persistence, but his greatest talent was that of the shoeshine artist, who could buff the toecaps of his foreign patrons to such brilliance that all they saw when they peered down at his labors was a quickening image of their own glory. And now he had summoned Angola back from the brink of change toward the intolerable waste and hardship that it knew by heart.

During his travels on the coast of Angola, Joachim John Monteiro, an Associate of the Royal Schools of Mines, was struck by the indifference of the local people to pain and death. In an account of his journey, published in 1875, he recalled having come across a young man lying in the middle of a busy market in Luanda. The "thronging crowd" did not notice that the youth was dead. Indeed, this was only ascertained when Monteiro gave the body an inquisitive prod with his foot. "His being covered in flies," Monteiro observed, "was too trivial a circumstance to attract any attention." In Ambrizzette, a fair way up the coast, he met a man who had been badly injured when a gun barrel blew up in his hands. His relatives had brought him in search of a surgeon to amputate the right hand. No doubt the enterprising Monteiro would have been willing to stand in; he had heard from several Portuguese doctors how the natives could withstand surgery without sedation. But he was preempted by a Frenchman, who sent the family off with some bandages and a sharp razor, to perform the operation themselves. An hour later, crossing the town, Monteiro came across the amputee "laughing and joking quite at his ease, with his left hand roasting groundnuts." Not only were Monteiro's Angolans spared the qualms of Christian conscience, they also lived in a paradise of physiological innocence, beyond the irksome reach of their nervous systems.

Had any of this been true, it would have served them well a century later, during their war of liberation against the Portuguese. It was one of the most costly of the modern wars in Africa, for the fighting continued after independence and rose to a pitch at the end of the 1980s. It was civilians above all who suffered; in numbers that were only guessed at, the war deprived them of their homes, their fields and their livestock. The hospitals of Angola were ledgers of far more serious loss, yet even here it was possible to see signs of resilience without celebrating Monteiro's bogus miracle of African insensibility. In 1988, at a clinic in the center of the country, a doctor introduced me to a young mother with her leg in a splint. She was propped up in bed, nursing a newborn child. Celestina was one of the fittest patients in the hospital, thin but not gaunt, with ample milk for the baby. Her leg had been broken by a bullet during a rebel attack on her village. Some of her neighbors, who were also in the ward, had more serious wounds. Celestina's chances of walking again without pain were fair. She was eight months' pregnant at the time of the raid and her child, a girl, was born in the hospital. Mother and daughter, said the doctor, were making progress. As we were leaving, Celestina rebuked me for failing to ask her daughter's name. She had called her Fracturada—meaning "broken"—after the injury that had marked the last month of pregnancy. On the way to his office, the doctor remarked that he could think of no better name for the country itself.

Angola's liberation was a complicated failure; its independence was nominal, mortgaged to outside forces before it was ever proclaimed. Its tribulations, however, were never in doubt. There were times when the country seemed broken beyond repair.

Yet in 1991, the Angolans embarked on the unfamiliar process of peace, with no guarantee that their act of faith would save them from the antagonisms in which they were caught. The ceasefire between the two adversaries was signed in May. The ruling party won elections at the end of 1992, but the losing side cried fraud and redeployed troops that should have been demobilized. Soon after the fighting began, the forces of the ruling party began burying the victims of their own atrocities. Whatever the next step in the peace process, violence seemed a likely form of political expression for as long as Angola held together. "He who has striven," runs a poem by Agostinho Neto, "has not yet lost, but has not yet won." By 1993, the author of these lines, the first president of independent Angola, had been dead for fourteen years, and the old definitions of loss and gain were no longer so useful.

The ruin of Angola was well under way in 1975 on the eve of independence from the Portuguese. With troops from South Africa, Cuba and Zaïre deployed throughout the country, it was already hostage to external forces. For many years previously, three anticolonial movements had been vying bitterly for control. The Movimento Popular de Libertação de Angola (MPLA) was equipped mostly by the Soviet Union along with Cuba, while the United States and China funded the Frente Nacional de Libertação de Angola (FNLA) and the União Nacional para a Independência Total de Angola (UNITA). The MPLA was not much of a military force but it had a big following in the capital and the north, among the Mbundu people. The FNLA drew most of its support from the Bakongo people of the northwest; its leader, Holden Roberto, enjoyed personal and political privileges in neighboring Congo (Zaïre as it had become in 1971) and the FNLA had bases there. UNITA was the youngest of the movements, led by the volatile but astute Ovimbundu politician, Dr. Jonas Savimbi. The Ovimbundu, the largest ethnic group in Angola, were concentrated in the center of the country; without their consent no democratic postcolonial government was possible.

By 1974, when revolution in Portugal made independence inevitable, the prospect of the three factions sharing power was remote.

The rivalry of their foreign backers was increasing; so too were the transfers of arms and money into the country. For their part, the liberation movements had learned to settle their differences with the gun. In negotiations, they were taciturn and suspicious. By the middle of 1975, with the Portuguese withdrawal already in progress, it was clear that matters would be decided by force. Whichever movement could control the capital would win the day. Luanda was the heartland of the MPLA and, after a period of intense street fighting, it drove its main adversary, the FNLA, from the city. UNITA too had retired to the center of the country to review its position. Savimbi responded to the MPLA's success in Luanda by forging an alliance with South Africa. At the time, it was a reckless move, unthinkable even, for in the moral registers of African liberation there was no greater evil than apartheid. Savimbi was a useful ally for South Africa, which had reasons of its own to deplore an orthodox Marxist faction seizing power in Luanda. In his anticolonialism, Savimbi had never been as scrupulous as the rival movements and his popularity among Portuguese settlers was well known, even in Pretoria. A month before independence was due to be declared, a column of South African armor crossed the Namibian border and made its way up the country with UNITA in tow. The South Africans had every intention of entering the capital but they were drawn up short by the first serious show of resistance from a Cuban expeditionary force. Cuban officers had been training MPLA troops in Angola for several months, and Fidel Castro had sent reinforcements in response to the news that South Africa was about to enter the field. The result was a standoff. However, the South Africans were still in the country in November, when the MPLA proclaimed the independence of Angola under its sole leadership. Despite the misgivings of the American business community—the oil companies in particular—Washington refused to recognize the new government, seeing it purely as an instrument of Soviet ambition in Africa.

With Agostinho Neto installed as the president of the People's Republic and Luanda under the control of the MPLA, the collapse of Holden Roberto's movement was only a matter of time. UNITA proved much more resourceful. The Carter administration cut off Savimbi's American support in 1976, but his relationship with the South Africans had already been sealed. Over the next fifteen years, they supplied his guerrilla headquarters in the south, providing combat training and weapons to his army, who in turn became the foot soldiers and, on occasion, the cannon fodder of Pretoria's own war in Angola. The MPLA, for its part, was buttressed by a steady increase of Cuban troops and ample military hardware from the Soviet Union.

South Africa's incursion in 1975 was a show of bravado, but its decision to commit itself for a further fifteen years showed that it did not take the evolution of Angola lightly. The source of anxiety was another liberation struggle, in Namibia, which South Africa had administered since the end of the First World War. The South West Africa People's Organization (SWAPO) was the main liberation movement in Namibia. It took up arms against South Africa in 1966 and sent its guerrillas down into Namibia from camps in Zambia, either directly through the Caprivi Strip or filtering across Angola. The logistics had been difficult. Portugal and South Africa were cooperating closely at that time and SWAPO was involved in regular clashes with the Portuguese army. After the MPLA came to power, however, the picture changed dramatically. Henceforth SWAPO had bases in Angola and better access to Namibia. Strictly speaking, there were two wars being fought in the country: an internationalized civil war between the MPLA and UNITA and a liberation war for Namibia. In fact the ideologies of the various combatants fused these wars into a single conflict. On one side stood the Soviet Union, Cuba, the MPLA, SWAPO and the African National Congress, who were also given bases in Angola; on the other, the United States (which restored Savimbi's funding in 1986), South Africa and UNITA.

But however complex it looked on paper, the war itself was often more perplexing. Many ANC members in Angola objected to fighting UNITA. They were detained in ANC camps for this and for other divergencies. SWAPO supporters, who had roamed freely in Savimbi's territory for several years, were suddenly obliged to do battle with UNITA, once he had thrown in his lot with South Africa. In Marxist parlance, which had become the dominant form of expression under the MPLA, these were "contradictions." But even the most scientific of Angolan Marxists felt that the term was not adequate to explain the full range of anomalies that took hold of the country after 1975. They had a better word: *confusão*, confusion. There was *confusão* in the fact that Savimbi, who railed against the MPLA's white and mixed-race composition, should collaborate openly with the regime that had murdered Steve Biko; there was *confusão* in the fact that Cuban soldiers defended oil installations worked by Texaco and Chevron against sabotage by a group that received its arms and money from the United States, Angola's biggest trading partner. There was still more *confusão* in the fact that Angola had a negligible private sector—it was a workers' state—and at the same time boasted thriving open markets, where you could buy anything from a half liter of palm oil in a rusting Fanta can to a resprayed pickup truck. The informal sector was massive and *candonga* played an important role in Angola's war effort, yet few officials would ever admit to it. By the mid-1980s, outside interests were moving the war along with a momentum of its own and the outcome had become crucial to the evolution of southern Africa as a whole. Such was the country's misfortune.

At the time I was introduced to Fracturada and her mother, the MPLA had been in power for thirteen years and UNITA had been in armed opposition for as long. Angola was a puzzling country. To enter through Luanda, on the government side, was to be cast as a tourist of the revolution, whose Marxism-Leninism was still quite orthodox despite a growing economic liberalism. The MPLA had constituted itself as a workers' party in 1977. The political culture of the capital was closed, hostile, fundamentally sullen. It was difficult to come away with anything of value. Yet it was obvious from the way that minders, bureaucrats and even casual acquaintances spoke that Angola had been running for years on an economy of recrimination, in which the past was the official currency. If you wanted even an inkling of what Angola had become, you had to listen carefully to the way people spoke about its recent history.

▲

It was not easy to persuade Justino Gonçalves to rehearse his part in the anticolonial struggle, although we had met through a mutual friend in the ANC. Justino was not shy; far from it, he was an eloquent man who took an interest in strangers. But he appeared to believe that the past was best forgotten. A bewildering earthworks, thrown up by the ceaseless excavation of Angolan politics, already concealed the present, and Justino feared that by taking this any further, he would obstruct his view of the future. He was one of the few Angolans who was happy to think ahead to peace and reconstruction. This little man with gray hair, a gray mustache and sad brown eyes was a stoic. He could look out over one of the most ravaged countries in Africa, from the edge of a capital city that had become intolerable to all but senior party officials, and smile with satisfaction. His house was a small, ramshackle affair of two stories with a walled courtyard. From one side you could see the beach, corrugated by the heat haze rising off the road that ran in front of it. On most days this strip of pale brown sand was frequented by bands of homeless children, plump Soviet expatriates who shooed them away like dogs, and convalescent soldiers back from the fronts in the southeast and center of the country. The *povo*—"the broad masses," as the government called them— liked to amble down to the beach to swim, or fish, or walk the tideline in search of cans and bottles. From one end of the beach to the other there was a smell of old prawn heads. Every ten minutes or so an

Antonov transport would grope through the sky above this vista of decay. But Justino would stand in silence and breathe deeply, as if he were savoring the crisp air of the fjords.

He would insist that a ceasefire was just around the corner. If the war were unwinnable by either side, then reason would end it. "Imagine this country at peace; imagine our oil revenues going into reconstruction"—Justino now worked for the state oil company, Sonangol—"and imagine what this city will be like. Before the war, Luanda was the Rio of Africa, I'm telling you." Luanda had been a kind of paradise for the Portuguese and a handful of others; it must also have been a promising, energetic place, as the Angolans of mixed race and those blacks acceptable to the Portuguese began to talk and dream of liberation.

Yet a revitalized Angola was hard to imagine. The war was such an insistent feature of daily life that there was no way to conceive of the country without it: the helicopter gunships thudding above the slums, the urchins in Luanda sifting through the rubbish, the unharvested crops, the wounded soldiers and displaced peasants sitting on municipal benches, and the sound of gunfire, even in the capital, where the army was trying to put an end to theft from the docks—or perhaps to secure its own share of the spoils.

Justino shrugged off all such objections. In the yard of his house, he would serve beer and hold forth in fluent English, while his children sat at the lunch table, swinging their legs with impatience. The subject was invariably the future of his country. It was a topic that made me restless and, in the end, I broke the rules of courtesy by urging him to talk about the past; his own in particular.

Justino was born in the north of Angola in 1941, twenty years before the oldest of the three Angolan liberation movements, the MPLA, took up arms against the Portuguese. When Justino was still a child, his father, a hardworking Portuguese settler, gave up his job as a timber conveyor to manage a coffee plantation. Justino's mother was a woman of mixed race; she was also a Protestant, which was not unusual in the north. Schooling in the countryside was often left to the missions, of which the most active tended to be Methodist. The administration itself was not interested in educating Africans; by the mid-1950s fewer than seventy thousand were attending schools, from a population of around five million.

Angola had prodigious natural wealth, in diamonds, oil, highgrade hematite, hardwoods and ivory. Grain and cattle farming in the center of the country were good. The northwestern slopes of the plateau, where Justino grew up, yielded plentiful earnings for owners and managers of coffee estates. Justino's father could afford a good education for his son. He sent him first to Luanda and then to Lisbon, where he completed his secondary education. He returned briefly to Angola, only to set off again, at his father's instigation, to study mining in South Africa. Justino arrived in Johannesburg in 1960. He enrolled at a technical college and acted as a site official for a large mining concern. That year there were riots in Durban and confrontations in the Transkei. In March the Pan-Africanist Congress called a rally against the pass laws in the Vaal township of Sharpeville. In a confrontation with the police, sixty-seven people were killed. At Crown Mines, many of the men were from Mozambique. Justino was appalled by their pay and conditions. As a Portuguese speaker, he was often an intermediary between the Mozambicans and their Afrikaner overseers. It was not long before he sided openly with the work force. On weekends, he passed his time in the Mozambican compounds, listening to the miners' tales from home, where their lot was indistinguishable from that of most Angolans. All Portugal's colonies had been deemed "integral parts of the motherland" in 1951, but only a fraction of the inhabitants enjoyed civil rights: for the majority of people there were no rights of any kind. At the mines, Justino had much to reflect upon and his conclusions put him at odds with the management. "The system got to me," he said, "and after two years in that terrible place I left. My eyes had been opened. In Angola I was brought up with a colonial mentality. We were taught to forget about the blacks, about their side of things, but South Africa awakened me."

Two years later, Justino handed in his resignation and set out for Europe. In 1964 he arrived penniless in Finland, wondering what to do next. The desire to return to Angola was strong. Two important events had occurred since his departure: an uprising against the Portuguese and a bloody confrontation between the rival liberation movements of the day. Justino followed these developments through the European press and an African grapevine that ran from Lisbon to Helsinki. The uprising in Angola was sparked off by the detention of fifty-two anticolonial activists, including Agostinho Neto, then a prominent intellectual in the MPLA, who was already familiar with prison. Neto had studied medicine in Portugal, where he was jailed briefly in 1952, and again in 1955, for his anticolonial activities. Yet he cut a modest figure; his expression, partly hidden by the thick lenses of his glasses, was in equal measure unassuming and unaccommodating. He was also a poet, who had stated his hopes and grievances in verse:

> I go through the streets
> groping

> leaning on my formless dreams
> in my desire to be.
> They are neighbourhoods of slaves
> worlds of misery
> dark neighbourhoods.

Neto returned to Angola in 1959 to practice as a doctor and he was detained within months of his arrival.

At Catete in the Icolo e Bengo region, where Neto was born, there were demonstrations against his arrest and the Portuguese army was sent in. Around thirty people were killed, and the incident brought matters to a head. Many Angolan peasants had been forced to move off their family plots and grow cotton on land designated by the authorities. Their labor was unpaid and their produce was purchased at low prices. A peasant insurrection, part Christian, part nationalist, began in Malanje in protest against this system. Bands of local people marched on the farmsteads of the Portuguese, slaughtering cattle and destroying property. The revolt spread and the Portuguese crushed it with troops and air raids on villages.

In the capital, Portuguese rule was also being challenged. Early in 1961 a group of militants from the *musseques*, the shantytowns, assaulted the prisons. They hoped, and failed, to release some of the country's political detainees; forty of the assailants were killed. Shortly afterward, enraged groups of Portuguese citizens armed themselves and set off for the *musseques* to teach the residents a lesson. When they left, the poor quarters of the town were strewn with bodies. One witness counted four hundred dead. The following month a peasant rebellion broke out in the northwest. Hundreds of Portuguese were killed and the colonial army was brought in once more, again with aerial support.

A core of MPLA followers now moved out of Luanda and began a guerrilla war in the hinterland. They had considerable support outside the capital among the Mbundu population, although the movement's enemies made out that Luanda was the MPLA's only constituency. The bush did not suit the MPLA, predominantly an urban movement with models of "struggle" and development based on an urban sensibility. Less than 15 percent of the population lived in towns during the 1960s, yet for the MPLA the "masses" of Angola were its "working class," that is, city dwellers. Eventually great stress was placed on the idea of the "worker-peasant alliance"; the MPLA even put a hoe, a machete, one corncob and a sprig of cotton in the national emblem, but it might as well have been two clods of dung and a chicken's head for all that peasant life meant to people in Luanda. To many intellectuals in the MPLA, the countryside was a disagreeable place, steeped in rural idiocy. From the outset, the decision to leave the capital and fight in the bush was not easy.

The MPLA's rival in Angola was the precursor of the FNLA. In its first incarnation, as the Union of Peoples of Northern Angola (UPNA), it had argued that the Bakongo lands in the northwest were separate from the rest of Angola. At the end of the 1950s it dropped the N from its acronym, but this did not change the regional character of its support. The UPA accused the MPLA of elitism and multiracialism. To the UPA, real liberation had to be as dark as the womb. Both movements had offices and bases in Congo-Léopoldville (now Zaïre). It was from here, in 1961, that the MPLA sent a column of guerrillas into Angola to make contact with its followers who had fled Luanda. On the way they were attacked by the UPA. There were no survivors. It is fair to say that the war for the liberation of Angola had begun. By 1962 Neto had become the leader of the MPLA and the UPA had changed its name, but not its politics. It became known as the FNLA and, shortly afterward, as the Revolutionary Government of Angola in Exile. The following year the FNLA was recognized by the infant Organization of African Unity (OAU). This was a blow for Neto, who intensified his own search for recognition and support, traveling to the United States, China, the Soviet Union and Scandinavia. Holden Roberto was also touring on behalf of the FNLA. Indeed, both men spent a great deal of time stepping from airplanes and mounting podiums in unfamiliar cities, looking for potential investors in the political future of Angola. Roberto found favor with the Chinese and Romanians, Neto with the Russians and, through Che Guevara, with Cuba.

For Justino, it was a period of change and difficulty. He had roamed Europe for two years, reveling in its exoticism, seduced by a culture that he had only dimly perceived during his school days in Lisbon. He was already an adult when he left Africa, having come of age in the miners' compounds near Johannesburg. Now, however, he underwent a second adolescence, acting and directing in fringe theater, writing poetry and living from hand to mouth by selling newspapers or working as a domestic. Everything he ascertained about Europe, in France, Holland and Finland, aroused his curiosity further. He drifted from one place to the next in a state of bohemian excitement. Yet Justino seldom doubted that he was an African; the question was how and when to acknowledge it. News of revolt and repression in Angola appeared regularly in the European press. Justino dwelled on the reports like a guest at a party who walks onto the balcony and remembers a troubling scene from his past.

In Helsinki, during a world peace conference, he ran into a group of Angolans, wearing MPLA badges, who urged him to make his decision sooner rather than later. "I told them, 'Please, I have to find myself first.' And perhaps they could see this," he explained. Justino was waging what he called a "within struggle" of his own, which could only evolve in its own time. He must have seemed a little fainthearted, even absurd, to his interlocutors, for the war in Angola was gathering momentum and, to add to the MPLA's difficulties, a third faction was in the offing. Jonas Savimbi had come to prominence as a follower of Holden Roberto, serving as the foreign minister in the FNLA's government in exile. He was a fluent, lumbering man, a charmer with a manic edge. After abandoning an early ambition to practice medicine, he had studied politics in Switzerland. He was a febrile letter writer, who signed his correspondence "Jonas Malheiro Savimbi, Licence in Legal and Political Sciences," adding occasionally "University of Lausanne." Savimbi broke with Holden Roberto in 1964, taking a small following with him. Two years later he reappeared at the head of UNITA. Savimbi's new movement entered the bush with a handful of arms originally supplied to the FNLA and very little in the way of outside support. But Savimbi was a man without scruples and he had one outstanding virtue as a guerrilla leader: he preferred the bush to the comforts of exile. Small units from all three factions now began to operate around the border areas of Angola. Justino read about the war with a certain disquiet, for it spoke of the day when his own struggle would have to be adjourned.

On the bookcase at the family home by the beach, Justino kept an album of mementos, a tattered, illustrious thing that I saw more than once and which his children loved. It was a photographic record of his life in Europe and his return to Angola, along with numerous letters and clippings. He had settled for a time in Holland at the end of the 1960s and had won a reputation as a theater director. There were several articles from the Dutch press about his work in fringe theater, which had drawn high praise from the critics. There was also a striking photograph of Justino on the steps of a basement apartment in Amsterdam with a parrot perched on his shoulder, like the personification of his African conscience, and another, taken later, on a metaled road in Angola with a wrecked military vehicle under a palm tree. It was in this disorderly book that Justino kept his first letter from the MPLA.

"It was a big step to think: Yes, I am ready to go back to Angola and perhaps get killed," he explained. "You have to imagine yourself as a dead man before you do a thing like that"—easier, he surmised, for the dispossessed of Angola. "It takes another kind of choice for a colonial like myself, who has not been through such hard experiences. I have lost the expression for what you do in a moment of decision. No, that's it. I want to say that I crossed the Rubicon in 1970. I wrote to Agostinho Neto and asked to join the MPLA."

It was Justino's way of applying for citizenship in a postcolonial Angola. Six years had elapsed since his encounter with the MPLA on the streets of Helsinki, but now he was ready to accept that his future lay in Africa. His upbringing in a colonial family did not disqualify him from being an African; quite the contrary. His letter ended up in Tanzania, where the MPLA had offices. The reply, which he unfolded and placed on the table now, was dated December 1971. Either he was incorrect about the date of his own letter or the movement was slow to respond. "Dear Friend," it began,

> I acknowledge receipt of your letter referring to your integration and participation in the struggle of the Angolan people, addressed to the MPLA.
>
> Unfortunately, Comrade Agostinho Neto is himself out of Tanzania for the moment. However, we will make everything possible for your letter to reach the hands of Comrade Neto as quickly as possible.
>
> Out revolutionary greetings.
> VICTORY IS CERTAIN
> Paulo Junior
> Representative, MPLA, Tanzania.

Wherever you went in Luanda, Neto's name was held in respect. He was a mythical figure like Nkrumah, Cabral, Lumumba or Mandela. If he was mentioned at the end of a long evening, inveterate drunks would straighten their backs and blink with an air of offended surprise at the glass they had just drained. If it came up in the course of a neighborhood meeting, women would ululate for a few seconds, brushing the dust from their T-shirts. Even Justino, disaffected with the MPLA though he now was, adjusted his glasses when he spoke of Neto, while his children, born years after the president's death, looked down at their feet with bored decorum as though in church.

For an outsider, hearing Neto's name, coming across one of his poems or catching sight of those kumquat eyes on the masthead of the daily paper was always an uncomfortable moment. The shortcomings of the MPLA were conspicuous throughout the capital. Thirteen years in government and they could not distribute food or goods to areas under their control. Nor could they organize basic services for the poor or ensure that a delivery of spare parts in the port at Luanda reached the tractors on a farming project fifteen miles away. It was hard to look well upon the icons of this dignified medic who had undergone so many trials for the sake of independence, or to see the general show of loyalty as anything more than an authorized version of regret. Besides, Neto's image too often invoked the activities of that other diligent practitioner in the south, Dr. Jonas Savimbi (University of Lausanne), without whom the vivisection of Angola might never have been possible.

Justino replaced the letter in the scrapbook and we browsed through the reviews. The clippings were all in Dutch; they had grown yellow down the years and now, in the afternoon sun, they looked like relics of an extinct civilization suddenly exposed to light. Justino paraphrased the odd article. "Here it says I have shown that text is unnecessary in performance. Sound and movement are more important. Here it tells that I was leading the way in children's theater and progressive drama."

There was a black-and-white picture, larger than the rest, with an area of heavy shade at one edge. A young soldier was seated with her back resting against a tree. Another, with darker skin and hair worn in a bun at the top of her head, was looking to the left. In the foreground was a third, with her face turned to the camera as though someone had called her name. There was a weapon cradled in her lap. She wore her hair in plaits, her skin was dark and her face expressionless.

"Her name is Katila," Justino explained. "I had a friend, we called him Saydi Mingas; his full name was Saydi Vieira Dias Mingas, a great athlete, and a poet. After I had joined the liberation movement, he came to stay with me in Holland and he showed me this photo. I think he took it himself. I saw Katila in this picture and I fell in love with her. Mingas was not sure where to find her. The picture was taken inside Angola but we thought we might contact her through the MPLA in Dar es Salaam. But that is another story."

I did not know what Justino meant by falling in love—not in this instance. It struck me as quaint: a mere notion, consonant with his interest in poetry and art. It was all part of the obstinacy that kept him in straitened circumstances, immune to the lure of corruption in a society where it was almost indispensable, and indifferent to advancement. Yet the photograph of Katila was undeniably powerful, and did much to excuse his wayward admiration. This picture of a teenage African guerrilla offered ample scope for a *coup de foudre*. Her features were delicate and well defined, and in her eyes there was a lack of enthusiasm for the task in hand—quite unlike Justino's, with their boyish vivacity. How easy it would have been, sitting in an apartment near the Magere Brug, to endow this image with a mythic force—the beauty of a people bearing arms, the simplicity and courage of a nation in the making. At that point, perhaps, the doctrine of national unity would have seemed more than a sober answer to the issues of tribe and race, as it took the strain of larger aspirations: the desire to belong, above all, as thoroughly as she appeared to do. The whole business was typical of Justino, with his roundabout way of making commitments. Perhaps the photo brought him closer to the heart of things, as he campaigned on the streets of Amsterdam for a boycott of Angolan coffee.

▲

The Press Center in Luanda had arranged a trip to the central provinces. If it materialized, I could expect to be away for several days. Domestic flights in Angola were unreliable and it was best to be at the airport before dawn. Even then you could wait beyond midday for a plane to take you into the provinces. It might be a military transport or a Boeing 737. The national airline, TAAG, had three of these in service. One looked in reasonable order; the rear half of the second was covered in an oily brown film and its tailplane had been patched up. The third was so filthy that you could barely distinguish the TAAG logo at all, as though it had been flying for thousands of miles on palm oil. As dawn broke over the airport, the dusty red lairs that housed the government's MiGs, and probably those of the Cuban air force, began to take shape in the mist. A long row of jet transports stood in front of a concrete terminal. The propeller transports were littered at random around the tarmac. Occasionally an unmarked Antonov hurtled down onto the runway.

A small electric towing vehicle with a trailer containing two tires and a mysterious cardboard box crossed from left to right in front of the protocol lounge and disappeared from view. A few minutes later it reemerged with the same load, passing the lounge from right to left, and sometime after that, from left to right. It was a very Angolan set of maneuvers—always baffling to an observer. As the sun came up another Antonov thudded onto the runway and drew to a standstill by the tower. The little vehicle, trailer, two tires and box approached with caution. A soldier jumped from the ramp at the back of the plane and spoke to the driver. The vehicle left and returned some minutes later with the same load. There were three soldiers by the plane now. They remonstrated with the driver. One of them went to the trailer, removed the box and threw it on the tarmac; the tires followed. The soldiers climbed back in the plane. With the ramp shut, it taxied away for takeoff. The driver of the towing vehicle now picked up the box and tires, replaced them on the trailer and drove off, crossing the protocol lounge from right to left. The MiGs brooded in their shallow bunkers.

There was no further activity for an hour or more. Then another transport landed and taxied out of view. The towing vehicle appeared once more with the same trailer and the same load, crossing purposefully in front of the protocol lounge, left to right. An hour later it passed the other way. The tires and the box were gone. In their place was a plain wooden coffin wedged in the back with a netful of grapefruit. Two soldiers were jogging behind this improvised hearse to ensure that the body and the grapefruit arrived at the terminal without mishap.

The doors of the second 737 were now open. A group of civilians, very poor, perhaps from the provinces, had come out of nowhere and run across the tarmac. Some of them were waving bits of paper, possibly tickets. By the time I boarded, a small crowd of disappointed people had begun to gather behind the starboard wing. Officials were trying to disperse them. The engines were turning over. The doors were slammed and the plane began to move at speed away from the terminal area. A group of women ran along the windswept grass at the edge of the approach, their hands pressed on their head scarves, but they could not keep up.

Half an hour into the flight a flight attendant brought orange juice and bread. Fifteen minutes later she collected the cups. Then the plane was over Huambo with no change in altitude. A minute later it plummeted, causing consternation among the passengers. The pilot leveled off and banked sharply. Then we dropped again, going down to the airstrip in a corkscrew, wings juddering and engines protesting. In 1986, Washington had decided to enhance Savimbi's bag of remedies for Angola with Stinger missiles, but the 737s were at risk from much cruder forms of weaponry. This determined the landing and takeoff patterns in the central provinces. Huambo, in particular, was a fiercely contested area.

We waited on the airstrip. In principle cars were brought for journalists, who were ferried, again in principle, from one place to the next with a minder from the Press Center in Luanda. But an hour went by without a car arriving. The hold of the 737 was opened and a soldier began tossing bundles of rags and sacks of grain to the passengers who had disembarked with us. The plane took off again, leaving another group of would-be travelers abandoned on the tarmac. It sheered up through the air at an alarming angle and leveled out against a wisp of grayish cloud. The airport was quiet now. An attack helicopter squatted on an apron of tarmac with its blades sagging around it. To the edge of the strip lay the wreck of a civilian carrier. Despite the gasoline shortage, a Soviet truck stood with its engine running and the cab empty. A dozen wounded soldiers sat patiently in the back. Two had bandaged heads, a third had pads over both eyes. There were crutches propped against the sides of the tailboard.

At length a car arrived. We were six in all: a minder, a South African filmmaker, her two English colleagues, a Cuban journalist and myself. After a lengthy stop halfway into town to pick up fuel, and a lot of coming and going that served to use most of it up, we arrived at a hotel. It was a grand colonial establishment with a magnificent dining room at the back; its windows gave on to the railway, which Savimbi had paralyzed. Had trains been running throughout the war, they could have carried food and medicine from the coast to the central provinces. But the railway had an important strategic role and Savimbi could not afford to let it operate. Now and again a train went past the back of the hotel, but it could only have been traveling a few kilometers.

Although Huambo was held by the government, the allegiance of the inhabitants was unclear. The Cuban journalist believed that the soldiers in Huambo were government by day and UNITA by night. This may have been an exaggeration, but UNITA certainly had a following in Huambo. On Independence Day in 1975, it was Savimbi who had stood in the football stadium and announced that the city was no longer to be known as Novo Lisboa. A huge crowd had cheered as the UNITA flag was raised. Huambo was near Savimbi's birthplace and it would have been odd if he had not continued to draw support from some of its inhabitants. He had eyes and ears in Huambo. In 1981 UNITA blew up the power supply. The following year it claimed to have blown up the MPLA's main assembly hall. That was the kind of war the rebels fought here.

The minder from the Press Center, a feckless young man with evasive eyes and a well-developed waistline, had no great affection for Huambo. He was edgy and careful to keep his initiatives on behalf of the foreign press to a minimum. His ideal assignment would have been a twelve-hour wait at Luanda airport followed by an announcement that all domestic flights had been canceled until further notice. Things had not gone so smoothly, however, and now that he was here the best he could do was to ensure that his charges sat in a hotel for most of their stay. Half an hour went by while we amused ourselves in the lobby. We were then ushered into the dining room, with its stout pillars and faded hangings, and down to a table, one among many, all impeccably laid. There were no other guests. A fine dust drifted in the light—not the familiar dust of Africa but a gray precipitate of the kind that gathers on the sills of European houses. The order of cutlery on either side of the plates, the buffet with its empty salvers, the conical napkins at a dozen tables or more—everything was as though the Portuguese had just stepped away for a few days. In Angola liberation felt obliged to keep up the most improbable appearances.

Three waiters hovered at the edges of the vast dining room, reluctant to approach, but in due course a jug of water and a vat of soup were brought to the table. The waiters now retired to the corners, napkins suspended on one arm, white jackets stained in places but neatly pressed, and watched us apprehensively. One of them disappeared and returned with a tray of smoked fish cut in half, followed by a tureen full of rice and a cold scrap of goat. A train came slowly past the windows and the cutlery rattled on a table near what must once have been the terrace. There were some sixty government soldiers in two trucks, swaying along with their heads bent and their rifles upright between their knees.

The meal was finished and we were ushered back into the lobby to wait until a little before dusk while the minder disappeared. The hotel was "not secure" and the search was on for rooms elsewhere. A car came; we got in, we drove here and there through the city with its crumbling projects built by the Portuguese during the 1960s. In one square there was a profusion of flowers and many of the smaller houses had patios adorned with creeper. In Huambo these little signs of endeavor were welcome but they also emphasized the general immiserization of the city.

The Almirante Hotel, our new quarters, stood across the way from a college or faculty of some kind, behind which the Soviet transport aircraft took a stately route, pouring out heat decoys like roman candles. The hotel smelled of sewage, overcooked starch and boiled goat. Almost every square inch of the interior—walls, columns, stairwell, as well as floors—was carpeted with a synthetic fiber, now old and greasy, that had absorbed this miasma for years. For much of the day there was no power and no running water. The hotel had become a billet for government troops and also the Cubans, of whom there were now over fifty thousand supporting the MPLA.

Before supper, I went outside to take the air, for the smell of the Almirante was demoralizing. The sun had dropped and the shadows of the apartment blocks were longer, fainter. A Russian jeep pulled up and a group of soldiers gathered to haggle over a case of liquor. Across a narrow road on one side of the Almirante stood a blackened concrete building, damaged by a UNITA bomb attack on the hotel in 1985, which was said by rebel communiqués to have killed twenty foreigners. A year earlier a truckload of explosives had gone off in the main street with still more spectacular casualties. UNITA boasted two hundred, including numerous Cubans and Bulgarians; Tass counted one hundred. The government news agency, ANGOP, put it at twenty-four. The Almirante and its surroundings were an obvious target, since expatriates and people of a less than pure black hue tended to gather here. Dr. Savimbi might be on cordial terms with the government of South Africa but he stuck to his diagnosis of Angola's ills, of which "half-castes" and foreigners were a part. The Cubans, he had remarked in 1976, were killing "our black people."

Dozens of diners sat in silence in the fetid gloom of the Almirante restaurant. An occasional clink of knives or the gurgle of water leaving a jug did not disturb the monastic quality of a place filled with men and women who had taken the orders of internationalism, or had these thrust upon them: mechanics from Bulgaria, Stasi types from East Germany, Czech immunologists, Cuban soldiers, Soviet military advisers. At one table were three Vietnamese who later introduced themselves as philosophers. They taught at the college and had done so for years. All three were mercilessly thin. Day after day they stepped lightly across the stinking carpets of the Almirante and over the road to the college—one of them wearing a pith helmet—where there were few lights, books or teaching aids and few students, to lecture on the philosophy of Marxism-Leninism.

Huambo, it seemed to me, was at once the loftiest and the hardest of callings for such people: a place where faith in the progress of scientific socialism was tested to its limits. Here, more than in Luanda, it was possible to believe that the war alone had wrecked the project of socialism, for the war was all around. Yet the people of Huambo, many of them, were still foundering in error; the philosophy course had not rallied the youth to the MPLA, which is why, perhaps, the diners ate in silence, making the same solemn choice day after day between the head and tail of that unlikely fish we had encountered in the first hotel.

It was dark by the time the guests had risen. A generator ran for a while, bathing the lobby and one landing in feeble light. Outside, there was sporadic gunfire and inside, nothing to drink but water from the pails set down by the lavatories.

The Portuguese census of 1970 counted nearly 62,000 people in Huambo, or New Lisbon, as it was then known. By 1983 the figure had risen to 203,000. The war was forcing the population of small farmers off the surrounding land and into the city. Here, they began to depend on food deliveries. By day they could venture out to cultivate plots within a few kilometers of the city, but it was not safe. In

Angola there were probably forty thousand men and women with missing limbs. Both sides used land mines to wage the war. Testimonies from victims suggested that the government sowed mines in the north without warning the local population. Casualties in UNITA care blamed the Cubans, but, in the country as a whole, people held UNITA responsible for the majority of injuries.

Bomba Alta was an orthopedic center on the outskirts of Huambo that could cater to a handful of patients at a time, modeling new limbs for land mine victims and teaching them to walk. The center was supported by the Red Cross, who claimed that it had been attacked twice by UNITA in 1982. Neither side was fastidious about civilians, but for UNITA soft targets such as schools or clinics were a strategic imperative, for they were symbols of the government's effort, however cursory, to manage and develop the country. As it happened, there were no casualties from these attacks. The center was hit again in 1985. A civilian night watchman was abducted and, according to the staff, UNITA burned half a year's stock of artificial limbs.

Inside the main room at the center, a young amputee called Josefa was learning to skip. She had been walking to school with her sister and a niece when she trod on a mine. Her sister had a severe ear injury and the niece was wounded in the face. Josefa lost her leg. She had nothing to say for herself but a member of the clinic's staff explained her case. She stood uncomfortably, waiting for him to finish, thanked him and returned to her skipping. "When she gets her artificial limb," said the doctor, "she will go back to school. Hers is a fairly typical case. It's typical for mines to be planted in such places, but these girls didn't know."

Many of the patients were women, many of them children. Those who had just received artificial limbs were being led across the floor by a physiotherapist. An older woman on two false legs grimaced with pain. Another group of amputees was doing exercises, one hand, sometimes both, gripping a long rail that ran at waist height down one wall of the main room. The sunlight drove in through the blank windows and there was a mocking hint of dance school about the center as it echoed to the thump of prostheses hitting the floor. Yet Bomba Alta was a success. Some of the patients, at least, had a chance of coming to terms with their disability. Moreover, to have lost a limb was a sign as much of good fortune as of ill, for it spoke of a narrow escape where others may have been less lucky. The doctors believed that Josefa, for example, would master her new leg and return to secondary school within a year.

Huambo was just the place for a government that was keen to show journalists the enormities of the war. The wards of the main hospital in the city were like dark tunnels from which one emerged blinking with anger and ill-disposed toward Savimbi's cause. I had visited two central hospitals already but the one at Huambo was the worst. It was understaffed, overcrowded and short of medicine. We were taken to a ward full of children. Some had uncles or aunts with them. One limbless pair of boys was attended by an uncle in rags whose own arm was missing. The rest of the family was dead. Another child, a boy, not yet twelve, was recovering from a bullet wound in the thigh after a UNITA raid on a village to the east of the city. There were few sheets; the children lay on bare stained mattresses with coarse blankets to cover them at night. Mosquitoes drifted purpose-fully between the beds and several of the patients were already show-ing signs of fever. Here it was harder to be sanguine than in Bomba Alta.

A Russian doctor by the name of Vladimir contrived to keep up appearances, smiling as he introduced himself in Portuguese and giv-ing a brisk case history at each bed. "We are really stretched here," he said, "there are cases that are even more serious . . ." and his train of thought faltered. "It's very difficult. There are children who have had their limbs amputated and who have returned to their homes without legs or without arms. It's very sad." Even he, I think, was dismayed by the patient in the corner of the ward. The injured child was with a wet nurse—its mother had died in the same incident, an attack on a village. It was no older than six months. It had been struck by a bullet between the knee and ankle of one leg, which in an infant is no longer than an adult hand, but infection had swollen it to the size of its own head.

On the way down the corridor an amputee on crutches stopped in front of us and performed an ungainly salute, whether in mockery or greeting I am not sure. Outside the sunlight was blinding. The minder from the Press Center leaned against the back of the car, stuck a finger in his ear and shook it vigorously. Today, at least, he did not need to drive home the government's point.

At the Almirante, the philosophers from Vietnam ate their sparse meal with subdued appreciation. They bade us good night as they passed our gloomy table. Outside there was small-arms fire until mid-night, some at the edge of the college. We rose early the following morning and, after an hour of delay, drove to the airport. There were too many people for the flight, some of them wounded military, who would get priority.

The plane arrived promptly; it was a 737, the one with the logo obscured by soot. When it was full there were still some twenty people fighting to board. They were pushed back by soldiers. The plane began to taxi and the stragglers, mainly peasants, jostled forward. The pilot braked abruptly, a soldier and an airport worker ran to the hold and opened it up. Two unmarked bundles were tossed in, followed by an oily cardboard box bound with dry grass. There was no way of knowing what these contained or why they were important. The hold was shut and moments later we were hauled up into the air. Huambo was visible at first, then there was nothing but sky, then it was visible again, smaller but still directly below. Around the city the sun was burning the mist off the ocher highland that stretched for miles.

A small child wriggled in its mother's lap and began to wail. The flight attendant served water. On landing at Luanda, the front tires burst and rubbery fumes filled the front of the passenger cabin, as the plane hurtled over the runway. A sudden lurch to the right and it came to a stop. I turned to look at the other passengers. They sat in silence, without making a move. Two minutes elapsed, the engines were shut down and an Ethiopian pilot appeared from the cockpit to say, in English, that the plane would be evacuated shortly. The child who had been crying at the start of the flight was fast asleep. A soldier carried her down the steps and held her astride her mother's back. The woman stooped and fastened the inert form in place with a length of orange cloth.

▲

Katila was sitting in one of the low armchairs in Justino's house. She wore a simple print dress. A gold chain hung from her neck. Were it not for her civilian clothes, she might have stepped from the photo taken more than fifteen years earlier by Saydi Mingas. Justino introduced us. A little later he produced the photo album and a map of Angola.

"I was sixteen then," said Katila, or Senhora Guedes as she now was. She spoke in Portuguese and Justino translated for my benefit. "I had already been in the forest for six years. This place was an instruction center run by the MPLA in a part of the country we called Zone A, near the border with Zambia. It was 1972; we were involved in an operation against the Portuguese base at Lumbala Kaquengue. I remember this photo, it was taken on the way back from the attack." Katila believed the operation had been a success. It took the Portuguese by surprise. She was close enough to see one man running for shelter with a towel around his waist and a foaming toothbrush clenched in his teeth. Reconnaissance parties from the instruction center had been observing the base for weeks. They knew when the soldiers would play soccer, for instance, or how long it took them to wash in the mornings. Katila belonged to a mortar crew, chosen for the

operation, she said, because of their "good behavior." They subjected
the base to a short bombardment. She said there were casualties among
the Portuguese. The guerrillas withdrew quickly and suffered no losses
themselves. It was a routine procedure. "I was a child living in the
bush," Katila explained, "and this kind of thing was not strange to me.
I was fighting for a cause and I was happy. That is all I knew." In a
liberation movement like the MPLA, there were important things to
learn besides aptitude with a weapon. One was the ability to go for
long periods without food, another was to master the art of walking for
days, perhaps months.

Katila was born in Moxico province. Her mother was a peasant
who spent her days tending her manioc and working in the local
colonial plantation. The peasants of Moxico were not wealthy; even so,
the hardships of her early childhood would not have prepared Katila
for life with the MPLA. The Portuguese referred to the remote south-
eastern provinces of Moxico and Cuando Cubango as "the End of the
Earth." Both contained great tracts of open land, a thousand meters or
more above sea level, scored by rivers and seasonal water courses.
Bordering on Zambia, Moxico was an ideal place for the MPLA to
operate, and they began to do so in 1966, moving back and forth across
the frontier. UNITA too began to mobilize anticolonial peasant mili-
tias in the province. The Portuguese were soon herding peasants into
strategic hamlets. The MPLA put those who were not fighting with
them into poorly camouflaged camps. "Where I lived," said Katila,
"either you stayed with the Portuguese or you went into the bush."

Katila never met her real father until after independence. She
lived with her older sister, her mother and an uncle. Harassment by
the Portuguese, interrogation and the prospect of forced resettlement
led many to flee to the bush. Katila's uncle was among them and he
took her with him. They set off while Katila's mother was away on a
visit to relatives. In 1966 there were groups of peasants wandering all
over Moxico, bound for the border, or hiding and foraging. Katila and
her uncle met up with a group of MPLA, who escorted them from one
safe place to the next. On their way they encountered other groups
who would alert them if the Portuguese were nearby. They walked for
days, covering nearly forty kilometers a day until finally they reached
a place on the Zambian border where Katila began the next stage of her
life as an MPLA cadre. Soon after their arrival, her uncle disappeared
while he was out in the bush and word came back that he had been
taken by the Portuguese. Katila, who was ten, entered a makeshift
MPLA orphanage at the movement's base camp in another of their
zones. The Vietnamese struggle was a model for the MPLA and the
camp was known by the guerrillas as Hanoi II.

Katila had an advantage over many peasant children, for she had attended a village school run by Protestant missionaries; she was literate and she enjoyed mathematics. In the classes given by the MPLA at Hanoi II she shone. She took quickly to the rhythms of life at the base, which resembled those of a large family. Américo Boavida was a figurehead in the community at Hanoi II. He had studied medicine in Lisbon, Porto and Prague, served as an intern in Barcelona and practiced for five years in Luanda. In 1960 he joined the MPLA. When Katila arrived at the base, he was running the medical service in the MPLA's eastern region. She was not yet in her teens and she came to regard Boavida as a father. He brought stability and contentment to her life at the base.

The Portuguese were campaigning in the area of Hanoi II in 1968, burning large tracts of bush and woodland, to make guerrilla movement harder. As the dry season came, a heavy silence settled on the countryside. The counterinsurgency effort had driven off the wildlife; there was no game to be had and no honey to be found in the wild hives. In September the Portuguese fell on Hanoi II with bomber aircraft, armed reconnaissance planes and helicopters. Katila joined the frenzied evacuation. Once they had reached safety, people scattered in small groups and hid. As the day wore on, the news came through that there had been no casualties and at sunset they drifted back to the base, only to find that Boavida was missing. His body was later recovered on the outskirts of Hanoi II. A minuscule fragment of shrapnel had lodged in his brain.

Katila wept when she spoke of Boavida and Justino comforted her. She said that later she had understood how hard life at the base would have been without this benign figure from the city, who had put his skills at the service of people like herself. In her mind, Boavida and the MPLA had been one and the same. "From Américo," she explained, "from the way he had lived, I learned what it was that I must do, what we could be, all of us Angolans. We knew him as Ngola Kimbanda—the *curandeiro* of Angola. There was nothing he could not cure. It was enough for him to be around for people to feel better."

War and resettlement were crippling food production in Moxico. By 1969 there was very little manioc in the province and barely a stalk of rice. Katila was thirteen but she was already adult. The MPLA decided to make her a "pioneer," sending her around the villages of Moxico, bringing word of the movement to the inhabitants. "We used to go with salt and cloth, which were kept in warehouses in Zambia," Katila explained, "and exchange these for food grown by the people. We walked for hundreds of kilometers. Sometimes the rains would hold us up in one place for a week and then there was nothing to eat.

Other times the heat made our water rations disappear too soon. Hunger and thirst were always with us during those years."

It was at the instruction center, where the photograph was taken, that Katila began her military training, under the command of Saydi Mingas. She had already taken a *nom de guerre*, common practice in Angola, for the fewer people who knew your family name, the lower the risks for relatives. She had chosen the name of Gloria. Mingas gave her the new name Katila, which in Kimbundu means "do not run." It was not long before Katila had her first experiences of combat. They were sporadic hit-and-miss affairs, nothing in themselves that could have won the war, but by now she was no longer simply a child caught up in the throes of a violent conflict; she had come to believe in the independence of Angola, and belief was a valuable resource, especially in the early years of the war.

Katila was at a loss when she tried to say more about this. Casting around for the words, her eyes settled on Justino's children. "How can I explain it? I had come to understand many things. At the beginning I was nothing, only a child. I was too young when things started to happen to the adults around me. Hard and terrible things that I did not see in their fullness. Gradually this feeling came to me, from my knowledge of what was happening to ordinary people in Moxico. I knew myself too as one of the oppressed. I would be the same now if I had not fought, for I was born at the End of the Earth. And at the End of the Earth, believe me, our lives under the Portuguese were somber."

There were friendships in the bush, she said, and the women would sometimes bear children. In Zambia they could even marry, but this was not common. Mostly casual contacts took place, children were born and groups of women took care of them. They became MPLA family. "I call that African society," said Katila with a wave of the hand, "not so different from the way we do things in the rest of our culture. Still, by the time I was fifteen I was aware of sex, aware that it was a problem. You see, I had no experience of this matter. At the age of sixteen I became pregnant. I gave birth to a boy, the fruit of an unhappy experience. His father was a young man, a year older than me. I can say that there were many other children born in this way. It was not until the eve of independence that health workers in the MPLA began to educate the women."

Not long after the attack on the Portuguese at Lumbala Kaquengue, Katila was singled out by her superiors for a course in the Soviet Union. She was transferred to Dar es Salaam, the capital of Tanzania, to wait for news of a scholarship. The year was 1973. Justino was still in Holland. He had joined the MPLA and was now a junior representative, taking orders from the movement's offices in Stockholm. In the east of Angola the fighting was so fierce that 22,000 people had fled to Zambia.

"I wrote to Katila in Dar as Saydi Mingas had advised," said Justino. In Dar a letter from Holland was worth a full investigation. It was intercepted and Katila was asked to account for it. She could not. It was opened and Justino's passion became a laborious entry in the early records of the MPLA's surveillance network—the DISA, or state security bureau, as it was known once the movement took power. Justino and Katila now corresponded regularly. He wrote her long avowals of love, with photographs attached, and poems to her grace and beauty. She wrote back in tones of modest encouragement.

Justino tried to visit Leningrad, where Katila was learning Russian and taking a course in radio maintenance, but he could not raise the money. Like most Africans on "technical scholarships" to the Soviet Union, Katila was doing her share of unpaid labor—assembling radio sets—but she was also picking up skills that she expected to use on her return to Angola. "It was a big happiness for me and a different life, coming out of the bush."

In Amsterdam Justino was hard at work. He made contact with Angolans in Europe, collected money, spoke at trade union conventions, student meetings, church gatherings. His taste for drama made him an able propagandist; this in turn led him to experiment with film. Then in the spring of 1974 a leftist military coup in Portugal overthrew the Caetano dictatorship. The hopelessness of the colonial wars in Mozambique, Angola and Guinea-Bissau had galvanized the Movement of Armed Forces, as it was known, and a majority of officers in Lisbon favored decolonization. The community of Angolan exiles was on the move.

Matters stood badly in Luanda on Justino's return. The three nationalist movements were jockeying for power. They met in Portugal in January 1975, established a coalition government and agreed on elections later in the year. Arms and money were now funneled to all three movements in alarming quantities. The head of the CIA's Angola Task Force reckoned that Washington disbursed over $30 million in five months to Holden Roberto and to Savimbi. Moscow was pouring arms into the MPLA—about $100 million worth, by one Western intelligence count, in the twelve months leading up to independence.

Savimbi was still only a marginal presence in the north and so the tension building in Luanda was confined to the MPLA and Holden Roberto's FNLA. There had been clashes between the two movements at the end of 1974 and by the middle of the following year they were fighting openly for control of the capital. The MPLA had a base at Caxito, an hour's drive northeast. It was attacked by the FNLA in March; fifty people were reported dead and the battle for Luanda had commenced. Caxito became a kind of front and the road from Luanda ran through a no-man's-land of anything between twenty and sixty kilometers. "One day it was held by the FNLA," said Justino, "the next by us. I was working in our office in Luanda, for the Ideological Commission, producing propaganda, seeing documents through the proof stages, but I managed to get all my office duties completed between dusk and the early hours of the morning. I had a car and at 6 A.M. every day I would drive out toward Caxito, to know the news. I was also assigned to take foreign journalists to the front. We had to show that Caxito belonged to us; that things were under control. We wanted reporters to see what they could. There was always great uncertainty. There was also a confusion over uniforms, for they looked the same to an untrained eye. So we would receive a ribbon in the morning to pin on one shoulder. The color would change from day to day or week to week.

"The liberation movements had many more armored vehicles than I realized. I discovered this on the way to Caxito. Some of our soldiers were moving on the road in a Soviet personnel carrier. They were surprised by three FNLA armored cars, I think they were Panhards, approaching from the opposite direction at about sixty kilometers an hour. Myself, I was behind when it happened. Our people kept going and there was a head-on smash. The Soviet vehicle rode right up over one of the Panhards. A Portuguese soldier and two Zaïreans got out of the wreck. They were shot dead and lying in the road when I arrived. There were many troops from Zaïre fighting with Holden Roberto; Roberto's bases were in Zaïre. The FNLA had a big army, bigger than ours."

In the capital the fighting continued. In June Neto's followers killed dozens of UNITA men in the suburbs, but Savimbi was already standing back from the far bloodier contest between the other two movements. Later that month all three factions met in Kenya to agree on a peaceful democratic transition to independence, but by July the street battles were raging in Luanda once again. This time they were conclusive.

Katila worked on at the radio maintenance course in Leningrad while her country went from one crisis to the next. She had an inkling of the confusion and she listened for news, in Russian, on the radio. Savimbi was in Huambo; he had won the support of South Africa for a defense of the city against an MPLA onslaught. The Cubans were arriving to bolster the MPLA in its bid for unilateral rule. The news was rare and clouded with rhetoric—*palavras*, as she called it. She thought it a waste of good radio technology. She heard no word of South Africa's October offensive until after independence.

In Africa there was speculation about what had stopped the South Africans short of Luanda; Cuban resistance at the Queve River or pressure from Washington. But in Leningrad the Cubans were indisputably the heroes of the hour. North of the capital, too, she heard that there had been a final FNLA offensive. It was backed by two battalions of Zaïrean soldiers, dozens of Portuguese Angolans and South Africans, and supervised by U.S. and French intelligence staff. The Cubans stopped this onslaught with Soviet artillery in the marshland of the Bengo River basin. It was the end of the FNLA as a military force. South Africa completed its withdrawal in March of the following year.

Tens of thousands of Angolans had sought refuge outside the country. Inside there were still hundreds of South African and Zaïrean soldiers, roughly twelve thousand Cubans and a large constituency to the south whose figurehead, Jonas Savimbi, had set his heart on confrontation. Most of the Portuguese settlers had left; what they could not take with them they had destroyed. Cement was poured down elevator shafts; cars were tipped into the bay at Luanda. The real legacy of Portuguese colonialism was an 85 percent illiteracy rate and a total lack of managerial skills.

Many students from Lusophone Africa were leaving the Soviet Union in a state of jubilation. Katila too was shortly to complete her course. In 1976 she flew to Zambia to collect her child. He was a few months old when she had left him in the care of the MPLA women and set off for Russia. Now he was nearly four. One woman in particular had formed a bond with the boy and she was dismayed by Katila's arrival. They argued bitterly and the matter was only settled when it was brought to the Zambian police. "I told this woman, 'All right, you must come with me to Luanda, we will live together.' But she had heard too much about the killings up there. She was afraid."

Having arrived in Luanda with her child, Katila found clerical work with the general staff of the MPLA's armed forces—FAPLA—and made plans for a visit to Moxico in search of her mother. "But before then," she continued, "something strange took place. There was a rally for the army and President Neto was making the first military promotions. It was hot and there were many people. Out of nowhere this man came up to me and put his arms around me. It was Justino—this very man. We celebrated then."

"I did not celebrate," Justino protested. "Of course I was overwhelmed to see her. I had never seen her in my life, except in the photograph. I was filming the ceremony for the department and growing tired of lieutenant colonels, so I looked for images in the crowd. Then I saw her." But by this time it was too late: Katila had taken up with one of her colleagues in the MPLA.

Shortly afterward, Katila was transferred from the general staff to work under her former commander, Saydi Mingas, who was now the minister of finance, and the following year she was given leave to look for her mother. She flew down to Moxico with the army and found her in Lumbala N'guimbo. "I had heard that she was there. The people of Lumbala could tell from my features that I was the daughter of Dona Maria. They brought her from the house and we wept. It was like a resurrection. We wept and then we feasted for a week. After we had eaten all the goats in the neighborhood, we started on the pigs. And when it was time to go, I left."

Saydi Mingas was murdered in May during a coup attempt within the MPLA. There had been a food shortage in Luanda and growing resentment against the leaders of mixed race in the government. The takeover failed but not before several figureheads in the movement had been killed. Katila was downcast by the death of Saydi Mingas. She remained in the ministry for a time and then transferred to work for the national airline.

"I learned city life," she said, "and I learned the goodness of silence. Nothing can come of complaining. It would only add to our misfortune. Now I am a mother and a wife; my children will enjoy a better life than me. My husband works for the ministry of agriculture and we have some privileges. Things are not right in Angola but God knows we are not the poorest of its people."

Justino shut the photo album and wiped his glasses on his shirt. He made to fold the map but Katila was hunched over the land at the End of the Earth. She was trying to calculate how many miles she had walked during her time in the bush.

▲

Since 1987, there had been a great deal of military activity at the End of the Earth, in the province of Cuando Cubango. Now, a few months into 1988, the long war with South Africa appeared to be ending in some kind of victory for the government and the Cubans. In any case, they must have thought so, since they now arranged for the foreign press to visit the front.

There was nothing to do in the protocol lounge of Luanda airport at 5 A.M., but the roar of the propeller transports made sleep impossible. The fighting in Angola was so widespread and intense that two or three could land in the space of a few minutes and be up again within the hour. As the dawn came, the sky over the airport was brackish with the fumes of aviation fuel. A dozen journalists or more paced the lounge while their phlegmatic minders from the Press Center settled into the scarred upholstery. The destination, they had announced the night before, was Cuito Cuanavale, a small garrison town with a strategic airstrip in Cuando Cubango province, about two hundred miles from the Namibian border.

During the early 1980s, the South African Defence Force (SADF) had launched three major offensives in the southwest of Angola, where SWAPO guerrillas tended to concentrate. The southeast, however, had become a more active zone in 1985, when the government and the Cubans embarked on a dry-season campaign against UNITA. It had failed because of logistical difficulties. Scant news of the fighting had reached the outside world, although the South Africans had followed up within a few miles of Cuito Cuanavale. The government repeated the process in the dry season of 1987, with more armor and more thorough planning. This time the combat had been harder and the casualties higher on both sides. It was now May of the following year and the series of battles around Cuito Cuanavale had only recently come to an end. In the interim, the little town had become famous.

The government offensive of 1987 had been directed at Mavinga, which lay between Cuito Cuanavale and Savimbi's headquarters at Jamba. Mavinga was administered by UNITA and protected by the SADF, who made unimpeded use of its airstrip. Since 1986, when the United States aid to the rebels was resumed through Zaïre, the movement's presence in the north had been growing. But the guerrillas still depended on supply corridors running up from Jamba. Cutting these was the main objective at the start of the campaign. As the government columns began to move—and there were eight brigades involved by August—they could rely on cover and supply from the middle of the country by what had become an effective air force. There had been considerable supplies of arms to both sides from Washington and Moscow.

When the South Africans realized that four government brigades would be committed to forward combat, they threw their weight behind UNITA. This took the form of the 32nd Battalion, known also as Buffalo, and the 61st Mechanized Battalion. Buffalo had been in and out of Angola for years. It was an assortment of capable soldiers and was renowned for derring-do, playing by ear and the kind of casual killing that was typical of the wars in southern Africa. During August additional South African units were brought into Angola and there was now a "force in being" in the field that South Africa's chiefs of staff referred to as the 20th Brigade. The most important weapon at its disposal was an artillery piece known as the G5, which had a range of about twenty-eight miles. The G6, also deployed in Angola, was a self-propelled version of the same gun. UNITA had the Stinger surface-to-air missile, but it was rarely used.

By January of the following year UNITA and the South Africans had launched a counteroffensive. The government's 47th Brigade had been routed west of Mavinga by a South African force about a quarter of its size. The government forces had pulled back and dug in around Cuito Cuanavale where the South Africans had pounded them for weeks with artillery fire. The town too was bombarded heavily and it was impossible for planes to land on the airstrip. For a time it looked as though the South Africans would take Cuito Cuanavale, although they denied that this was their objective. The government could still put up air cover from Menongue, to the northwest, and move supplies by road. Then in March the government announced a breakthrough. FAPLA had held up a major South African offensive and was at last confident of its position beyond the Cuito River.

In theory we were going to inspect a piece of recent history. It was a fair guess that the battle of Cuito Cuanavale was over; that the serious fighting had shifted to the southwest and center of the country.

It was already light when we boarded an Antonov and flew to Menongue. It was bright and warm when the plane put down, but there was a delay: confusion perhaps, or a dispute about whether to take us on the second leg after all. It expressed itself not in open discussion between the military and the apparatchiks, for example, but in a curious series of maneuvers on all sides. A minder disappeared around the corner of the control tower and reappeared with a soldier, neither of them speaking. A jeep breezed up to the journalists standing around the Antonov; more soldiers got out, made as though to greet them and then decided against it, piling back into the vehicle, which then disappeared, but in another direction. Once they were almost out of sight, the minder waved at them to stop. Ten minutes later the same jeep was bumping across the tarmac with the same driver but a different set of soldiers and the process was repeated, only there was a brief conversation between minders and military. Then, after half an hour, two jeeps arrived and we were driven away for breakfast.

The old colonial building was in a state of decay. A leafless creeper had nudged the plaster from the facade. Inside it was clean and bare. We were ushered into a room with two tables and several chairs. Breakfast was already laid: three tins of Planter's nuts, several packs of lager and a dozen bottles of vodka and scotch. A handful of Cokes and a lone bottle of mineral water stood aloof from the main body of the meal. The military sat at one table, the press at the other and breakfast was consumed to the last drop. Both groups now clambered into the vehicles and the airstrip materialized through a haze of alcohol, dust and engine oil. A MiG took off and brazened its way across the lower half of the sky with heat decoys spilling from beneath its tail. As it rose it shrank to the size of a pinhead but the land surrounding the airfield still seemed to shake.

The scrub at the side of the strip began to shine and ripple like water as the first helicopter, a Hind gunship, took off, nose down as it lifted. I watched it level off from a window as the blades of our own helicopter dragged us into the air and we too were on the move. The Hind sped down ahead of us clearing a path. The Angolan pilots were in good spirits after their breakfast, and we browsed the forest at high speed. Once there was a splintering crash as the underside tore through the top of a tree. Rich woodland extended on either side, thinning gradually to a pale green blur of savannah; the pilots took us lower still.

A group of soldiers had boarded with us, one in his late teens or early twenties, who spent the journey scanning the land to our right with the muzzle of his rifle protruding through a window. A couple more were dozing; one of them was a tall woman in her thirties with plaited hair. A spruce lieutenant colonel sat by an empty machine-gun mounting at the cabin entrance. He was known as Ngueto; a major until recently, he now held the regional command. He gazed out beyond the scrub beneath us. After a time, a weapon was put in the mounting. We were flying over a road now. On one side of it were trucks, armored personnel carriers and armored cars, forming a long column.

The helicopters put down on a rise in the road. An armored vehicle and a truck with an open tailboard were waiting to take us into Cuito Cuanavale. It was a five-minute ride. You could see the town below full of military, the signs of bombardment visible in the streets and houses. The land stretched away from the town, immense and oddly untroubled, falling to the Cuito River, running flat beyond it through a flood plain and rising again to the east in a shallow scarp with thick vegetation. Two or three peasant settlements at the edge of the town lay abandoned; one large hut had its roof blown in. The fields around were overgrown and cratered.

In the town itself, Ngueto pointed to a school destroyed in the shelling, and then a clinic, going on to explain that South Africa had suffered a significant defeat in March; it was a turning point. "They lost five Centurion tanks," he said. "Three of them were destroyed and one, which we've got here with us, still goes. We also shot down one of their planes." The young soldier who had sat with his gun sticking from the helicopter took a cigarette from one of the journalists and tucked it into his top pocket.

The South Africans had launched three armored assaults in February and March and failed to drive the government back across the river. They had gotten bogged down in the minefields, taken casualties and lost armor, including Centurion tanks, or Olifants as they were known, although their own count was only three. It was the end of a heavy engagement: eight government brigades in the early stages and thousands of Cubans; at least three thousand South Africans and many UNITA; meanwhile, to the west, units from the liberation movements with bases in Angola—SWAPO of Namibia and the ANC—had been fighting on behalf of the government. For Africa, this was war on a massive scale but in Cuito Cuanavale, with the third South African assault repulsed, the heat of battle had gone. For FAPLA it was victory. That was the meaning of the silence which hung like crepe across the Cuito River and up into the woods. It was why the lieutenant colonel could admit to a certain satisfaction. "It's not easy to organize an army," he told the journalists. "You've got to keep at it. It's the work we've done over a long period that is bringing us results now."

We were put back into the vehicles and driven slowly down a steep, rutted dirt road to the bridge. At the bridge we got out and the drivers turned the vehicles around, the open truck now nearest the water. They left the engines running. The journalists walked around the bank of the river to inspect some of the wreckage. The bridge had been hit by G5s; it was sagging in the middle. To its side lay a rusting pontoon. On the far bank there were a few Angolan soldiers and a small detachment of Cubans. Some of these men were making their way toward us across the battered bridge, which looked like a roller-coaster accident. There was really nothing here to dwell on. Ngueto ordered the journalists back into the vehicles but nobody paid attention. He gave the order a second time and a few people climbed aboard.

There were still several stragglers when a South African shell landed, raising a column of mud beside the bridge and forty meters from the open truck; then we were hauling people onto the tailboard with the truck already jolting forward. The armored vehicle raced ahead of us with soldiers clinging to its sides. The ruts on the road tossed the truck about and more shells were now falling behind us. Indeed we seemed to be drawing them forward like some courtier trying to bow out of an ill-judged audience. We tore straight through the town, up to the crest of the hill and stopped.

There were no injuries in the truck, although it had been nearer the bridge; the armored car, however, had taken part of the blast—and casualties as a result. Two soldiers hanging on to the side of the vehicle had wounds, light enough but with high blood loss, and a third was seriously injured. He too had been clinging on. He had received a large piece of shrapnel near the hip and the blood had drained from his body into the vehicle. He had slumped across a hatch and been held there during the frenetic retreat from the bridge by anyone inside who could get a hand to him. A medical unit took him away and we waited around, mostly in silence. Ngueto must have hoped to strike a lighter note by bringing up one of the captured Olifants for inspection. When they brought back the soldier on a stretcher I saw for the first time that it was the boy who liked to trail his rifle out of the helicopter. I asked his name but this was not viewed well. Ngueto was dismayed by the injury. The casualty was a hero of the armed forces, that was all there was to say. We waited around as the Hind put down, followed by our own helicopter.

He was lifted in with a blood drip on his arm and a drainage tube in his torso. The other casualties boarded with a little help, one copiously bandaged, the other holding his own saline bag. There was nowhere to secure the packs and people took turns holding them up above the wounded. The boy on the stretcher was unconscious during most of the journey—a piece of good fortune, for the pilots were erratic, jerking the aircraft up over the woodlands and down again as the bag of plasma swung above him. A wild surge toward the ground and a steep recovery brought him around. The first stirrings in the inert body were a relief, for we were all willing the life back into him. He grimaced and raised an arm. Our eyes moved from the drip to the forest and back to the drip. As the sun sank, the province of Cuando Cubango was a solemn red. Then, in the twilight, you could pick out cooking fires, glowing in the woodland below. Many were military, no doubt, but nearer Menongue there must also have been families, hundreds of them, resourceful, enduring—hidden beneath the bulk of the war like lizards under a vast stone.

In Luanda we learned that the Cubans had deployed in the southwest of Angola, on the border with Namibia. Washington had assembled the three main adversaries—UNITA was excluded—at a meeting in London. Both developments were crucial markers on the course toward peace. After two days of discussion, the parties agreed to meet again and did so at the end of the following month in Cairo. Two days after the talks in Cairo came to an end, a successful air raid by Cuban MiGs destroyed a strategic bridge on the Cunene River and damaged the Calueque dam, which services northern Namibia. Eleven South Africans died in the attack. On the same day, just before midnight, the South African task force in Cunene province was ordered to leave Angola.

▲

In 1990, nearly two years after the South African withdrawal, I was given permission to return to Angola. It was with some reluctance that the Press Center issued invitations to foreign journalists. Broadly speaking, the purpose of the center was to obstruct the practice of journalism whenever possible. Its goodwill in the last days of the war in the southeast had been a momentary lapse, for which remorse had now set in and, as a result, most of my time would be spent waiting in Luanda for the center to set up appointments with junior government ministers.

There was an American by the name of Donald in the Hotel Turismo. He was tall, fair and prepossessing, though he had difficulty keeping his balance as he searched his baggy trousers for his business card. He introduced himself in a garbled mixture of French and English, with a dash of Spanish, apologizing finally for his incoherence with the single Portuguese word, *desculpe*. We agreed to meet for a drink at eight o'clock that night. I was late and rang the room from reception.

"What time is it?" he asked. I told him it was 8:30.

"Eight-thirty? Shit. *J'ai du travail à faire.* I'll catch you at lunch."

I hinted that it was not yet morning and, with some relief, he asked me up. In the middle of his room was a pile of cut ginger and an empty champagne bottle. The rest was chaos. I read the paper while he splashed some water on his face. An editorial disguised as a news item warned against "excessive zeal by party organs and the tendency to confuse social and mass organizations with party organizations." *Man of Action* was playing at the Atlantico Cinemo: "Directed by Craig R. Baxley. With Carl Withers and Craig T. Nelson. American action film." Finally there was a tally of recent UNITA bombings—twenty in all. Savimbi was closer to the capital now and the lights were often going out.

Donald dragged himself from the bathroom, asked me politely not to smoke and then put some rock music on a small recorder with portable speakers. He handed me a beer and he produced a joint. I asked how long he had been in the country.

"Three months. No, four. No, *momento por favor*. Shit. Anyhow, I feel like I've been here my whole fucking life." I never found out quite what Donald did in Angola and I'm not sure he knew either. "It's a U.N. thing," he said, "but kind of private. I've been teaching business skills to some guys in the government"—he swayed about in a moment of irresolution, quickly overcome—"who did not know jack shit in the first place and never will. *Excusez-moi, desculpe*, I think we should change the subject."

Donald's views about Angola were robustly optimistic. "Now the South Africans are all but gone," he said, "and the Cubans are going, you're about to see the end of this horseshit. *Tu vois*, big changes. It's a great country and you can do a lot of things here. First you pay off Savimbi and send him to live in Morocco with King Hassan. He likes it up there; he's got a villa in Rabat. Then you throw out the president, take the ruling party and stick it, which is no problem, because everybody hates the MPLA, I guess you've noticed; and what are we left with? Some smart guys in UNITA, some honest guys from MPLA, a bunch of Portuguese who'll leap back in here once the peace is signed—and plenty of liberal professionals who've been lying low. Well, that's not bad for starters. It's enough to put a democracy on the road."

Much had changed since South Africa's withdrawal. It had loosened a kind of regional lockjaw. Now it was possible to articulate the present and, if you cared to, the future. Even Donald was a new phenomenon in Angola—an amiable character with wholly "antisocial" views, whose presence was only possible with approval from the government he roundly despised.

After Cuito Cuanavale and the Cuban air strike on the Cunene River, it was generally assumed that South Africa had suffered a military defeat in Angola. In Cuba, Fidel Castro even approved a Cuito Cuanavale exhibit at the military museum. The South Africans could not accept this view. They invoked their devastation of the 47th Brigade in October 1987 as one of the South African Defence Force's greatest victories. Then they argued that they had fought with their hands tied behind their backs by the politicians in Pretoria and Washington. They had said much the same in 1975.

It was no bad thing for the future of the region if both sides could claim victory in a war that no longer mattered. In the Soviet Union, perestroika had sounded an ominous note for the military regimes in Angola and Ethiopia. NATO estimated Soviet aid to Angola during the first half of the 1980s at $8 billion. Washington had pushed for a settlement in southern Africa whereby independence for Namibia was contingent on a withdrawal of Cuban troops from Angola. This was unpopular in Africa, even though, by the end of 1988, Dr. Chester Crocker, then assistant secretary of state for African affairs, had turned the policy into a success. The South Africans had pulled back to their own country, SWAPO had won a democratic election in an independent Namibia and the Cubans were leaving Angola. In February 1990, Nelson Mandela was released from prison.

There was no peace for the Angolans, however. The effect of the settlement was to tilt the region like a tray so that the residue of the war in southwest Africa clattered into Angola. The MPLA still had plenty of Soviet hardware and several thousand Cubans. UNITA, deprived of serious South African support, could still count on supplies from Washington through Zaïre. By 1990 there were reported to be three C-130 transports making two airlifts a week into Angola. They were under contract from a company in Florida. The planes were thought to leave Zaïre from a place called Kamina, but Donald had been in Zaïre and said he'd seen C-130s discharging onward cargo in Kinshasa. "I mean, what do you think they were offloading—rubbers for the *povo*? Michael Jackson tapes? *Mon ami*, come on!"

The heaviest fighting was now in the north, in the province of Uíge, once full of coffee estates and palm plantations. Donald was leaving Angola at the end of the week but he planned to return and use the war in the north to make some money. There was still food being grown in the area but the fighting had disrupted the local markets. People were desperate to get their produce to Luanda. Donald planned to buy a truck, take out two insurance policies on it, one with the government and another with Lloyd's, and work the road to Uíge. Even with the stunning premiums he could expect to pay, he reckoned there was a $500 profit to be made on each trip. "Producers are already paying in dollars to run their stuff to Luanda," he told me. As with most things I heard in Angola, I had no way of knowing whether this was true. "And, of course," he added, "if UNITA take out the truck, I simply collect on the insurance."

This was a short-term enterprise, he told me, because the war would be over by the end of the year. (Donald was wrong on this score.) In the longer term he planned to open an investment service for foreigners wishing to put money into Angola. Potential investors would need to be shown the ropes in a puzzling and solipsistic culture such as this. The service would offer briefing papers, risk assessments, introductions to the relevant ministries, accommodation and field trips. It would provide office space in Luanda with a telex machine, a fax and phones that worked. It would take care of the daunting paperwork and legal formalities that a prospective investor was sure to face, even as Angola liberalized. "And," said Donald with emphasis, "it would ask for a fee. Maybe a flat fee. A businessman comes on the phone to me and I say, 'Sure, we can do it. But I want to see $100,000 deposited in such-and-such bank before I even think about you.' Then, once the business starts up, you can negotiate a second contract as a troubleshooter. Meanwhile new clients are flowing down the pipeline . . ."

Donald was of the opinion that the president would be keen on schemes like his. New laws guaranteed foreign investors the right to

transfer net profits abroad and repatriate capital in the event of sale or
liquidation. Profits were taxable at a modest standard rate of 35 percent, plus a puzzling surtax that, in deference to the days before perestroika, was called the Popular Resistance Tax. Donald knew all
about this. The president, he said, was the force behind the reforms,
bulldozing them through the objections of the hard-liners in the party.

It transpired that he had even met the president, and although
he had difficulty recalling the circumstances, he gave the impression
that he was in Angola at the presidential behest. "Sure I met him,"
he told me, rising to his feet and relighting the joint. "That's what
he wanted. We shook hands. I said, *'O senhor presidente, desculpe,'* you
know, because my Portuguese is shit. And because I'm an American.
Je suis un américain. The president replied in perfect French, *'C'est un
honneur de vous recevoir dans notre pays.'* " Donald swayed in silence for
a few seconds, shrugged his shoulders and collapsed onto the bed. I
went out to the balcony and when I came back, he handed me a
Polaroid photo of himself and a young African woman, with glasses
and a studious expression. "That's Cecily," he said. "She's my wife.
I haven't spoken to her in weeks. She's in Paris and you can't get a
line to Paris."

I was not sure that Donald would ever succeed in a business
venture in the new Angola. He lacked the folly of the really ambitious.
There would be better contenders for the pickings in Angola when the
time was right. They would come from South Africa and Portugal,
and they would know much better how to "deal with Africans." All
that, however, would have to wait until the war was over.

▲

In Angola, and perhaps in other parts of Africa, a visiting journalist rarely has much to do with the vast majority of people—the
peasantry—unless they are hungry or working at a government
project. Indeed, to most African governments landed populations are
an embarrassment—obdurate, superstitious and resistant to change.
The MPLA had a word for these tendencies: *obscurantismo*—it even
appeared in the Constitution as something the people's republic was
resolved to "combat vigorously."

There are probably between nine and ten million people in Angola, of whom at least six million depend on the land. The government
always claimed that the war had disrupted farming massively. One
had only to think of the antipersonnel mines in the country to suspect
that this was accurate, but unless they knew you well, the MPLA liked
you to remain in the towns. As a result, I had no notion whatever of
the land, of this enormous mass that must have asserted some conti-

nuity for its people, despite the disruption of crop cycles, the displacement, abduction and injury that came with war.

When the Press Center offered a trip to Benguela I had high hopes of flying further inland on a light plane. The government had announced a drought in the province and even though people would be in miserable circumstances, their spokesman might give an account of what had happened to them during the war.

My new minder was a fluent French speaker called Augusto. His skin was so black it had a violet hue of which Savimbi would surely have approved. He was from the north. His parents were peasant farmers; simple people, he explained, "even without a bank account." They were supporters of the MPLA. He had spent his childhood in Congo-Léopoldville. When Neto's people shifted their offices to Brazzaville, the family moved there too. Later they returned to Angola and were now living in the province of Uíge, where UNITA was concentrating its attacks. Perhaps Augusto's abnormally strong dislike of Savimbi, which was clear the first time he spoke about the war, had something to do with the fact that his relatives were now in the thick of it.

The old Fokker Friendship was packed and as usual there were disappointed customers. A handful of *povo* who managed to board were wrestling with the frayed seatbelts, but after a few minutes in the air they were relaxed and chatting, as though on a bus. The plane sighed down the coast to Benguela and for quite some time Augusto said nothing. When I broke the silence by remarking on the elegance of his beret, he thanked me and explained that it was a matter of style, which in Africa was important. In a pedagogic tone, he added, "Even when we are suffering, we must have this thing that we call style, for it gives us dignity." He sat back and stared straight ahead down the cabin. We both listened anxiously to the pitch of the engines for a while. Then he said:

"Why do you think Kenneth Kaunda has a handkerchief? I will tell you. It is purely a question of style. I agree, he does not suffer, even when he weeps, but he has great style. I am like Kenneth Kaunda. You see me now with my own two handkerchiefs." He plucked at the worn sleeve of the donkey jacket—*"Premier mouchoir"*—and then tapped the beret: *"Deuxième. Force réserve."*

Parts of Benguela were badly run-down but it had stood to one side of the war, unruffled. It had open squares, tiled roofs and grassy tramlines that were now pedestrian thoroughfares. The large shunting yards were full of twisted locos, destroyed by UNITA, with bindweed proliferating around the wheels. Benguela had been one of the big slaving ports on the Atlantic coast. In his memoir, Joachim Monteiro described how older people that he met had seen "as many as ten to twelve vessels loading at a time in Luanda and Benguela." Monteiro himself had witnessed the arrival of a caravan of slaves in the city. A century later it teemed with a new dispossessed, forced out of the interior by war and, at present, drought. Many, no doubt, were resettled as a matter of policy. Stretching thirty kilometers up the bay to Lobito there was a corridor where the railway line still operated, running parallel with a usable road. The area was fertile and well tended. When you drove the potholed blacktop, an endless drape of banana fronds hung to one side of you. The plantations ran back from the corridor to a depth I could not judge.

The drought was inland, to the east. We waited for a day to know if we were going. On the next, an official from the party headquarters in Benguela arrived to tell us that we would now be able to see what was happening with our own eyes. Shouldn't we pack first? The official laughed as he led us toward a diesel pickup. We drove across town to a whitewashed apartment block in the suburbs, several stories high with a transmission mast on the roof. The building was badly damaged, and a trail of blood led from the landing of the second floor to that of the third. The elevator was broken; a woman with gray hair at her temples walked ahead of us up the open stairway carrying a pail of water.

On the top floor were the offices of the city's radio and television station. They contained a video suite with a working air conditioner. Suddenly it was chilly and we were sitting in front of a monitor with two technicians and an Angolan journalist, watching scenes of degradation from Cubal, 150 kilometers east. The camera moved up the legs of exhausted mothers, across the threadbare *capulanas* tied tight above the hips and came to rest on infants tugging at wrinkled breasts. It darted into a dark hut where there was nothing but eyes and the sound of brushwood snapping under the cameraman's feet. A young blond man in jeans and a pale blue T-shirt, an aid worker perhaps, was taking notes in the background. All the while strange music, like the score of a spaghetti western, played on a grinder's organ, was running underneath. The air-conditioning had turned the room bitterly cold.

The local official told us that UNITA had made it hard for relief to reach Cubal. He looked at his notes. "Until March this year," he informed us, "2,659 people have died." Augusto gave a high-pitched whistle, adjusted his beret and wrote down the figure on his notepad. The official added that when aid did get in, the statistics improved. "But we have very few trucks and the roads are unsafe."

There was something worse, undeniably, about seeing hunger on a monitor than in real life. For journalists in Africa, mass starvation was hardly unfamiliar. You could stumble through feeding centers in Sudan, Eritrea and Mozambique, but in its representation on screen—this one in particular—it was suddenly more dismaying. The music, the aid worker, the scrutiny of the camera—all this seemed to compound the misery of the *povo*. Cubal might have been anywhere in Africa; we were studying the image of some generalized African peasant, with no kinship or lineage, whose fate was eternal indignity, handed down like a name or a ceremonial object.

The official asked to be left at the municipal headquarters. We walked with him up the stairs of this huge and exquisite colonial building and went through the usual courtesies on the landing, surveyed by black-and-white portraits of Marx and Engels, and the beautiful Déolinda Rodrigues, a heroine of the revolution murdered by the FNLA. Almost everything to do with women in Angola, including the junior ladies' handball tournament, was named after Déolinda. Lenin was there too, pouring over a text like a grand philologist.

"Les patrons du marxisme," said Augusto with a cheery wave of the hand, as we made our way down the staircase.

The car wound through some rocky hills, passing a complex of small farms, until we were back on the coast, following a narrow road below an uneven rock face. In the dusk the sea looked gray and agitated. We pulled up at a row of small bungalows fronting the beach and were led to a room behind a small veranda. It was crammed with chairs, which the official accompanying us rearranged. Four young men shuffled in and stood behind the chairs. They were followed by two MPLA men, older and better dressed, who ordered them to sit down. Augusto looked the younger ones over with an air of disdain, his eyebrows raised to the rim of his beret. They were short on style and, as far as he was concerned, they were still in some sense the enemy.

There was a plan for the reintegration of UNITA fighters who had been captured or had given themselves up under an amnesty, and these four men were in it. There were said to be about ninety such people in Benguela, but since Savimbi's army was thought to number anything between twenty and sixty thousand, the figure was not impressive. Rehabilitation appeared to involve isolation, for they were kept far from the center of the city. A short man in an orange T-shirt began a prepared speech thanking God that he was no longer with UNITA. He had been in the bush for several years after the rebels destroyed the village where he lived, near Huambo. Everyone, he said, had been taken into the forest. He had fought for the movement and then run away in 1987. The MPLA had sent him to Luanda and now he was here; he was well; he had no complaints.

Next to him sat a burly youngster in an off-white T-shirt with vertical black stripes down the front and behind them a picture of Michael Jackson. In red lettering near the neck was the legend: "Bad." He could not give even a rudimentary account of his past except to say that though he had a large family in Huambo, it was too dangerous for him to visit them. Perhaps he had become notorious in the area during his time with UNITA. He lay crouched in the center of his big body, troubled and unavailable.

A smaller man in a white shirt said he had been abducted almost seven years back. The "bandits" (for one was not allowed to use the name UNITA) had arrived at four in the morning and taken everyone from his village. He had been tied up and led into the bush, along with his wife. "Since you're here with a woman," they had told him, "she stays with us and you go to the front." He was five months in training with UNITA's army and five years in the military. He said he had "suffered too much."

One day he was ordered back to Savimbi's main bases at Jamba; he was going to start work as a radio operator. He found his wife in such a bad condition, sick and abused, he suspected, by other members of the movement, that he wanted to leave. "Don't worry," his commander told him, "peace will be coming. You must be patient. You must wait." A few days later he took his wife and three children and his weapon and crept away from the base. He had decided to give himself up. He went back to his village in order to greet his parents, but it was still in UNITA hands and he thought better of entering. "We walked on to Huambo," he said, "a journey of several days. I was received by the offices of the party without incident. I requested a pass to Luanda but this was refused and instead I was ordered to serve with the FAPLA for five months. Then, as you see, I was brought here to Benguela, although my wife remained in Huambo." He seemed to have finished his story until one of his guardians leaned across and spoke to him in Umbundu. "It is here in Benguela," he added, "that I lack suffering. When everything is settled I will call my wife from Huambo to be with me." It was a thumbnail sketch of a life in the central provinces that had gone awry. It had a ring of authenticity to it. Above all, it was not discouraging. This man had survived more than five years of combat, his wife was still alive, he had his wits about him and all of his limbs. It was a safe bet that he would have nothing impartial to say about UNITA in front of his keepers.

As we rose to leave, the big, uncomfortable boy began to speak with difficulty. It was a jumble of thoughts that Augusto translated into French as we remained standing with our bags on our shoulders. The boy began with a complaint about a chicken leg. One scrawny piece of a bird that you happened to find: you would have to give it to your commander. You were tired, you had not eaten for days, you had been in combat and then, after you entered a village, perhaps you found the remains of a meal in a pot. But if you did not hand it in, they would shoot you. He glared at me and went on. Worse than that was the walking. You walked for a day without food, you slept; in the morning you picked up your bag and your gun and began again. *"Và,"* exclaimed the boy. *"Sempre: và, và!"* Now he was shouting. You begged for clothes, he went on, to replace the rags on your body, but you were told by spruce commanders that you would have to wait. If you said a word against the political line you could die as you died for eating chicken. As a soldier you went a little crazy in that situation. The boy's eyes were smarting and he rolled his big head so that one ear rubbed against his shoulder. He mumbled something and clicked his finger joints. "That is all he remembers," said Augusto, "and now he asks your permission to stop."

On the way back, I asked Augusto whether there wasn't a system of merit for the boys: might they not be rewarded with privileges of some kind for denouncing UNITA with alacrity? Hadn't the boy, seeing us on the point of leaving, plucked up his courage? Augusto drew in his breath. It was not like that, he said, not at all. I thought of the noise of the waves on the beach and the young men being led into the cramped room. It had all been like a trial of castaways conducted by the chiefs of a remote island.

"That business of the chicken," I said aggressively, "if it's true, it means UNITA has discipline. No theft; good relations with the people."

"UNITA is not a movement," Augusto replied. "They are *fantoches*—puppets—and they kill without thinking. This is common knowledge. They take whatever they see. People who visit our country have much to learn but they are always coming to conclusions before they have a chance to look."

Many peasants had fled from the war to Benguela. The drought too had brought them into the city. The production of corn had been disrupted and the government had distributed three hundred tons of seed to get it back on its feet, but the rains had failed again and there was no point in planting. Most of the seed had been eaten. Now livestock were dying; the province had lost as many as 23,000 head of cattle through lack of pasture.

Once more we were climbing the grand staircase of the municipal headquarters. The office we entered was big and bright, and the governor of Benguela was seated at a large desk from which he rose to greet us. His name was Paulo Jorge. He had been in the province for eight months. His was an appointment with strong presidential backing, for just as Benguela had stayed at the edge of the war, so Paulo Jorge had lately kept his distance from the conservative elements of the party, although as a former foreign minister, he had been one of the best Angolan negotiators the U.S. had faced.

Of course the drought was the first subject to be raised. The governor spoke responsibly and knowledgeably about it. He said that there was now a local emergency committee to monitor the crisis and channel the aid to the worst affected areas. He had negotiated the purchase of one thousand tons of flour and fourteen thousand tons of corn from the European Economic Community, over and above the allocation from the central government. The war was not so hard in Benguela, he said; even so, UNITA was sorely tempted by food aid, for its own system of supply was unreliable. With food aid taking to the road, UNITA had stepped up its ambushes. All this, said the governor, meant delays on delivery, for it took days to arrange proper security for convoys. I caught Augusto's expression of high satisfaction from the corner of my eye. He was writing down the dirt on UNITA.

Paulo Jorge was a vigorous and impressive man, even a good man, but he was also a dreamer, like Justino, or Neto and the other poets of the MPLA—or Donald for that matter. He was handling the drought as best he could but it was clear that he wished to pass on from this to discuss the future. The governor could already see a nation in which the war was over and the old ideas of the MPLA about a regulated economy were not only dead—new laws had been killing them off for several years—but buried. He saw a land of thriving private farms, like those of the Portuguese, and state plans to support the peasant farmer with credit and the provision of tools and seeds. He saw nurseries and seed multiplication centers, irrigation projects, hectares of rippling corn, and above all, a dynamic market for this produce, with price liberalization as the great incentive for the peasants to grow surpluses. "It's under discussion at this stage," he said with a professorial wag of his finger. "If it goes ahead, we will be fine."

Then he moved on to the subject of the Benguela railway line, which extended hundreds of miles into the interior, linking Zambia and Zaïre to the Atlantic coast. It must be rehabilitated, said the governor; it was part of a regional complex that would unite the new southern Africa in a vast trade partnership. Millions of dollars in foreign aid had already been pledged for the rehabilitation of the port at

Lobito and, with peace, the donors would invest in the redevelopment of the entire line: 1,305 kilometers! Lobito would be flourishing.

"My starting point, my very premise," he went on, "is one of the pillars of our society: man. The priority of priorities is to get enough for man to eat, to clothe himself, to have shoes on his feet. To be able to exercise the basic right to medical care and an education."

It was a candid admission that the scientific socialism of the MPLA could now be abandoned in word, as it has been in deed. Suddenly the whole thing had begun to look like an acknowledged write-off and in its place stood a new enthusiasm—the liberal enthusiasm, the faith in markets and free exchange. Market philosophies might well be closer than the doctrines of Soviet socialism to the forms of exchange preferred by peasant farmers. They might even suit them better. Yet there was no reason, it occurred to me, why a peasant in Benguela province should share Paulo Jorge's belief in any economic system. Peasant culture might be highly politicized but it didn't squander *belief* on frivolities of that kind. It was altogether less fickle about the things it believed in: birth, purification, death and communion with the ancestors. In Angola the distance between the people with plans and those for whom the plans were laid was daunting.

"For your information," said the governor, returning to the drought, "we still need sixty thousand tons of corn to cover the emergency needs of the population."

Augusto adjusted his beret and led the way to the top of the majestic staircase, where we passed *"les patrons du marxisme."* Angola had arrived at what they might have called a state of maximum contradiction.

▲

At 6:30 in the morning we were at the railway station in Benguela. Before the train pulled in, trucks began to gather in the square below the facade. I counted around ten, with long wooden tailboards once brightly colored, blue, red, yellow—faded now and peeling. Then three cars pulled up and waited with their engines running. A ceiling of fine red dust and gasoline fumes filtered the harshness of the morning sun. When I turned to the station, the train was moving along the platform. It was hard to tell how many cars there were as the engine drew alongside and past. I could not see to the end of the train and the view was obscured by *povo*, hundreds of them, pouring from the tops and sides of the cars, or releasing the handrails from which they'd been hanging, to ease down into a run. First the children, then the men. Sacks, baskets, crumpled suitcases were ejected behind them; they turned with their arms up and caught them on the move; shouting, jostling passengers ran for the exit, but the train had still not come to a halt.

A grinding of metal and a shocking jolt down the length of the train brought it to a standstill. A flood of human beings began to pour through the wooden stile at the side of the station building. The old were propelled along by the young; the lame and limbless came hurtling through on their crutches, buoyed up by the people around them. Objects seemed to rise, suspended above the crowd: buckets of kale, oily cardboard boxes, bundles of cane, string bags of green tomatoes, a very old chrome standard lamp with fabric flex; lagging fifteen yards behind it, a mauve shade with torn gold trim; more boxes, a basket of melons, an enamel tub, three cans of butter oil and a ripped bolster. An old man bobbed past us like a cork, with three straw hats stacked on his head. There were women of all ages coming through now, their head scarves obscured by the loads on their heads and the dyes of their *capulanas* glowing through the dust-clogged cotton.

From its waist down, the crowd seemed to be wading through a river of saffron, red, viridian, orange and every variety of blue. Above this was a jumble of T-shirts with improbable legends—"Jack Daniels," "Joggers for Jesus," "Madonna," "Suzuki," "Tonight's the Night"—torn at the nipple or riding down below the shoulder. Collarbones and tendons braced to their burdens. Many women carried children, strapped at their backs with lengths of flannel, *capulanas*, even fishnet. Some were gaunt and undernourished, others stout; very few wore shoes.

They fanned out into the square, packing the trunks and cars, which now rolled off in ragged convoy, leaving many more people shouting and gesticulating.

Augusto said the people were coming from Lobito to work and to barter in Benguela. Hundreds of them, though, were going along the coast to Baia Farta, where the small fishing boats came in. There must have been a roaring market trade that lasted until sundown. He said the vehicles would come back for a second load, maybe a third. "This is how we are living," he added. He found it hard to answer whether trade of this kind was illegal. In the past, yes, most of it, he said, but such things were a fact of life. "*Je suis réaliste*," he added. In Luanda, the government had even given the big markets a formal status and a name: People's Markets. The people themselves stuck to the outlandish names of their own devising. One market was still known as Roque Santeiro, after the title of a Brazilian soap opera.

"But this is the *povo*," Augusto exclaimed after the crush had thinned. "What do you think of them? I think you have never seen them in such numbers."

I was lost for a reply, as though I had just witnessed a miracle.

"They are something," he answered on my behalf, with a broad, ingenuous smile. "They have impeccable style. That is my opinion and on this matter, believe me"—he touched the collar of his donkey jacket—"I am an expert."

▲

Not seeing the war was strange. It made you doubt the solidity of things, because at the bottom of the new dispensation in Angola, at the bottom of the regional peace, lay a bitter lee of killing. The Cold War was ending everywhere. Angola was no exception, even if the government could still rely on a dwindling Cuban expeditionary force—over half had gone—and a few deliveries from Moscow. In a sense, it was now Washington's war, pursued to dispel any illusions among the MPLA that Savimbi was defeatable. The Cold War had wreaked havoc in Angola, but at least a proportion of the fighting had been confined to military fronts. Now the fronts were nominal; in fact they had blurred beyond recognition. This loss of definition meant more torment for civilians, especially in the north, where UNITA was heavily armed and fighting wherever it saw the chance. Reports coming in from Uíge suggested that the province was ravaged. Figures for civilian casualties were posted regularly at the Press Center and often they were high. Bomb blasts—*"exploitations"* as Augusto called them in an unusual departure from his perfect French—were more frequent.

There was one more textbook campaign in the southeast, a last FAPLA push against the town of Mavinga, in the manner of the old war, but on this reports were wildly at variance. On the very day that the South African president F. W. de Klerk announced the impending release of Nelson Mandela, the government claimed to have taken Mavinga. UNITA disagreed and in March Savimbi invited journalists from South Africa to have a look. They reported evidence of government losses. Savimbi announced that the burned-out government tanks were destroyed by Toyota four-wheel-drives with mounted antitank guns. They had been flown in by the United States, through Zaïre and down on transports to Savimbi's bases: fast vehicles with no protection, harassing the enemy's armor—the same tactic had worked in Chad for Hissène Habré four years earlier. Later I saw a news agency picture from Mavinga, allegedly taken at the time. It showed a group of wooden crosses marking government graves. Hanging from each was a ration can with a section cut out of the front. Inside that was another, smaller tin containing tallow and an improvised wick.

Where military information was hard to come by, rumor flourished. One version in Luanda held that the government had broken

Savimbi's corridor to the north and captured a quantity of UNITA material at the Mavinga airstrip before withdrawing. This was plausible. Savimbi called anything Mavinga, and if the government had the airstrip, that was not to say that it had overrun the entire UNITA complex. The offensive was headed by a Soviet-trained officer, João de Matos, and conducted without Cuban units, perhaps too without air power—there was disagreement on this. The whole operation may well have been devised to show the United States that, even without the Cubans, FAPLA could pose problems for Savimbi. But few people, and certainly no journalists, knew quite what had happened.

In the capital, it was said that other motives were in play. The party was due to hold its third congress later that year. Change in the air would mean battle in the plenum. The old guard had already been weakened in 1985. Its survivors would feel themselves under threat as the president laid the groundwork for a new organization that must face up to peace and power sharing. The military had enjoyed immense political prestige in Angola and was still an integral element of the party. In the future it would have to reconcile itself to becoming a national army, without party privileges; or more accurately, one element of a national army, since an end to the civil war would mean the integration of government and UNITA fighters. Mavinga was a bid to strengthen the hand of the officer corps with a success in the south. When the congress came, this would be the surest ground on which to defend their interests, long after the lamps had guttered on the crosses at Mavinga.

▲

Luanda seemed to me ravaged. Yet, like Benguela, it had seldom been touched by the war. Most of the apartment blocks had a mysterious sickness, a kind of weeping psoriasis that had spread across the exteriors. It must have happened in stages. First the flaking—a gradual loss of paint and sealants; then discoloration as the air conditioners, long since out of action, had stained the exposed surfaces with rusty discharge; then a seepage of moisture from within, followed by an outbreak of fungus. The concrete seemed to rot with the acquiescence of wood, or fabric.

There was pro-UNITA graffiti on the benches along the bayside road. From there to Justino's house was another half hour, following the edge of the bay. I had meant to ask after Katila, but I arrived in the middle of a heated controversy. Two young Angolans, escorted by a large man with a damaged face and fiery eyes, a white Angolan called Rangel, were working their way through the bottles on Justino's table. The argument had started over the subject of the Russians. Someone said that they had moved on to the best section of beach in 1975 and cordoned it off, so that no Angolans were allowed there. Someone else said that all Russians were racists. They had once discovered black people swimming in a pool in Lubango and had ordered it to be drained and refilled before they would use it again. Someone else said that the Russians should have been thrown out years ago. This attitude, said another, was tantamount to emptying a dozen pools. There was more controversy about the precise time that the beach had or had not been taken over.

The youngsters were cartoonists and Rangel had made them his protégés. There was censorship in Angola and unauthorized cartoons were only just starting to appear. Even so, the difficulty and cost of publishing anything, even on a samizdat scale, were considerable. Rangel was planning to sponsor a booklet by the young men—a comic strip reviving an N'dongo warrior who had risen against the Portuguese three centuries ago. He would come back and lead a satirical attack on corruption, shortages, black marketeering—"a new revolt."

Rangel had served in the Special Forces of the Portuguese colonial army, running counterinsurgency operations against the liberation movements. Then, like many officers after the coup in Lisbon, he had thrown in his lot with the MPLA. It was at least a decade since he had seen action, but the old days still fascinated him. He was a swashbuckler and a romantic, for whom war was both a sensuous and a proper pursuit. He talked about the quiet, dangerous nights in "Kapa-Kapa"—military shorthand for Cuando Cubango province, the End of the Earth—lying in a hammock as the Southern Cross hung above him. He told stories about dropping by helicopter into the middle of UNITA bases and flushing out the rebels, picking up chickens as he scurried from hut to hut. "They were not good soldiers," he said with disdain. Before independence, he claimed, UNITA had worked with the Portuguese. If they were caught near the Zambian border, the Portuguese would attack them, but toward the center of the country, they left them alone. UNITA was freer then to harass the MPLA and steal their food and weapons—and occasionally to inform the colonial administration about their movements.

Through the mists of alcohol, I thought I saw who Rangel was. He would have been on the ascendant in FAPLA until the end of the 1970s, when Portuguese military philosophy in Angola, set at the disposal of the MPLA by a young and committed elite from the Portuguese Special Forces, was finally overshadowed by Soviet and Cuban thinking. Until then the best approach to UNITA was the one taken by the colonial Specials against the MPLA and Holden Roberto's movement during the 1960s and 1970s, moving in small, highly trained airborne units on operations of the kind that Rangel liked to recall. But once South Africa had pulled UNITA back to the southeast and reassembled it as a large auxiliary force of its own, there was no reason why the Russian doctrine of heavy armor should not prevail. Yet it did so with a dreary vengeance, leaving little room for special operations, despite the need for them in the center and east of the country. Rangel's decline into seedy dissent was also the decline of a remarkable alliance between skilled officers and anticolonial leaders— the end of a specific vision of Angola, blurred and finally extinguished by *force majeure*. It was clear why a good soldier like Rangel held UNITA in casual contempt and reserved his real bitterness for the comrade advisers.

After his guests had left, Justino cleared the debris from the table and we sat together for a time. Then I told him about the railway station at Benguela. "Broad paths," he said, when I had finished, "full of people, full of people. Full of people." He removed his glasses and started to polish them on his shirt. "This is from a poem by Neto," he explained. Without his glasses, Justino looked quite blind, although younger and sadder.

Before leaving the house, I copied out a poem by Justino. Back in the hotel I skimmed it, unable to concentrate. Altogether there were too many poets in this stricken republic and I wondered how broad the paths through the nation really were. Had they been few and wide, there would have been more scope, in the country's different cultures, for movement and encounter. As it was, too much was unclear; no one was sure who anyone else was or where they were going. The gifted peasant girl in the photo had not been staring out at Justino after all, but at a track that led away from the bush toward the city and the hopes it embodied—democracy, education, development; it was the place from which Américo Boavida had come, with his love and knowledge. From the moment Justino had set eyes on the picture, however, his own imagination had led him in the opposite direction, toward that pastoral monochrome of revolutionary difficulty. Now both Justino and Katila lived similar lives in Luanda—and how fitting that Justino chose to stay in a tumbledown house without running water, at the city's edge. They shared the same sense of disappointment with the country, the Russians, the Americans, Pretoria and Savimbi. Yet they had not met on the same road, merely on routes that had intersected. One might criticize the old radicals of the MPLA for their romanticism, and their own *obscurantismo* when it came to peasant life, but it was not accurate to say, as Savimbi did, that they had run the country to the detriment of the majority, or that they had not cared. Everything, UNITA included, had conspired to blight Angola's prospects, one by one.

I was about to return to Justino's poem when the power went out. As the night drew on, the Antonovs droned overhead, and just after curfew gunfire started down by the port.

Whatever similarities there were between the city during the closing days of the war with South Africa and the city now, the quality of the place was different. Previously the decay, the poverty, the sullenness of the bureaucrats, the blank look on the faces of so many people, even if they moved with purpose and elegance, had seemed to be functions of the war, and nothing but the war. The South Africans had been running a big operation inside the country and everything was secondary to holding them back. The dreadful state of Luanda thus made sense as a kind of asceticism; the mind of the city was concentrated elsewhere, in the Sixth Military Region, and had no time to attend to its bodily disorders, which, in any case, were simply repercussions of the epic struggle in the southeast.

In this light, Luanda had seemed an impressive place. Its very degeneration was heroic, and even its poverty. So was the perversity of the system, the arrogance of the party, the ruthless unavailability of ministers and officials. It was all the monolithic offspring of necessity. Pretoria had drubbed Mozambique, squeezed Namibia and punished its own opposition, but Angola had stood its ground. It had also paid dearly, in lives and in oil revenues, for supporting the ANC against apartheid and SWAPO against the occupation of Namibia.

Without the extenuation of war with South Africa, Luanda was no longer a great Stalinist endeavor, rotting nobly in the tropics for a noble cause. It looked instead like a testimony to years of neglect. The poverty was primitive, the decay was reckless, the indisposition of ministry officials seemed suddenly suspect; on the outside of a political culture that kept its own counsel, one inclined to think the worst.

Objectively—and this was often my experience of Angola—the facts should have led me to see things differently. If anything, Luanda was feeling the proximity of the war as it had not since 1975. The rebels were breathing down the city's neck with pestilential results. They had set off six bombs in Luanda since the start of the year. They had brought down the power lines from the Cambambe dam and sabotaged the water pipeline from the northwest twice. By the end of the year the number of known cholera cases, already high in 1988, would rise to 25,000. This was not the best moment to try disentangling the failures of the MPLA from the wantonness of the rebels.

▲

Augusto was in gloomy spirits. He had lost his beret. It had "walked away" from the café on the ground floor of the Press Center. In real terms, Augusto earned $20 a month in cash and was also entitled to some basic foodstuffs as well as government-subsidized purchases from duty-free shops that could then be traded on the parallel market for their real value in cash or kind. He was a poor man and the loss of the beret was a blow. He sighed and grimaced and paced around for most of the morning, but since we had given up all hope of any further trips or appointments, it was all the same what we did. Besides, we were both running a fever.

We walked to the offices of the state oil company, but Justino had already left for lunch. On the way back we passed a "small *candonga*"—an old woman with wrinkled forearms selling cigarettes and obscure sundries from an upturned box.

"These people," said Augusto, who was still in a foul mood, "are something we want to get rid of. They spoil the aspect of the place and, moreover, what they're doing is not yet legal. Far from it."

"Should they starve," I asked, "or just go where we can't see them?"

"It's simply a question of the law," said Augusto.

"And the aspect of the place? The famous ambience of Luanda?"

"Yes," he said. "That too."

We sat in the lobby of the hotel and read the paper. A long feature accused Zaïre of backing UNITA in Uíge and a report on the front page was headed "Puppets Assassinate Defenseless Civilians." It claimed that an attack by UNITA on a township in the province had killed ten and wounded twenty-five. Forty people had been abducted. When I queried these figures, Augusto grew exasperated, reminding me that he knew Uíge well, that this was where he had come after the exile of his family. He insisted that UNITA attacks had a pattern. One night they would overrun a village. They would destroy the party buildings, then the hospital and school. He raised his finger, lest I interrupt. Party members were eliminated on the spot. Various inhabitants were taken as porters. Some were allowed to go when they had served their purpose, others were shot, others still were enrolled in UNITA. Two of his cousins had disappeared in exactly these circumstances, he said. The older was ten and the younger seven. The local militia was no match for UNITA. The next day the government moved in and reoccupied the village. The air force was called in to identify UNITA targets, but when the pilots spotted them, UNITA placed the people it had abducted in a circle around its fighters. That was several years ago, he said. "Since when, no news of these cousins." People who came as visitors to Angola, he added, had much to learn. I could only concur.

The night before I was due to leave, we said goodbye. We were both unwell and pleased to see the back of each other. Augusto wished me a pleasant journey. I thanked him for his help and told him that my visit had been mostly fruitless.

"Ah yes," he said, "but you do not complain, which means that you are in a strong position to return, should you wish to." He looked disparagingly at me and wiped the sweat of fever from his forehead.

"It's not a test of patience," I protested.

"There," he replied, "I am obliged to disagree with you."

▲

The Soviet commitment in Africa ended in May 1991 with the fall of Ethiopia's president, Mengistu Haile Mariam and the signing of a peace agreement between UNITA and the MPLA, in the presence of James Baker and Eduard Shevardnadze. Jonas Savimbi arrived in London a month before to advertise the forthcoming peace in Angola. Twice on the same day, I went to hear him speak. Unlike Mandela, whose release he praised, he could not fill Wembley stadium. However, in Britain he had a dedicated following of extreme conservatives. Before both his audiences in central London Savimbi cut an impressive figure. The fatigues and the gun were gone. Instead he wore a dark collarless suit and plentiful gold on his fingers. About him there was an unsavory mixture of pomp and conviviality that one had come across before in the roll call of African dictators. Now, however, every humor, every mannerism was bent to the task of diplomatic sobriety; of dignity in victory, or at least, in the absence of defeat. As he spoke, I remembered the sound of artificial limbs on the floor of Bomba Alta and the smell of the central hospital in Huambo. The rapture of his foreign supporters was remarkable.

Savimbi had never fallen into the trap of addressing strangers as though they were his own rank and file. On the contrary, he had the skill of a salesman opening up a box of samples, and today he listed the great opportunities to be had in Angola: "oil, petrochemicals, pharmaceuticals, agriculture, forestry, fishing, industrial processing, civil engineering and tourism." He paused for effect. "We need to join hands to develop all these to our joint benefit." In the hope that he would assume the presidency of Angola, he was already putting the country up for auction. He feared, of course, that investors would be more tempted by the crumbling Soviet bloc. "We offer more, in some cases," he insisted, "than Eastern Europe. The region's superior physical infrastructure, in South Africa, Namibia and Zimbabwe, and its potential in Zaïre, Mozambique and Angola, are impressive; the financial infrastructure in South Africa is vastly superior to that in Eastern Europe."

De Beers had already persuaded Angola to market her diamonds through its central selling organization and was planning to work the Angolan kimberlite deposits that had not yet been exploited. Three Portuguese companies had signed up to rehabilitate the hydroelectric dam at Lomaum that Savimbi sabotaged in 1983. Another had been engaged for the restoration of battered rolling stock. There were riches to be had by repairing the war damage in Angola.

There was no question that a vigorously capitalist Angola—a culture of "markets"—would improve the state of the country beyond recognition, but the drift of Savimbi's ideas was not reassuring. A nation in collapse was now to develop largely according to the logic of foreign incentive. This might square with many of Angola's needs, yet some basic element was missing. Savimbi was such a seductive speaker that it took a little while to realize what it was. The Angolan peasant, brutalized by the Portuguese, ruined and persecuted by the MPLA, abducted and murdered by UNITA, bombarded by the Russians and South Africans, was now being consigned to oblivion in the shallow grave of "joint ventures," "economies of scale," "sectoral and regional priorities" and "principles of economic efficiency." The closest Savimbi came to acknowledging that Angola was still a country of peasant farmers, a fact that his following was apt to overlook, was a promise of rural development and a passing reference to unspecified numbers of Angolans "engaged in subsistence agriculture." In its day, the MPLA had made a similar, worthless promise.

Savimbi's vision of a civilized El Dorado still presupposed two nations: a peasant nation gradually restoring its land and a nation of money spinners rapidly founding a modern economy. In principle there was no reason why the two could not coexist. Yet there was no precedent in history for coexistence of such a kind. On this new frontier, what recourse would the one nation have against the bustling depradations of the other? Savimbi had been a Maoist, a democratic socialist, a rampant capitalist, a black racialist and a diligent friend of apartheid, a fawner and a braggart by turns—in short, an inventive man. But as a likely president of peacetime Angola, he could not produce the bold, imaginative outlines of a new African polity that extended rights and respect to the peasant majority and wealth to the country as a whole. The best he could envisage was an African version of Brazil.

His ideas did not win overwhelming support in Angola. The elections a year and a half later gave the MPLA a clear majority. Dos Santos won the presidential vote by a narrower margin and the runoff was delayed by a return to fighting. Savimbi was not a good loser. In Cabinda, near the offshore oil deposits, a handful of long established separatist groups were reviving their "armed struggle," while Angola's diamonds were leaving the country in a freelance operation of such scope that De Beers was forced to buy a percentage to keep control of the price. Inside Angola, the value of democracy could not be artificially sustained in the same way. I wondered if Justino even bothered with the word, as he turned from this new defeat to scan the future for signs of hope.

2

NAMIBIA

▲▲▲▲▲

I chiefly fed mine eyes with beholding the destroyers of tyrants
and usurpers, and the restorers of liberty to oppressed and
injured nations.

Swift, *Gulliver's Travels*

Across full rivers—through forests and bushes
My children are walking

Nguno Wakolele, *Southern Africa*

T he southern African linocut artist John Mua-
fangejo died in 1987. His pictures won international recognition during his lifetime, becoming even more fashionable, and expensive, after
his death. Many spoke eloquently about South Africa's occupation of
Namibia, others invoked the lost time of African village life, before the
intrusion of the white man. Muafangejo was born in southern Angola
and, in his early twenties, moved to a Lutheran mission inside
Namibia. He did not regard himself as Angolan or Namibian, but as
a Kwanyama—a large group of Ovambo whose lands extend either
side of the border. One of his most famous pictures is entitled *Angola
and South West Africa (Namibia)*. It is constructed like a map, with the
Cunene River pouring down the left-hand edge and the Okavango
River to the east. Running through the middle of the picture is a
horizontal bar, marked "Artificial Boundary." To the north lie striped
flanks of savannah and forest, and a few important landmarks in Muafangejo's life: "Ondjiva where our Chief Madume was"; "Etunda la
Nghadi where I born in 1943." South of the border a huge elephant
grazes and a clutter of planes marks out the airport.

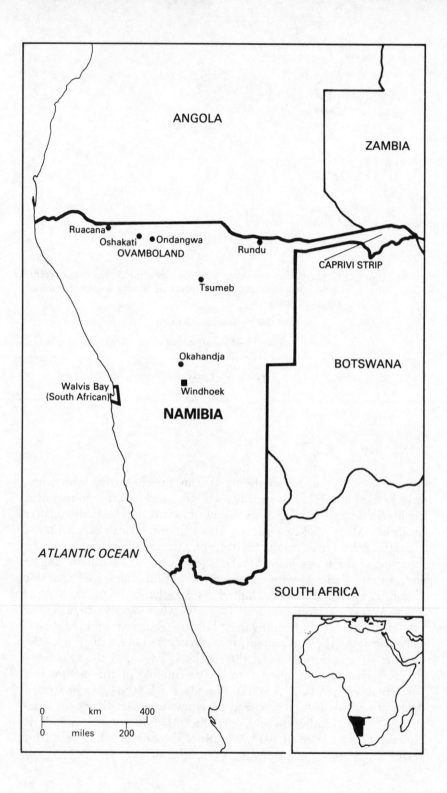

   Like all borders on the continent, the colonial frontier between Angola and South West Africa was drawn up with no thought for the communities it would cut in two. It was decided along with the rest a century before Muafangejo's death, at a congress of European powers in Berlin. The Portuguese were already installed on the coast of Angola, where they had enriched themselves and a small number of northern chiefs on four hundred years of slaving; they now took formal possession of the hinterland. South West Africa was made over to Germany. Resistance in the country was fierce—and put down with greater ferocity still. Between fifty and a hundred thousand Africans were slaughtered in the revolt of 1904–1906. South West Africa remained a German colony until the First World War, after which it came under the League of Nations mandate, administered by South Africa. In fact many German settlers continued to farm the south and center of the territory. Growing numbers of Afrikaners too were moving westward from South Africa. Antisettler resistance revived and, yet again, was suppressed. South Africa took advantage of the role it was given in the territory to turn it into a colony of its own, despite the misgivings of the League and the protestations, after the Second World War, of the United Nations, whose "trusteeship" system should have applied to South West Africa, but South Africa refused to comply. South West Africa—or Namibia, as it was renamed during the 1960s— would remain under South African sway for nearly fifty years. Toward the end of that period, devolved rule from Pretoria was little more than outright military occupation—especially in the north of this sparsely populated country where the Ovambos, the largest ethnic group, were based and where the main liberation movement, the South West Africa People's Organization (SWAPO), enjoyed its strongest support.
   Namibians always argued that they suffered oppression twice over: first as a colonized nation and then as victims of apartheid. If Pretoria's creation of "Bantustans," or homelands, in South Africa was received as a cruel absurdity by the world, its pursuit of the same policy in Namibia was an outrage. The first of the Namibian Bantustans was announced in 1967, a year after SWAPO took to armed struggle. It was Ovamboland—which went on to bear the brunt of the occupation in the years to come.
   Muafangejo's picture of *Angola and South West Africa* is dated 1976. By then the border was active. Thousands of young Namibians were moving up the clandestine trails into Angola to join the armed liberation movement; the South African Defence Force was rebuilding UNITA into a well-armed insurgency and unknown numbers of Kwanyama were crossing and recrossing the frontier in order to avoid

escalating conflict in the one country and mounting repression in the other. By the start of the 1980s the flight from disruption was less easy: fighting had spread over a wide area and northern Namibia was patrolled by a large army of occupation. Whether this arc of hostilities constituted one war or two was, like the border itself, something of a technicality. The Angolan government, the Namibian liberation movement and the Cubans were marshaled under a single banner; UNITA, the South Africans and the Namibian territorial army, with its killer counterinsurgency force known as Koevoet ("Crowbar") under another.

Until 1988 Namibia was a pawn in Washington's Cold War strategy. Once the time table for the Cuban withdrawal from Angola was agreed, the old German colony was on the way to independence. Elections took place at the end of 1989. SWAPO secured the necessary majority to form a government, and the following year independence celebrations were held. They were rapturous. The chances of Namibia achieving stability and a measure of prosperity were fair. There were fewer than two million people in a country more than double the size of North and South Dakota. The concentration of Namibians in Ovamboland carried risks in terms of food security and environmental damage in the north, while large tracts of the coast and center were already uninhabitable desert. But the wealth of natural resources, diamonds, zinc, uranium and some of the best fishing in the world meant potential benefits for nearly all Namibians within a decade of independence. SWAPO did not embark on a large-scale nationalization of the country's assets; much of the mineral wealth has remained in private hands.

On its return from exile, SWAPO was briefly involved in a cleansing of conscience, when the detention, torture and elimination of alleged "traitors" and "South African agents" in Angola during the war were aired in public. Some argued that this was not enough, but the symbolic importance of broaching the subject was immense. It took France more than twenty-five years to admit to the rivalries and betrayals within the French resistance and the country reeled as it tried to come to terms with the truth. Two years after his release, Mandela would follow SWAPO's example by expressing deep regret for similar crimes by the ANC against its own members in Angola.

At independence, Namibia also rid itself of a sinister shadow cast by European history. On the eve of the Second World War, the white parties of South Africa had found themselves deeply divided between opposition to Nazi Germany, appeasement and outright sympathy. The tradition of German settlement in South West Africa was fertile ground for pro-Nazi sentiment and, after 1945, the territory remained

a place where admirers of the Third Reich could idle along in a prosperous, low-key way with no real challenge to their racial doctrines—a
kind of African Paraguay, not for war criminals as such, but for those
who shared their views. SWAPO's Marxism, and its radical Christian
infancy, simply encouraged right-wing extremism during the war.
That is over now, although Namibia is the only country where I have
seen an antique Nazi flag displayed with pride and, in a one-horse
town on the Atlantic coast, a pristine reprint of the Führer's water-
colors, from which I turned with pleasure to the works of John Muafangejo.

I had not planned to travel in Namibia in the wake of independence. I went on impulse, unprepared, and left with a sense of calm,
despite a brief acquaintance with the problems that the country faced.
The Ovambo were not the only ethnic group in Namibia—there were
the Kavango, Herero, Damara, Nama, white men and bushmen.
Namibia was a quilt of peoples, like any African state, where the
possibility of splitting and unstitching could not be ruled out. Nor
could an administration that put the circumstances of war behind it
and settled in to the pomp. In 1992, during a drought in which
Namibia was appealing for relief aid, the president spent nearly $25
million on a private jet and one of Namibia's Scandinavian donors
responded by causing a stir. Status symbols of this kind evoked a
somber past in Africa, where newly vested leaders had a habit of
throwing away their mandate in a torrent of self-indulgence. Perhaps,
too, it was a self-indulgence on my part not to leap on the stories that
I heard in Namibia about small-scale corruption in the government.
But I had come to think of war as a far more heinous affair. Namibia's
freedom was tinged with bitter memories of the past; there were omens
too that it paid not to ignore, yet the sweetness of the thing was
unmistakable.

P enny Hango was a fortunate woman. To meet her
was to recognize this almost at once, although she was neither rich nor
settled, and had no immediate prospects of work. She lived in a small
house, owned by the brother of her common-law husband, in Katu-
tura township, just outside Windhoek. The husband was no longer in
evidence and had left Penny with a child of eighteen months. Space in
the house was at a premium, the front room doubling as a bedroom for
the children of her in-laws, who marked out their territory with a large
poster of the English football player, Brian Robson. The most impor-

tant picture in the room, however, was a photograph of Sam Nujoma, the leader of SWAPO and, lately, president of independent Namibia. It hung opposite the front door, next to a plaster of Paris relief that read "As for me and my house, we will serve the Lord." Nujoma had brought his people home from Angola and Zambia in 1989 to win a two-thirds' majority in Namibia's first proper elections. Penny Hango was one of them.

We were introduced by a mutual friend who suggested she accompany me to Ovamboland in the extreme north of Namibia, where most of the country's population was to be found. SWAPO's roots lay in Ovamboland, and it had borne the brunt of South African occupation. Penny would be an excellent guide, according to our friend, and would welcome the chance to go. She had spent sixteen years in exile and, on her return, stayed briefly in the north, but work was scarce up there and she had been forced to move to the capital. There were still some relatives she had not had a chance to see.

Penny was keen on the idea and set a date later in the week for her departure. She would make her own way north and we would meet in Oshakati. While we were talking, her sister-in-law came in and Penny told her of the plan with obvious pleasure.

Oshakati was the biggest town in Ovamboland, a four-hundred-mile drive from Windhoek, along a high, rocky plateau that sloped down after a few hours to the habitable spaces of the north. In Africa, travel by road in broad daylight was one of the privileges of peace and it felt exhilarating. I met up with Penny in Oshakati as we had planned. The following day we drove to our first appointment in a village near the Angolan border. On our return, late in the afternoon, we stopped by the frontier post, leaving the car near an old South African military base and walking up toward a cattle grid, with a metal gate on one side and a piece of string across the other decked with SWAPO colors. Penny was cautious; she was not sure where the border began. The customs house had been destroyed and rebuilt further back. Before we were thirty yards from the grid, an irate SWAPO soldier with a red beret and shades hustled us away. Then a policeman in a gray uniform intervened and we were let past the string. Penny trod with care, measuring each step. She was carrying her child. She adjusted the baby's hat to cover its neck and pointed across the frontier, whispering in his ear, "Ngola."

The air was dry and sour; the heat hung above the tarmac road, but beyond the border, in the upper half of the sky, there was a faint discoloration, as though it would rain. A couple of Angolan government soldiers were chiding a group of civilians, one with a large tub on her head, outside a shoddy frontier post, beyond which stood another building, severely damaged. The flag of the People's Republic of Angola drooped from a pole to the right of the little group, as though this were an elaborate folk performance of the national pastime: argument, delay, the transformation of a simple thing into a labyrinth of prohibitions. It had been the same in Namibia under South African occupation.

I had come to Namibia because I wanted to travel in a country where life was gradually acquiring value again, after a war of twenty-three years, which had ended with independence and electoral victory for the country's biggest liberation movement. I didn't know Namibia before SWAPO took over in 1990, but even for a newcomer there was a bright, intoxicating quality about the great spaces of the north and the gradual repopulation of the land. You had only to see the damage done to the roads by military convoys, or pass an abandoned base with its gaunt reconnaissance towers and bleached carapace of sandbags, to grasp the nature of the South African occupation.

The number 435 was sacred to African liberation. It identified the U.N. Security Council resolution on Namibia adopted in 1978, which called for a ceasefire between SWAPO and the occupying armies of South Africa, followed by U.N.-supervised elections. It took a further eleven years to implement the resolution. The delay was not only the result of South Africa's belligerence and Angola's open support of SWAPO. The United States's insistence that independence could only come about with a Cuban withdrawal from Angola also meant that Namibia was a hostage to the MPLA's war with UNITA and South Africa, and to the broader evolution of superpower relations.

The implementation of Resolution 435, when it came, was a success. The Reagan administration regarded its share of the U.N.'s implementation budget as a good price for Cuban withdrawal. It was also a moment of glory for the U.N., which had enjoyed precious few until then. Something had gone wrong, however, at the outset of the peace. It happened on March 31, 1989, although I once heard it referred to as the April Fool's Day massacre.

The main practical problem with Resolution 435 was simply that it had been shelved for twelve years. To monitor the peace process, a U.N. military force of over seven thousand had been proposed. By the time Washington was ready to go ahead, the South African administration in Namibia had created a large territorial army—perhaps as many as twenty thousand—and also the small but competent counter-insurgency team, Koevoet. The logical response should have been to increase the U.N. force. When the time came, however, the Security Council was determined to halve the original budget of more than $800 million and reduced the troops accordingly. The final dispositions were only agreed six weeks before the peace plan was due to come into effect.

Furthermore, the demobilization procedures for SWAPO were open to abuse. After Cuito Cuanavale, when the regional settlement got under way, a protocol was drafted to the effect that SWAPO fighters inside Angola should remain there, well north of the border, until the South Africans had withdrawn from Namibia. But earlier documents appended to Resolution 435 stated that SWAPO guerrillas in Namibia itself should report to the U.N. Technical Assistance Group and hand in their weapons. Either side could, in theory, take advantage of this ambiguity: SWAPO guerrillas in Angola could infiltrate and claim that they had been in Namibia all along, while the South Africans could engage any SWAPO fighters on sight and allege that they had filed across the border.

It is not entirely clear what happened on March 31. SWAPO claimed that guerrillas based in Namibia were searching out U.N. groups for a handover of weapons. It was conceded that units did indeed come across the border, but that they were impatient to have done with Angola, where the SWAPO leadership was harsh on its rank and file, and return to their homes. Others said that the leadership had ordered them across. On the morning in question there were dozens of SWAPO units wandering around Ovamboland. Wherever they had come from, they were probably looking for U.N. teams. The U.N. had lost its nerve, allowing a battalion of South African troops to go into action after complaints from Pretoria that SWAPO had breached the new Protocol. Within hours the ceasefire had been broken and some three hundred members of SWAPO were dead. It left an ugly mark on the peace, but it was probably the last of the big sacrifices entailed in "linkage." Penny Hango, who had returned to Namibia three months later, would only say that it was a piece of South African chicanery, a parting shot by vengeful losers. "Oh yes," she declared, "they were planning for that disaster. Most definitely."

We traveled for the best part of a week, plying the roads to the villages, meeting people, listening, moving on. We were accompanied throughout by Penny's little boy, who had a ravenous appetite for the breast and an ability to sleep anywhere at any time. Almost all the people we met were Ovambos, like Penny, who had grown up in the north. Many had been educated at the missions—SWAPO was nurtured in the Anglican and Lutheran churches—and many had stayed throughout the war.

One morning we made a brief stay at the place where Penny was born, a little village with one water pump and a general store. Most of the villagers depended on subsistence farming. As soon as she was old enough, Penny had planted, harvested, pounded grain, cooked, drawn water and looked after the other children. She also attended school nearby, but by the time she was fifteen, the patterns of life in Ovamboland had been disrupted by the war. Attendance declined and school became a political forum. Small groups of pupils would disappear and not be heard from again. It was generally the case that they had gone into the bush. As time went on, the pressure increased on all young people to do the same.

At an early age, Penny, like many thousands of Africans, had chosen exile in the name of liberation. She set out in 1974, with a group of classmates, for the provisional headquarters of SWAPO in Zambia, a journey of about a thousand miles. They found a man with a truck and arranged to begin the journey with him. By the time the driver was ready to leave they were nine in all. They took the road to Ondangwa, and on to Oshikango, where they transferred to a large beer truck that was crossing into Angola. They arrived early in the morning in Xangongo.

It was only a few months after the coup in Lisbon. Angola was a relaxed place by comparison with Namibia and the Portuguese soldiers were well disposed toward Penny and her friends. Two boys in the party had money and shared it with the others. They took a bus to Lubango, 150 miles north. From here they hoped to travel east to Zambia—it was five hundred miles to the border—although they had no idea how. They slept that night in the bus station at Lubango. Next morning they took another bus to Huambo, or Nova Lisboa, as it was still known. Someone in the group seemed to know what to do. They rode a train 250 miles up the Benguela line to Luso, a staging point for new SWAPO members. Here Penny found herself in a group of eighty. After a day or so, the Portuguese army put them in trucks and drove them to a border post.

Penny had come a thousand miles with the greatest of ease. She was a nineteen-year-old girl who had barely set foot outside her narrow world. This journey was an exciting thing. It took the edge off her sadness at leaving home, while fear of the unfamiliar was allayed by her companions, and by the fact that she was joining up with growing numbers of Ovambo youngsters who had gone ahead of her. The next stage of the journey was harder. At the Zambian border, Penny spent the night in a tent encampment. In one of the tents there were rows of bodies, but she did not know how these people died—perhaps in clashes with the South Africans near Caprivi, for Pretoria was deploying troops along the length of the Namibian frontier with Zambia as well as Angola. She was shocked and frightened.

The next objective was Lusaka, another three hundred miles or more. The Portuguese soldiers issued their charges with tinned rations and sent them off into the bush to complete the journey on foot. They divided into groups, with members of the SWAPO Youth League, the elite of the young opposition in Namibia, leaving first. As long as they headed straight, they were told, they would reach their destination.

"We thought that liberation would probably take a year and we would be home in 1975," Penny explained. "In the meantime we must walk. We walked on and on, and when we were getting tired we had to leave those tins that the Portuguese gave us. For water we found small rivers where the animals used to drink, and for food we sold our clothes to the local people. When I was hungry, I gave one dress for a bunch of bananas. I thought, 'Enough is enough, let me not have this dress.' I became frightened crossing the rivers. Until now, I cannot swim, but we were obliged to cross in canoes with the villagers. We were never lost, for we could follow the tracks of the first group, but we were always tired. We went and went and soon we were hungry again. At last we were remembering the tins we threw away."

The pace became steadily slower and at the end of the second week of walking, the youngsters from Ovamboland, who were used to trekking for firewood and hiking miles to school, had to slow down for their companions from the south. At length they came to a SWAPO base outside Lusaka where the journey ended. They were fed and welcomed. Transportation was brought from Lusaka to fetch the first group, the SWAPO Youth League members, who were set to work organizing a proper system for receiving and accommodating further arrivals. Young Ovambos were coming across in ever greater numbers to enlist in the liberation army now that the Youth League's leaders had been detained inside Namibia.

Penny's group stayed on at the base for a time and was then transferred to another in western Zambia, where she remained for almost a year. There was food, there were classes, there were other exiles to receive and pass down the line. Support for these activities came from the U.N. High Commissioner for Refugees and, after 1975, from the Commonwealth. SWAPO also received modest funds from the OAU Liberation Committee. For the boys, there was military training. Some were sent overseas, to North Korea, others on operations in Angola, where there were many casualties. In the bases, nonetheless, there was too much time and precious little organization.

SWAPO was overwhelmed by the numbers coming in. Indeed, by 1976 the situation had led to a revolt in one of the camps, for there were shortages of food and medicine, and the young men, chafing at the lack of arms and ammunition, were naively eager for battle. They would find it soon enough in Angola, now that the MPLA had taken SWAPO under its wing. Penny, however, had already been issued with a passport and told that she would be traveling to Nigeria.

"The Boers gave us to understand," said Penny, "that women cannot fly. If you fly you may not have children." There were fifty Namibians on the flight, shepherded by a SWAPO journalist. They eased Penny's mind about the dangers of flying. When the refreshment service came, she emptied a packet of salt into her tea. The U.N. Development Program sponsored Namibians to study in Nigeria; it was basic secondary education with a strong emphasis on English. Penny was ashamed of her age and her lack of education. She was twenty by now, but she claimed that she was seventeen. Her English was not good; it amused the Nigerians in her hostel. "One day I wanted to clean the dormitory but I could not recall that word broom. 'Where is the sweep?' I said, and afterward the people were laughing for several days."

In 1979 Penny was sent to Angola. It was the year after Operation Reindeer, a South African airborne assault on a SWAPO settlement in the south. Six hundred Namibians had died at Cassinga. Penny had heard about the massacre while she was in Zambia. Now she met several of the survivors, who crowded in with their accounts.

"At that time I did not know what to tell them," she said. "They could only remember this one place, Cassinga. Everything else was a dream. At last, I told them, 'You must stop or it will make you mad.' " Their recollections were with her as she boarded a plane for Leipzig at the end of the month.

Penny and her friends had left Ovamboland with every confidence that they would return to an independent Namibia in 1975. Five years had passed and she was now traveling thousands of miles in the opposite direction. The East German government offered scholarships to many southern Africans. Penny spent a year at the Karl Marx University, learning German. She went on to do a general course in science. After that, she was told that she would be studying agriculture. The idea did not appeal to her; instead she was sent to Weimar for a three-year course in agronomy, which she completed in 1984, before returning to Luanda. In Angola, SWAPO placed her in charge of food production on a handful of farming projects but her work seldom brought her into contact with Namibian guerrillas, who had plots of their own on bases whose whereabouts were kept from non-combatants. By the mid-1980s, there were ninety thousand refugees from Zaïre and Namibia registered in Angola, but the figure may well have been higher. The majority of exiled Namibians were civilians. Penny made occasional trips to SWAPO farms in Zambia and, in 1987, she went to London for three months, to attend a course in agricultural management.

In 1989, Penny gave birth to her child in Luanda. The South Africans had withdrawn from Angola, the Cubans were preparing to go, and the U.N. Technical Assistance Group was arriving in Namibia. It was not difficult to name her son; she called him Tuyeni, which means "let us go home."

▲

Windhoek seemed a long way from Ovamboland. For the SWAPO government installed in the capital, it was a period of glory. Ministers acquired large cars and generous salaries; the president assembled a motorcade of lunatic bikers—Angolans, rumor had it—who drove around Windhoek like the messengers of hell in Cocteau's *Orphée*. There were mutterings about corruption. In Ovamboland, meanwhile, the U.N. had a food program that was keeping SWAPO returnees alive, but this was due to end shortly and there was no clear plan to regenerate the north, where thousands of repatriated Namibians were settling.

Not everyone could put the war behind them. Near an accommodation center, an hour from Oshakati, we met a blind man in his late twenties. He had lost his sight during combat in Angola and protected his eyes with wraparound sunglasses. His wife was older. Her face was a boneless mass of scar tissue, in which the eyes were the only feature. She had suffered this injury in a land mine explosion. Her husband had been spared the horror of seeing her. They had two children and lived in fear of the U.N. food plan coming to an end. The young man was sure that he had no chance of finding work and that they would soon be sleeping rough, for he had no relatives in the district and was afraid, ashamed perhaps, to go back to his own village, where his disability would not pass unnoticed as it did in the center. One of his children sat with him on the *stoep* of the little hut where the family was quartered. With braided hair, and eyes set wide apart beneath straight eyebrows, she was a handsome child whose features one was bound to scrutinize for hints of her parents' looks, which the war had masked forever.

In the center there was a cement building with more than one room. Like the rest, it had no amenities. Penny led me across the threshold to find a small, wrinkled figure in a straw hat and glasses sitting in a wheelchair by a high bed. He introduced himself as Jacob and bade us welcome in a hoarse, irritable voice.

"This place is smelling like a dead dog," he declared once we were seated, "or so it was until the water came."

A truckload of water had come that morning, but it had done little to improve his disposition. He must have taken us for U.N. people, for this was the first in a string of complaints about conditions at the center, which he ended with a sincere appeal on behalf of "the returnees."

"Who will look after these children?" he asked. "These fighters who forced South Africa into a roundtable conference?"

We sat in silence. The old man pulled down the brim of the straw hat, obscuring his face entirely, and added, in the manner of a scholarly footnote, "Not on their own, mind you. We also have to thank the tireless fighters of the ANC: Umkhonto weSizwe." "Umkhonto we-Sizwe" meant "spear of the nation." It was the armed wing of the African National Congress.

Jacob had been at the center for at least five years. He told us he was born in 1932, but he looked much older. When he discovered we were not from the aid agencies, he was visibly disappointed, levering the hat back on his forehead and slumping down in the wheelchair. Penny whispered his surname to me, but it meant nothing. Jacob Kuhangua was one of the founders of the Ovamboland People's Congress, which had been set up in Cape Town at the end of the 1950s. It was the forerunner of SWAPO, in which he was later to serve as general secretary. There were many Namibians in the Cape at the time. They were contracted to work for the mining companies around Johannesburg but the terms were notoriously bad and moonlighting in Cape Town was a better option. On his arrival in Johannesburg, he had contrived a transfer to the Orange Free State, where he worked in a clinic at one of the miners' compounds in Kimberly.

"I just couldn't stomach it after one or two weeks," he confessed. "The miners would fight on the weekends. People were being stabbed with knives and what have you. I requested a transfer to clerical duty."

After six months in the compound he slipped away and headed for Cape Town, equipped with a pillow and an English dictionary, which he had brought with him from Ovamboland. It was a prize, awarded at the end of his teaching practice by the staff at St. Mary's, an Anglican mission in Odibo. Penny and I had seen the mission the day before. During the war, security forces had laid explosives on the property, destroying three buildings but leaving the church intact. The ruins did much to sanctify the role of St. Mary's in Namibian history. For half a century or more, it was a cradle of resistance. The likes of Jacob Kuhangua had left it with a taste for universal suffrage, education and independence.

The Ovamboland People's Congress was formed with the idea of abolishing contract labor in Namibia; since South Africa administered the system, it was by the same token an anticolonial movement. Its young figurehead had started off with Kuhangua as a clerk in the mines and traveled with him to Cape Town. Herman Toivo ja Toivo was intrigued by African nationalist politics and soon developed contacts in the ANC and the Communist Party of South Africa.

"In Cape Town we attended ANC rallies, Toivo and I, but I didn't care for them, not at first," Kuhangua recalled. "I was looking for money, for super-wealth. Even Toivo, at the outset, he too was hunting for diamonds, but there was this idea of liberation building in South Africa and finally it was quite infectious."

It was suggested that an ANC branch be set up in Windhoek, but ja Toivo and the others already preferred the idea of a national movement of their own. In 1958 ja Toivo was expelled from Cape Town for smuggling a tape recording to the United Nations advocating proper trusteeship for South West Africa. Ja Toivo concealed the tape in a copy of *Gulliver's Travels*. Thereafter, a steady stream of petitions began to arrive from South West Africa. Jacob Kuhangua followed ja Toivo to Windhoek and founded the Ovamboland People's Organization. Sam Nujoma was installed as president. In 1960 the organization changed its name to SWAPO. Kuhangua traveled around the territory, building the membership and spreading the word. The South Africans detained him and on one occasion tried to deport him to Angola.

"They took me across at Oshikango," he remembered, "and told the Portuguese that I was an undesirable Angolan making trouble in South West Africa. 'Punish him hard!' The Portuguese took me aside and I explained my situation. They went back and told the Boers who had brought me, 'Look, this young man has declared he was born in your country. Don't you have jails of your own?' Finally I was taken back into Namibia and left in Odibo, which is my birthplace."

Shortly afterward, Kuhangua crossed the Angolan border of his own free will. He made his way to Nova Lisboa and then to Benguela, after which he headed east toward Zambia and Tanzania, hitchhiking, walking and riding buses. His destination was New York, where he hoped to petition the U.N.'s Fourth Committee in person. He obtained a visa in Dar es Salaam but flew first to Addis Ababa, to collect his onward ticket and $150 in cash. It was a gift from Emperor Haile Selassie, an active friend of the cause.

He told the Fourth Committee that apartheid "had its roots in the same concepts as Nazism" and he was bitterly critical of British and American complicity with the South Africans in Namibia. After a short period of travel, he was recalled by SWAPO to Dar es Salaam, when his career as general secretary of the movement was cut short by a knife wound that left him paralyzed below the waist. He would not say who was responsible or why. Perhaps he assumed that we knew.

"The cause of the knife in my back is difficult to define," he said. "I didn't fight him; he loomed out of the dark."

I learned much later of an obscure dispute between Kuhangua and SWAPO's vice president, which had been settled by force. Louis Nelegani was not convicted by the courts in Dar but SWAPO relieved him of his duties. Henceforth, Kuhangua was little more than an observer. In 1966 SWAPO took to the gun and the U.N. voted away the vestiges of South Africa's mandate. The following year nearly forty of the movement's leaders stood trial for terrorism in Pretoria. Kuhangua's old friend ja Toivo was sentenced to twenty years' imprisonment, and in the period that followed, Pretoria put the finishing touches on its "incorporation" of Namibia, imposing a homelands policy and further drastic restrictions on all forms of freedom for non-whites. Kuhangua had by now returned to the United States to collect his degree—"with marks of distinction, in a wheelchair for that matter." He remained there for several years, undergoing a series of operations, to no avail. In 1977, he returned to Ovamboland. He had one last brush with security, seven years later, when ja Toivo emerged from Robben Island. The occasion touched Kuhangua deeply and he wrote a short text that fell into the hands of the security forces. To them, it was proof that he was still a seditious spirit.

"They arrived and accused me of terrorism. I told them, 'You see me. I can't even touch the ground. It would be difficult for me to plant a bomb.' They replied, 'You have soldiers to carry out your mandate.' Nothing came of it. But for many years, I must remind you, our dignity was trampled underfoot."

Jacob Kuhangua looked us briskly up and down. Then his eyes roamed over the bleak little room to which misfortune had confined him in the nation's hour of freedom.

Jacob was unusual in Ovamboland at that time. Most disabled people were half his age. Penny and I saw many fighters with injuries sustained in Angola. They were men for the most part, living together in groups, waiting for some change in their circumstances—decent accommodations, overseas aid for prosthetics, the arrival of trained physiotherapists—and they did not take well to intruders. If they had the use of their eyes, they played cards. If there was chicken with the corn porridge, they cracked the bones appreciatively. If tobacco was available, they smoked. Once in a while there might be beer or *dagga*.

The ablebodied were luckier, for whatever happened in Ovamboland over the next year, they would receive a hero's welcome on the streets, inside the little drinking establishments known as shebeens and around the cooking fires. Koevoet, the antiterrorist special unit, of whom large numbers had been recruited from Ovamboland, had been paid off by the South Africans. They received handsome stipends for their efforts and were now flaunting their money in the bars, which was a source of tension, since SWAPO guerrillas had yet to receive any pension. There were incidents. Arms caches were found almost every week. The British had started training integrated companies of SWAPO fighters and their former enemies. The future might be uncertain but the present was good for the fighters who had come home with their minds and bodies intact. They moved through the stages of Ovambo hospitality like moths in a gallery of lamps. Their very presence was a daily cause for celebration; and even if their hosts began to count the cost, they gave no sign of it. The country had grieved for much too long.

Those who had remained in Ovamboland throughout the war were not in an easy position once the fighters returned. Ovambo civilians had suffered under South African occupation but this was unacknowledged in the welcome extended to the exiles, who included most of the leadership. Since the start of armed hostilities in 1966, life at home had been hard and unglamorous. There had been hunger, sickness, poverty, detention and, as a direct consequence of the war, many of the elders believed, there had been drought. Preventable diseases had become fatal: diarrhea, whooping cough, measles. There was no clean water, fresh vegetables were rare. Yes, said the doctors in a clinic near Ondangwa, there were bullet wounds, land mine injuries, beatings, but the worst problem was common illness. Under the occupation the people had nothing, and neither did the hospitals. In the end they had to charge. Three rand for a consultation, one rand for follow-up; three rand for admission, five rand for surgery. The war claimed twenty thousand Ovambo lives in casualties alone, but deaths through poverty and sickness were probably as high. It was a time of indignity at home, coupled with fear for those who were in exile; relatives disappeared for months in detention and the bodies of dead fighters were hung like game from the sides of armored cars parading the road from Ondangwa to Oshakati.

Traveling on my own one evening, I could tell that nowadays the highways of Ovamboland were joyous places. Africa's newest nation was finishing its business for the day. The road to Oshakati was packed with overcrowded trucks and pickups heading for town. Occasionally a big sedan would pass them, honking and forcing oncoming cars to slow down. Along the shoulder, children were driving livestock back to kraal. Goats strutted through the dust and the cattle ambled forward in their own time, their dewlaps rocking from side to side. Everywhere you looked there was activity. It was overwhelming and soon took on the aspect of a whole continent in motion: a vast population, walking, running, gunning mopeds, hanging on to tailboards, bearing tremendous loads, driving cattle, making their interminable way, as the sun bulged in the west and shadows raked the glowing ground. Perhaps it was just an expression of the mood in Namibia, where the spirit of Nkrumah had been roused from a long sleep. The road seemed to contract as the sun dropped and a few fastidious drivers switched on sidelights. Abstracted, slightly frightened, I pulled over and sat with the engine off for a few minutes. The people of Ovamboland thundered past, waving, sometimes staring suspiciously, for even now it was hard to trust white men in stationary cars.

It was almost dark as I drove by the big South African base outside Oshakati. There were rock martins, diving and rising around the empty watchtowers.

▲

Penny Hango had an uncle outside Oshakati whom she had not seen since her departure for Angola. Mr. Shiimi was a contented-looking man, despite the ills that had befallen him under South African rule. He rose from his desk in the doorway of a large warehouse and came out to greet us. A Parker pen was clipped to the pocket of his shirt. He said he had heard that she was back and thanked God that she had returned safely. Then he praised her contribution to the family, taking Tuyeni in his arms and looking him over. He called to one of his staff for some chairs and sat us down at the desk.

The warehouse did not belong to Mr. Shiimi but the furniture business was his. He had started the business in 1976, buying tables and occasionally a wardrobe from Windhoek and transporting them four hundred miles or more to Ovamboland, where an eventual sale would allow him to repeat the process. He already had a small general store by the time he was detained in 1979, so it was not a fatal blow to his family that the furniture venture had to be abandoned for a while.

In Ovamboland, SWAPO was as much a milieu as a movement; for prominent figures in the community, membership was almost a matter of course. Mr. Shiimi was born in the same village as Sam

Nujoma, and he had joined in 1965, on the eve of armed struggle and intensified repression. By the time he was detained, most activists were in danger of their lives.

Mr. Shiimi was driving one day to Oshakati when he came upon the remains of a skirmish between the army and some SWAPOs. Two members of the security forces were dead. When the army saw Mr. Shiimi on the road, they assumed he had helped to plan the attack. He was held for thirty days under an AG 9. During this time he was given shock torture, locked in a mortuary and shut up in a small chickenwire cage containing a snake. In the simple cell where he spent most of his detention, he was chained up by both legs. Mr. Shiimi survived this ordeal without visible damage. The AG 9 was not renewed and in due course he returned to his family.

Nothing went well after that. Threats to his life and constant surveillance marked the start of a persecution campaign. One day Mr. Shiimi's wife came home from the shop to find their second child, Philip, playing in a strange mound of earth in the yard. He was digging up a land mine and had already broken two of the detonators. Mr. Shiimi phoned the police, who referred the matter to the army and a team was sent to remove it. Shortly afterward, the family found a rocket-propelled grenade in the grounds of the house; they concluded that it had been put there to incriminate them. At night there were often noises in the yard outside, footsteps, murmuring, and then, one evening, a knock on the windowpane. Mr. Shiimi went to the door and the intruders ran. A few nights later he heard the same knocking and walked to the window. Through the reflected image of his own living room he could just make out a figure with a raised gun. He threw himself to the floor as the glass shattered and the bullet entered the wall behind him.

For three years Mr. Shiimi hid out in the south, to protect his family as much as himself. With the help of his lawyer and an influential doctor, he won assurances from the security forces that he and his family would not be harmed if he returned to Ovamboland. When these were given, he rejoined his wife and children. After that, there was only one more incident. The doctor who had helped him to come out of hiding asked to borrow Mr. Shiimi's car for a trip down to Tsumeb. A few miles out of town, he was stopped by plainclothes members of Security and asked to show his papers. One of the men climbed into Mr. Shiimi's car and pulled a gun on the doctor. He ordered him to follow the security vehicle, driven by his colleague. After a mile or two the car in front turned off the road down a track leading deep into the bush.

"It was a simple misunderstanding," Mr. Shiimi explained. "You see, they thought that because it was my car, it must be me, and our names, mine and that of the doctor, were not the same but they were similar. When my friend, that doctor, told them his name, they were thinking it was me. Then at last he began to protest and showed his identity papers once again, to prove that he was none other than himself. They looked at him and told him to go away from there." Mr. Shiimi chuckled. "Now, my friend is in the Permanent Secretariat for Health."

Mr. Shiimi congratulated his niece on her child once more, taking the boy's hand in his own. For a while he spoke with Penny in Ovambo, while two men in overalls moved between the rows of furniture. There were a dozen wardrobes with vinyl surfaces, an array of kitchen cabinets and three big sofas in plush with matching armchairs. Now that the war was over, Mr. Shiimi planned to develop the business. With the changes in South Africa, there was already more freedom to maneuver. He and his colleague, Enoch, who owned the warehouse, were now buying direct from Johannesburg. "All this here," he gestured round the room, "is from South Africa. It's good stuff, you cannot get the same quality up on this side. I know a chap in Okahandja who makes beds and I would like to buy them, but I must tell you truthfully that right now I can find better in South Africa."

Despite the peace, there was not much of an economy in Ovamboland; the South Africans had seen to that. The occupying army had given a boost to small trade but nothing more. When the U.N. Assistance Group came, there was a brisk boom in the north; now they were leaving, it was back to hard times. But Mr. Shiimi managed to do business here and there. Sometimes he even bartered his furniture for livestock.

"The first thing, very important, is the peace that prevails in our country," he said. "Do you know, that one who planted the land mine at my house, I discovered who he was. After independence he came to apologize, in person. He told me, 'I put that same mine in your house. I am the one who did it.' " Mr. Shiimi said that he saw him often. "We pass in the street and he greets me. And so I greet him back."

We went up once more by the Angolan border to a clinic near St. Mary's mission. Our travels in Ovamboland were almost over. As we made our way back along a track through the scrub, I could only think that Penny's future in Windhoek did not look bright. She wore it well, yet even her contentment seemed for a moment to be a ponderous thing, in no way assumed, but a burden nonetheless. To be happy for one's country was not a state of mind I understood. Despite the vagaries of the road, she sat quite comfortably while the child clambered about her like a devotee exploring some monumental bronze of motherhood. When would she find steady work? Why wasn't she at her wits' end? Perhaps she had a promise from SWAPO, or more likely, she knew the extent of her own resourcefulness. In the meantime, there was much to catch up on. I had always imagined the return of exiles as a swaggering affair. For days, Penny had listened carefully to everything our hosts had told us, as though she were feeling her way back to Ovamboland, mile by mile.

Tuyeni was standing upright now, one arm on my shoulder and the other thrust in front of my face, pointing across the flat scrub that ran to the border. He seemed to know where we were—and even to recognize the nebulous thing that Penny had shown him on our earlier trip. She repeated the word "Ngola" several times, as she retrieved him and sat him firmly on her lap. Ten minutes later the track bore south and joined the tarmac road to Oshakati.

▲

In Windhoek there was a visiting rugby team on tour from the United Kingdom; majority rule meant the end of the sports boycott. It was one of the ideals of independence that a B team from an overseas national side and a party of players from Namibian clubs could share bar space at the Kalahari Sands Hotel with the assortment of African delegations who had come to celebrate the liberation. The rugby players had dined with enthusiasm in the hotel restaurant and were now gathered in one corner of the bar, drinking their way to oblivion. By ten o'clock the singing was fulsome. There was more than a hint of bad manners toward the bar staff and dismay among the other guests, who took this as a bad omen. But allowances had to be made, especially when it came to rugby—one of the pillars of white culture in southern Africa. The barmen handled their charges with the skill of nannies ministering to fractious children.

Representatives from other liberation movements were in Namibia in force to express their solidarity with the government of a new African nation. There was still a fraternity of liberation and you might run into its members anywhere. It was seldom clear where they might find themselves next, and in this respect, although they lived more comfortably, they were no different from people like Katila or Penny whom the struggle had taken thousands of miles from their homes, transforming their lives in the process.

Mohamed Sidati was one of these itinerants. For several years he had been the representative for the Western Saharan Polisario Front in Europe, but lately he had been recalled to Algiers, where the movement was grooming him for a new post. We met by chance in the bar of the Kalahari Sands. Sidati was in Windhoek to see some SWAPO ministers. He bought drinks and asked for a briefing on the rugby players. Were they South Africans? Russians? Policemen? A touring troupe whose performance had been canceled? Whoever they were, he shouted to make himself heard above the din, they lacked modesty. I explained their business and argued that this was a kind of cultural evening. Sidati looked across at the party with incredulity.

He went upstairs to his room and returned a few minutes later with a black-and-white photograph of himself standing arm-in-arm with Nelson Mandela. He inscribed it in French with a felt tip and handed it over. "With best wishes, Sidati. Windhoek" and the date. Mandela looked tired but authoritative, Sidati looked relaxed. Both were aristocrats—Mandela from a renowned Thembu chieftaincy, Sidati from a distinguished Reguibat family on the Saharan coast. Mandela had a constituency of several million, Sidati fewer, probably, than 200,000.

Polisario's war with Morocco was a standoff and had been for ten years. There was movement on the diplomatic front, however, and a referendum destined to settle matters was almost in sight. It would be supervised by a team from the United Nations, just as the peace in Namibia had been. Independence here was an encouraging sign for Western Sahara, but it required exceptional generosity of spirit for someone in Sidati's position to revel in its success while his own people were still under arms in an obscure war. Amid the deafening festivities, he smoked half of a Havana cigar, shouting his conversation across the table. He raised a glass of fruit juice and drank to Namibia, then he retired. Two of the sportsmen were being helped off the field by the hotel staff.

Sidati's photo was in the paper two days later. He and a SWAPO minister were signing a document. Formal diplomatic relations, said the report, had been established between Namibia and the Saharan Arab Democratic Republic "at ambassadorial level." SWAPO had always maintained relations with Polisario and its nominal state, sending delegates up to the Saharan refugee camps in southern Algeria whenever occasion demanded. Now that SWAPO was in charge of a country, the little liberation movement in the desert would be posting a mission to the capital.

At the U.N. offices in Windhoek, junior staff were packing crates and shifting them out to the car park. A Scandinavian in shorts engaged me in conversation. He was leaving the following day. "By the middle of next week," he said, "most of us will be gone." He pointed to the sumptuous array of vehicles, dozens of them, all white with the blue disc on the door that proclaimed their origin and mission. Land Cruisers, Land Rovers, trucks, pickups and sedans. "All these will be a gift to the Namibian people," he said, but of course he meant the government. He was bound for Geneva and then New York, but was adamant that the U.N. would be back in force in Africa before the year was out. "In Western Sahara," he said, "the referendum will take place this year."

3

WESTERN SAHARA

▲▲▲▲▲▲▲▲▲▲▲

Had God pleased, He would have united you into one nation.
But he confounds whom He will and gives guidance to whom
He pleases. You shall be questioned about all your actions.

The Koran

For us, this is a closed matter.

Spanish Foreign Minister, May 1976, six months
after signing of the Madrid Accords

As it turned out, the optimistic Scandinavian in
Namibia was wrong. By 1991, the United Nations had indeed moved
a team of monitors into Western Sahara to prepare for a political
solution to a long and fruitless war, but the process was soon compromised by pressure on the ground and in New York. Some of the
members of the U.N. team were seconded to the Western Saharan
town of Tifariti, where the slow demise of the peace plan gave them
ample time to reflect upon the situation they were sent out to resolve.

Tifariti is one of the most memorable places in Africa. It was
abandoned less than twenty years ago. Picking a way through the
empty settlement, climbing to the roof of a surviving block and looking
out over the shimmering landscape beyond, it is easy to imagine that
the desert itself reduced this place to its sorry state. An abrasive wind
wears away at the exteriors of the empty houses. Inside, it sings
through the remains of the rooms, where loose flanks of corrugated
iron clatter in broken doorways and nets of pale sand shift over the
floors.

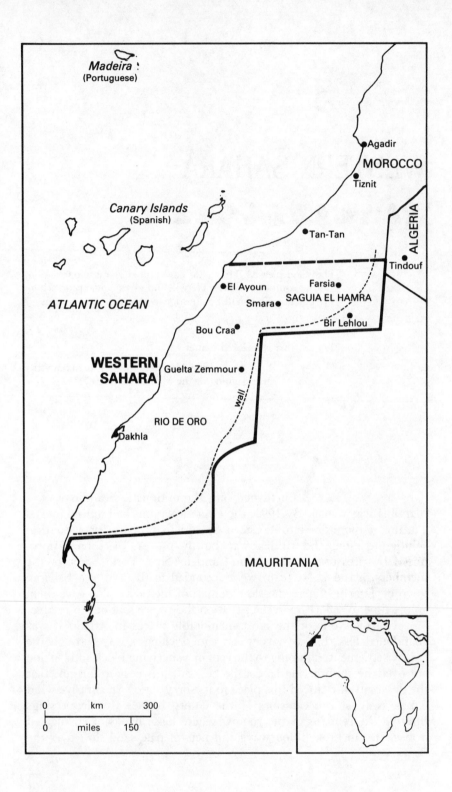

Madeira
(Portuguese)

MOROCCO

● Agadir

● Tiznit

Canary Islands
(Spanish)

● Tan-Tan

ALGERIA

● Tindouf

ATLANTIC OCEAN

● El Ayoun

Farsia ●

Smara ●

SAGUIA EL HAMRA

Bou Craa ●

Bir Lehlou ●

**WESTERN
SAHARA**

Guelta Zemmour ●

wall

RIO DE ORO

◆ Dakhla

MAURITANIA

| 0 | km | 300 |
| 0 | miles | 150 |

But Tifariti did not succumb to the harshness of its surroundings; it was wrecked by Moroccan bombardment in the mid-1970s, at the start of a war that would continue for another fifteen years and develop into a game of diplomatic hide-and-seek between the king of Morocco and the United Nations. The object of conflict was a former Spanish possession that Morocco believed was Moroccan and the inhabitants of the territory did not. On one side stood old and peremptory ideas of the nation as a vague space defined by archaic loyalties; on the other, a more modern, secular sense of national identity, based on the axioms of African liberation. In Tifariti, and other settlements in the hinterland, the results of this dispute were abundantly clear: dispossession, ruin and waste.

▲

Many African liberation movements came and went through the Maghreb. During the closing stages of the French-Algerian war, they congregated in Morocco. The Algerian Front de Libération Nationale (FLN) was an imposing exile presence in Rabat. Even before it was over, the war was an inspiration to the other independence struggles on the continent. The anticolonial movements of Portuguese Africa set up a center in Morocco in 1961. The following year, Nelson Mandela arrived for a week of briefings on guerrilla strategy from an FLN commander. After the French withdrawal from Algeria, the movements tended to congregate in Algiers. This was a period of energy and hope, in which every freedom struggle conceived itself as an expression of some larger continental destiny.

The guerrilla movement in the Spanish Sahara, which came late to African liberation, called itself the Popular Front for the Liberation of Saguia el Hamra and Río de Oro (Polisario), after the two administrative areas into which Spain divided the colony. Polisario held its founding congress in 1973, proclaiming itself to be a "unique expression of the masses." If Polisario had models of struggle, they were to be found in Cuba and Palestine; in the writings of Frantz Fanon and Che Guevara. Like the Lusophone African movements, Polisario was pitted against a Western dictatorship and derived no support from the democracies that held General Franco's government in qualified esteem. Nor did this unpretentious, minimalist guerrilla movement win direct patronage from the Soviet Union. In the mid-1970s Spain withdrew in disarray from its Saharan colony, ceding it to Morocco and Mauritania. The inhabitants were not consulted and Polisario fought on against its new adversaries. Mauritania withdrew after a few years but Morocco was more tenacious. The Spanish Sahara was rich in phosphates, which did much to explain King Hassan II's interest in the territory and the Soviet Union's indifference to Polisario. Morocco had phosphates of its own, which it traded at high prices; it was eager to bring the deposits in the Sahara under its sway. The Soviet Union needed a steady supply and was happy to contract for these with Morocco. When the U.N. protested about the fate of the Spanish colony, the Soviet delegation in New York dutifully voted for the self-determination of the Saharan people, but in 1978 Moscow signed a thirty-year contract with Morocco for the supply of phosphates and agreed to finance a new mine at an estimated cost of $2 billion.

The collapse of the Iberian dictatorships—first Caetano, then Franco—had disastrous results in more than one part of Africa. The liberation movements were not fully prepared and the arrangements for orderly transition were inadequate. Spanish Sahara was a less notorious case than Angola, but the process had some similarities. Four months after the coup in Lisbon, Spain announced that it would hold a referendum on self-determination in its Saharan colony and the U.N. agreed to monitor the process. The Spanish Sahara was already an anachronism: Morocco had won independence from France in 1956; two years later it regained a southerly strip of territory that had been administered from Madrid; independence for the French colony of Mauritania followed in 1960 and for Algeria in 1962. Morocco's integrity was further consolidated in 1969 when King Hassan persuaded Spain to hand over an enclave on the Atlantic coast at Ifni. Since 1973 Polisario had been fighting and negotiating with the Spanish at the same time. They were the logical heirs to the Saharan colony. But by the fall of 1975 metropolitan Spain was in turmoil: Franco was dying and the country was preoccupied with its own political hopes, after thirty-six years of Fascism.

King Hassan, like most of his subjects, believed that the Spanish Sahara belonged to Morocco. Alert to Spain's difficulties at home, Hassan prevailed on the U.N. to delay the referendum while the International Court of Justice at The Hague deliberated his own claim, and that of Mauritania. He also deployed troops along Morocco's southern border. In October, the court advised that there was nothing in either claim to qualify the case for self-determination. In November, King Hassan dispatched 350,000 Moroccan subjects over the frontier in a well-orchestrated show of popular commitment to the annexation of Spanish Sahara. The "Green March" forced Spain's hand: a military confrontation with Morocco was out of the question. On November 14 a partition agreement was signed.

The U.N. and the OAU stood by as it came into effect early in 1976. By then many civilians were in flight. There is evidence that the Moroccan air force used napalm and phosphorus to evict them. Polisario rallied the refugees in Algeria. Then, in a small desert settlement, briefly secluded from the Moroccan army, it proclaimed the independence of the former Spanish Sahara and declared its intention to continue fighting until the occupation came to an end. With Spain's ignominious departure, most of the world now referred to the territory as Western Sahara. The Moroccans and Mauritanians regarded it as Morocco or Mauritania. Polisario chose to call it the Saharan Arab Democratic Republic (SADR). Their constituency, the Sahrawi people, was one of the smallest nations in Africa, numbering fewer than a quarter of a million, and at this stage it was little more than an assertion of faith.

After 1975 Algeria was Polisario's only dependable ally. The FLN had a tradition of support for liberation struggles in Africa and, in this case, the colony lay at its doorstep. Besides, Algeria had its own grievances against Morocco, a conservative monarchy with whom it was vying for regional influence. It provided Polisario with arms, bases, offices and communications, a site and food for tens of thousands of refugees. The FLN even sent troops to fight alongside Polisario as it recovered from the Madrid agreement.

Throughout the 1970s and 1980s, King Hassan played skillfully on Cold War rivalries in order to get the most out of his allies. At home he was an absolutist endowed by the grace of God—the "Defender of the Faithful." To the West he projected himself as a champion of the "free world" and his opponents as enemies of the Western democracies. He was a friend to UNITA and to the conservative monarchy in Saudi Arabia. The Saudis provided financial support for the occupation of Western Sahara. France too was an old friend and ally. From 1980 onward a good proportion of the costs of the occupation were met by U.S. federal tax dollars. By 1992 the price of holding on to Western Sahara was reckoned at around $3 million a day.

By then the king had agreed with the United Nations that a referendum should be held—this was Polisario's central demand—but as the date approached he was able to delay it by trying to swing a rule change in the voters' roll. There is perhaps no single figure who has succeeded as conspicuously as King Hassan in making fools of the U.N. Security Council, with a well-thought-out mixture of prevarication, corridor lobbying and obstructionism on the ground: when the U.N. team was dispatched to Western Sahara to prepare for the referendum, supplies were interfered with and access to many parts of the territory was denied.

Since the end of the Cold War, Morocco has found it harder to ingratiate itself with the West, although it can still invoke the threat of fundamentalism as a good reason for the U.S. and others to continue their patronage. It may be that support for the king is no answer to the rise of extremist Islamic groups in Morocco—on the contrary, it could even encourage it. Repression in Morocco is severe. The pages of Amnesty International's reports on torture in detention are terrifying and the king is often more precarious than he seems. Until now, his greatest skill has been survival, however, and many in Polisario who once argued that discontent inside Morocco would bring down the regime and, in so doing, provide a solution to their own problems, are no longer so confident.

The suspension of the referendum process leaves more than 150,000 refugees from Western Sahara stranded in camps across the border in Algeria. The new world order has done as little for any of them as the old. In the U.S. Congress opponents of aid to Morocco have had a tough battle. When the Clinton administration took over this year, it inherited a request for appropriations totalling nearly $75 million in aid to the kingdom, of which $47 million was military assistance—not a serious incentive for Morocco to abide by the peace plan. It may be harder, too, for the U.N. to revive its enthusiasm for the referendum in a climate of change which is undermining the idea that colonial boundaries, like those of Spanish Sahara, should form the basis of Africa's nation states.

This chapter tells the story of the conflict from one side only—Polisario's—on the basis of two visits to the refugee camps and the "liberated areas": a small portion of the territory in which Polisario still has freedom of movement. I had a brief glimpse into Morocco at the end of 1991, when the Moroccan dissident, Abraham Serfaty, addressed a meeting in a church in London.

Mandela's release from prison in 1990 had made Serfaty Africa's longest-serving political prisoner. He was incarcerated in Morocco in 1975 and released in 1991. There was no comparison between the prison conditions of the two men. Serfaty was handicapped by severe beating on the soles of his feet and, he told me, by a bout of polio. He made his own way to the steps beneath the choir stalls and addressed a few words of thanks to the international community—to Amnesty International, above all—for pressing his case. There was an implicit tribute, too, to the United States: Serfaty's release had been a precondition for King Hassan's state visit in 1991. Washington no longer had grounds for ignoring the plight of such an obvious Cold War hostage.

Serfaty was a secular Moroccan Jew, a mining engineer whose political party had been banned: he was a bitter opponent of the king. Serfaty was a Marxist when he went to jail for treason in his late forties, and a Marxist when he limped out at the age of sixty-five, having clung on through oblivion to emerge in a very different world.

Yet little had changed for the majority of people in Morocco, and Serfaty, who had never had much faith in Soviet communism, was confident that his beliefs were still a match for the absolutism of the king and the growing threat of Islamic extremism.

Serfaty would not repent his greatest sin: he was one of the very few Moroccans who had denounced the annexation of Western Sahara in writing and in person—he had even spoken out against it from the dock in 1976. A week after he left London, Serfaty sent me a Xeroxed tract he had written and smuggled out from prison, welcoming the independence of Western Sahara and calling on Moroccans to mobilize for freedoms of their own. King Hassan could not forgive ideas of this kind. On his release, Serfaty had been deported and stripped of the very thing that he was not prepared to see imposed on others: Moroccan nationality. Conferred by force and revoked in anger, citizenship of Morocco was one of Africa's most dubious honors.

I n February 1986 Polisario celebrated the tenth anniversary of its notional state. At least sixty countries now recognized the Saharan Republic and most of them sent delegations. Journalists were also invited to attend. Visitors were flown from Algiers to Tindouf in southwest Algeria, where the Sahrawi refugees were settled under Polisario's exile administration. They had been there since the Moroccan invasion and their numbers had grown steadily. The procedures for guests at airport security in Algiers were streamlined. Anyone traveling on to Tindouf with Polisario was waved through and met on the other side by a group of men in suits with a lengthy manifest. I waited half an hour, no more, until the minders had raised enough guests to fill the bus. Delegations were arriving on almost every scheduled flight. Algiers was wrapped in the fog of a Mediterranean winter night, deepening the mood of curfew that always seemed to hang over the city, even in summer.

Late the next night, a military transport put us down on the runway at Tindouf. An assortment of foreign delegations, European support committees and journalists was led across the airstrip to a row of trucks and driven out into the desert. The wind was up but the sky was clear and filled with stars. There was a roadblock, a head count and then a burst of speed, as we moved through a veil of fine sand thrown up by the vehicle in front.

At dawn, a pink light washed the camps on the Tindouf plain. Patched tents of khaki, brown and faded green stood in rows as far as the eye could see. The sun climbed from the rim of the desert, daubing the camps with angular shadows. Within an hour they were shrinking; another thirty minutes and the plain was bleached with bright light. The chorus of restless livestock and clattering pots that had brought in the morning died away. With their shadows trimmed, the tents seemed precarious, stripped of some vital support and only held in place by the thick buttress of heat riding up from the ground. The settlements rippled in the haze.

The camps were organized in four sections, separated by several miles of flat desert and bounded by an infinity of sandy rock. Each section was named after one of the towns in Moroccan-occupied territory. Polisario claimed that there were now 165,000 refugees on the Tindouf plain, but the figure was impossible to verify and vigorously denied by the Moroccans, who also argued that the camps were full of people from Algeria and Mauritania.

Besides the refugees there were now several hundred foreigners to be lodged, fed and shown around. The journalists were in search of stories, the support committees must see the results of their fund-raising, while the delegations had to be indulged at every opportunity. At first the whole complicated procedure went smoothly. Then one evening the wind changed and blew stronger; within hours an implacable sandstorm had descended on the camps. It drove for two days, howling around the tents, lashing at the vehicles, veiling the great canopy of light above the plain so that the lower half of the sky was a pale dun and the upper limits, barely discernible, were the color of ground coral. The sand flowed into the tents, clinics and schools. It thickened the water and the food. It found its way into every orifice, scratching the eyes, lining the ears and settling so thoroughly into the mouth that one was forever chewing on the granules like minuscule seeds. At times it reduced visibility to a matter of yards. Dozens of tents began to rip. The elderly became sick with chest infections, and inside the tents children coughed and shivered, the mucus on their upper lips full of grit. The stronger refugees went about their business swathed in cloth, from which the sand trailed like smoke. The plain resembled an inferno crossed by small groups of penitents.

The officials were in despair. *Haboub* was going to wreck the celebrations. They waited and watched as one event after another was canceled or postponed. The gale had made it unwise, as well as difficult, to show the foreigners around. Two visitors were nearly injured at an exhibition of women's handicrafts when the high awning over the entrance gave way. A thick wooden beam, about twenty feet long, crashed to the ground at their heels as they ran from the whole falling edifice. On the way back to the car, the Polisario guides confessed their relief. For them too it was a narrow escape—from a piece of damaging publicity. For the rest of the day, the delegates, support committees and journalists were left to sulk in their tents with small glasses of sandy tea. Then, quite suddenly, the storm let up.

The air still rubbed at one's throat and lungs like pumice but the wind had dropped somewhat and the sun shone faintly through a smeared sky as the day of the anniversary fell and we were taken to attend the celebrations in El'Ayoun camp. A stand had been erected in the middle of the plain, a hundred yards from a promontory hung with a large text in Arabic: *"Koul el watan aou shahada"* (The whole land or martyrdom). From dozens of posters pinned to the stand or held aloft by the crowd, the eyes of Lulei surveyed the proceedings—El Ouali Mustapha Sayed, the first secretary-general of the Front. He had long, tousled hair and a bright gaze. Sometimes he wore a turban wrapped around his neck, sometimes just a shirt and jacket. El Ouali was one of the founders of the Front and a martyr, no more than thirty when he was killed during a raid against the Mauritanian capital. Today, ten years later, he was everywhere; nothing escaped his scrutiny.

The foreign dignitaries were shown to their seats in the stand beside the president of the Saharan Republic, and soon the procession of honor began. A cohort of small children marched by, the boys in blue shirts and white shorts, the girls in yellow dresses, their tops emblazoned with the colors of their notional country: black, red, green and white. The secondary school pupils and teachers, the women's union, the health workers, the mechanics, the liberation army and a long column of armor. A cage of doves was released, their wings rasping the sandy air, and a group of children dressed in white ran to the stand with Xeroxed copies of a text they distributed to the delegates, and then to the press, in French, Spanish and English. The "Opened Letter" had a floral decoration at two corners. It asked all the visitors, "loving peace and justice persons, to support our people to stop this devastated war. Our hope is also on you." It was signed "the Sahrawi Children."

The speeches from the stand seemed to last for a long time. The wind was still strong enough to cause discomfort, gusting at right angles to the parade, so that the crowds of refugees on one side were obliged to bandage their faces with their turbans, leaving a thin crack for the eyes. Algerians, Nigerians, Indians and Cubans extended their fraternal greetings to Polisario at length. Translators whispered into the president's ear. Now and again he nodded his assent. "We and the people of the Sahara," said a delegate from the ANC, "are confronting a common enemy—by this we mean international imperialism, which supports both apartheid and Morocco." A representative from

SWAPO spoke to the same effect. Finally the president himself rose to address his people, amid wild ululation, which lasted for several minutes.

Mohamed Abdelaziz had an air of reserve, a gravity that held him from the rhetoric that inspires so many rallies in Africa. To make good his shortcomings, this small, dark-haired man in battle fatigues addressed the crowd for over an hour. Morocco was warned that failure to negotiate would end in humiliation. Abdelaziz called for direct negotiations and a ceasefire, so that a referendum could take place. He gave his thanks to the ANC and SWAPO, and to the president of Algeria, "our brother and friend."

"The Sahrawi people," the president concluded, as the wind shook the tarpaulin, "will not abandon a single inch of their national territory and will pursue their struggle until all their land is liberated, in accordance with their vow; the whole homeland or martyrdom." Tens of thousands of Sahrawis rose on the plain to cheer. Tattooed women whooped like owls and rheumy children with matted hair braced their fingers in a field of victory signs.

The weather had relented at the critical time and in the camps that night there was celebration. The imams recited from the suras; drummers and composers performed until dawn and women danced in shallow crescent formation in the awnings of the tents. There had been four days of ardent ministration to the needs of the guests, and at last their straitened hosts could feast on the remaining meat.

Many people were now ready to go home. Indeed the delegations were visibly eager to do so and left by a shuttle to Algiers which began that night. Some of the journalists and most of the support committees went with them. The remainder showed a marked reluctance to leave. They had eaten this impoverished community out of mutton, vegetables and grain, and now they wanted to stay on. A handful of journalists hoped for a trip to the liberated areas and a few support committee stragglers waited with them, their hopes, if any, more obscure. The moment came when the exhausted officials began a summary triage. The remnants of the support committees were bundled into a truck and packed off to the airstrip. The minders were clearly delighted as the truck disappeared behind a screen of beige dust.

Those of us who remained were moved to a single-story brick building with a large courtyard. At four the following morning an official woke me with a shove of his foot and ordered me to pack. "You have two minutes," he said and clapped his hands sharply. There were several journalists waiting by the Land Rovers outside. The drivers began the journey with headlights on but doused them after a time and made their way through the desert like bats. Now and then we would take a sharp angle as though we had come to a junction in the middle of a city, but there were no roads, only tracks through the darkness. There were several turns of speed, for up to fifteen minutes at a stretch, during which a white cold set into the body. We would then slow up and one of the drivers would switch on his headlights briefly; the other would respond with his own. Twice they stopped, left their engines running and conferred. We continued in this way until dawn, which began as a sliver of light behind us and widened to reveal an immense red floor of sandy rubble, sloping gently upward to our right for twenty miles or more. We stopped at midday, ate and drank, and then continued. We must have entered the liberated areas—a thin stretch of Western Sahara running down the border with Algeria and then with Mauritania—after an hour's driving. The rest of the territory was enclosed behind the Moroccan defense.

For five years Polisario had excelled in unconventional desert warfare on open terrain. By 1979, Mauritania had relinquished its claim on Western Sahara, allowing the guerrillas to concentrate on Morocco's army to the north. This they did with such success that King Hassan, backed by friends in France and the United States, conceived the idea of an immense shield that would span the desert and keep the guerrillas from the habitable areas now under occupation. Within a year the first bulldozers had crossed the border, and by 1986 the sand wall had become a fact. It was now over seven hundred miles long; there were at least 75,000 Moroccan troops based at regular intervals along its length and many more to the rear. As it had grown, moreover, it had crept steadily nearer the Algerian and Mauritanian borders of Western Sahara, reducing the area under Polisario's control as it went.

I had heard any number of stories about the wall, its size, its character and aspect, but none of them prepared me for this cryptic blemish on the body of the desert. I had imagined a structure that would be visible from a long way off; the bases situated every twenty or thirty miles along its length would surely dominate the landscape. The whole thing would rise out of the desert, effortless and magisterial. But in Smara sector, which we reached after two nights, it required hard work with the binoculars and guidance from the local Polisario commander to pick out the defense at all. In the event, it was a thin band of pallor standing out from the rest of the terrain, which was darker by a shade. At the crest of a hill where the defense rose with the contours of the land, there was a base, a wide circle of ground, paler still. Twice Moroccan soldiers appeared on the perimeter, little black dots quivering in the heat.

To reach Smara sector we must have covered several stretches of desert in full view of the wall, although much of the traveling took place after dark. The terrain offered minimal cover, and the Land Rovers, which were Polisario's most dependable form of transport, had almost certainly been exposed, even if our guides had no intention of saying so. Now, however, we were no longer conspicuous; it was our turn to observe, which we did for an hour or more, from a rise in the ground. The wall shimmered in the lenses—a mute and intractable thing. Its languor was exasperating and perhaps a sign of strength. Later we retraced our steps down a watercourse littered with the remains of American fragmentation bombs. We drank tea, ate and slept. The next day Polisario brought up two mortar crews to a line of gravel bluffs within a mile or so of the base.

It required a brisk bombardment to rouse the wall from its inertia. The guerrillas dropped a volley of 120mm shells just short of the base, and some beyond. Once they found the range, the shells began falling one after another within the base perimeter like a drip from a rafter. When the Moroccans replied, their rounds fell comfortably wide of Polisario's positions, which were too close and low for the gunners on the wall to get an accurate trajectory over the steep gravel hills and down onto the mortar crews. But the units on the wall responded with feverish extravagance, filling the air with thunder. Then abruptly it stopped. We waited two or three minutes before scrabbling down the gravel to the Land Rovers. Some of the fighters had been shouting at us to move faster now. Their voices were harsh and excited. One of the guides, his head bound in a long turban, waited politely as we stumbled over the gravel. "Yes," he said, "let's go, yes." His impatience was just discernible under the veneer of protocol.

An hour and a half later we were drinking tea in a dry riverbed. It was prepared with care by one of the men, who transferred it backward and forward between a set of small glasses and an enamel teapot on a bed of coals in the sand. The fighters were devoted to their tea; always the ritual three draughts. The first, they said, should be sweet, like love; the second bitter, like life; and the third soft, like death.

Smara sector took its name from the town that lay some distance to the north, cut off by the Moroccan defense. The hills were bearded with a fuzzy gorse; on the low ground a small purple flower grew in profusion among the green-tipped acacias, but the vegetation thinned as the land fell away to the horizon. In places the sand was moist throughout the day and during the night there was heavy dewfall. At dawn dark shadows lay on the hillside; the air smelled damp until six or seven in the morning. The hardships of Tindouf felt a long way off and the fighters were at ease here, laughing, unwinding, breathing freely.

The town of Smara was founded at the turn of the century by Sheikh Ma el-Ainin—the name meant "water of the twin springs"—an impulsive spirit who presided over the tribes of the western desert. He had settled for a time in Tindouf but later fixed on Smara as a more appropriate site for a religious center, which would also be a monument to his life and lineage. To accomplish this ambition he sought help from the boy sultan of Morocco, Moulay Abdelaziz, and completed the work in 1902. The city added to his reputation, already great by virtue of his descent. Ma el-Ainin had performed the haj, the journey to Mecca, and was said to know the Koran by heart.

Although Spain had acquired a foothold in the region at the Congress of Berlin, its forces were no match for the warrior peoples of the hinterland. The Spanish founded a settlement on the Saharan coast and left the interior to its own devices. For France, this was most unsatisfactory. Whatever Spain could not administer became a pasture of revolt, from which raiding armies sprang up to defy the French in neighbouring Mauritania and Algeria. France, rather than Spain, was the sheikh's great enemy.

If anyone could raise an army it was Ma el-Ainin, and in doing so he relied on his friendship with the sultans. Abdelaziz's predecessor, Moulay Hassan, had seen no harm in supporting a vehement anti-Christian to the south, especially in view of growing European designs on Morocco. In 1904, as French forces pushed into the desert from the banks of the Senegal River, Ma el-Ainin rallied his tribes against the unbelievers with a call to jihad, holy war. The following year, the sultan sent arms to Smara for the campaign. Ma el-Ainin responded by declaring that the vast, ungovernable lands running south from the Draa valley to Timbuctu, and east from the coast to the great dunes of the Chech and the Khenachich, were part of Morocco.

In the end, the jihad collapsed, not only because the French fought with courage, but because the sultan himself, and then his successor, Moulay Hafid, gave in to European pressure. By 1910 Morocco had signed away control of its seaboard and parts of its administration to France and Spain. Moulay Hafid was then forced by the French to cut off all assistance to Ma el-Ainin and his followers. The sheikh, now garrisoned on the edge of the Anti-Atlas, made a final, impetuous gesture and declared himself sultan of Morocco. On their way to join battle with Moulay Hafid, Ma el-Ainin's armies were intercepted and crushed by a French force. Four months after his defeat, Ma el-Ainin died in Tiznit, but his descendants carried on the struggle and the Spanish Sahara was not fully colonized—the term was "pacified"—until 1934. Three years after the sheikh's death, a French force entered Smara. The town was deserted and they stayed for two days, setting off explosives in the old man's council chamber and vandalizing his library. In 1930, a more affable Frenchman reached the town. The poet and adventurer Michel Vieuchange did not set foot inside Smara but took a series of photographs of its surrounding walls and wrote in his journal, "I have seen you completely. Truly, you are the work of man, of Ma el-Ainin at the zenith of his powers."

The sheikh of Smara is still invoked by both sides in the dispute over Western Sahara. The Sahrawis see him as an indomitable anti-colonial figure who was sold short by Morocco. They regard his declaration that the desert sheikhdoms of the south were part of Morocco not as a binding pledge to the sultan, but as a provisional call for unity against the colonial forces of France and Spain. Mohamed Sidati, the senior member of Polisario whom I had met in Windhoek, claimed direct descent from Ma el-Ainin. Like his forebear, Sidati was a poet. He once wrote that his nation would rise back out of the desert "like a rose of sand."

For Morocco, however, there was no Sahrawi nation. On the contrary, Ma el-Ainin's declaration proved that every people in the southern wastes was fundamentally Moroccan. In the 1950s, a fierce nationalist current took the modern kingdom to include the Spanish Sahara and Mauritania in their entirety, parts of western Algeria and a northerly section of Mali—the very lands that Ma el-Ainin had nonchalantly bestowed on Moulay Abdelaziz half a century earlier.

The situation was further complicated by the fact that in 1956, on the brink of independence, the Moroccan nationalist leadership appealed to the people of the Spanish Sahara to join its liberation army. Many Sahrawis responded, crossing the border to Morocco to take up arms against the French. With Moroccan independence secured, the Sahrawi contingents simply bore the insurrection home to the Spanish Sahara and beyond, to Mauritania and western Algeria. They survived for two years and were then thoroughly subdued by a large force of French and Spanish troops; in the aftermath of Operation Hurricane, the remains of the Sahrawi armies made their way back into southern Morocco, where many were integrated into the Moroccan military and others lived on in aimless penury. The events of this period were grist to the mill of Moroccan expansionism. Would so many Sahrawis have rallied to the Moroccan army of liberation if they were not, in some transcendent and decisive sense, Moroccan?

One of the men who had come on the journey to Smara had an

answer to this. Nuruddin was the Polisario's representative in Sweden, relaxed, articulate, fluent in English and keen in argument. He maintained that Morocco's claim over Western Sahara was prehistoric nonsense. The Sahrawi people were a proper nation who belonged to the twentieth century. Under Spanish rule they had taken on a modern identity. Many, and perhaps most, had given up their nomadic existence as Spain worked the phosphates and developed the coastal towns in the 1960s, encouraging a steady drift from the desert. "Already," Nuruddin said, "we had moved beyond this tribal business— 'You are from this place, I am from that place'—when our fathers went to fight for Morocco. Then, as many Sahrawis moved into the cities, it was even less important."

In the process, the Sahrawis were granted a measure of political autonomy and went on to form a nonviolent anticolonial movement with strong support in the towns. Harakat Tahrir, as the movement was known, came out on the streets of El Ayoun in 1970 and was summarily repressed. Its leader, Mohamed Bassiri, a journalist and teacher, was detained and never seen again. The vigor of Spanish reaction drew younger activists like Nuruddin toward armed struggle. Their figurehead was El Ouali Mustapha Sayed. El Ouali's parents had taken him with them when they moved to southern Morocco after Operation Hurricane. He went on to study in Rabat, where he headed a loose association of Sahrawi students. The Moroccan authorities did not approve of Sahrawi nationalism and El Ouali left the country in 1972. The following year, in the ill-defined borderlands of Mauritania and Spanish Sahara, he presided over the founding congress of Polisario. Ten days later the movement launched its first attack on the Spanish. Nuruddin had been a member since the early days. When he was not debating with the journalists, he wandered with his head down and his turban wrapped loosely around his neck, in search of fossils. These he handed out with a phlegmatic smile, as if adding some obscure weight to his arguments.

It was obvious that matters had reached a strange pass in Western Sahara. Morocco maintained the sand wall with an array of up-to-date equipment, most of it from the big Western defense technology houses: Racal, Royal Ordnance, Vickers, Dassault. Yet the case for occupation was archaic. Polisario was a less modern fighting force. They fought their war with Kalashnikovs, mortars, Land Rovers, 23mm anti-aircraft guns, a few SA-6 and SA-7 missiles, and any material they happened to capture; they used the old tactic of the desert tribes—the long-distance raid. Yet their claim on the territory was a modern one, consistent with the thinking of the OAU. In 1964 the organization had laid the cornerstone of its doctrine on the future of the continent:

respect for the "tangible reality" of colonial boundaries. Without it, Africa could not cohere. During the long years of exile, this principle did much to sustain the Polisario Front and the refugees in Tindouf.

▲

Lamine Baali became the Polisario Front representative in London in 1984, moving to a small apartment in Pimlico, from which he sought to rouse British opinion against Morocco's occupation of Western Sahara. Convincing the public that the conflict in Western Sahara had any bearing on its life was a difficult task. Why should Britain be interested in a former Spanish colony in Africa, when it had so many former colonies of its own? By the time Lamine Baali took up the post, the fighting had been contained by King Hassan's wall. As the war dragged on, so the defense reduced the military options, and also the renown, of Polisario's guerrilla army, which had enjoyed five years of success in the field against the Moroccans.

For a delegate from the Sahara, London had two conspicuous features—an indifference to the conflict in the desert and prodigal rains for much of the year. Solitude was a constant tribulation, although there was always work to do and there were plenty of other liberation movement exiles in London. The Sudanese People's Liberation Movement had a representative on the Finchley Road, the Eritreans ran their offices in Battersea, the Tigrayans were set up two hundred yards from Stockwell tube station, the PLO had premises in South Kensington, the ANC was barricaded into chaotic offices opposite a police station in Islington, and SWAPO ran an establishment piled with stupefying documents near the Arsenal football ground. The Polisario Front was on cordial terms with the last two. Now and again Lamine Baali addressed trade union meetings. Much of the time he was to be seen around Westminster, making his way through the drizzle in a light gray suit to the Houses of Parliament.

On the whole, progress was slow. For all liberation representatives, the first step was to recruit a core of supporters in London, whose own sensibilities required delicate handling. Someone might want to bind the struggle to a worldwide ban on animal experiments, for instance; another might urge the forging of historic links with the Fourth International through the Haringay section of the Socialist Workers' Party. With their odd passions and disreputably wide horizons, support committee people were quite unlike most ordinary British citizens.

One of Lamine Baali's duties was to maintain a regular flow of press releases that he typed out on a telex machine. "Stepping up its victorious operations against the Moroccan monarchist troops of the occupation, the Sahrawi Popular Liberation Army launched a violent attack against the Moroccan army based in El Aydiatt. . . . During the attack our brave fighters destroyed and occupied the Moroccan bases and they shot down a fighter plane (F5E no. 91931) and captured many Moroccan prisoners." He ran off twenty copies and sent them to the editors and correspondents on his mailing list.

When he went to see the politicians in Westminster they would tell him that the great thing was to get more information into the press; that way the issue of Western Sahara would appear on the parliamentary agendas with more frequency. The journalists said exactly the opposite. Now and then the impasse would be broken and the press would run a story.

When King Hassan II of Morocco paid a state visit to Britain in 1987, many newspapers raised the issue of the war and urged that the king should only receive more British armaments in return for a guarantee to negotiate peace in Western Sahara. This was due largely to Lamine Baali's diligent efforts with the press. The fact that, seven years earlier, Hassan had kept the queen of England waiting for an hour was a welcome bonus. The memory of the affront incensed the British public in a way that the plight of the Sahrawi people could not. The *Sun* called King Hassan "the Rude Ruler of Morocco." Once again, the paper claimed, he had been unpunctual; this time he had kept the Duke and Duchess of Gloucester waiting thirty minutes at a banquet. "If he hadn't decided to go home early," the *Sun* said, "we would have told him where to stick his fez!" Lamine Baali sought clarification from the support committee.

By this time he was already attending fringe meetings at the autumn conferences and had begun to make headway in the hardest posting that the movement had to offer. But the war went on in a desultory way. In Morocco, the king was stalling on negotiations and the people of Western Sahara were stranded.

Lamine's mother was in prison in Morocco; she was a prominent Sahrawi nationalist who had been detained since the mid-1970s; there was no news of her. Two thousand miles from home, in a complex and insular culture, it often seemed that a war was only a war by virtue of its being reported.

▲

In 1987, at Lamine Baali's instigation, I traveled to the camps in Tindouf and to the liberated areas. It was a year and a half since my previous visit, but in that brief interval the settlements had taken on an air of permanence. Over seventy countries now recognized the Saharan Arab Democratic Republic and there were more resolutions at the U.N. and the OAU, but the conflict had reached a nadir of obscurity. Twelve years had elapsed since Morocco's annexation of Western Sahara and the Sahrawis were still waiting for King Hassan to come to the negotiating table.

Their patience was ambiguous, for every additional school or clinic that went up in the settlements suggested that a new level of permanence had been reached, as though the exiles were gradually adjusting to the idea of life in Tindouf. They had become an embryonic nation, and the camps a country, on which it was possible to try out various forms of social organization. While these ensured that life remained orderly for the time being, they were almost certainly devised with an eye to the future. When the time came to return to Western Sahara, the administration would be easily transferred, like so many pots, pans and blankets.

In Tindouf it was possible to look around without the darkness of spirit that usually attends the sight of displaced people, although the winter of 1975 had been terrible. The refugees had left their belongings behind them, and often their livestock. Casualties from Moroccan air strikes had been carried to Tindouf but there was little to be done for them. Medical supplies were pitiful; food was desperately short. Hunger and disease crept through the camps. By the end of the year it was said that sixty children were dying each day from measles, whooping cough and diarrhea.

Now, in 1987, there were basic medicines, trained people to administer them, and food. The war was fought well to the west of the camps, across the border, and the refugees were quite safe. Other family members, unheard of for years, might still be in the occupied territory, under Moroccan rule, in prison perhaps, or harassed, or complicit. Since 1986 another section had been added to the wall, bringing it right down to the Mauritanian border. Polisario believed there were now 140,000 Moroccan troops in the territory. Even so, they argued, Hassan's army was overextended.

Morocco could ill afford the high expenditures of the war, but it had allies who were ready to assist. The Reagan administration regarded the king as a "traditional and historic friend" and supplied him generously. In 1981 Washington extended $33 million in military credits to Morocco, delivered $136 million in arms and licensed the commercial export of further weapons to the value of $68 million. In return, the president's Rapid Deployment Force was given transit facilities in Morocco; UNITA commandos received military training and, quite possibly, some of the weapons that the United States supplied to the king. France kept an uneasy relationship alive with Polisario's main provider, Algeria, and also with Morocco. It was the principal trading partner of the first and furnished the second with weaponry, mostly attack aircraft. Saudi Arabia was a dependable friend of the Alaouite monarchy and suspicious of Algeria; during the first ten years of the war Riyadh provided anything between $500 million and $1 billion a year. But by the middle of the 1980s, Morocco had an external debt of U.S. $13 billion. Hassan II traveled the world with the pomp and trappings of a king, but the occupation of Western Sahara had made him little more than a glamorous beggar.

Mouloud had never been to the wall. As an Algerian, and a journalist, he knew a good deal about it and was keen to set eyes on it. When I took sick in the camps, he was very concerned; perhaps he thought that if I did not recover in time, Polisario would not bother to take him and the other visiting journalist—an American—to the front. Three were worth the trouble; two might not be. His face fell as though he were sick himself. The pale cheeks sagged with the weight of apprehension but the sleepy eyes were unusually alert. "Ask for more medicine," he said in French, peering down at me by the light of a hurricane lamp, "more injections." As a rule, he spoke little, ate less and smoked rarely. He wore faded gray trousers that fluttered over his bony legs when he was standing still and clung tightly around them as soon as he started to walk, which he always did at a furious speed.

Mouloud was a Kabyle berber with a measure of contempt for the ways of the Algerian littoral. He had dissent written all over him, a bohemian indisposition to authority of any kind; he was a Muslim, but deeply suspicious of imams, a revolutionary with a disdain for political parties and, above all, a reluctant ascetic. The sight of an elegant woman in the camps, where the chador was seldom worn, sent him into a foment of delight and despair.

The night before we left for the front there was singing and dancing near one of the tents. A young refugee, half Mouloud's age, had taken the floor, moving slowly with her eyes fixed on her outstretched hands, as the women stood in a crescent behind her, clapping and singing. It was impossible to watch this performance without some obscure sense of regret taking shape at the back of the mind as the steps proceeded. I lay back and shut my eyes. Abruptly the musicians doubled the beat; there was a flurry of clapping and loud laughter. I sat up to find Mouloud dancing opposite the young woman. Soon he was flying around the girl like a length of rope.

Some of the audience stopped clapping and studied this supple outsider encircling the girl as she lowered her eyelids and drew in her stomach. One of the younger men leaned across and replied to a question from an elder, who nodded with an air of misgiving. The Sahrawis were reluctant recipients of Algerian goodwill. They would rather have waged their war and raised their nation without help or interference. As an Algerian, Mouloud put them in a difficult position with this outlandish behavior, for if a benefactor should overstep the bounds of propriety, who among the beneficiaries will bring it to his attention? Mouloud removed his turban, flung it over the top of the young woman's head, let it droop to her hips and began to draw her toward him. A provocative smile appeared on his face. Three Saharan women emerged from the crowd and started to dance. A group of men followed. The tension was broken and the audience, courteous to the end, was visibly relieved.

The following day we left for the liberated areas. Farsia sector was in the northeast, about four hours' drive from Tindouf, over the frontier into Western Sahara and on to another great plain of rubble stretching south and west as far as the eye could see. A dry wind scorched our faces. The fighters had stripped the windshields, and any other reflective material, from their Land Rovers. A flash of sun on glass could alert the soldiers on the wall. Besides the driver, there were two Sahrawis in the car—a cook and a minder, by the name of Bachir Ahmed, a small man with a squint, who was probably in his late thirties or early forties. Bachir spoke several languages and went about the tiresome business of escorting visitors without a hint of fatigue.

At first, the route over the brown rubble was scored with tire tracks that revealed a lower membrane of light sand. We kept a steady course southwest for a time and, as the tracks thinned out, we turned due west. There was no change of aspect to the place; only the wind seemed less harsh. Further still to the west lay the territory's phosphate deposits. Within a year of the occupation, Polisario had brought production to a virtual standstill, but the defense had soon enclosed the mines at Bou Craa, as well as Smara and El Ayoun.

The vehicle rolled on, over flat ground, where the going was good. After a while, Bachir took my elbow and drew my attention to the wall. It hung a few miles to our right, thin and innocuous. We traveled for some minutes holding it dead level and due north. The consistency of the rubble seemed to change; the stone was coarser and the plaintive whir of the shale under our wheels dropped by a semitone or more, while the flat ground that slid away into the emptiness of the south began to pucker and dilate through the heat haze.

Mouloud seemed unimpressed and Nelson Smith, the congenial journalist from New York City, shrugged his shoulders. The cook, however, had braced his rifle across his knee. The wall disappeared from view as we slid gently behind a gradient and the three Sahrawis began an animated conversation, shouting through the turbans wrapped around their mouths.

Under the supervision of the local commander, Lih El Hadj, we set up camp in a dry watercourse, running a tarpaulin between a thorn acacia and the back of the Land Rover. About a dozen fighters were eating and drinking tea with us. One of these men was called Mohamed Kori. He remained with us until we returned to the settlements. Throughout the journey he presided over the complex protocol of making and drinking tea. A man with a broad face and well-delineated features, Mohamed Kori was clearly respected by his comrades. He was a poet; among the Sahrawis, composers had long enjoyed a cultural status beyond their social rank, which, in precolonial times, was scarcely higher than that of the slave. Mohamed Kori also took charge of loading the Land Rover when we broke camp.

As the day grew hotter, the rubble around us turned darker by degrees until it went black—charred at first, then glossier, like wet tar. The heat seethed out of the ground. In the shade, Lih El Hadj lay back and covered his face to sleep. It was quiet apart from the flies and the enamel teapot rattling on a bed of embers. Bachir too lay down and spread his turban over his head.

Later in the day a brisk wind got up, generating dust devils that pirouetted along the shale and then guttered. Bachir took this opportunity to make fun of Mouloud, comparing him to a small gyre of dust bouncing toward our watercourse. Perhaps he had seen him dance that night in the camps. Like Mouloud the dust devils were reckless and mercurial. They were also a hazard, for they could draw Moroccan fire—dust meant movement, which in turn suggested guerrilla activity. The desert was a great trickster, but there was no doubt whose side the fighters felt it was on.

The sun had dropped to the rim of the desert; a pair of large birds hopped around in the dry watercourse. Bachir told us to leave whatever was not essential with a group of fighters in another Land Rover. Mohamed Kori served a third glass of tea, which we drank as the drivers made the Land Rovers ready. He stood up and tightened a few packs, complimenting me, as an Englishman, on the virtues of the Land Rover. Bachir interpreted. Mohamed Kori stood back with his hand outstretched to the vehicles, like a salesman. Then he shot me a glance full of mockery and muttered something in Hassaniya that made the others laugh.

Nelson Smith was asked to remove his black canvas jacket. The darkness had a milky, incandescent quality that made black stand out. In its stead he was given a green shirt. Lih El Hadj said something to

Bachir, who checked that none of us was wearing a watch. Night had fallen by the time we climbed into the vehicles and set off toward the wall, one car behind the other, moving at about fifteen miles an hour. They eased over the rubble incline that had shielded us all afternoon, and on toward the point where they would be detected by any thermal imager in the sector. At the crest, the drivers cut their speed to about three miles an hour, the engines barely turning over.

It was a fair guess that there were gaps in the Moroccan surveillance, and that for twenty-four hours a day, month after month, the guerrillas had been probing the whole structure for flaws. After all, the wall was not precisely a wall. It consisted of two sand-and-rubble parapets, one behind the other, separated by a flattened alley where mobile artillery and armored personnel carriers could deploy. Every twenty miles or so was a base containing one Moroccan company. Between each base was a series of alarm points, each of these containing roughly forty men. There was radar and there was night-vision equipment. On or in front of the wall were ground sensors. There was a barbed-wire terrace way in front of the first parapet and a random scattering of plastic land mines. According to Bachir, the barbed wire had been cut months ago and Polisario sappers had recently removed the land mines.

Holding a course at ninety degrees to the wall you were at your least visible. This geometric conflict of inclines and protractions required precise judgments. Polisario had to approach a lookout point or a base in a straight line. Any deviation, by even a degree or two, would present the Moroccans with an increasingly visible target as the guerrillas drew nearer. But then there was only ever one point on the wall toward which they could run at ninety degrees, and in doing so, they were approaching others—an adjacent base, for instance—obliquely. Perhaps the drivers and unit commanders had a good idea of what they were doing.

We paused briefly. Bachir climbed down without opening the door, crept to the other vehicle and whispered to the driver. He then returned to our Land Rover and told us that from now on there was to be no talking. The vehicles took up again at a snail's pace. After a few hundred yards, our engine stalled. We sat without speaking, afraid and slightly embarrassed. The driver tried the starter; there was a half-hearted cough beneath the hood. He tried again, to no avail. The third attempt was equally useless. Was this why Mohamed Kori had gone through the routine about the great British Land Rover, his broad face carved with mirth and a hint of derision in the eyes? The driver climbed out and raised the hood. When he returned and tried again, the engine responded with a noisy bark and, as it settled down, we started to inch forward once again. It was strange that the Moroccans had not yet got wind of us—so strange that I thought the whole excursion was a hoax; we were being taken to an abandoned stretch of the defense in order to discover, and then report, that the multimillion-dollar fortification was easily breached.

Mouloud announced in a low voice that he was frightened. He spoke as though he were reporting his experience, years later, to a learned society. "Just then," he said, "I had a sensation very like fear." When he sat back, he found it difficult to breathe; a short cough turned into a wheeze and Bachir's turbaned silhouette swung around in admonition.

There was a second party of fighters near the wall. They led off through the darkness in single file and we followed. For several minutes, my boots churned clumsily in the gravel until one of the guides fell back, caught me by the wrist and led me over the ground with such skill that I was no longer making a sound. We were moving roughly parallel with the wall toward a point where we would be able to climb onto it at a comfortable distance from any base or alarm post. The ground was rising slightly now and it was sandier, which suggested another dry watercourse. After a few minutes, we passed a mysterious well of light about two hundred yards to our right. Later one of the guerrillas said it was a distant flare; but Mohamed Kori insisted that it was a beam from a nearby searchlight. Whatever its source, this light was inimical.

We had described a long curve, bringing us closer still to the wall, when we were ordered to lie down. Bachir moved back to ensure that each of us was lying flat. I inquired in a whisper what was going on. "We're waiting," he said. "Lie down." It grew cold and the silence spread through the night like a chilling dew. About three yards ahead I could distinguish the prone body of Mouloud in the sand; beyond him, Nelson Smith, and beyond him, Mohamed Kori and another fighter. The minutes dragged by as everyone lay quite motionless. A thin wailing began up ahead. It was a despondent, animal sound, which rose to a pitch and then stopped. A few seconds later it began again, this time for longer. Three of the fighters sat up rigid. In the dark, Mouloud's legs were just visible, beating quietly on the sand.

A less appropriate place for this mysterious convulsion was hard to conceive. By the time Mouloud began to wail again, Bachir and Mohamed Kori were crawling down the file to attend to him. Mouloud struggled to check himself. He gave a cough, then a wheeze, then a series of staccato gasps. When the two Sahrawis reached him, they squatted beside him, one with his hands on Mouloud's forehead and the other seizing him around the chest. They placed his face in a turban and hit him hard on the back. Mohamed Kori whispered into his ear. There was a short bout of muffled coughing and Mouloud was breathing regularly again. He gave out a very low chuckle and rolled onto his side. Bachir and Mohamed slid away to the front of the file and lay down. Ten minutes later Bachir crept back, whispering that we should listen carefully and we would hear Moroccan voices.

"Where is the base?" I asked.

"One hundred and fifty meters," he replied and pointed to our left. I could see an outline; perhaps it was the perimeter of a base. It was better, I supposed, to be close to a base than an alarm point: the base perimeters were big and doubtless poorly patrolled. I listened intently. I could hear something, some imprecise sound, but that was often the case in the desert. "I can't hear them," I said, and Bachir went to check on Mouloud.

It was another fifteen minutes before we climbed the wall. We edged along the sand for a few hundred yards and then, abruptly, it was in front of us. Like a child in a dark garden startled by a sheet on a clothesline, I felt my heart racing absurdly. Pale and wrinkled, suspended in the darkness, the rampart even looked like drying linen. In a few moments we were over the first parapet, walking gingerly along a set of tank tracks. Slowly we climbed the second parapet, sending trails of rubble from our heels. If Bachir was to be believed, we were now in occupied Western Sahara; there was nothing but sand and the darkness pressing down on it. Within a few yards of the defense, the feeble radiance emanating from the ground had been extinguished.

Our guides waited while we stared into occupied territory. In the blank night one imagined a land of bitterness and confusion. It had been stuffed with settlers from Morocco and borrowed money that would woo the local population. Those who were not susceptible were detained. The whole country was a kind of penitentiary, surrounded by armed men and military matériel, divided from the Polisario by the fantastic structure on which we were sitting.

One of the fighters tugged at Mouloud's arm. We moved off as quietly as possible, retracing our steps along the curve we had taken, until the wall began to blur into the milky darkness; the drivers were waiting by the vehicles with the engines running. Bachir was pleased. Indeed, there was a general feeling of relief among the Sahrawis, for they had carried out their duties without mishap. The military situation may have turned against Polisario; but they fought the propaganda war with skill and commitment, and this brief foray onto the wall had been a victory.

According to Bachir, raids behind the defense were now possible. Two units might be mobilized opposite different points of the wall, several miles apart, to draw the Moroccans, while a third launched an assault on quite another place. Operations had to be short and sharp. Once the wall was breached there was not much time in which to carry out an attack—on an alarm point, for instance—before Moroccan reinforcements arrived in the area. Moving through a breach to travel deep behind the wall was dangerous, for the exit could be plugged quickly, leaving the guerrillas trapped. In the last publicized assault on the wall, Polisario claimed to have occupied an eighteen-mile stretch near the Mauritanian border and pursued Moroccan forces to a depth of eight miles behind it. This was modest by comparison with the days when light guerrilla columns could wreak havoc on the other side of the Moroccan border.

    If the men in the field could tell you the specifications of the weapons they had captured in the last engagement—a litany of initials with suffixed numerals—they could also rattle off the resolutions adopted by the world bodies in their favor: 34/37, 35/19, 36/46, 37/28, 103 (XVIII), 104 (XIX), and so on. These were much more important than captured weapons to a man like Bachir, who knew that while Morocco's military resources were finite, it had enough to be going on with, and that while the wall was reducing Polisario's room for military maneuver, it had done as much, in diplomatic terms, to cramp the king. The more effectively Hassan impeded Polisario's war of liberation, the more thoroughly he became immured in the problem of the occupation.

    The U.N., the OAU and the Nonaligned Movement all favored a ceasefire followed by a referendum. Five years into the war, in 1980, Polisario's African allies moved to award the Saharan Arab Democratic Republic membership of the OAU. The result was a fracas at the summit in Sierra Leone. The Mozambican delegation led a furious attack on the Moroccans, who threatened to walk out if the plan went ahead. However, two years later the SADR became the fifty-first member of the OAU. This time Morocco did walk out, and took eighteen members with it. The landless little state offered not to take up its seat if this would repair the rift. In 1983, the OAU adopted the resolution on which all subsequent peace moves would be based.

    Polisario officials knew the wording by heart and could recite it like a mantra. It called for direct negotiations between the two belligerents "with a view to bringing about a ceasefire to create the necessary conditions for a peaceful and fair referendum for self-determination of the people of Western Sahara, a referendum without any administrative or military constraints, under the auspices of the OAU and the United Nations." In 1984 the Saharan Arab Democratic Republic took its seat at the OAU. It represented tens of thousands of people stranded on a miserable tract of desert in Algeria.

This was recognition of a high order, even if the OAU, like the United Nations General Assembly, had little power to bring about a settlement. Polisario had won a secure place in the conscience of the developing world while canvassing successfully for friends in Europe and the United States. Real influence lay with the permanent members of the U.N. Security Council, two of which backed Morocco.

There had been several official declarations from Polisario about the need to "demystify" the wall. It was not clear what this meant, except that it was part of the process of sustaining morale until the cost of Hassan's occupation reached a critical pitch and the fortification collapsed. It was, however, an admission that the war had turned against Polisario. The great years, at the end of the 1970s, when they had dogged Mauritania and taken up forward positions in southern Morocco, were over. The "strategy of walls" was a blow. Hassan's foreign advisers had conceived the idea of a conventional shield and it had worked. Year by year, old sections, and sections of sections, gave way to newer, forward sections, or adjusted sections, constructed under the protection of large troop and mobile artillery deployments. The defense began to swell, and the guerrillas were unable to stop its progress toward the limits of Western Sahara.

Bachir explained while we were up at an observation point that the best they had managed was delay—delay and diversion. The guerrillas could mount operations against a section under construction, he said, and force it off what they took to be its preordained course. If a new section—and there were now six major sections—had looked set to run southwest, for example, the guerrillas could impede the construction work and nudge it west. But the time would come when the Moroccans built another section further down.

If "demystification" meant coming to terms with the new situation, you could see it at work in the field. Bachir, Lih El Hadj and Mohamed Kori were relaxed and confident during their lengthy studies of King Hassan's defense. Hour upon hour of observation, while they themselves went unobserved, seemed to give them a psychological edge. They drove from one incline to another, scrabbled up on all fours and took turns to study the wall through an old pair of Russian binoculars, talking incessantly as they did so. At one of these positions was an upright shell casing with a scroll of paper inside it giving precise distances from the position itself to points along the fortification. It must have been left for the mortar crews. Here, we remained on the lip of the gradient for an hour. As long as the guerrillas watched and talked, handing the coveted binoculars from one to the other, the onerous threat of the wall seemed to subside. In this obdurate structure sprawling across their land, they seemed to see options and eventualities, evolutions and weaknesses, all infinitely debatable. At times it was even an object of mirth.

Around noon, Bachir looked up at the sky and drew our attention to a thin contrail, losing definition at both ends. We had been driving due south, away from the wall, or we would have seen the aircraft earlier. Everyone turned to watch the vapor trail rise slowly along the vertical like a strip of lint unraveling. It continued to extend in our direction and then curved back, leaving a white loop in the sky that was still intact an hour later when we stopped to rest. Bachir said it was a reconnaissance flight, although it had not looked high enough for that. In the bright glare of the day one tended to forget that the sky was a useful place from which to prosecute the war of observation.

As usual we ate pilchards in tomato sauce, mashed into a dough of rice and a diced onion. The water had a salty cast. The Sahrawis were all in good spirits. Nelson Smith asked Lih El Hadj what he hoped to do after the Moroccan withdrawal. He said that he wanted to stay in the military. A good-looking man of indeterminate age with a wife and children in the camps, he seemed oddly content with his situation, as though he could keep moving up and down the wall, attacking now and then, in much the same way as an Englishman would once have tended an allotment or kept a pigeon coop. The fact that his work sat well with his character was simply a privilege—the luck of the draw. As an officer in the sector, he enjoyed the full respect of his men and was free of vanity or bluster. His slight form and easy gait evoked the name by which the tribes of the western Sahara had been known: Sons of the Clouds.

Bachir was older. For years he had taken his duties as a guide in earnest, ministering to the needs of foreigners who complained, or took ill, or were restless and churlish. His gravity distinguished him from his comrades. Polisario's national movement was an agreeable fusion of two trends: on the one hand, austerity—the spirit of the beleaguered collective, reconciled with the desert precisely by being at odds with it; on the other, the supple, easygoing internationalism that enabled them to quote from a back issue of the *Herald Tribune*, or to embark on a discussion of some strange piece of global gossip. How many pairs of shoes did Mrs. Marcos really have? Was the Reagan White House really advised by an astrologer?

Bachir was not much interested in gossip. He was devout but, like the rest of Polisario, critical of institutions such as polygamy. His wife was a teacher in one of the settlement schools and he had a great panoply of relatives; it was likely that he came from an important family. The struggle was nationalist in character, strongly opposed to the tribal groupings that had defined the peoples of the Sahara for centuries—the Reguibat, the Tekna, the Oulad Delim, the Tidrarin. Adversity had brought them together as a modern national entity, but the process cannot have been straightforward. For Bachir, I imagined, the revolution was a large, unfamiliar house that he had entered after a long journey. At first, propriety had kept him from investigating every recess. After a time, however, he had begun to explore it, room by room, object by object, until he had satisfied himself that he was not dreaming. Even so, his diffidence meant that he was never entirely at home there, which was what made him such an able diplomat.

It was nearly dusk. The inclines had begun to throw shadows, the acacias in the dry watercourses were sharply defined against the sky and the barren terrain beyond had become a field of reds and russets. This was not a safe time to be traveling—the air was clear and the evening light seemed to flood through it—yet we were on the move. We'd just drawn the two Land Rovers up behind a shallow gradient and some of the men were praying with their backs to the descending sun. "When you are exposed to danger," says the Prophet, "pray on foot or while riding." The fighters knelt down with their legs folded under them. Mouloud leaned against one of the vehicles and gazed dreamily toward the south. His skin was badly scorched by the wind and sun and his jaw was dotted with black stubble. He looked tired after his ordeal at the wall, which he claimed to have been an asthmatic attack. I had come to see it as the very opposite of breathlessness: a fit of inspiration. Whatever demon had possessed him, it had chosen the perfect time and place to rail against the folly of the king's defense. It had made a mockery too of Polisario's surefootedness and put the fighters at risk. Very likely this querulous spirit had found a home away from home in Mouloud, whose interest in the struggle would always tread a margin of danger: it had a wild, sacrificial quality. He turned and caught my eye, jerking his head at the kneeling fighters with an air of resignation. About half a mile behind us, a third Land Rover was approaching. I watched the dust unwind in its wake as it headed toward us. When I could hear the engine I turned back to watch Lih El Hadj and two of our group at prayer.

A high, facetious whistle was interrupted by the muffled bang of a large door closing miles away; then it resumed, nearer and louder. It was followed by an angry, splintered clap. A spout of brown dirt went up a little behind us, to our left. One shell, casually delivered at a dust column, and now silence—an improbable silence that seemed to flatten and extend sideways; the further it spread, the more capricious the single round began to seem.

Bachir gave the order to pull out. There was some shouting, perhaps some remonstrating with the men in the third Land Rover, I couldn't tell, and soon we were driving toward another rubble shield, just to our east. We turned due south a mile later and skated across the shale with darkness gathering in front of us and a curtain of subdued orange light closing across the horizon where the sun had set. For a moment two enormous flying beetles held a parallel course with the Land Rovers, their silhouettes rolling along like black coins through the house of fortune.

Bachir had spoken the proverb once before and he repeated it now: "To the west is the house of fortune; to the east is the house of fire. You must journey south from time to time. As for the north, it is best forgotten." To the north lay Morocco, the annexationist, "the thief," as Bachir also liked to call it. To the south lay a vast, uninterrupted field of rubble.

"Later," Bachir announced as we made camp, "we will observe a harassing operation against the wall." Two Polisario units would engage a base and probably an alarm point with light fire—automatic rifles and 23mm machine guns—from separate positions. The coals writhed beneath the teapot, tended by Mohamed Kori, who was speaking out in his customary style, the blunt features drawn into a downcast expression as the monologue began. In due course his voice assumed a more declamatory tone and the others responded with approving sounds at the back of their palates. The words fell into regular groups, distinguished by little intervals. He was crouching with his head raised, eyes askance at the sky.

Mohamed Kori had inherited the gift of poetry from his father. Both men could recite in Arabic and compose in Hassaniya. He began with a poem of his own. It was a simple nationalist text and Bachir translated it once it was finished:

> You are resolute and that is a pride
> to outdo all other pride.
> However he is armed your enemy
> will not withstand this resolve
> you carry in your hands,
> this steadfastness.

He recited another in Hassaniya. It was long and we caught little of it in Bachir's condensed translation. The others enjoyed the recitation. I asked whether it was normal to inherit the gift of poetry. Bachir was unsure but Mohamed Kori responded quickly: it was a sign of respect to your father, he said, not to discuss poetry with him once you became an adult. He leaned back conclusively and stared at me while Bachir interpreted. Had his grandfather been a poet too? Certainly not, came the assured reply, merely a verse maker. Mohamed Kori stared up at the sky for a few seconds and then began attending to the tea things. The first glasses were distributed, drained and collected again, and after the final round we made ready to leave.

We stopped the single Land Rover in the darkness and trudged up the merest hint of an incline. "Here is where we will observe the engagement," said Bachir. We sat down in what appeared to be the middle of a vast gravel plain and waited. The ground glowed faintly in the starlight and I could see the silhouettes of the others when my eyes were used to the dark. "You will see how things are when it begins," Bachir informed us.

It began with brisk tracer fire to our left, a few bursts, and the sky darkened again. Then to the west came some longer volleys from mounted 23mm guns; the Moroccans fired back, their own tracers arcing down onto the guerrilla positions. The eastern guerrilla unit opened up a second time and immediately the Moroccans replied. The exchange of fire continued for a time. Then the Moroccans put up a flare. It wafted slowly down, throwing a pool of rosy light in front of the wall. The firing stopped and a second flare went up.

"Too high," said Bachir, and it was true that the light was weaker, like the beam of a flashlight through muslin. To our west, the firing resumed and the tracers moved busily through the darkness. Then a flare rose directly in front of us. Bachir and Lih El Hadj ordered us to lie flat with our faces down. A rim of light began to ease across the rubble until every shard was glinting. With it came an intolerable feeling of exposure.

We lay still with our faces to the ground, waiting for the light to subside. But I could imagine no end to it, and no end to the ways of becoming visible in a conflict where invisibility was everything. Polisario's war had been waged for years in this fashion, beneath the gaze of the sweeping, inquisitive technology up on the wall, an alien vision scanning the plain for their presence, day and night.

After a time we returned to the Land Rover. I lay back on the juddering packs and looked up at the sky. The constellations hung over us in a grand conspiracy of surveillance. A star shot low across the sky and lingered a fraction too long for my nerves. I found myself groaning with panic. Mohamed Kori laughed and played the fool, but the sense of exposure persisted.

The wall disappeared to our left in the afternoon heat haze. It was the last we saw of it. It had kept the guerrillas away from their towns and forced them into a strategy that did not suit them, yet it was a clumsy affair. To block the aspirations of a tiny desert nation, the wall cost Morocco something in the order of $1,000 a minute. Vast sums of money had been deployed against an army of some fifteen thousand guerrillas with little more than an intimate knowledge of the territory, a fleet of Land Rovers, a low-technology arsenal and two Third World backers, one of which, Libya, had now eased off its support. Mouloud preferred to think of the wall as *"la bêtise marocaine."* There was something to be said for this summary view of it.

Bachir stripped some kindling from the large acacia under which we were sitting. The final leg of the journey would take us across the Algerian frontier and into the refugee settlements. There was a makeshift well, an oil drum sunk to its neck in the ground. Below the film of dust on the surface the water was cool and clear and I drank it in handfuls. The cook and the driver lit the fire and Mohamed Kori began work on the tea. Mouloud asked me to take a photo of him holding a Kalashnikov; Mohamed Kori and Bachir made fun of him. He scoffed and lay down by the tree. The wind got up again and the dust devils started to gyrate across the flats. Bachir walked away in the scrub. I lay with a cloth over my face and slept.

When I woke, the wind had dropped away and the land was still. Mohamed Kori stood up and attended to the packs. Nelson Smith refilled his canteen from the sunken oil drum and doused his face with a red handkerchief before we set off for the camps.

▲

Tindouf was sheltered by long mud walls and breaks of plaited grass on which the wind drove with such ferocity that the weave itself had become distorted. Within lay forty hectares of garden, an aberration for a nomadic people who had only recently become settled. The walls and windbreaks hid the gardens like a closely guarded secret from the godforsaken plain, which could only howl with derision: the sons and daughters of the great desert tribes, raiders, herdsmen, poets and prodigious wanderers, were squatting in the mud and planting turnips!

For the Sahrawis, this was no disgrace. They had been working at the project for ten years now. Under small palm and pomegranate trees, radishes and beetroot grew in rows; there were onion patches and even stands of tomatoes, anything with a tolerance for the salts that fouled the local soil and much of the water. After many triumphs and failures, a hectare of cultivated land in Tindouf was yielding fifteen tons of carrots—not much less than a hectare of land in Egypt.

The Sahrawi Nile was a saline water table thirty feet below ground. The water was sometimes raised by diesel pumps, but normally the gardeners used the shadoof, a hand pump with a long arm and counterweight. It was then sent down a network of irrigation channels lined with plastic sheeting. Men and women worked together in the gardens. Each administrative section of the camps had a plot and every year Polisario sent young Sahrawis abroad to train as agronomists. In the gardens, elderly men and women without much formal education, graduates in shirt sleeves with rolled-up charts tucked under their arms, and veteran combatants all worked together. There was no shortage of work and plenty of people to do it. As the cultivation spread, the mud walls and windbreaks were extended.

The problem was salt; in one of the camps the sandy earth was full of it. To leach the soil required large quantities of water but the immediate sources were so high in salinity that it had to be brought from other parts of the plain. In some areas the water failed to drain properly, sitting instead on a shallow base of compacted sand; in others it ran straight back into the underground supply, introducing even higher levels of salt than before. The refugees solved the first problem when they received a machine that had been used to dig drainage conduits underneath peat bogs in Scotland. The second problem was harder to cope with and suggested the Sahrawis were running against the clock.

The gardens were part of the war effort, requiring imagination and patience. They were as much of a challenge for the civilians in Tindouf as the wall was for the fighters. Horticulture was a symbol for the little nation bound together by adversity, its nomadic life enriched by cultivation, just as tribal loyalties had been set aside in a common cause. The gardens evoked Sidati's "rose of sand," even in the ungainly guise of a carrot, but there were more practical considerations. On the aid diet, the sick and elderly, pregnant women and children ran nutritional risks that the gardens were intended to minimize. In the eyes of the nation, everyone mattered; moreover health meant population growth. For the dispossessed there is always virtue in greater numbers.

A few hours before we left for Algiers, we ran into Omar Hadrami, one of the founding members of the Front, who had conceived the administration of the camps and been in charge of "external relations" on the SADR's National Council. He was also a member of the Polisario's Political Bureau. Hadrami was a stout man with a round face, jocular and solid, a man of the people, in whom the art of the platitude had been carefully refined.

"What do you think of our nation?" he asked us.

Mouloud opened his arms wide and grinned approvingly. What was there to say?

Hadrami knew the answer. The Sahrawis were a small nation, he told us, but a great one at the same time. Which was a paradox. He waited to see if we would commit this thought to paper. Bachir looked Hadrami up and down in an odd way. There was no clue in his expression as to what he might be thinking.

Nelson Smith brought the discussion around to the sixth section of the wall, which clipped the Mauritanian border. Hadrami criticized Mauritania for its docility. It had tried to keep out of the war and Morocco had seen this as a "green light," he said. Now the war was at Mauritania's door. He told us the king had ambitions for a trans-Saharan road through Mauritania that would link it to Senegal. "It's an economic and political dream," he said with a dismissive smile. "Of course, France and Saudi Arabia are telling Mauritania not to worry. All will be well. But I say, 'Be careful.' Look how Spain partitioned us."

After this we all shook hands and Hadrami took his leave. I remember thinking him a decent sort of person. If he was uninformative, it wasn't that he had something to hide, or that he couldn't be bothered, but that he was a stalwart—a little dull, though probably dependable. This was a woeful error of judgment. Two years later in Washington, Omar Hadrami decided that for fifteen years he had been laboring under a misapprehension: he was not a Sahrawi after all but a Moroccan. His new motherland—"clement and merciful" to those who have strayed—gave him the use of a villa in Rabat, where he settled down to denounce his former comrades in the Polisario Front.

He described a vicious antitribalism in Tindouf. When Polisario officials sat the people down for meetings they would ask some poor man what tribe he was from, whereupon if he named it, he would be stuffed in a sack and dragged around the camp for public abuse. He told of a pro-Moroccan tendency in the Front, mostly among the Tekna tribe, who wanted to end the impasse and seek a deal with the king, referendum or no referendum. "The people have had enough," he said. "They've been there for a long time; they want to get away, they want money, they want to buy things for their children, they have no salary." Hadrami now concurred with the official Moroccan view that there were fewer than fifty thousand refugees in Tindouf, of whom only twenty thousand were from Western Sahara, the rest being Mauritanian and Algerian. However many genuine Sahrawis there might be, they were ready for home. He also argued that their first leader, El Ouali Mustapha Sayed, had never wanted an independent state in Western Sahara. El Ouali had been for integration with Morocco until Colonel Qaddafi's pan-Arabism seduced him into a "much bigger deal."

Hadrami told of being detained for seven months by Polisario security in Tindouf. It was 1988; he had been offered a post as SADR minister of information, and when he refused he was accused of being pro-Moroccan and of taking money, perhaps from the Saudis, during a trip to the United States. Hadrami maintained that half the camps began demonstrating against the leadership. All they wanted was to go home. There was a big clamor for his release, a minor uprising. On the walls of one of the camps an insolent piece of graffiti appeared: "Long Live the King." Stiff repression followed. Hadrami claimed that there were over seven hundred arrests. When he was released, he requested a post in Washington, which Mohamed Abdelaziz granted. From there he forsook the cause and began lobbying for the integration of Western Sahara within Morocco.

Whether it was revelation or invention, Omar Hadrami's story cast doubt on the very notion of reporting from the camps: no visitor to Tindouf would ever get far beyond the appearances that the refugees were obliged to keep up. There was a certain truth in this. Polisario's arrangements did not differ much from those of other liberation movements. They had the advantage, however, of operating in an isolated, well-organized domain, where outsiders were unlikely to encounter divergences of opinion. Hadrami was now on Morocco's payroll and though this added nothing to his credibility, it did not mean that his story was entirely mendacious. The issue of tribalism was so sensitive for Polisario that you could not inquire into anyone's origins without a sense of breaking the rules. The history of the tribes was not taught in the settlement schools. It was possible that as the years went by, with the refugees no nearer home, cracks in the edifice of national consciousness had begun to appear. On the leadership too a certain weariness may have descended. Elsewhere in Africa, 1988 was a dramatic year. Three thousand miles to the east, the Ethiopian garrison of Afabet fell to the Eritreans. The South African Defence Force withdrew from Angola and the implementation of 435 in Namibia was at last a reality. Hadrami called it a "period of reconciliation" but the Sahrawis had little to show for it. When it came to discussions with outsiders, the nagging problem of the salt beneath the gardens was a likelier topic than the underlying strains in the camps.

Yet, just as time appeared to have run out for the Polisario, King Hassan agreed to a referendum, in accordance with the resolution adopted at the OAU's nineteenth summit five years previously. A quarter of a century had passed since the U.N. mooted the idea. It was not the first time Hassan had promised peace. Now, however, there was reason to believe that he might be in earnest. The tone was set in May 1988 with the restoration of diplomatic relations between Morocco and Algeria, which suggested a growing sense of realism on both sides. The Algerian government was running into deep economic and political difficulties, making an indefinite commitment to the Sahrawis harder to envisage. Morocco's debt, meanwhile, had risen to more than U.S. $20 billion and the cost of the occupation was crippling.

Morocco and Polisario agreed to the U.N. peace plan in August. The following year the king met with a senior Polisario delegation. By the summer, the U.N. secretary-general was in the region and a time table for the referendum was under discussion. The vote would be for independence or integration with Morocco and in June a commission met in Geneva to determine who would be eligible to take part. The only basis for the voters' roll was a fifteen-year-old Spanish census, which had counted fewer than 74,000 inhabitants in the colony. If the figure was low, this had to do with the retreat of the Sahrawi army to Morocco after Operation Hurricane and, later, to a drought in the Sahel that forced many nomads south to Mauritania. The U.N. proposed to update the census with information from the camps in Tindouf and the occupied territory, which the commission, composed in part of Sahrawi elders, would help to verify. In so doing, it was authorized to deal with individual pleas of unfair exclusion from the roll. In the summer of 1991, the U.N. had approved a budget and a mission force, the two sides had agreed to a ceasefire date and the secretary-general had given notice that the referendum would be held in January 1992. As it happened, there had been no fighting since the end of 1989.

The old Spanish census was a curious yardstick with which to take the measure of Sahrawi nationalism, but partition and occupation had paralyzed all forms of due process inside the territory. Indeed, a sizable Moroccan presence still posed dangers for the U.N. plan. There were probably 100,000 settlers and at least that number of troops and security personnel in Western Sahara, which implied the presence of "administrative or military constraints" on the referendum campaign and the voting itself. The partial troop withdrawal, which Morocco was supposed to complete within three months of the ceasefire, would still leave 65,000 soldiers under arms while Moroccan administrative structures would remain intact. There would be fewer than three thousand U.N. personnel and, if Morocco could have its way, no independent observers. There was scope for corruption and even out-right coercion. Polisario, nonetheless, put a brave face on the arrange-ments. Their mistrust of Morocco was as keen as ever; the king was a clever man whose difficulties only served to sharpen his wits. He had always fought the diplomatic war with spirit; should all be lost, he would bare his throat in a show of ritual compliance. At home, how-ever, quite another part of the royal anatomy would be exposed to the inquiring eyes of New York and Addis Ababa as the king appeared on Moroccan television to announce that he would not give up a grain of Saharan sand. Polisario regarded him as a dangerous adversary: behind the wall, as they knew, lay a revetment of arrogance and guile, no less formidable. In June 1991, the king released a batch of detained Sahr-awis, perhaps three hundred, but there were many more who were still detained or who had disappeared. Then, in July, Morocco sub-mitted two vast lists of names for inclusion on the voters' roll. It was an indication that the king was back on his feet and fighting. The U.N. had proposed to judge each submission on its merits; the Moroccans calculated that 120,000 claims would keep it busy well beyond the scheduled voting date. The U.N. rejected the list wholesale. But in August, as Polisario began moving refugees from Tindouf back into the empty sliver of territory under its control, Morocco launched a series of air attacks and followed up with troop deployments beyond the wall. It was determined that no voting would take place in the liberated areas. The fighting had begun again after more than a year and a half. Then, as the day of the ceasefire fell due, a disingenuous silence settled over the field.

By the end of 1991, the peace process was in deep trouble. Mo-rocco had threatened not to cooperate with the U.N. unless the names it had submitted to the commission went onto the voting register. In December, the mission was embroiled in a scandal and the officer in charge resigned. Polisario had provided the U.N. with information that would help to update the Spanish census. It included the names of those Sahrawis, registered in the census, whom it knew, or alleged, to have died since 1974. At some time in the late summer or autumn, a member of the U.N. mission made this information available to the Moroccans. The only plausible motive was financial gain—perhaps of a high order, since information of this kind could delay the referendum indefinitely. The names of the dead Sahrawis had only to be submitted as living and eligible, for instance, for immense confusion to prevail. At the beginning of 1992, the new U.N. secretary-general, Boutros Boutros-Ghali, called for a three-month hold on the peace plan while the problem of voter eligibility was reassessed. It was a dismal per-formance by the great community of nations. I saw Lamine Baali in his apartment a few weeks later. He prepared tea in an enamel pot on a portable electric ring and we watched the news on television. In 1989 the SWAPO exiles had begun to drift home; the following year the South Africans were on the move; the year after that, the Eritreans and Tigrayans had gone, but the Polisario delegate was still living in Pimlico, waiting on the king.

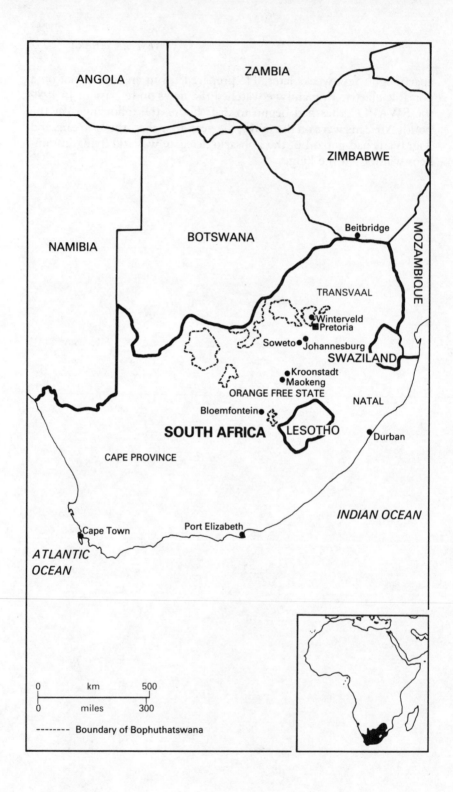

4

SOUTH AFRICA

▲▲▲▲▲▲▲▲▲▲

> The simple lesson of religions, of all philosophies, and of life
> itself is that, although evil may be on the rampage temporarily,
> the good must win the laurels in the end.
>
> Nelson Mandela, letter from prison

> Little leopard, who goes about preventing
> other little leopards at the ford!
> Finisher off! Black Finisher off!
>
> From a poem praising the military
> prowess of the Zulu emperor Shaka

If apartheid began to crumble in the 1980s, it did so
slowly. Beyond its borders, South Africa was teaching Mozambique a
cruel lesson for supporting the ANC—this was not expensive—holding on to Namibia and running regular campaigns inside Angola: a
sign of confidence that proved well founded until its last bid for Cuito
Cuanavale. At home it withstood the longest uprising in nearly forty
years of National Party rule. Abroad, the moral order of combat had
scarcely changed since the early days of the anticolonial wars against
the Portuguese in Mozambique and Angola, when NATO supplied
weapons to the dictatorship in Lisbon and the communist bloc gave aid
to the main guerrilla movements. Despite the momentum of the anti-
apartheid lobbies in the West, the governments of the United States
and Britain regarded apartheid as an acceptable price to pay for Pretoria's staunch anticommunism—but by the middle of the decade,
perestroika had begun to undermine this view, and in Washington, the
move for comprehensive sanctions was afoot.

In the townships of South Africa you could find any number of Cold War recruits. They were the young men, prematurely adult, who took to the streets against the security forces and threw rocks at military trucks, in return for which they were beaten and incarcerated. This much was simple. But their account of themselves went far beyond the dusty limits of the townships. The rank and file adopted the cry of liberation rallies from Angola and Mozambique—Viva!— in homage to their exiled comrades in the ANC. More eloquent members of the resistance at home spoke of a war against capital, of control of the means of production, of a world in which human and workers' rights were synonymous. They could chart the phases of the struggle with zeal, as though they were reciting the stations of the cross. Beyond the passion lay the resurrection and the workers' state.

Like so much of the debris from the Northern Hemisphere inherited by Africans—high-tar tobaccos, substandard medication and castoff shirts with goose-wing collars—this language was already spurned by most of the developed world, including the Soviet Union, by the time it was common currency among township militants. The dispossessed of South Africa had a use for it, just as they did for the gospels, cannibalized cars and second-hand clothing: they could turn their hands to discarded ideology in the same way they could fix and wear a damaged Walkman. They made use of it because they were an urban underclass in an industrialized society where old doctrines recovered a lot of their meaning. The ANC had strong links with the South African Communist Party, one of the last in the world to qualify its Marxism-Leninism, and this connection meant that there was plenty of doctrine to recycle. Even so, the youth of South Africa fought the Cold War less by conviction than default. They wanted voting rights and social justice: and then they wanted new ideas, not old ones; respectable living standards, not hand-me-down lives. The benefits of modern consumer society screamed out at black South Africa from the redoubts of white privilege. To the township youth, socialism meant that either they would get some of this or, in the end, nobody would have any of it.

The real apartheid Cold Warriors were easy to find, and they were not in Soweto or Alexandra. I had occasion to meet one in 1986—the congressional representative for Indiana—while compiling a radio report on the comprehensive sanctions bill in Washington for the BBC African Service. One of Dan Burton's aides fixed the interview on the misunderstanding that I was from BBC television. There was grave disappointment when I appeared: the representative for Indiana was not much interested in broadcasting to Africans. But he gave the interview, in which he set about the ANC with the two words that came most naturally: communist and terrorist and sometimes, "communist-terrorist."

At the end of the session he declared that the BBC was, in his view, too well disposed to communists and terrorists. His opposition to sanctions against South Africa was founded on an unswerving sense of the global communist conspiracy. He argued that no more than a fraction of South Africa's black majority supported Nelson Mandela and the African National Congress. Burton was a Buthelezi man; he liked the sound and smell of the ANC's rival, the Zulu Inkatha movement, and felt that it could stop the rot of an ANC takeover. I would think of him again, six years later in the African winter of 1992, as I walked past the freshly dug graves in Sharpeville, where many victims of a massacre by Inkatha warriors in the nearby township of Boipatong lay buried. Much had been lost by then. But Dan Burton was in some sense vindicated: Chief Mangosuthu Buthelezi had held his own, in his own inimitable way.

Burton and his colleagues conceded defeat in 1986. The daily satellite feeds of the burning townships had swung the American conscience against this new and deeper South that evoked so many of the issues of the 1960s. The vote for sanctions was solid and the presidential veto, which had been brandished at the Congress, was never exercised.

In the longer term, the Cold Warriors won a kind of victory, based on a spoiling game from which southern Africa will need time to recover. In Angola they forced the ruling party deep into the Soviet camp, where it was committed to policies that bled the remains of a damaged economy, all the while cheering an unscrupulous tribalist through war to defeat at the country's first election. Reconciliation in this battered country has been hard. Complicity through the early 1980s with Pretoria had a different effect. It led to the consolidation of a state security system with thorough control of the apparatus of government. By the time de Klerk took office and announced his package of reforms in 1990, almost all areas of civil society were administered by the security elite—a mix of army and police—that his predecessor had allowed to flourish. It was a conservative force with no accountability. Its use of death squads and criminal violence sowed confusion on the streets of South Africa, before and after the reforms, and its sinister influence in most matters of state led South Africans to suspect that de Klerk could not carry through his promises, even if he meant to do so.

In South Africa, I tried to work as much as possible in the townships, away from the buzz of conspiracy theories and forecast journalism, in the murk of ordinary South African life. I would have been out of my depth anywhere else. But by 1990 there was such mayhem in the townships around Johannesburg that "ordinary life" was no longer a useful term. Forty years of travesty were coming home to roost and the results were frightening: young men with no education, no money and no family allegiance were now in charge of the "revolutionary process"; they listened to Mandela speak but then they went their own way, through the twilight of the townships, in a world where gangsterism, violent crime and personal feuds were all subsumed under the broad heading of liberation. Like everything else at the end of the 1980s, the struggle itself was becoming deregulated; there were growing numbers of freelancers and the townships began to bristle with firearms. By 1992, South Africa's murder count was six times higher than that of the United States, although its population was a fraction of the size.

The street leaders of the young urban dispossessed, who may have been detained and who had given up their education for the struggle, were fiery individuals. Many of their followers smoked *dagga* and drank beer to keep their nerve up, for the growing anarchy of township life required courage day after day. Moving in the townships as an outsider was also much harder after 1990. Previously, the press were regarded as allies who could show the world what was happening in South Africa. By 1990, I believe, people were not convinced that the world cared any longer. They felt quite abandoned. Frustration at the lack of real change, and the upsurge in violence, meant that the press were fair game. In large tracts of Soweto and many other urban areas, you had to trust to chance and, in moments of confrontation, to probe very fast at the nerve of reason in your challengers. That it was numb, not dead, was an oblique tribute to the township youth. It meant they had a chance of outliving their anger—and so did you.

Within a few months of Mandela's release a new and terrible element entered the equation in the townships of the Transvaal. There had been war in the eastern province of Natal for several years between Chief Buthelezi's followers, Inkatha, and Mandela's. It was a war of allegiance conducted in the Zulu heartland, where the chief was opposed to recruiting drives by ANC loyalists. His aim was to build a firm Zulu base that could give him leverage in constitutional negotiations. But he had lost potential followers to Mandela's cause and the fighting had claimed four thousand lives. Now Inkatha carried the war up to the Transvaal, which was ANC territory, to challenge Mandela in one of his strongest constituencies. By the beginning of 1993, a further ten thousand lives had been lost in this violent urban confrontation.

I was in Soweto for most of the week after the fighting erupted. Early one Saturday morning I was crossing a squatter camp where an angry crowd had gathered. They pointed up the way to a development of detached bungalows occupied by wealthier Sowetans. A party of Inkatha warriors had ransacked the crescent during the night and some of the residents had come back to collect their belongings. There were two pickup trucks loaded with coffee tables, kitchenware and three armchairs in dark green plush. These were prosperous people who had wrought lives from an intractable system; they had bank loans and jobs; quite probably their children went to school. They had survived the upsurge in crime and the desultory drift of rumor that turned you overnight from a respectable citizen into a "sellout" or an "agent of the state," often for no good reason. They were the kind of people I used to think of when South Africans said with pride that their townships were "not yet Lima." But the new war in Soweto had dislodged them. A man in a suit came out of one of the houses carrying a radio-cassette player in one hand and, in the other, a picture of Christ on the Mount of Olives. Solemnly, he placed them in the back of a pick-up.

Further down the project was a house with a small yard at the back, where a wake had been in progress when the attackers arrived. The family had lost an older relative in a car accident and the mourners had come to eat meat and drink through the night. Two of them had been stabbed to death during the attack. There was a ceremonial sprinkling of earth in the front garden to cover the blood. In the yard the tables full of food had been overturned and fresh-cut vegetables, prepared for the second wave of cooking, were scattered on the ground. The huge, horned head of a cow lay sideways on a broken trestle table with its glassy eye staring up at the neighbor's wall. As I went back through the squatter camp, the crowd were calling for Inkatha's blood.

South Africa has an active press and a fixation with violence—the bloodshed in the townships often seemed to happen twice over, once in fact and a second time, spattered underneath the headlines, where it froze the resolve of a country on the edge of constitutional change. Five months after the Boipatong massacre, de Klerk announced that some form of representative election would take place by 1994. To Mandela, this was too far ahead. Another season of doubt and chaos could make elections very hard indeed. There were those, besides, who had ceased to see South Africa as a country at all. A small white colony had been formed in the southwest; Afrikaner extremists were clamoring for another, larger white homeland; and the leaders in two of the older, "autonomous" apartheid mini-states known as bantustans had begun to guard the status of their artificial fiefdoms with a jealous eye. Buthelezi too wanted no part in a unitary South Africa where majority rule took precedence over ethnic rights. Just as Savimbi had threatened to "Somali-ize" Angola after losing the elections, so Buthelezi spoke of triggering a "Yugoslav" scenario by leading the Zulu nation out of South Africa by force. The talk was more alarming than the prospect: it suggested that Mandela's vision of a single, multiracial state would only bond through further violence. In this dark period, there were people on all sides who opposed the armed patrol, the death squad and the panga. They were, in their way, the staunchest defenders of Mandela's ideal. Ironically, more than one of them had crossed into Angola in the heyday of the old South Africa to see that this ideal was never realized.

South Africa's war in Angola was remote, waged in a penumbra, but the fitful news from the End of the Earth was always of interest to the rest of Africa. Naturally the continent was less attentive once the South African Defence Force had gone. For the South Africans, the long struggle at Cuito Cuanavale was no longer a source of concern or a point of honor. In South Africa, less than eighteen months after the withdrawal from Angola, it was clear that the whole episode had been consigned to the past.

Stephen had served in southern Angola during the closing stages of the war, but he was slower than most to put it behind him. Indeed, the army was still an inescapable point of reference, now that he had become a conscientious objector and refused to complete his national service with a stint of duty inside the republic. His case had been written up in the *Weekly Mail* and while I was in Johannesburg I arranged to meet him. I borrowed a car and drove to his family's home in the northern suburbs of the city. It was a big but unpretentious house set back from the road. On the gate, unusually for this area, there were no security signs or pictures of guard dogs. Stephen came down the garden to let me in. We walked around the back of the house, entered by the kitchen and sat in a large room with very little light. Stephen was a thin young man with an untroubled face, although his manner was diffident and sometimes halting. He wore a ring, or a stud, through one ear. He said he had disliked the army from the moment he was conscripted in 1987. There was still a state of emergency in South Africa at the time and he had spent two months patrolling the township of Mamelodi, outside Pretoria, before he was sent to the Army Battle School at Lohatla in Cape Province, where he trained on the artillery range. In November he was flown to the big

South African base at Rundu in northern Namibia and from there to Mavinga, to join a battery of eight G5 guns in Angola. Quebec, as the battery was known, had been deployed in August. Stephen now spent four months as a junior gunner in Cuando Cubango province checking the sights of the battery's G5s with a theodolite and helping with their maintenance. It was a period of boredom, discomfort and above all anxiety; Stephen did not like the idea of killing people. By Christmas of that year the battery was often in action. The G5 was South Africa's most effective weapon. With its range and accuracy, it could keep the troops away from the thick of things. In theory, each gun could discharge over one hundred shells in the space of an hour, but a much lower rate was prudent. Before Stephen arrived, a shell had exploded in an overheated breech, killing one of the crew and seriously wounding the others. The same thing occurred on Christmas day during preparations to move the battery after Angolan MiGs had bombed much closer than usual. Stephen and his colleagues were fortunate that a pile of nearby charges was not ignited.

The shells, however, were deadly over their proper destinations, where they burst into around four thousand fragments with razorlike facets; the entire surface was covered with tiny spines. The battery could fill the air over a target with about one million such fragments in an hour. To sit under a G5 barrage was an ordeal that thousands of FAPLA troops had gone through. Sometimes they were pinned down for hours among their own dead and, when the guns were silent, there was only the certainty that they would resume. I recalled the incident at the bridge of the Cuito River and the dismay of Ngueto's face when his men were wounded. Stephen asked for a description of the terrain beyond the river, and said at once that there would have been spotters in the high woodland, where the plain rose to the east. He stared between the curtains at the garden, inclining his head and fingering the lobe of his pierced ear. He said that the bridge must have been a regular target. There were plenty of targets, he added, and dozens of them could have been civilian. The units in the field and the observation posts ahead of the guns would simply radio back at the slightest sign of movement; the coordinates were then logged into a computer and assigned a code number with the prefix T. Once the entry had been made, the code number could be punched again and the elevation automatically set. At the beginning of 1988 the battery remained on one site for two months with its target options rising from T1, Stephen recalled, to a three-figure number. Each of these stood for a small zone of ruin in the rolling savannah between Mavinga and Cuito Cuanavale.

The "force in being" in Angola was an improvised affair, impressive in its way, but its supply lines were ragged. There was seldom enough water, Stephen remembered. They would search for it in the area, but FAPLA—"the enemy," as he called them—had put bodies in many of the water holes. There were periodic shortages of ammunition and parts. The men in the battery often had to fend off a creeping sense of isolation from the rest of the force, and from the world. Stephen was never sure of his whereabouts; the strangeness of this foreign country, which he had entered in order to subdue, drained the landscape of detail and context. It was apprehended through a veil of acronyms and digits that spared the South African Defence Force a view of the chaos that threatened to engulf it in Angola. Stephen said it was as though he and his colleagues in the battery, half a dozen to a gun and large group of auxiliaries, had succumbed within days to the extremity of their situation, jabbering in recondite numbers over the din of the guns, which kicked shallow weals in the ground and scorched the cover as the shells flew toward their enigmatic destinations. The battery was also active at night, but in the dark it was easier not to think about the nature of the target. There was only the ritual of carrying, loading and firing, as young men labored in the dark like stokers.

During the day the Angolan MiGs could come in low but the bombing, said Stephen, was inaccurate—"seldom closer than two kilometers." Sometimes he'd see South African Mirages fly over and then, within the hour, they would be coming back, pursued by Angolan planes. The superiority of Angolan government air power put the South Africans at a disadvantage. They had already drafted in a team of Israeli technicians to develop an attack aircraft, but the project was outpaced by the diplomatic settlement.

The threat of air attack added to the strains on the battery. Back in South Africa during basic training, Stephen recalled, the pacifists and the patriots had come to blows. Now, under pressure, Quebec began to divide, but the fissures were shallower and the animosities unspoken. Half a dozen of Stephen's friends from basic training went with him into Angola and formed up against the lieutenants and bombardiers who had been through the junior leadership courses and felt obliged to defend South Africa's presence in Angola. Stephen believed that these men had trouble convincing themselves of their own arguments, which is why the discussions in Quebec battery petered out as the men returned to their books by Alistair MacLean and Stephen King, which were handed around irrespective of differences about the war. Moreover, in Angola, the South Africans had a whipping boy. In public the SADF liked to heap praise on UNITA, and there was a genuine admiration for the commanders, but on specific points the Boers were far from enthusiastic. Savimbi's men were shabby in reconnaissance, they said, and covered ground at a snail's pace. They did not realize how easy it was for the Angolan government troops to cross the rivers in the south. Sometimes they ran away in the face of the enemy. Certain officers would get furious about the way UNITA did things and a disdain for its rank and file underlay the camaraderie between the two forces. Stephen saw little of UNITA in the battery but he remembered that, when they were around, they were a focus of ridicule and sometimes anger. "They used to read our magazines," he said, "and I remember one of the gunners showing a UNITA guy an advert for a bed. The guy was amazed by the bed. He'd never seen one before. He took a real joshing for that." Whenever anything was lost or mislaid in the unit—food, magazines, radio batteries—UNITA took the blame. Once Stephen's colleagues accused a UNITA man of stealing a magazine. He was slapped several times and, finally, punched hard in the face.

Stephen was granted leave from Angola about the time of the South African assaults on the Tumpo Triangle, the decisive phase of the battle for Cuito Cuanavale. These ended in failure, although the details had not yet entered South Africa's reservoirs of neglected common knowledge. The Tumpo Triangle lay a few miles east of Cuito Cuanavale. There was an MPLA strategic base in one corner, at the confluence of the Cuito River and a short tributary. The SADF made three assaults on the triangle in an attempt to drive the government forces back to the town. The first, at the end of February, was wrecked by the failure of 5th Reconnaissance scouts to detect one of the mine fields in the excellent defense at Tumpo. The commander's vehicle hit a mine, giving away his position, and the South Africans were forced back under a heavy barrage. The casualties, especially among UNITA auxiliaries, were high. A few days later, a second attempt was called off, once more under heavy fire, after a series of tank breakdowns. UNITA casualties were again high. Finally, at the end of March, after careful planning, the SADF took a final crack at the triangle, bringing in a fresh brigade from Namibia, complete with two new tank squadrons. The air force flew preliminary strikes and two UNITA battalions were ordered west on a series of diversionary raids. On the day, the main assault force swung around the triangle and approached from the north but here it foundered in a mine field under tremendous bombardment. Savimbi's troops suffered the brunt of the defeat, with more than a thousand casualties. Most of the South Africans completed the retreat, plowing over the bodies of their allies as they fled.

I told Stephen how Ngueto had brought up the captured armor from the final rout to show off at Cuito Cuanavale. Stephen was struck by this and nodded as though it confirmed what he believed but could not prove. He was sure that South Africa had lost the war. "If they had got that territory," he said, "they would never have moved out."

For a moment he could not remember whether he had done two tours in Angola or one. Then he snapped his fingers and told me that after his leave he had been sent for a few months to Ovamboland. He remembered only that there was more abuse of black people, more punching—this time an Ovambo interpreter who failed to stand at the back of the mess queue—and the routine burning of kraals, expulsions from villages and seizure or slaughter of livestock. He said the army in Ovamboland was "jumpy." They would blaze away at a rustling bush or the sound of a twig snapping in the dark. On his return to Johannesburg he had been struck down by a frightening inertia. It came suddenly, on his third or fourth day, a sort of paralysis. The light in the garden was too bright, the inside of the house was too stifling, his parents were too pleased to see him, his friends seemed unavailable. A few months later he registered with a national organization for conscientious objectors. He had been listed for three weeks of township duty, probably in Natal, but he had made it clear to the authorities that he would not go. If his call-up was confirmed, he risked a spell in prison. He pinned some hope on a recent finding in Bloemfontein that there was no enforceable minimum sentence for violations of the Defence Act. Stephen was nervous but he was not prepared to back down. He wanted no further part in soldiering.

His mother and one of his sisters returned to the house and I caught a brief glimpse of them as Stephen ushered me out. His mother greeted me with a suspicious nod. As we walked down the garden, Stephen explained that she respected his beliefs and was ready to support him, whatever happened, but his father was a conservative man and would not react well to his decision. For the time being he was in the dark. At the gate I asked Stephen what he planned to do, if he did not go to prison. He said he wanted to work in industrial relations; preferably to represent a trade union. Modest, circumspect but principled, Stephen would be an asset to the new South Africa, unless it went awry.

My second appointment in the Transvaal had as much to do with Angola, and the old order in the subcontinent, as my first, but it jolted me out of my obstinate interest in the war. Louis Breydencamp lived in Pretoria. I telephoned him from Johannesburg and he asked me up, giving me directions to St. Alban's Cathedral, in the center of town, where he would be attending a meeting that night. He was an active member of the national campaign against conscription. The country that I had entered a few days earlier was an exuberant, hopeful place.

Nelson Mandela was a free man; the ANC was a legal organization; the state president, F. W. de Klerk, had embarked on a series of changes that appeared genuine and perhaps irreversible. The state of emergency, in force in the townships for several years, would soon be lifted. Young white men in living rooms with drawn curtains could talk with a measure of freedom about their unwillingness to soldier for a racialist state. I had no doubt that Louis Breydencamp too would speak his mind.

The N1 highway cuts straight up from Cape Town, running northeast through the Orange Free State, on to Johannesburg and Pretoria, and then up through the northern Transvaal to the border with Zimbabwe. For all its vastness, South Africa can seem small and suffocating, like a narrow garden with high walls of the kind one might have entered in a dream, through a door that promptly ceased to exist. I rarely strayed north of the capital, and had little idea of the communities in the low veld—Warmbaths, Nylstroom, Pietersburg—beyond Pretoria. Here the countryside had a gloomy affinity with the American South—the land was heavy and grand; it put the blunt arguments of nature at the disposal of rash ideas about godliness and chosen races; anyone who begged to differ was a fugitive by definition. The towns were thus like staging posts to Mexico. Beyond the river—the Limpopo or the Rio Grande—lay another world and, no doubt, for many the possibility of a clean break.

The idea of transgression is strong in South Africa. If it once had the simple sense of stepping across, this was now buried beneath the weight of Afrikaner custom that lends such force to the breach, and the observance, of the country's racial codes. It was by crossing out of the Cape and up to the interior that the Afrikaners assumed their identity. But in this traversing of land there was something of the politician who crosses the floor; it was a gesture, as much as an act, of defiance, and the drift away from the Cape became a founding transgression in a more complex sense. The renegades who proclaimed the white republics of Graaff-Reinet and Swellendam at the end of the eighteenth century did so in response to a belated attempt by the Dutch East India Company to impose its authority on the small settler community that had dispersed into the hinterland. By then the settlers were pushing further east into Nguni pasture; the border wars that ensued between African and Afrikaner were a matter of some anxiety to the company. So too was the harshness with which the settlers were treating their African workers. The two republics were short-lived but the delicacy of the situation beyond the Cape persisted. Several decades elapsed before the issue of master and slave was raised again in earnest, this time by Britain, which had superseded the company as the new authority on the southernmost tip of the continent. It was the antislavery laws of the British that prompted the Great Trek. By 1845 nearly fifteen thousand Afrikaners had made their way across the Vaal and Orange rivers, equipped with firearms, farm tools and Bibles, in pursuit of the righteous obscurity, and the supremacism, to which they felt they were entitled. At that point in Afrikaner history the hunger for solitary devotion and the habit of trespass became inseparable.

As Xhosa resistance strengthened and the British spelled out their disapproval of further Afrikaner expansion eastward, the attractions of the north became stronger. Moreover, the rise of a powerful military state during the 1820s under the Zulu chieftain Shaka had caused massive displacement in the interior and there were now empty lands for the taking. Where chieftaincies survived, the Afrikaners challenged them. Modern weapons gave them a great advantage over the African armies they encountered and, more often than not, it was decisive. In 1838, at Blood River, they overcame a Zulu force of ten thousand men. The pace of infringement and dispossession was only interrupted by the discovery of gold in the Boer republic of the Transvaal half a century later, which revived Britain's flagging resolve to bring the Afrikaners and their mineral wealth under the unconditional sway of the empire.

Beleaguered and provoked, the republics of the Orange Free State and the Transvaal declared war on Britain at the end of 1899. The Afrikaners fought with ingenuity, and when the empire outgunned them, they turned defeat to their advantage. The annexation of the republics, the scars of military defeat and the outrage of the British concentration camps, in which at least twenty thousand Afrikaners died of hunger and disease, bound a wandering and disputatious people into a nation without a state. Like the Zulu nation forged by Shaka, then robbed of its lands and further homogenized by the British, it was an agglomeration of subjugated clans. Many of Africa's "tribes" were creations of empire, and the Afrikaners were among them. Moreover, in Afrikaans they had a common language, which assumed a sacred status at the end of the Boer War when the British suppressed it in schools. The Afrikaners would have to wait for more than seventy years before they could redress this indignity by imposing their own language as the medium of instruction in the apartheid curriculum. The result was an uprising in Soweto, followed by reckless repression and an exodus of young black South Africans, who crossed the borders to join the armed struggle. At the time, the N1 through the northern Transvaal could not serve as the route for black transgression; it led across hostile redneck territory to the frontier with Rhodesia, which was still manned on both sides by officers of white minority rule.

Not even twilight could flatter Pretoria. On the contrary, it gave the city a stricken air, poised on the horizon, with one angular edge of the university bathed in red, as though its life were ebbing away through the fabric of invincibility. Over the brow, sheer faces of cladding and reinforced glass were draped in evening shadow. Every few seconds I would look up from the road and check the lineaments again. Each time Pretoria was nearer but a touch darker. One imagined a city consisting only of mezzanines, vaults and security precincts, held together by thousands of elevator shafts. I scoured the traffic for the sight of black drivers or black passengers, to reassure me in some nebulous way, and to remind me of my whereabouts. This prospect was the nearest I had come on the continent to a heart of darkness. I glanced in vain at the BMWs and Mercedes going by in the fast lane. By the time I was off the motorway, slats of ominous fluorescent light had begun to appear in the city's foundering bulk.

In the center the streets were almost deserted, as they would be this time of day in the financial district of New York, or the richer residential areas of London. Here and there were men in uniform and the only traffic seemed to be military or paramilitary. I was early for my appointment with Louis Breydencamp and parked the car by a Portuguese restaurant. The waitress was from Mozambique; she had left at independence. She brought *peri peri* chicken, the bird splayed flat in the Portuguese manner. A policeman came through the door, glanced around but did not stay. There were no other customers.

At the cathedral I made my way down the aisle to find a group of people, less than a dozen, seated in a circle in the transept. Louis Breydencamp introduced himself and motioned me to a chair, explaining to the others that he had arranged to meet me here. He seemed out of place among his anticonscription colleagues, most of them thinner, a little paler, and the men long-haired. Louis had blue eyes and a ruddy hue to his cheeks. I put him in his early twenties. He was dressed untidily, in jeans and a tattered combat jacket. He had a shock of corn-colored hair, but the back and sides were short. As the meeting drew to a close, it was Louis who tied up the loose ends, summarizing the tasks that members had undertaken for the week and steering them toward a compromise on the date and time of their next encounter.

Once the meeting was over, I drove with Louis and one of the other campaign members, a medical student called Thomas, through the empty streets of the city that were now largely dark, until we arrived at a comfortable house in the suburbs. It belonged to Thomas's parents and was empty apart from a small dog that shuffled around the kitchen floor. Here we sat and talked until two or three in the morning:

Thomas had the house to himself for the weekend and there was a faintly conspiratorial air about the two young men taking it over. Thomas was younger than Louis and less assured. He dressed in a homespun style that gave him the look of a medieval player. Altogether his appearance suggested the idea of return—to an idyll of some kind, an eccentric notion of innocence.

Louis Breydencamp was opposed to conscription but the difference between him and Stephen was a big one. Certainly, the benefits of liberal Johannesburg had to be weighed against the objections Stephen's father was liable to raise, but Louis lived in the bastion of Afrikaner consciousness. Besides, it was harder for an Afrikaner to stand against the Afrikaner consensus because there was no ground to retreat to, just as the nation itself had nowhere to go. Other whites had escape routes, to England, America, Israel, but the Afrikaners were a defensive, parochial people whose interest in land and nation stood between them and the refuge of cosmopolitanism. The Afrikaners also had a keen sense of treachery among their own. It was precisely for these reasons that an Afrikaner who dissented was a more serious proposition. If he could stand his ground, as Louis seemed to have done, he could not be lightly dismissed.

Louis had been conscripted in the mid-1980s and trained in the northern Transvaal, where the South Africans were also equipping and organizing Renamo, the insurgency against the left-wing government of Mozambique. He saw a good deal about race relations in the military that struck him as improper. He went on to serve in Angola, where he began to question the objectives of his government at the End of the Earth. Still, Louis said, the army had troubled him less than his return three years ago to Pretoria. He said he had taken a dislike to it. He had been out of sorts, just as Stephen had in Johannesburg. There was also the brutal torpor of the city to contend with.

"It was dead," he said decisively. "You know, a very dead place"—to which Thomas assented with a grin.

Angola had changed Louis and, now that he was a young adult, Pretoria no longer suited him. It was so segregated by comparison with Johannesburg or Cape Town, so dangerously stockaded against the realities of African life that it was almost unbearable. He took some comfort from his father, however. Louis Breydencamp, Sr., was a liberal, a building contractor based in the "homeland" of KwaNdebele, north of Pretoria. His work and contacts also took him to the neighboring township of Mamelodi. He had always refused to differentiate his acquaintances by skin color and was in the habit of whiling away his time after work with friends in Mamelodi, whom he and his wife invited back to their house in Pretoria. He believed in a just wage, freedom of movement and association; he chose his business partners without regard for race. Louis Senior had introduced his son to people in Mamelodi and Louis soon made friends of his own in the township. He and Thomas were going over to Mamelodi for a party that weekend.

"Some nonsense started," Louis explained, "because my father had a friend in Mamelodi who ran a nightclub. He introduced us and I spent quite a bit of my time there, but people started to tail me on my way in—whites, security people I mean, from Pretoria here. On the edge of the township I was forever being stopped and searched. Several times in the nightclub, the SADF came in with guns and cased it. The owner and my friends in Mamelodi told me it only happened when whites were there. Then security would make a big show with their guns and spoil the occasion. They didn't want us to have black friends. Definitely not. At that time I was living in Pretoria in a kind of a commune, a shared house, and I began to get these telephone calls with heavy breathing and, you know, threats. The last one I got, this voice says, 'Stay away from Mamelodi. Necklace! Necklace!' Incidents like that made me angry. I started to consider the whole situation in South Africa and it changed me. I was definitely upset."

By 1988, things had eased off a little. Louis was studying for a degree in microbiology and had joined the university chapter of NUSAS, the National Union of South African Students, which shared the goals of the ANC. At Pretoria University the members had to call the union by some other name, because it had been outlawed, Louis explained, on the grounds that it was "inconsistent with the Afrikaner character." They settled on Students for a Democratic Society. By enrolling, Louis had chosen to identify himself with the radical minority at a conservative university. The movement was now running an education project in Mamelodi. Both Thomas and Louis taught at the weekends in the township. In a world of hostility to projects of this kind, support came from their families. Thomas's father was a doctor, another liberal, Thomas said, although he was disparaging in his use of the word. He said his father was a good man but the older generation were still victims of "propaganda, socialization."

"That's such jargon, man," said Louis, who took people as he found them. His uncle, for example, was a member of Eugene Terre'Blanche's Afrikaner Resistance Movement, but he had no interest in accounting for this: to him all neo-Nazis were merely bigots and the movement a public nuisance. In 1989 Louis became involved in another SDS campaign, this time over the segregation of the buses in Pretoria. The SDS traveled with black people on the buses in defiance of the law, but the campaign was soon curtailed by large deployments of police at the bus stops and Louis was arrested. The family began to receive threatening phone calls. A crackling voice told him in Afrikaans that if he persisted with the campaign, he would get into trouble; that the trouble would "make Blood River look like a tea party." Louis knew that Afrikaners are given to hyperbole; even so, he took the precaution of sleeping in the lounge. Not long afterward, in the small hours of the morning the house was hit by gunfire. Louis was shaken but unharmed. It was not the first time: many years earlier, someone had tried to shoot Louis Senior and his wife. There had also been a gasoline bomb in the garden. By the beginning of the following year the buses were no longer segregated. For the time being, people left the Breydencamps in peace. Might it not be, after all, that they were the ones with foresight; that they had weighed the alternatives and decided that the price of apartheid was too high for their beleaguered nation?

Louis proposed that I stay over at his house and accompany him the following day on an SDS outing to the homeland of Bophuthatswana.

"You'll see," he said, "the kind of people who study at the university in Pretoria."

The SDS was laying on the tour to show their fellow students the anomalies of the new South Africa. Some of the worst poverty on the continent was to be found in Bophuthatswana and the SDS believed that the trip would be salutary for their fellow students.

As we prepared to leave for his house, Louis raised the subject of Angola. He had vivid personal memories of an earlier South African failure to take Cuito Cuanavale, in 1986, when he had served as a paramedic with the Special Forces. After he had been in the field a few weeks, Louis was attached to a force of UNITA infantry for an attack on the town. It was winter and they were tired and cold when they arrived. They were supposed to link up with an SADF mobile unit but it got stuck in a mine field, he said, and they lost radio contact. An armored car and a recovery vehicle were damaged by mines and had to be abandoned. A UNITA soldier lost his foot. Louis's detachment, perhaps a hundred men, was meanwhile supposed to engage and "eliminate" FAPLA forces at the bridge but they came under fire, in the darkness, after their UNITA guide lost his bearings, and there they remained, pinned down until morning. At first light FAPLA sent out tanks. "I swear to you," said Louis, "when those UNITA guys saw those tanks, they were gone." Louis was left to fend for himself, along with a signalman and one other South African. They crept away after a time and walked forty kilometers until they were picked up and returned to their base, whereupon Louis was told that he would be going back again that night.

The second attempt was a failure, although this time they went with vehicles known as "ground shouts," which blasted recordings of tank and armored maneuvers through large speakers across the river while Louis's detachment fired mortars. The procedure was designed to give the impression that an armored division had assembled in front of the town. FAPLA was supposed to run away. "First thing in the morning," said Louis, "out came the tanks from Cuito Cuanavale and we withdrew. We were bombed on the way but luckily there were no casualties."

At a forward resuscitation point about fifty kilometers from Cuito Cuanavale, Louis was informed that he was to be sent back, yet again, to blow up the bridge. He set off with a hundred UNITA troops, each one carrying a small brown briefcase of explosive. "We walked for ages and ages. We had one water bottle each. I was tired by now," Louis explained, "almost asleep as I marched. We were moving in a column. Suddenly someone tells me, 'Sshhh!' Our guide had led us right into a FAPLA bivouac on the east side of the Cuito River. We crept back and around and eventually we could see the bridge. I'd expected something like London Bridge, a big thing, you know, but it was dark and ordinary-looking. There were two patrol boats under the bridge. Our intelligence was that the boats were empty. A group was sent up to check the boats and just started shooting at them. When that happened, the whole of the opposite bank lit up with fire." Louis and his group were on the retreat again. They crawled and then they ran and then they started walking until Louis felt he could go no further. There was no water, there was never enough of it. Like disillusioned trainees leaving a sales conference, the UNITA men began to dump their briefcases, one after another. "I could hear it," Louis said, "Plop, then plop, and then a few yards on, plop, until none of them had explosives anymore." They walked for another seven hours before the dawn broke. With the gray wash of darkness still in the sky, the MiGs came. Louis ran for cover in high grass and as soon as his body hit the ground he fell asleep from exhaustion.

Once, not long before he left, Louis was tuning his radio in to a South African station and heard Magnus Malan, the defense minister of the day, deny that there were any South Africans in Angola.

"Radio Five," said Louis, "you could pick it up in Rundu." In the car to the Breydencamp house, Louis told me he had been awarded a commendation for his service in Angola but he had burned it. He stressed his admiration for the officers in the field. As far as he was concerned, they were professionals who would as easily have soldiered for a democratic state, although on this score his judgment turned out to be too generous. When President de Klerk held the white referendum on constitutional change in 1992, Colonel Jan Breytenbach, under whom Louis had served in Angola, advised strenuously against a vote in favor of reform. Perhaps Louis had taken Breytenbach's demeanor in the field to indicate a courage and propriety in civil life that were simply not there.

"I enjoyed the army in some ways," he concluded, "and I could see myself in a future military force, serving a democratic cause."

The following morning we drank tea in the house with Louis's mother and father. She was a quiet, adamantine woman, her face furrowed with difficulty. Her husband was bluff, but beneath each observation one could sense a stoic offering a stream of hostages to fortune. The Breydencamps were the kind of people one would have wanted on one's side in any circumstances.

Louis and his colleagues in the SDS had found an ANC man to give the running commentary on the bus as it trundled out of Pretoria toward the margins of Bophuthatswana. There were some two dozen students on board, divided almost evenly between SDS members and those whose attitudes were, quite plainly, more consistent with the university's idea of the Afrikaner character. The "Characters," as I came to think of them, gravitated naturally to the back of the bus, as far from the tour guide as possible, leaving the SDS members in a huddle of their own at the front. Five minutes out of Pretoria the SDS had a brief conference, after which they redeployed among the others. After all, the idea of this trip was to plant the seeds of change in obdurate ground and no occasion should be wasted.

Before long the view from the bus window took on a drab, underdog aspect. The terrain was dry and depleted, crammed with matchbox developments and semishanties. I had been in this part of the world two years earlier with rural aid workers who were trying to defend a group of township residents against mass eviction. It was a sorry place, where the sun beat down on a gray suburban waste with no central city. This was the essence of the apartheid strategy: the extension of a bleak limbo in which large populations were forced to live as a city folk without proper towns in the manner of a peasantry without proper land. In 1988 the police had thrown us out of the township with a reminder that "serious accidents" happened to people who took undue interest in the welfare of its citizens.

Until the tour guide pointed it out, there was nothing to suggest that we had left South Africa and entered the demesne of Chief Lucas Mangope, president of the Independent Republic of Bophuthatswana, sometime minister for economic affairs and head of the Bophuthatswana Democratic Party, which held all of the seats for most of the time in the National Assembly, except a handful controlled by a party that opposed the very existence of the state and a further dozen awarded by the president himself. Bophuthatswana contained well over a million people, deprived of their South African citizenship in 1977 and awarded membership of a fantastic entity, composed of seven separate enclaves and recognized only by Pretoria, which subscribed generously to its exchequer. Most, but not all, of the people who lived in this racial homeland—which had since been enlarged to include even more ex–South Africans—were Tswana speakers. Many commuted from the imaginary state to other parts of South Africa for work. The inhabitants of South Africa's four independent homelands were not the first people to have nationality thrust upon them, but these lamentable republics, which concentrated power in the hands of influential chiefs and confined unwanted black South Africans in marginal South African land, were among the most reluctant nations on earth.

The ANC man gave the facts and figures in English as we journeyed on through this carefully managed deprivation known in South Africa as "Bop." The Characters were inattentive, except to his accent, which amused them, and perhaps, too, to the fact that he was black—a clever man, "cheeky" therefore, of whom they might well be wary. They showed a keen interest in the view from the bus; perhaps they had signed up knowing that they might never have a chance like this again. One youngster endowed with enormous ears repeated a couple of the tour guide's words, mimicking his accent loudly, to the embarrassment of several Characters and all the SDS members. The ANC man abused him genially under his breath. As the shepherd of this disparate flock, Louis reviewed the situation with an anxious eye, turning to left and right, as he apologized for the state of the bus, stressing that the SDS was short of funds.

We were headed for an area known as Winterveldt. The guide explained that there were over half a million people on about 225 square kilometers of land. The population of Winterveldt began to soar after the Group Areas Act of 1956. Large numbers of South Africans were removed from designated "black spots" around Pretoria and dumped there. The majority were not of Tswana origin and had to negotiate with the local landlords for accommodation. There was already a history of tension between the landlords and the non-Tswana tenants before 1977. Thereafter the bogus statehood of Bophuthatswana formalized the discrimination against non-Tswana residents that had begun while everyone was still a citizen of South Africa. Any Zulu, Xhosa, Pedi or Shangaan who had the misfortune to live in Winterveldt—and today fewer than 20 percent of the residents were Tswana—was now at the mercy of Tswana ethnic rule, conferred by the Afrikaner bureaucracy in Pretoria. This malignant strain of tribal devolution would haunt South Africa long after apartheid was gone.

We got down from the bus at a modest community center where members of the Winterveldt Action Committee, solid for the ANC, would address us. Cheerful nuns in gray habit flitted around us with tea in plastic cups. There were two short speeches about the injustices of Winterveldt that seemed to pass the Characters by; they were restless and whispered among themselves in Afrikaans. Then an elderly gentleman by the name of Hans stood up and described an incident that took place at a nearby soccer field in 1986. "The place I am telling you about is called Makgatho," he began. "It is not far from here." The local community leaders had called a meeting to protest against their situation and almost everything they took the Mangope regime to stand for: corruption, ethnic preference, connivance with Pretoria. Hans explained that he had been at the community center when he received word of confusion at the rally. "I got in my buggy," he said, "and I drove to that place known as Stadium." When he arrived people were already running. Mangope's police had opened fire on the crowd; two hundred were wounded and eleven dead. He described the arrests, his return journey, his anger and grief and then, quite suddenly, the story had come to an end. It was nothing, just those deaths and the gunshot wounds, and his own dismay, four years later, in the telling. The students looked embarrassed. An awkward silence fell on the room but as one of the nuns stepped forward to keep the proceedings afloat, Hans remembered something else. The police had refused to release the bodies of the dead for several days. They had put the houses of the bereaved families under guard. Three young men had been shot dead returning from a vigil for one of the victims, a pastor. Hans stood for a moment longer, as though he were waiting for a phrase that would reveal this matter in its proper fullness to his young listeners, but his patience was fruitless. He sat down and wiped his forehead. The nun stepped up again, thanked him and asked if there were any questions. That Hans's story had died in the telling was consistent with the spirit of the new South Africa, in which old grievances appeared to have no place. Even as he broached them, the storyteller hesitated, as if on the brink of impropriety. Yet why, if the present had pronounced them dead, could they not lie down?

We made two more stops, one at a market and another by the side of the main road. To our left was a row of poor housing, to our right, below the road, a flat, smoldering garbage dump, which extended as far as the eye could see. Thin twists of smoke rising between the heaps of rubbish gave it the air of a field a few hours after battle had been concluded, but to the students, I am sure, it was worse than that. They sat in the parked bus staring out through the windows while the inhabitants of the dump, perhaps a hundred, shuffled from mound to mound and returned with a handful of trophies to their plastic tents, setting out again a few moments later across the smoking moraine. After a time the spectacle no longer seemed like battle so much as punishment. The man from the ANC remained standing in the bus, with his back hunched, gazing out with the rest of us. Then with Virgilian authority he ordered us down. The ordeal of fascination was over and the students filed meekly from the bus. For the next hour they walked in small groups through the garbage, crossing paths with the inhabitants, who reacted with an elaborate mixture of acknowl-edgment and disavowal to this impromptu delegation. At first they went about their business without a murmur. Then they ventured an ironic greeting in Afrikaans. Then they returned to their pickings. They were dirty and downtrodden—debased, in fact—some of them in rags, consumptive-looking, gray-skinned men and women with burning hangovers, earned by the garnering, sorting and resale of bottles, tin cans, wood and paper. Their leaders were articulate, with a reasoned grasp of their downfall. When the tour guide introduced them to the students, a middle-aged man with bare feet in a tattered three-piece suit explained that most of the people on the site had once been tenants, or relatives of tenants; after eviction they had become squatters and then, driven off yet again, they had reached this final pass. They were not wholly to blame. A group of rubbish pickers gathered around him, nodding as he spoke. The students were quite defenseless out here in the stench and heat of the dump. Across the drifting smoke, the old bus up on the roadside seemed beyond reach. There was no choice but to pay attention and the students did so, SDS and Characters alike, equally shocked, equally intent on the faces of the dump people, from whom it was now quite foolhardy to divert one's gaze to the desolation around them.

We walked back to the road, led by Louis, the ANC guide and the man in the suit, who stood at the edge of the dump with a farewell hand raised while we clambered up the gravel bank and boarded the bus, looking out as we had before at the little colony of men and women plying the gray, circular paths. Then the bus pulled off. On the way back to Pretoria the passengers were subdued and the two groups altogether indistinct. Louis Breydencamp sat with the ANC guide but, after a few minutes of business, they both fell silent. Louis slept. The closer we came to the city, the more I was inclined to think that the culture of the trek was not entirely finished. The new trans-gressors were the Afrikaners who had begun to wheel around in a steep arc, heading away from the solitude of the past toward a country they would have to share. The bus wove through the suburbs of Pretoria to the university and there was a general dispersal.

The violence in South Africa always seemed intelligible from a distance. In Western Sahara, for example, you could see a line of armored cars sold to Morocco by Pretoria and captured by Polisario. They were stubby, aggressive little vehicles with angular contours. Their very economy spoke of the streamlined, militarized state, which produced quantities of armor for its own purposes and marketed the rest to governments of like persuasion. To be shown around these contraptions or to stumble on G5 shrapnel in Angola was to recognize the nature of the South African regime and, at the same moment, to align oneself instinctively with its opponents.

White rule in Pretoria took on a more ruthless character when the armed struggle began in 1961. For fifty years the ANC had been a well-organized mass movement committed to nonviolent means, but this was no longer possible after the Sharpeville Massacre, when the ANC and the smaller Pan Africanist Congress were outlawed. Both developed armed wings and both were henceforth at war against apartheid.

From outside, South Africa remained a cut-and-dried case of state brutality. Yet south of the Limpopo, after 1976, political life was undeniably more complex. Peaceful change had proved impossible, but the new doctrine of armed struggle was fraught with perils, for the figureheads of the movement, who might have explained to their followers what was at issue, were in prison or exile. A steady stream of younger political talent was drawn away from the townships into detention or across the border to training camps in Tanzania, Zambia and Angola. Many of those who emerged from detention were mentally and physically debilitated, while the exiles were gone for the duration. Thus it fell to an ever more youthful and headstrong leadership to interpret the revolutionary war against the state. During the 1980s the security apparatus had assumed thorough control over most aspects of South African life. Its intelligence was good; it was adept at sowing confusion and suspicion among its opponents. It could arrest half a dozen township leaders in an evening's work, leaving even less seasoned individuals to step into their place.

In the mid-1970s apartheid had opened a front in education by trying to impose Afrikaans in schools. It was natural for the youth of the country to continue doing battle on this patch and boycott was the obvious weapon. Over the next decade education was replaced by mass truancy or deliberate provocations that ended with the forces of the state closing down the schools. When they were open, they became the political clubs of the revolution, in which argument and recrimination were hard to distinguish. Classwork was abandoned and teachers were vilified if they should think of objecting. Those pupils who expressed the wish to go on with their education drew down the wrath of the others. By the 1980s the term "sellout" had gained an ominous currency among the younger township militants. As the great wave of unrest broke in the townships in 1984, it became an important lexical addition to their armory of terror. A sellout could be a town councilor, whose palm was greased by Pretoria, but it might equally well be a diligent pupil, a father who begged his children not to confront the army on the streets of the township, or a shopkeeper who was loath to hand out free goods to the baffling number of youngsters claiming to be comrades enrolled in the freedom struggle. The penalties for being a sellout were severe: beating, house burning or immolation, yoked in a tire full of burning gasoline, known as a "necklace."

It was a piece of good fortune that I first saw the townships around Johannesburg at the end of 1987, when the military pressures were easing and war weariness among the comrades and residents had led to an interim calm. I had stayed in a prosperous area of Soweto, Orlando West, at a Methodist manse. Here a young Afrikaner minister, the Reverend Paul Verryn, had opened his premises to young comrades in danger of being picked up by the army or in need of convalescence after detention. There was much coming and going at the house, which nonetheless had a stable feeling, a definite air of sanctuary. One of the boys was recovering from a harsh detention near Pretoria, during which he had suffered brain damage. The others appeared easygoing, although they might sometimes be seized with bouts of anger or hilarity that suggested otherwise. They were courteous to strangers, escorting me to church with Verryn and showing me around Orlando. One night the army came up the street, moving from door to door, and most of the children in the manse fled through the yard at the back, leaving only one youngster turning the pages at the piano in the parlor, while Verryn played over a metrical setting of Psalm 23. I stood at the front window and watched while a man was picked up and flung in the back of an armored truck. When the hymn was finished, Verryn banged the lid of the piano shut and strode into his study. The army presence in Soweto angered him; he believed that what happened to people in detention was "blasphemy." Later, after the boys returned, there was an altercation at the end of the garden among a group of residents. They went outside to see about it and a shot rang out. Nobody was hurt, but they scurried back into the manse, laughing and breathless. It should have alerted me to the impending chaos in Soweto, and the steady rise in the number of firearms. However, I still thought of the Transvaal townships in terms of the epic conflict between the state and the dispossessed.

After the Soweto uprising in 1976, the ANC's international appeal became its strongest card. Its leadership was severed from the realities of the townships, and had no military strength inside the country. But it made good these things with a skillful public relations campaign, presenting its case to the international community with such success that presentation became the bulk of its work. Just as the tall figure in dungarees holds the body of Hector Petersen in the famous photograph taken after the Soweto massacre, so the movement held South Africa up to the world for reprimand, until the state could no longer be so unrestrained in its business. Indeed, the country as a whole was becoming vividly self-conscious. The struggle remained harsh and terrible, but it was at the same time a kind of theater, in which a regime trying to conceal its intentions sought to overcome a population actively divulging theirs.

Video cameras and tape recorders made the state by turns more sensitive or more censorious, and people more careless of their safety. When the press were not restricted by the emergency laws, the comrades took absurd risks, protracting the running battles, burning more cars, stoning more police vans and speaking out with greater anger, although the penalties were severe.

In Soweto, at the beginning of 1988, I attended the funeral of the young activist Sicelo Dhlomo, who was murdered shortly after he appeared in a CBS documentary giving details of his torture in custody. I was accompanied by two of the boys from the manse and a striking, fearless woman from KwaThema who was staying in Orlando West. Xoliswa Falati rebuked me for my faintheartedness. I did not have the stomach for showdowns with the police and she regarded this as doubly reprehensible in a foreigner. She wore a Mandela T-shirt with the ANC colors under her funeral dress and vaunted it before we set out for the manse. At the time, these T-shirts were banned. Her gesture of defiance was modest compared with that of the youngsters who found their way through a tight security cordon to brazen it out with the police at the entrance to the Regina Mundi church. Half a dozen wore their ANC colors openly. As the cameras rolled, they were rounded up, whipped, beaten and bundled into the back of a police van, while a Boer with a loudspeaker announced that the press had five minutes to disperse under the emergency laws.

Two years later, in the new South Africa, self-consciousness seemed to have turned into self-absorption. The press, especially the

Johannesburg Star, took gloomy care over the details of the growing and apparently senseless violence, as though it were studying wet entrails for signs of impending failure in the country's transformation. Tales of pure criminality, or crimes committed in the name of the struggle, or ritual murder by warring factions in Natal—the ANC on one side and Chief Mangosuthu Buthelezi's Inkatha movement on the other— adorned the pages of the *Star,* serving lurid countermands to its lame editorials in defense of the new order. That this was self-absorption rather than prurience seemed clear enough. If the changes were successful, South Africa would return to the fold of nations. The violence seemed to suggest that the process was unworkable. In its fascination with murder and disorder, white South Africa was exercising its right to turn away from the cheap redemptions of the world community and walk back the way it had come, over a bloody terrain that proved the point it had been making for decades. The black newspapers took a more positive stance on the changes but they were also captive to the spectacle of growing violence in the country.

Somewhere in this pessimism lay a longing for peace, as though in some recess of the national spirit, South Africa could not wait to throw off the whole sorry history of supremacism and join the rest of the world on its rugby pitches and cricket grounds. The promise of an end to the sports boycott, which came two long and dreadful years after de Klerk announced the reforms in 1990, held the allegiance of millions of people, black and white alike, to the new dispensation. The sports coverage in the press was the only antidote to the horrors encountered on the other pages. The murder rate was climbing, Kalashnikovs and handguns were pouring into the Transvaal townships, and the war in Natal between Inkatha and the comrades showed little sign of abating.

Liberation was no longer the discipline it had aspired to be. In some sense it was no longer even a useful term, except to define a period of African political culture that was coming to a close. A few days after my arrival in Johannesburg, I had heard Mandela address a rally in Soweto. The crowd was eager and attentive. Mandela spoke in the language of the past—simple, dignified, Marxist—yet with a limpid faith in the future, and in the people. The very anachronism of this lingua franca, which the rest of the world had decided to purge or jettison entirely, gave the rally the warmth and intimacy of a meeting between familiars. Here, at least, since others were no longer fluent in the language, South Africa could speak to itself without being overheard. Tens of thousands left at sunset, in buses and trucks, wafting a great blanket of dust into the sky, singing, swaying, waving as they passed. "AMANDLA! AWETU!" (Power to the People!) Yet it was like the end of a family gathering. Not long afterward, Mandela set off for Algeria where the president awarded him the country's highest honor, the Wisaam al Athir medal, for his role in the freedom struggle. It was thirty years since his military briefing by the FLN in Rabat. The present visit seemed to bring liberation full circle and so to beg another definition of struggle with new practices and new myths. Yet the next step in South Africa was fraught with perils and this elderly man had returned to a country that could only agonize over whether and how to take it.

A definition of "the violence" remained elusive. The phrase suggested only that there were now greater risks to life and limb in South Africa than from state brutality. It had made its mark on my own circle of acquaintance, narrow though it was. In 1988 the manse in Orlando West had come under attack from a prestigious quarter. The Mandela Football Club, based a few streets away at 8115 Orlando West, was also the residence of Nelson Mandela's wife, Winnie. The club was in essence a violent gang, distinguished from dozens of others in Soweto—Jackrollers, Ama Japan, Ninjas, AKs—only by the august patronage that gave it greater criminal leeway. You could see the members hanging around the house, decked out in ANC colors, and they were not the people to whom one would want to entrust the future of a country, or indeed a bit of scurrilous gossip about a neighbor. Nevertheless, it was to them that Xoliswa Falati, whom I had last seen at Regina Mundi, made her way a few months later to put it about that the Reverend Paul Verryn was taking sexual advantage of the young men lodging at the manse. On hearing the news, Winnie Mandela had five of the boys abducted to her new house in Diepkloof, where four of them were grievously assaulted. The incident became a *cause célèbre* when the body of one of the boys, James Moeketsie Seipei, was unearthed some six weeks later. Two of the others, who would later testify in court, claimed that Winnie Mandela had taken part in the beatings. It was said that a famous Soweto doctor was summoned to the scene to examine "Stompie" Moeketsie and advised that he should be taken to the hospital. Abu-baker Asvat might have been a key witness at the trial, but at the end of January 1989, almost a month after his alleged visit to the Mandela home, he was shot dead.

Stompie Moeketsie was fourteen, a little township general who organized piecemeal resistance to the police and army. He was staying at the manse because at home he would have been picked up by Security. Quite possibly, too, he was at risk from rival comrades, for the word had gone around that he was an *impipi*—a police informer. In Soweto, jealousy or personal dislike was well served by such accusations, which did not necessarily have a bearing on the truth. It seems that the club was familiar with the rumors and chose, having once got hold of Stompie, to take them seriously, but its prompt reaction to Xoliswa's stories suggested that homosexuality was sufficient pretext for summary justice. This was all the more curious since, during my stay, there had not been the slightest evidence of sexual relations at the manse. And supposing it were true? Clearly, if the Mother of the Nation disapproved, it could not go unpunished. But why was the penalty extreme physical violence?

There were youngsters in Soweto who argued that the alleged homosexuality was a red herring. Stompie's misfortune was to have been branded as an informer. Once uttered, the words "informer" or "sellout" had a sinister way of detaching themselves from the accused and alighting on the shoulders of others. It was thus in the interests of those present when the charge was repeated to ensure that it stuck, and, if they could, to place themselves beyond suspicion. Beating was a fairly regular activity at Winnie Mandela's place, a center of informal "people's justice," and anyone desisted at his peril. This logic drew committed comrades into situations that they must have loathed, although there were those who clearly had a taste for it.

Xoliswa had fled to Soweto after her house in KwaThema had been burned to the ground—by police, she said, but it was also rumored in Soweto that she had been driven away by local comrades, who regarded her as a sellout. True or false, the rumor put Xoliswa in danger; it made sense to ingratiate herself with the most dangerous elements in the area, by whatever means she thought plausible. That is the gist of what was said in Soweto. If it was true, then Xoliswa's gambit was well thought out, for it was also said that Winnie Mandela was deeply unhappy with the existence of an effective sanctuary for young comrades run by an Afrikaner, a short distance from her own home. That a respected activist like Stompie should have gravitated to the manse rather than her house was an affront. Verryn's ideas of the struggle and those that enjoyed currency across the way were very different. He had always discouraged the boys from useless sacrifice and preached the sanctity of human life; any other way was degrading and degradation was the cornerstone of apartheid. He challenged their assumption that political victory would open on to an earthly paradise and did his best to wean them from the dangerous axioms that made them clubbable in revolutionary Soweto—and to which, in the end, they fell prey. Verryn had founded a minor apostasy on the territory of an acknowledged saint.

The murder trial of Jerry Richardson, the Mandela gang's leader, was in a more important sense the trial of Winnie Mandela, although on this occasion she was not called to give evidence. However, when the judge rejected testimony that she had been two hundred miles away at the time of the assault, it was clear that she would later have to stand trial herself. Richardson, meanwhile, was found guilty of murdering Stompie Moeketsie. Xoliswa repeated her allegations about Verryn, for whom this occasion was also a kind of trial although, unlike Mrs. Mandela, he was not spared the indignities of the witness stand. One Sunday, while the Richardson trial was adjourned, I made my way to Soweto, where Verryn was preaching to a packed congregation. I do not remember the details of the sermon, only its unerring movement from one New Testament text to another, invoked like formulae in a mathematical proof, and its conclusion that apartheid was a sin against mankind and the Trinity. Township services are a lengthy affair. Many hymns are sung, then the choir must demonstrate how the congregation might have performed better; community business is broached and the sign of peace exchanged; the state president and the leaders of the struggle are blessed. In this instance, the proceedings were interrupted and Paul Verryn came forward to make a statement. He cut a diminutive figure. The pomp of the cloth, which had revealed his passion and wit in the pulpit, now seemed to conceal them. He was visibly nervous; the blue-gray eyes, greatly magnified by his glasses, gave him the air of a gifted schoolboy. I could see how this might have tried the patience of a rival saint. The pews creaked under the shifting weight of apprehension and a child let out a short, spluttering cough. Verryn's address was short. He raised the subject of the trial and reminded the congregation of the testimony against him in court, summarizing Xoliswa's allegations and going on to deny them. He offered to answer any queries now or after the service. When he finished, there was a long silence. Then the congregation broke into spontaneous applause. For this protagonist, at least, they had no questions.

▲

Pane Moshounyane was not from Soweto. He was living in the township of Tembisa, northeast of Johannesburg, but he knew about the Stompie Moeketsie affair and, as a church worker, he knew Verryn. Indeed it was through a friend of Verryn's at the headquarters of the South African Council of Churches that we met. Pane was employed by the council's Justice and Reconciliation Department as a fieldworker for the township residents of the Orange Free State. In the Free State, one of the two impenitent Boer republics, the basic problems of dispossession were compounded by a strain of white racialism that was both more virulent and more easily expressed than in the Johannesburg area. The smaller townships of the Free State were less well protected than a place like Soweto with its complex defenses of disobedience and volatility. There were parts of the state where it simply required less courage for a white man to enter a sleepy township and redress some imaginary grievance. There was little to fear in the event of an outcry from township residents; it might even be that the police were party to the violence, or at its very center.

My new acquaintance faced just such a case in the township of Maokeng, which lay at the edge of Kroonstadt, some two hours south of Johannesburg on the N1 highway. The details of the incident, which had occurred less than a week before, were vague, but the workers from the Council of Churches in Kroonstadt had contacted the head office in Johannesburg with a request for funeral subsidies. Apparently two youngsters had been shot dead in Maokeng when they had thrown stones at a commercial van that turned out to contain police. For the mourners, the funerals would be charged with political significance, and since the council was a politicized body it would offer what it could in the way of funds. The source of the current conflict in the Free State was the reluctance of the Afrikaners to concede the changes in the country and the exuberance of the township youth, who were quick to affirm them and were now bent on carrying them forward. The comrades had called a consumer boycott in several Free State towns. In Maokeng, they had set up checkpoints to enforce it. This had led to trouble, first with the township police station and then with officers drafted in from the white areas. It was Pane's understanding that Maokeng was in a state of siege, which had only lifted after the shock of the killings. His job was to visit the bereaved families and to see that the funerals were properly funded. He held out little hope of bringing the offenders to justice.

It was ten o'clock when we left the council's offices in Johannesburg and made our way across the town to join the N1. Pane would normally have traveled in a shared taxi but I had a rental car at the time. Maokeng lay a hundred miles south of the Witwatersrand. Like most townships, it was not on the map, but it was only a ten-minute drive from Kroonstadt, which was marked. Once we had passed the Soweto turnoff and settled in to the journey, Pane put his paperwork down by his feet and sat back. He did everything, even this, methodically and slowly, with an exaggerated precision of the hands. He even seemed to put some thought into whether or not to lean back. When he spoke, he held his hands stiffly in front of him, as though entrusted with a fragile ornament. The fingers were thin and the thumbnails long, like those of an Oriental sage.

Pane told me that the two youngsters had been killed at a junction known as Beirut. The use of such nicknames was common in South Africa. Comrades would fight with the police and army in a particular place and, if the battle were long and hard, it would be renamed. The battle too could acquire a title. In Alexandra, for example, there was a Six Day War when the army closed off the township and tried to take the uprising apart. There were plenty of Beiruts and Vietnams dotted around the country. The one in Maokeng had been fought over for weeks before this recent incident. I was troubled by the name Beirut and Pane too pronounced it with cautious disapproval, as though it betrayed a relish for the old myths of township struggle that he could not share. Once spoken, it seemed to mark our journey, like a password, dropping us through the floor of the new South Africa into a network of somber passageways that led away from the future. This sense of being trapped in the vaults of the country, dark and full of perversity, never quite left me from then on.

A haze hung over the bridges and gantries, though it was autumn now. Beyond the Vaal River and into the Free State we stopped for gasoline. Pane remarked that it had once been usual for black people to sit in the back of the car when they traveled with whites in this part of the world. He had grown up here and his mother had sat with him in the back when they accompanied their landlords, the Coetzees, whose farm they had worked during his childhood. He laughed. He was in good humor and enjoyed traveling south. For all its iniquities, the Free State was his home. As a boy he had been to school here, as an activist he had been detained here, and later he had married here, though his work kept him away from his wife and child, who lived near Bloemfontein. It struck me that having spent most of his life here, he must have understood the Afrikaners well. He replied simply that he thought they were a part of the future. "For them," he said, raising his hands to about chin height, "there is nowhere to go. Only Africa." He added that they had "some problems" to do with sharing the country and that this was one of the reasons that youngsters were killed in the townships.

South Africa was full of images of fallen warriors but Pane's remarks reminded me of one in particular—a painting I had seen in Johannesburg two days earlier and now tried to describe. It depicted a British cavalry charge at Laing's Nek in 1881. Two officers in blue tunics held the foreground. The middle ground was full of grass and rock and young foot soldiers. One of the officers had lost his helmet and his horse had collapsed beneath him; another was shouting at him, spurring his own horse forward. The picture bore a caption: "An eye-witness of the attack on Laing's Nek thus describes the incident depicted—'Poor Elwes fell among the 58th. He shouted to another Eton boy (adjutant of the 58th whose horse had been shot) "Come along Monck! *Floreat Etona!* We must be in the front rank!" and he was shot immediately.' " The Boers drove back a British column at Laing's Nek and a month later at Majuba, just south, they annihilated it. The enemy of these two Etonians with identically rosy mouths had been the taciturn Afrikaner who clung to the earth facedown, arms outspread, like Raskolnikov prostrate at the crossroads; only this was a posture not of repentance but tenacity. He was still there in the Free State today, limbs spread as far across the veld as he could stretch them. His progeny were passing by us in the fast lane, watched cautiously by Pane from the corner of his eye; they owned the land on either side of the highway, they hired and fired, or sold their own labor at a high rate. They were the descendants of the first properly armed anti-imperialist guerrilla force in Africa.

Afrikaner liberation was an anomaly. Unlike later liberation movements, it aspired not to the city but the veld. The Afrikaners could not put enough space between themselves and the imperial mammon. They had lost the war but they came to win the peace by cultivating a strain of bitterness that gave them enormous political energy and a strong position in the Union of 1910. Two years later the dedicated nationalists split off from the party of government to form the National Party; anti-British and antimetropolitan, it was a vanguard movement with an unshakable sense that Africa rather than Europe would be the ground of Afrikaner identity for the foreseeable future. The South Africa Party remained in power throughout the First World War but the depression that followed gave the National Party a great boost and deepened its hostility to capital. By 1924 it was governing in coalition. Pane too believed that capitalism was unjust and ungodly. On the road he told me that the land "does not belong to this one or that one" but to God and, since all South Africans were children of God, they had equal rights to it. The Afrikaners' rise to absolute predominance after 1948 had been affected by means of policies that he, with his allegiance to the ANC, would have endorsed. The difference was that in 1990 the ANC still hoped half-heartedly for socialism in one country, whereas the Afrikaners had imposed a narrower version still: socialism for one tribe, which guaranteed jobs for whites in a burgeoning state sector and ensured that black South Africans fell away from the people's state into an abyss of poverty and landlessness. Pane's father had worked for the right to live in a shack on the Coetzee farm, but his ancestors would once have reaped their own benefits from the land. In 1934, a purified National Party took shape under the leadership of D. F. Malan, who preached the end of capitalism to his followers. He held that a system based on "self-interest and the right of the strongest" was surely doomed. Malan had formed a government in 1948, at which point apartheid became a state philosophy and the Afrikaner project was brought to fruition. We spoke briefly on the road to Maokeng about Malan and the strong, centrist state. Pane, a man in his mid-thirties, knew no other system so thoroughly. When it came to the alternatives that he and his comrades could envisage, this was worth bearing in mind.

Kroonstadt was small, with a Midwestern air, and tense. Prolonged trouble in the townships had bred a dreary, dangerous ill feeling. Sidelong glances from the townspeople turned into stares; stares became longer and less inquisitive. We stopped at the Council of Churches' local office and met two of Pane's colleagues who would accompany us to Maokeng. Four black men were sitting disconsolately just inside the entrance. They were from a township further north where the comrades were fighting the police. The police had now sealed it off and the men felt that the risks of trying to cross the cordon were too high. They would have to wait overnight, possibly longer, in Kroonstadt, or perhaps they could be lodged in Maokeng. In the yard of the next house, at the back of the council offices, there were two black policemen keeping a hostile eye on the premises.

It was fifteen minutes to Maokeng and then, in the township, another hour going from place to place in search of people who might be able to tell Pane what they knew about the incident in Beirut. The results of the fighting in Maokeng were visible in the smashed windows on one street, a burned-out car in another and, in the center of a dust patch, the badly damaged house of an Anglican clergyman who would have been able to help us but was not there. The front of the house was blackened and one window was boarded up. We went inside to inspect the charred bedroom, empty apart from an iron bedstead beneath a set of blackened rafters. Someone had smashed the window, poured gasoline into the room and set it alight. The minister had been away at the time. A few weeks earlier he had moved his children from their own bedroom, which he thought unsafe, into this very room; on the night of the attack they had been staying with relatives. But who was responsible? "The police," said Pane's colleagues in unison. They explained that the minister had been organizing an interdenominational march against police harassment in this part of the Free State.

Maggie Mahlatsi's house lay in a long row of bungalows facing some waste ground. In the yard next to hers a group of children were clambering over a blue pickup. One of them was sent to fetch Mrs. Mahlatsi from the back of the house. She was thirty-eight years old, dressed in a pink sweater, red skirt and red beret. Below her eyes were the remains of some skin lightener smeared over the cheekbones. We went indoors where her daughter was brewing tea on a paraffin stove. Her son Michael was almost fourteen when he died. That morning, she told us, he had left for school as usual. He was attending lower primary school, for in Maokeng too the boycott has slowed children's education to a crawl. When he failed to return that afternoon, she thought that he must have gone to her sister's place. Beirut was less than a mile from her house and that day there had been a lot of activity. The comrades had taken possession of the area and burned some cars. It became a matter of interest for other adolescents, not necessarily comrades, to go down and have a look. "What happens," said Mrs. Mahlatsi, "is that when people are coming with this *toyi-toyi*, other people just follow along." (*Toyi-toyi* is a kind of militant dancing, swaying and chanting; often the dancers hold imaginary guns in their hands; sometimes wooden Kalashnikovs. It is a call to arms.) Was Michael a comrade? "Michael was a young boy growing up in South Africa," she said with a shrug. At about 4:30 a furniture van pulled up at the junction known as Beirut. The back of the van was covered with a tarpaulin and it looked innocuous enough. But the children in Beirut recognized the vehicle. It belonged to a white company and so they stoned it, for it had no business there.

"Everybody knows that this furniture truck was full of police. I think you have read it in the newspapers," said Mrs. Mahlatsi. The police threw back the tarpaulin, stood up and sprayed Beirut with live rounds and birdshot. They were wearing uniform. Someone came to the house and told Mrs. Mahlatsi that there had been shooting in Beirut, that several people were seriously injured and that Michael was one of them. She inquired about her son at the hospital but the nurse she spoke to was not sure she had seen him. When Mrs. Mahlatsi described Michael's clothes, the nurse lowered her head. "I know him now," she said. "You must look for your son in the mortuary."

"I went straight in a taxi to the mortuary. When I arrived, they told me still there is one who is not identified. And so . . ." She trailed off. Her daughter was by the paraffin burner, crying. Pane broached the cost of the funeral, which was set for the following weekend. He took some notes, conferred with his colleagues and rose to leave. Mrs. Mahlatsi did not understand what a man from England was doing in Maokeng. "Has God sent him?" she asked. "He is with us," Pane explained, "to see the conditions we are suffering here in South Africa." Mrs. Mahlatsi gave a nod of assent and shook my hand.

On the way to the house of Isaiah Tau's mother we passed Beirut. It was a dust patch with a few burned cars. "This is the place where that truck was standing when the police fired," said one of Pane's colleagues. We had stopped the car at a T-junction. "Only it was not a furniture truck; it was owned by a merchant of scrap metal." A woman was crossing the dust patch with a bag slung over her back and further away some others were waiting at what appeared to be a taxi stand, but there were no taxis. The comrades were nowhere to be seen.

Laura Tau came home from work at three in the afternoon on the day that Michael Mahlatsi was killed. Her son Isaiah was in secondary school; he was at home when she got back but left shortly afterward. Less than two hours later one of his schoolfriends ran into the house and told Laura that the police had shot her son. I asked whether Isaiah was a comrade. Laura Tau looked at me with immense suspicion. She didn't know if he belonged to an organization; they didn't discuss politics, but there may have been activities in school of which she was unaware. Then she said, "He fell into a yard. They shot him and he fell into the yard of this crèche worker. It was she who told me. There was no demonstration, nothing."

As the sun sank lower, the far wall of the room turned a luminous red. The bare sitting room seemed more manageable in the dusk. At the same time, I had the impression that it was shrinking. Everyone, even Pane, looked fragile and confined. A transistor radio stood on the shelf to the left of the table. It was inscribed in black lettering: "Orlando Pirates. Up the Bros." The Pirates were a football club from Soweto. Her son had watched plenty of soccer on television but he was never a player, he wanted to be a businessman. "Maybe," said Laura Tau, "to own a big shop. And he was always listening to music." She shrugged her shoulders, as Maggie Mahlatsi had done, and showed us out.

A reliable newspaper had reported the death of a child called Seiso Mangwenjane, aged nine. Neither the church workers, nor Laura Tau, nor Maggie Mahlatsi had heard of Seiso. Other confusions had also emerged. Contrary to Mrs. Mahlatsi's account, Mrs. Tau had said there was no demonstration in Beirut on that day. As for injuries, nobody was sure. Joseph Tshabalala, aged thirteen, had his genitals and thighs filled with birdshot and another boy, a friend of Isaiah's, had his lower arm blown off by a bullet. The newspaper had referred to the scene of the shooting as "Vietnam" but Pane's colleagues and most residents knew it as Beirut. The report said the vehicle used by the police belonged to a company called Barnett's Auto Spares. It was not that the newspaper was wrong, but that information was easily refracted in the murk of the townships, making it hard even for residents to establish the facts. Pane was satisfied, however, that there were two funerals to be dealt with.

We drove to the house of a local civic leader, our final port of call, where a heated discussion was going on between two women and a handful of well-dressed men. Now and then one of the men would go to the window and check as a car drove by. The women were saying that a stop had to be put to the violence in Maokeng. One of them deplored the idea of a large, politicized funeral on Saturday. "The police will kill more of us, that is all," she said, turning to Pane for support. It was dark outside and the next time that the man drew back the curtains to survey the street, the dusty night had transformed the men and women of Maokeng into wraiths. Moments later a man in overalls, with a round face and scrubby beard, was shown into the house. His forehead was creased, although he looked no more than thirty. He sat down and embarked on a long story to the church workers. One of them took notes and Pane sat with his eyes fixed on the wall, interrupting the tale with a murmur every now and again. At the end, he sat back with his notebook on his lap and his hands raised. "This man," he explained, "is the brother of a man who was killed last night. The shack was burned to the ground. His brother, his brother's wife and three children were inside the shack." The man in overalls nodded. Pane said that he wanted us to visit the shack and the man nodded again. "So now we will go," he said, "because he has asked us."

"We are afraid that it was the police who did this," Pane remarked as we drew up at the remains of the shack. Apparently it was dark when the neighbors ran to the burning shack. They were beaten back by men with masks but no uniforms and by the sting of tear gas in the air. We got down from the car and left the engine running. The headlights picked out the site but the shack itself had been burned to the ground. A tall refrigerator, stripped gray by the heat of the blaze, stood on the flat rubble. A few feet in front were five plastic sacks. Pane's feet crunched on the coarse ash as he walked with the bereaved brother, both men crossing and recrossing the headlights in front of the bags and the terrible, solemn fridge: all that remained of the home in which Johannes Mokoakoe, his wife, Mittah, and three of their children—Lydia, aged fourteen, Daniel, aged eleven, and Lucia, aged nine—had burned to death. There was one survivor, the youngest child, David, who had escaped from the blaze. He was in the hospital with serious burns.

Pane sat beside me in the car. He had not spoken for a quarter of an hour. The dipped headlights probed the edge of the wide highway and once, about twelve miles out of Kroonstadt, they seemed to pick out the fridge again. Pane broke the silence with a long "Ya-aahhh." I could see his profile without looking at it—composed and a little haughty. When he spoke, it was to say that the dead man, Johannes, had belonged to the union of railway workers and harbormen. Perhaps there was an industrial action about to start in Bloemfontein. Perhaps the police felt they needed to teach the militants a lesson. Was the dead man a union activist? Apparently not—or not according to his brother. He merely worked in the shunting yard. Perhaps he was a leader of the rent boycott campaign in Maokeng? Perhaps, but Pane was listless and unwilling to think about it. The journey back promised to be long. For another ten minutes he said nothing. I turned to see whether he was still awake, and found him sitting up straight with his eyes on the road. At length I asked how he had come to work for the Council of Churches and slowly he began to talk about his life, removing us far from the road and the Mokoakoe shack.

Pane had been politicized during the 1970s, with the rise of militant Black Consciousness. In those days, he admitted, he had scorned the multiracialism of the ANC and had been an ardent admirer of the "BC" student leader, Steve Biko. After Biko's death in 1977 and the ruthless suppression of the movement, many of the young South Africans whom it had inspired began drifting toward the ANC. Pane was among them, but in his case, faith in the idea of multiracial democracy coincided with conversion to Christianity. The early 1980s was a time of revival both for the churches and for the ANC. Twenty years after it had been announced, the armed struggle was still a negligible affair. But the vacuum left by Black Consciousness and the new courage of the churches, with their rejection of racial politics, created an opportunity for the ANC to recover ground. Civic organizations and a multitude of small activist groups sprang up in the townships with a set of minimum demands based on the Freedom Charter of 1955.

There was a poignant legend, which Pane reiterated, that Stompie Moeketsie had been able to recite the charter by heart—if not the many subclauses, then at least the preamble and the basic tenets. It was adopted by an alliance of opposition groups, including the ANC, when Pane was a year old. It demanded quality before the law, the redistribution of land, the right to work and housing. "All the cultural treasures of mankind," it declared, "shall be open to all, by free exchange of books, ideas and contacts with other lands."

Pane's family was already on the Coetzee farm by then. He grew up in virtual serfdom, tending cattle and fetching in the harvests in return for his parents' right to stay on the farm. His mother's diligence secured him a place in a nearby school, where he quickly learned to read and write. His secondary education was intermittent. The nearest school was ten miles from the farm and there was no transportation. In due course his parents decided to leave. They put out the boy to a distant relative who could help him finish his education in a series of local schools.

Pane had reached Standard Seven in a Bloemfontein school when a cousin, a young man from Soweto, came to stay. He was a member of Biko's South African Students Organization and he had a profound influence on Pane. He preached an uncompromising doctrine of black pride, with heroes as divergent as the Emperor Shaka and Malcolm X. Pane and his schoolfriends were impressed by these ideals. Later that year the school boycott came to Bloemfontein. The police reacted violently. They visited Pane's home and demanded that he name the leaders. Pane told them he had not been at any of the student meetings. They said from now on he would have to attend, and provide them with information. He refused politely and a few days later he was detained. "I was beaten," he said, "but not like the others, who were badly assaulted. After some weeks we were released. There was no charge against me."

Detention did as much to radicalize him as the visit of his cousin from Soweto but life was quiet for a year or more and he continued with his studies. When the next round of the education boycott was called, this time on a national scale, the schools in Bloemfontein were closed for an entire year. Pane was more active in the boycott now and when the police came to his house, to make the same proposal as before, he was less courteous. He was taken into detention and for the first week interrogated daily. He was asked to supply the names of activists who were suspected of burning down the houses of police and other "agents of the system." He refused. He was repeatedly assaulted and subjected to electric-shock torture. His inquisitors called it "shaking hands with the boss." A piece of flat, live metal wired to a transformer was set in front of him and he was forced to extend the palm of his hand until it made contact. One day he was drive to a kind of gym and two bodybuilders were paraded before him. He was told that they would be allowed to work on him if he did not incriminate his comrades. Prepared statements were given him to sign but he refused. In the end he wrote his own and, although the police were not happy with it, they decided to release him. Before doing so, they took photos of him. For one of these Pane was forced to pose as a "terrorist," with an automatic rifle in his hands.

This labor of perversity by the police had a kernel of truth, for Pane was by now ready to bear arms against apartheid, and thought seriously of leaving the country to enroll in the armed struggle in Zambia or Angola or Tanzania. Instead, however, he turned to the old battlefield of education, this time to writing. He started a small writers' group in the township with a few friends—they read books and wrote texts that were then discussed by everyone present. At the end of the year Pane was detained again and the writers' group fell apart. Several members, who had also been associated with the boycott, left the country but Pane stayed on, finding himself quite isolated, simply because people were now afraid to be seen with him. He drifted aimlessly for a time and then, in 1983, he found work as an unqualified teacher.

Since his first detention, the churches had become far more outspoken in their condemnation of apartheid. The Anglican church, like the Communist Party, was bitterly opposed to any form of racial politics and the revival of the ANC's fortunes gave it a firm footing in the movement. Pane was impressed by the Christians he met, both black and white, and the doctrines to which he was exposed. In the hands of the Church militant, the gospels became validations of struggle. He explained, for example, that Christ's exhortation to turn the other cheek was a way of measuring up to your adversary. "If first you are struck on this side of your face, the one who strikes you is doing so with the back of his hand. It is logical. And it is a kind of playing, or testing. It is only a light blow. So you must offer the other cheek to discover if he is serious. Now, he can walk away or he can hit you with the palm—again it is logical—and if he strikes with the palm, it is certain: he wants to fight you. So now you must challenge him." In Europe, I replied, nations used to do the same thing, only with telegrams. And we had rarely invoked the book of Matthew. Pane believed that Christ had allowed his disciples to bear arms. When the high priests came to arrest him, Simon Peter had cut off the ear of one of the retinue. "There was no reason he was armed especially for that day," Pane explained, "and Jesus did not rebuke him for carrying a sword. He only told him to put it away. It is told that way in John." These arguments were cunning, but I could not help thinking of Verryn and how much he would have disapproved.

While he was teaching in Bloemfontein, Pane attended a meeting called by the clergy to demand the release of detainees in the Free State. He spoke up and suggested that a committee be formed. One Lutheran minister, one Catholic priest, one Anglican and Pane became the backbone of the "Crisis Committee." Pane was twenty-nine years old. The committee secured the release of dozens of activists and persuaded the students to end the boycott. Word had reached the school inspector that Pane had been seen in a "Release Mandela" T-shirt. His time as a teacher was up, but he had been welcomed into the fold of the Church. Within a year he was working full-time for a local Anglican group and soon afterward he was at the offices of the

South African Council of Churches in Johannesburg, where he began to coordinate church activities in the Orange Free State. "From then on, I think, there is nothing more," he said, "because those offices are the very same place that we have met."

In Johannesburg we broke our journey for a meal and then I took Pane on to Tembisa. "Tomorrow," he said, "I will be in the office early to recommend a contribution to the funerals of Isaiah and Michael. As for this Mokoakoe business, I cannot think about it tonight. I am afraid there are no proper remains. Some are in those bags that you saw and they are still confused with pieces of the house."

We reached Tembisa after midnight, another sprawling arena of abjection, lit by raised orange floodlights. Outside Pane's place two boys huddled by a brazier. The nights in the Johannesburg area were cold now. A slight man, obscured by a few feet of township night, Pane passed through the front gate with his plastic briefcase under his arm, disappearing around the side of the house. On my way out of Tembisa an armored personnel carrier rumbled along behind me on the main road, turning off to the right a mile beyond the township.

Not long after our trip to Maokeng, I left South Africa and did not return for nearly two months. Things had grown very difficult in the meantime. In Natal, the war between the comrades and Inkatha continued, while Chief Buthelezi proceeded with a plan to turn the Zulu movement into a formal political party. Elsewhere several small Afrikaner jihads were in the offing. Fanatical rallies were interspersed by bomb blasts in places where black citizens crowded together—an explosion in a Johannesburg bus station at the onset of winter was followed two months later by another at a taxi stand in Pretoria. Inkatha were not the only righteous tribesmen on the march. Yet the defeatism that had long been at the heart of Afrikaner belligerence still dogged the modern paramilitaries. Their cause appeared quite hopeless. Two years later, in the weeks before de Klerk's referendum, there were eighty right-wing bomb blasts in South Africa, but this frenzied defense of the *volk* failed to convince most Afrikaners. Even the Orange Free State voted for reform. It was a brave step. One had only to think of a preacher like Verryn or a family like the Breydencamps to know that the future of the Afrikaners would demand courage and a steady nerve. For the moment, however, it was impossible to tackle the more serious spread of anarchy in the townships.

The sky curved down to the edge of the flatlands, and up ahead the N1, straight as the eye could see, seemed to peel away from the ground like a dry rind. We were again southbound on the highway, driving away from the Limpopo and the rest of the continent. Pane Moshounyane lay back in the passenger seat with his hands resting on a sheaf of papers, his briefcase on the floor at his feet. It was his first trip to Maokeng since we had seen the disaster at the Mokoakoe shack. We stopped in Kroonstadt at the offices of the Council of Churches to pick up a local worker for the Justice and Reconciliation Department, a gaunt but youthful man called Oswald. Together we made our way into Maokeng. Today Pane would confirm the costs of burying Isaiah Tau and Michael Mahlatsi and try to establish those of the Mokoakoe funerals. Perhaps the cruel expenses incurred by the survivors could now be defrayed. I waited outside while business was done with the Beirut families. I knew from Pane that there had been no proper inquiry into the Beirut killings but now, back in the car, I asked Oswald whether anyone had been dismissed from the police in connection with the Mokoakoe family deaths. It transpired that the local feeling about this incident had changed. The police were no longer thought to be involved and Oswald believed that this was correct. His account, however, was no less terrible.

We turned onto a narrow track and pulled up in front of a compound. Johannes Mokoakoe's mother, Lydia, lived here with the only survivor of the fire, her grandson David. We sat with the engine switched off and the windows up, a crowd of children gathering around the car, while Oswald explained that the Mokoakoe shack had been burned down by the comrades. In Maokeng there was one young man who was greatly feared. He was a *tsotsi*, or ordinary hoodlum, with political pretensions. He had the nickname For Yourself. The residents believed he was behind the murders. They argued that Johannes Mokoakoe's wife had seen this man and others setting fire to the mayor's house in Maokeng earlier that year. The mayor was thought to be a sellout. "That is not all," Oswald continued, "for she was coming with water to put out the fire. Some days later the boy was detained. Then it is said that the wife of Johannes is a police informer and a good friend of the mayor. So this is what everyone believes to be the truth. Even her"—he waved in the direction of the compound— "but she will not tell it to you."

An elderly woman in a green head scarf stood at the entrance, squinting anxiously at our car. Around her midriff, fastened by a safety pin and covering her blue dress, she wore a length of rayon tartan. We got out and Oswald introduced us to Lydia Mokoakoe. By her side stood her grandson David, horribly transfigured by the fire. He put out his arm with great effort and grimaced as our hands touched. He had undergone plastic surgery but it had not yet done its job and, once Mrs. Mokoakoe had led us indoors, she confided her doubts that it ever would. Some weeks ago he had been discharged from the hospital without another appointment. She sat on a red wooden chest and spoke to Pane in a mixture of English and Sotho. On the wall behind her was a photograph of Mandela, fist clenched, framed in the colors of the ANC, and near it a needlework sampler, with a legend I had seen before: "As for me and my house we will serve the Lord." For some time Pane discussed the details of the funerals and the expenses of keeping little David, who had just turned five. Lydia's husband had died in 1975 and she received a monthly pension of 150 rand ($50) from the state, besides what her two unmarried daughters could bring home. Since the fire, she had been suffering from memory loss. She had not slept well for three months. She had been to the doctor, who prescribed some pills, but they were not much use. At first, with the fire and then these afflictions, she thought she had been cursed, but she refused to go for a consultation with a traditional healer, or *sangoma*. It was against her principles as a Christian.

Pane made some notes while I looked through a photograph album that Mrs. Mokoakoe had produced from the red chest. There was a portrait of Mittah, subscribed with the words "Love Me," and opposite, one of the infant, David, captioned "Love My Baby." Further on, Johannes was drinking a long can of Castle stout with three friends. Among the pictures the album contained blank areas with the paste-on corners still in place. The police had removed some of the prints for their desultory investigation, as though, if they studied the images of the dead for long enough, the identity of the killers might slowly dawn on them. These rectangular gaps in the album, slightly darker than the rest, said more about Mrs. Mokoakoe's bereavement than the portraits of family life that remained. When she had finished talking with Pane, she ran her fingers over the photos, naming each family member, but her memory was damaged and she could not recall the name of one of her dead granddaughters. She put the album in the chest, closed the lid and sat down on it again. Once she was settled, she informed Pane that there had been trouble at Johannes's shack before. A year ago, she recalled, while he was attending a night class in carpentry, someone had tried to burn it down but only the door had caught fire.

"I am going to ask her," Pane informed me in a soft aside, nonetheless quite audible to Mrs. Mokoakoe, "who she thinks has killed her family." She shifted on the chest as he put the question. At length she shook her head and said that she had no idea. Then she gestured at the picture of Mandela and spoke in Sotho. With a heavy heart, Pane began to translate. Johannes had presented the photo to her on Mother's Day, he said, and they had hung it on the wall. But now she could no longer respect it. "The comrades do not listen to appeals from our leaders and if this is so, it is because our leaders themselves are weak. Who will redeem my family? Not this man. Only God can bring peace and justice to our country."

Pane lowered his head in dismay. On another occasion Mrs. Mokoakoe might have said these things differently, but today she had reached for the idiom of anger, like so many South Africans who felt that the language of reason no longer served them adequately. Pane too, it seemed to me on the darkened freeway back to Johannesburg, was angry now. He had been in Maokeng to see to the needs of three families, not to pinpoint the various culprits, yet he had been overwhelmed by hearsay and was unable to shake off its persuasive ring. I put it to him that he was upset and, being a generous man, he did his best to respond. As a Christian, he began, he believed in forgiveness. If the comrades, or comrade *tsotsis*, had burned down the Mokoakoe shack, they must be forgiven. The same went for the white men who had shot Isaiah Tau and Michael Mahlatsi. "When you cannot forgive," he reflected, "you develop a spiritual hardness." Yet there must also be justice. Mrs. Mokoakoe was speaking the truth when she said that only God could bring it, but were we not made in his likeness? Was it not therefore our duty, as children of God, to see that his wishes were observed? There was a man, Pane went on, whom he could not bring himself to forgive: the Afrikaner policeman who had asked him to inform in the days of the boycott. "When I refused, he made a promise to me that he would punish me. And he succeeded. He and a friend of his, a colleague, arranged both my detentions. These were the ones who tortured me and refused to let me have water for six weeks, so that I had to wash from the toilet."

Just south of Johannesburg it began to rain lightly, but not enough to stop the wipers chafing against the windshield. The road ahead began to smear until I turned the wipers off and we were squinting at a myriad of brilliant orange dots. It was unusual for rain to be falling at this time of year, but as we reached the city it let up and the stars shone clearly high above the haze of Soweto.

▲

When I dropped Pane at Tembisa that night, the Inkatha Freedom Party, as it was now known, had already decided to carry the war against the comrades up from Natal into the Transvaal. It began a fortnight earlier in Sebokeng, when several busloads of Inkatha supporters arrived from Natal to attend a "peace rally" at the local stadium. In Natal the conflict had been going on for four years and hostilities between the comrades and Inkatha were fierce. The ANC in Sebokeng greeted the news of the rally with suspicion and a group of comrades smashed a hole in the stadium wall to keep an eye on the proceedings. General disorder followed and eyewitnesses claimed that the violence erupted when a comrade was seized by the police and handed over to Inkatha. He was set upon and stabbed. The comrades responded by marching on a Zulu household in Sebokeng and burning it down. By the end of the following day twenty had died in the township. An ominous lull followed; then, a few days later, the township of Katlehong erupted after a game of dice in a squatter camp. There was an altercation and a Zulu resident was stabbed. He was avenged with the death of a Xhosa, most of whom supported the ANC, and soon the camp became a battlefield. Within weeks, the townships around Johannesburg were at war.

As the death toll rose, the ANC insisted that there was a "third force" at work: the security apparatus, or elements within it, were inflaming the violence and perhaps also organizing Inkatha, as they had in Natal. There was some truth in this, it later transpired, but at the onset there was no proof. Even so, there were other forces in play besides Inkatha and the comrades, of which the most conspicuous was once again South Africa's equivocal relationship with its own future. Grafted on to the rising criminality of the townships, a war between two of the country's biggest political factions was fair evidence that peace would not be attainable. If the procrastinations of minority rule were compounding the country's problems, majority rule could well be worse. From one day to the next the authority of the ANC was being weakened as it slid from disarray into disrepute, and all the while a national fascination with the conflict seemed to sustain its dreadful energy.

The war came to Soweto along the railway line. On a cold winter morning in August a group of Inkatha fighters massed on Inhlanzane railway station in Soweto and attacked the 5:30 train from Naledi as it pulled in, full of commuters and zealous comrades who were moving up and down the carriages on their routine duty of consciousness raising. Inkatha fell on the train with spears, pangas, sharpened crowbars, the same "traditional weapons" they had brought to the peace rally in Sebokeng. The first reports that came through announced four dead and dozens injured. The next, in the early afternoon, put it at nine dead, but thereafter the casualties at Inhlanzane were lost in the growing figure for Soweto as a whole. A similar attack had taken place a few weeks earlier, on the same line, but at that stage the mood was still one of random animosity. The train was an obvious target to Inkatha, for whom the idea of the comrades educating people in the ways of the ANC was anathema. They had already taken offense in 1986, after a drive by the United Democratic Front in Natal won keen support among Zulus for the ANC. This was tantamount to theft: Zulu allegiance was being spirited away from Inkatha right under Chief Buthelezi's nose, which is how the war in Natal began. As it crept into the Transvaal, however, it became a different thing. It was a struggle about constitutional democracy: whether this should come about, what it might be and how much the Zulu leadership stood to gain or lose from it. The picture of senseless violence painted by most of the press was misleading, but then the papers were at the forefront of the national fascination, which made reflection difficult. Chaos was only another "traditional weapon" in this new phase of conflict; once unsheathed, it was a force in its own right, yet, cut for cut, the violence had a meaning. It was Chief Buthelezi's war; he was fighting for influence in the talks between the ANC and the minority government, which threatened to marginalize his movement. There is no doubt now that he found allies in de Klerk's administration and the security forces. These were not people to throw up their hands in equivocal dismay. On the contrary, they hoped to abort the new South Africa, in the same energetic spirit as their predecessors had destabilized the post-colonial governments of Angola and Mozambique.

Within a few hours of the killings at Inhlanzane station, a large crowd of Soweto residents had massed outside the Jabulani single men's hostel in Soweto and another outside the hostel in Merafe. There were thousands of ordinary Zulu residents in Soweto, but in the hostels it was a different matter. These places were isolated barracks for Zulu migrant workers who had no stake in the community. They were there to work and send home slender remittances to their kin in Natal. When the ANC called a stay-away from work, the hostel dwellers were loath to observe it. Their labor conditions were poor, but they were rarely unionized. Most residents associated the hostels with Inkatha; they were the obvious place for an angry crowd to gather after an Inkatha foray.

That morning Edward was reluctant to travel from Orlando East to Jabulani, and he warned in no uncertain terms that this was war. As a man of middle age, too old to be a comrade, but solid for the ANC, he did not look kindly on Inkatha. The answer to Inhlanzane, he said, was to fight back without quarter. He told us that "blood must be shed" and that any other course was folly. The conversation took place in the parlor of his house, where I had come with a reporter from the BBC. Edward had said earlier that he would accompany us to Jabulani—for our safety, he claimed—but now he seemed troubled by the idea. The reporter waited while Edward had me drive him across Orlando to his *sangoma*. The healer was in bed with a bad knee but

Edward was allowed inside to receive a blessing and perhaps some magic, to safeguard him in the presence of Inkatha. After a time, I was ushered into the room. The old man lay covered in blankets with a one-bar heater by the side of the bed. The room was scattered with glass bottles containing barks and powders. When I asked how he treated the knee, he burrowed in his bedside table and produced a large tube of Deep Heat. He held it up and Edward stepped forward to squint at it. Outside, Edward told me that magic, or *muti* as he called it, was an important resource in Soweto. The same *sangoma* had once provided him with chameleon *muti*, which allowed him to disguise himself in the event of danger. He added that the old man had agreed with him about Inkatha—blood must be shed.

On the road to the hostel the township residents had put up barricades under the supervision of the comrades. We stopped where the crowds became impenetrable and left the car. There had already been a clash with a party of Inkatha men, but no one was clear about the outcome. Instead they were making ready for the next round. A large woman in her mid-forties launched into a tirade against Inkatha; she was an eloquent figure in a bright dress who evoked the virtues of the old Soweto. A chorus of younger women cheered her on as she declared that the hostel system was a creation of apartheid and South Africa was supposed to have finished with apartheid now. It was a discreet way of saying that the hostels should be burned down. As I turned away, a youngster in ripped check trousers and a wide-collared shirt ordered us to drive him to the Merafe hostel along with three others.

The dust patch that separated the eastern edge of the hostel from the rest of Mapetla was occupied by the security forces. It was about the size of a township football ground. A yellow police van was unrolling yards of razor wire across the front of the hostel and, when it came to a stop, two policemen got out to survey their work. About a hundred Inkatha men looked on from the perimeter of the hostel area. They wore red headbands and carried bundles of homemade weapons: axes, metal staves, swords, knives, pangas and spears. One or two had traditional shields made of hide. The razor wire only stretched two thirds of the way across the dust patch and could not prevent a confrontation between the Zulus and the residents assembled opposite. It was simply a question of who moved first. In due course, Inkatha started to sing and clap their hands. They danced their martial dances, full of sullen virtuosity, which I had seen before outside the Zulu hostels in Johannesburg. A single dancer came forward from the rest, leaped, squatted, spun impeccably in the air, slowing mysteriously at the top of the trajectory, and fell to the ground, as though struck.

Then he stood up, swathed in dust, his face a mask of tranquility, and made way for another dancer. The main body of men were chanting and beating the plastic covers of the makeshift vendors' sheds behind the razor wire. I walked closer to the wire and stood beside a pair of black policemen, the three of us transfixed. The television crews moved closer. The BBC reporter went past us and up to the wire, his microphone in front of him. Most South Africans had watched Zulus dance for recreation but this performance was another matter. The nation was being summoned for battle; old regiments were assembling as the dancers stamped their feet against the dry earth, which seemed to age and wrinkle beneath them. One of the policemen smiled, folding his arms in a show of indifference. Then, in an instant, it was obvious that the dance had served a tactical purpose as well, rallying all the dancers up at one end of the wire. From here they threatened to spill around it and onto the dust patch. The police too had moved up, preparing to contain them. There was remonstrating and some jostling, after which the knot of dancers broke up, deploying along the length of the wire, thrashing the vendors' stalls with their weapons as they went. An elaborate feint had been taking place: way over to our left at the other edge of the dust patch a host had emerged from Moroka Street and it was marching on the residents.

How many Zulus were there? A hundred? Two hundred? It was impossible to tell. They were huddled together with their weapons flailing above them like the rods of some archaic engine. Twenty feet ahead of them a single warrior led the way, moving in a crouched position, knees bent, head and neck thrust forward. He was brandishing a panga in his right hand, high over the concave sweep of his back and trailing his left hand in the dust of Moroka Street. Two white police in uniform knelt and loaded tear gas charges, firing them at the head of the levy. For a moment dozens of tall silhouettes writhed in the smoke. When they reappeared, the ranks had broken and a retreat to the hostel was under way. At this point a great shout issued from the residents and they began to advance through the thinning tear gas. A hundred of them, no more, led by young men armed with knives and clubs, were striding over the dust patch like angry workers marching on a mill.

The police acted again; this time they fired a volley of tear gas into the residents. More silhouettes were twined in white smoke, from which a desultory shower of rocks emerged. Then the comrades, who were always in the vanguard of the residents, were running backward, merging with groups of women and older men to start a general retreat, the entire crowd ebbing off into the dirt roads and alleyways of the neighborhood. We got into the car and followed, making our way back through a maze of barricades toward the Jabulani hostel. A red sedan full of white men, plainclothes security, raced past us with shotguns protruding from the open windows.

The idea that the police were as much a part of the problem as they had been in Natal seemed a facile view of the conflict here, but in Bochabela Street it was hard to resist. It was a shortcut to Jabulani that, according to one of the passengers in the car, would avoid another round of barricades. A handful of children let us through and closed off the street behind us with piles of bricks and stones. Twenty yards further on, I brought the car to a halt; the top end of the street was in flames. We hesitated for a few seconds and a rock came flying in our direction. Then a spectral combie (minibus) emerged from the smoke and hurtled toward us, pumping tear gas and plastic bullets from its windows. A woman appeared at the side of her house, pulled open a gate and beckoned to me to get the car in, while the other passengers, most of them comrades, yelled a variety of instructions. We got in with a few seconds to spare before the combie flew by and smashed through the brick barricade at the bottom of the street. The woman's house was also a shebeen and there were two customers in the backyard, drinking and peering around the corner to keep track of things on the street. Here we were trapped for an hour or more while a battle ensued between the police and the local comrades. It had a laborious rhythm to it. Once the combie was gone, the children rebuilt the barricade while groups of defiant comrades hovered in the smoke at the other end. They saw it as their duty to reassert control of the street. But the combie was circling around to a point just beyond the fire, so it could take the flames at speed and make another sally. This process was repeated several times. The comrades played it by the book as they had for the last five years—the barricade, the projectile, the cloth over the mouth—but there was a lassitude now to their dismal coming and going through the smoke. The police, on the other hand, went about their work with more conviction. They had made four or five runs down the street now and it was all but clear. They had only to refrain from another and the battle would be over, yet they seemed to want to pacify the very bricks. A single lurking figure at the top of the road or a child hurrying into a yard would be enough to bring a hail of gas and plastic bullets from the combie as it flew over the dust.

In the backyard of the house the air had grown intolerable. The tear gas cartridges had blown out the windows in most of the neighboring houses and bullets had grazed the paintwork. After every run the women had emerged at their gateways and cursed the police. Then they had attended to their business, with scarves over their faces, until it was interrupted again—taking in washing at the back of the house, putting more to soak in zinc tubs, handing empties across the wall of the shebeen and collecting fresh beers. At length the combie did its final run. It discharged a single tear gas cartridge—for luck, no doubt, because the street was quite empty. The children were inside with the women, the injured comrades had been lifted over the wall into Limakatso Street and the fire at the top of the road was dying down.

The following Friday in Johannesburg, the press was waiting for news of a peace forum mooted by the Soweto police. In less than a week, 150 people had died in the Transvaal townships and a thousand had been injured, yet the trouble had only just started in Soweto. The police intended that local leaders from Inkatha and the ANC should discuss the situation and calm their supporters. The mood in Soweto made this impossible and, besides, the leadership of the ANC had no control over the comrades, who in turn did not intend to give up the fight. Their suspicion that the security forces were in cahoots with Inkatha was mounting with every new incident, and they would not walk away from anything that hinted at the old conflict between the state and the dispossessed. By eleven o'clock that morning the initiative had failed. There had been fighting around Merafe during the night. At 3 A.M. a band of Inkatha had crept from the hostel and hacked a resident to death with pangas in her yard. Mrs. Lenah Modibedi was seventy-two. The comrades had later caught a Zulu, possibly an Inkatha, whom they had stabbed and set on fire.

As we drove from Edward's house toward Jabulani at noon, he was sure that the hostel was on fire. In the distance, a column of thick smoke rose above the area. We burst a tire on the remains of a roadblock and, as we changed the wheel, Edward was surrounded by a crowd of hostile comrades. A pair of young men intervened on his behalf and climbed into the car as we set off again toward the source of the smoke. As we approached, we could see that the fire was not in the hostel, but in the sprawling quarters of the municipal police. A hole had been broken in the concrete perimeter and the residents were peering through at a waste dump that was burning. Someone said the police had started the fire to deflect attention from the hostel. Others said it was the work of the comrades, who were now on top of the railway cutting half a mile away, starting another. A resident pointed and turned me by the shoulder so that I faced in the right direction. There was the smoke of a new fire, pure and minimal for the moment; and there were the comrades, tiny figures far from the hostel or any other object or recrimination, silhouetted against the sky.

The two young men who had come to Edward's rescue at the roadblock suggested that from now on we travel in the township with them. Their names were Zeek and Wide World. Zeek was a Xhosa in his late teens or early twenties, portly, with a gentle, anxious face. He had fallen through the educational system, failing to complete the basic grades that could secure him a place on the engineering course he had wanted to do, and was now looking for work. The recent death of his father was another blow to his ambitions, since he was now in charge of the family's welfare. Wide World was older and leaner. He made a living, when there was work, as a bricklayer and plasterer. He was a Zulu, one of millions for whom Chief Buthelezi did not speak. He regarded himself as a true comrade and denounced Inkatha with ferocity. The pair lived close together in one of the tougher parts of Soweto, but they now abandoned their homes for most of the day and much of the night, roaming the streets as the war escalated. This they did from a sense of duty—a mixture of "vigilance" and curiosity, the last by no means idle. They wished to take stock in Soweto, to hear what was said, to move and listen and respond, to be with the residents as a point of honor, and finally, to fight if necessary.

After the scenes we had witnessed at Merafe hostel earlier in the week, it was undeniable that the policing favored Inkatha over the residents: Inkatha could be contained by being driven back into their hostels, while the residents had to be pursued through a sprawling network of streets where any innocent victim was at risk from police violence, just as he or she could be from the depredations of Inkatha. But it struck me as a bold leap from here to the assertion that elements of the police were with Inkatha, although many made it. At the time the answers were not to be found on the streets, which was where Zeek and Wide World urged us to remain. I was happy to concur, for there was something to be said for listening and watching, even if nothing could be proved.

We moved away from the burning dump with no clear sense of where we were going. Wide World sat in the front of the car, directing us and inclining his head to confer with Zeek, who was sitting in the back. Both were slightly stiff and uncertain what to do with us. At length, a decision was reached. "I think if you're quite aware," said Zeek, who prefaced many of his suggestions in this way, "we must go to Jabulani hostel to check on the residents."

The single men's hostel lay beyond the railway above a deep section of the cutting. On the residents' side, a street led straight up to a bridge over the line, but the houses stopped at a junction some way in front of it. As we arrived, the police were working their way along the bottom end of the street and the residents were shouting at them. The air was full of tear gas, and canisters had been fired through the windows of two houses, in which fires had started, perhaps as a result.

Some local comrades took us into one of the houses, where we found a small man standing beside an upended green sofa with a burn in one of the arms. The floor was covered with synthetic padding, water and pieces of glass. He was looking out through the broken window and scarcely registered our arrival. He was oblivious of the tear gas, although the air in the room was unbearable for more than a minute or two. I went out to the back to draw breath and found a woman leaning against the yard wall, examining a heap of burned, waterlogged cushions.

The police left the end of the street after a few minutes and a party of children ran up toward the bridge with oranges from a looted pickup wedged in their mouths. At the junction, a crowd kept watch on the railway line and a woman approached us to explain that her cousin had been arrested at the bridge. "He was doing nothing," she said, "and when his sister protested, they arrested her too." There was a hush in the crowd. A few Inkatha had appeared on the other side of the embankment. A small girl spotted a tear gas cartridge on the ground and tried to pick it up. It was still very hot and she started to cry. A rifle shot rang out from the hostel and the crowd scattered, leaving her alone in the middle of the junction until a comrade came back and snatched her up. There were further shots and accusations from the crouching residents that police gunmen were working with Inkatha. A reckless youngster stood on a mound below the bridge, in full view of Inkatha, and tucked one end of a stick into his right shoulder, looking down imaginary sights at the warriors on the embankment. Their heads, in distinctive red bands, disappeared from view. He gave an imitation of gunfire and the residents applauded. Then he spread his arms wide, with the stick in one hand, and shouted something in Zulu, stepping lazily off the mound as a sinister thing, perhaps some kind of homemade bullet, came singing from the direction of the hostel. Lying lower still, the residents laughed nervously and praised the young man with the stick. Zeek answered the shot with a contemptuous whistle. Wide World was commiserating with the little girl who had burned her hand.

The reporter from the BBC was in touch with his office in Johannesburg and heard that by noon the death toll in Soweto had risen. The police were said to have killed two people already, an unidentified man with a gasoline bomb and an innocent teenager. Police units had also come under fire from comrades somewhere in the township. The armed struggle had only recently been suspended but the margin of interpretation was wide. Everywhere we moved now, we encountered roadblocks; Zeek and Wide World were finding it difficult to negotiate passage with the comrades, some of whom were very intimidating.

Edward was quiet, as we made our way to Jabavu. We were not far from the Jabulani hostel when we came across a pair of police vans and, as we turned out of the street, an angry crowd of residents surrounding about two dozen armed police. There was tremendous confusion in the air and when the residents were not arguing with the police, they stepped back, quite stunned, and began reproaching one another. Edward shook his head and walked back to the car, where he sat with the door open. The police were not drawn up in lines but stood in groups with their weapons over their shoulders. The road was narrow and descended to a track, which ran straight for a few yards and then curved out of view. At the bottom of the slope lay a dead man, his body under a brown tartan blanket and his head covered with newspaper. Beside him two women were seated. We tried to find out from the residents what had happened. One said the young man had been hacked to death, several others that he had been shot. There was agreement that a party of Inkatha had crossed the railway line some distance from the bridge, crept down through the bushes and come around by the track to mount an attack. There were several of them, but the witnesses were unsure how many. Nor were they sure how many had been killed: two residents and some members of Inkatha, perhaps three, whose bodies had already been removed. Inkatha had been armed with AK47s and one of the residents asked how the guns got into the hostels, if not with the knowledge of the security forces.

The police, however, were maintaining that there had been no gunfire. The residents challenged them and now someone stepped forward to allege that there had been shots from the bridge. Other residents pressed behind her, hands raised in support of a bitter argument that could not be resolved here. In due course, an ambulance arrived and the crowd parted. As the orderlies lifted the body of the young man onto a stretcher, a television crew began to film. The bloodstained newspaper fell away to expose the head and the two mourners rose to their feet, supported by a third. When the doors of the ambulance had shut, the women began their lament, setting out behind the ambulance with the television crew and a party of photographers. Zeek and Wide World watched in silence; the residents had also stopped arguing with the police to look on. Later that night, after the television crew got back to Johannesburg, much of South Africa would see the incident too.

We began driving toward Wide World's house in Mtetwa Street at about 9 P.M. It lay on the edge of Jabulani, bordering another district of Soweto known as Zola. Edward, who had remained in the car throughout the altercation between the police and the residents in Jabavu, was loath to stay over in this part of the township and I sought to reassure him. The night was quiet and there was an air of provisional truce. With Zeek and Wide World, he was in good hands. For years, Edward had assumed the guise of brusque criminality—I took this to be the meaning of "chameleon *muti*"—in order to survive, but he was not so young anymore and it seemed wrong, if he was uncomfortable, to bring him here. But he was unwilling to abandon us. As we approached Jabulani, he regained his confidence. "I can strike Inkatha dead with lightning and make the clouds cover the stars," he explained. Wide World laughed and said that this would not be necessary.

Wide World's father was an *inyanga*, a skilled herbalist with less status as a magician than Edward's *sangoma;* he and his wife ran the practice at the house. Wide World lived in a small one-room shack in their yard, to which he led us now. Most of the room was taken up by the bed, on which lay a pair of trousers, a bag and a T-shirt. "Before I met you," Wide World explained, "these were the clothes I was wearing to fight the Zulus and since that time I just left them here." I asked why he called them Zulus; after all, he was a Zulu himself. "Excuse me," he said. "We must call them Inkatha." Zeek went across to his house and washed. We sat on the bed and the BBC man played a game of chess with Wide World. At 10:30 Zeek reappeared. "If you're quite aware," he said, "our comrades are on that side, near the hostel, and we must go to see how matters stand."

It was a ten-minute drive through the darkness, following instructions from the two men. We parked the car on a road with a high curb and walked down toward a group of comrades standing over a fire. It was a cool night and they were wrapped around with scarves. Their weapons lay stacked by the fire and they drank from a bottle of brandy to fortify themselves. Even so they were shivering. They pointed to the likeliest spot for an Inkatha attack—the hostel was about a quarter of a mile away and they said they would be standing guard until two or three, when they hoped to be relieved by another group. They had a brief discussion with Zeek and Wide World. "The name of this street," said Wide World as we left, "is Masingafe. It means: 'We must not die.' " At the car, Zeek turned and cast a glance at the young men around the little fire.

Back at his house, Wide World produced a folder full of qualifications from a college in Pietermaritzburg. For four years after leaving, however, he had worked as a laborer and might well do so for the rest of his life. Zeek challenged the BBC reporter to a game of chess. "I do not toss for white," he smiled as they set up the pieces, "I always take black." Wide World put on the radio and began dancing slowly to "The Ghetto" by Donny Hathaway. Later, he showed me some photographs of Soweto in the early 1960s, with evident regret for the passing of an age that he had never known but which had a semblance of normal life to it. "We believe," he said, "that civilization begins and ends with Soweto." For the next hour a trickle of comrades came and went. Zeek walked Edward and me to his house in Dlangamandla Street—the name, he said with a laugh, meant: "Eat with power"—and made up a bed for us at the back, in a room containing a wardrobe and a portrait of his father.

At six in the morning Zeek came to wake us. "Gentlemen," he said, standing over the bed, "the night has been peaceful on this side and Wide World is preparing tea for you at his house, if you're well aware."

Saying goodbye to Zeek and Wide World that day was like abandoning them to some furious storm from which we had decided to shelter. The ease of the morning and the sweetness of the hospitality had been a short respite. Within a few hours we were confronted with evidence of new atrocities. By early afternoon much of the township lay in a twilight of smoke and disorder, and it was on the edge of this world that the two young men shook our hands and vanished. As we drove toward the calm streets of Orlando East, Edward remarked that they were "good boys." There were two things that one needed in Soweto, he said: courage and dependable *muti*. He asked how much we had paid Zeek and Wide World for their time.

Despite the presence of great wealth and a substantial middle class in the township, it was a labyrinth of penury through which most inhabitants had constantly to maneuver for survival. Here a household of sixteen might earn a combined income of $130 a month, while a domestic worker could put in a six-hour day for five days a week to bring home $10–$15 if her employers could see their way to paying some of her transportation costs. To keep body and soul together, residents were constantly on the move, performing basic tasks that someone with a moderate income and a telephone might achieve in a matter of minutes: Delay was a fact of life in the township. It was difficult for the comrades or the civic associations to convene meetings on time because most people who were due to attend were involved in a series of complex missions that took them around the township, mostly on foot, in search of other people who might in turn be absent on missions of their own: borrowing money, arranging the use of a car, finding a house with a telephone and, since death and sickness were so common, being called away on "family business." Even in times of comparative peace, the residents of Soweto lagged a good many paces behind their own lives. There were whites in South Africa, even liberals and ANC supporters, who ascribed the lack of punctuality among township people to the character of "Africans," when a more obvious explanation was to hand. It was also argued in some quarters that the ANC's incompetence in the new South Africa was the result of an abiding taste for chaos.

The virtue of South Africa's rapt attention to the violence was now more questionable than ever. A country that could only contemplate the same object, day after day, was condemned to the same deeds. Moreover, when the war broke out in Soweto it meant that the epic struggle with poverty, in which people like Zeek and Wide World and their families were locked, took on a new intensity. For those people with jobs, it was harder and more dangerous to get to work, while the informal arrangements by which tens of thousands tried to get by were severely disrupted. The mayhem in the townships tended to obscure this fact. The great majority of people in the most capitalized nation in Africa were forbidden access to the century, even as it drew to a close. Their closest affinity was not to the citizens of Mozambique, Botswana, Swaziland or Zimbabwe, but to the poor of Henry Mayhew's London.

Edward did not come with me to the township of Kagiso a few days later. Had he done so, he would probably have refused to enter the Zulu hostel. Throughout the Johannesburg area, anger and fear reinforced the material gulf between the hostels and the township people and, though Edward had plenty of Zulu friends, he now used the word "Zulu" with evident disdain. The people of Kagiso claimed that the police had been ferrying Inkatha members into the township for about two weeks. The residents had been forced to take refuge in the local churches. Now humiliation had turned into fury, and at one intersection the comrades were standing around a house in flames. It belonged to a Zulu. A levy of perhaps two hundred residents was marching on the single men's hostel with swords, staves and pangas. It was brought to a halt by a bristling cordon of modern technology: thirty or more police, mostly Afrikaners, with automatic rifles and tear gas, and behind them, the press, with a bank of Japanese newsgathering equipment. The residents camped down a few yards in front of the police, taunting them with Xhosa songs and rattling their weapons. They were bounded on one side by a brick foundry and, on the other, by a large billboard with the words, "Free Enterprise Is Working." Here they remained until an ANC official from the Krugersdorp Residents' Organization arrived to try and calm the situation. Nomvula Mokonyane was a confident speaker, quick to dissociate the movement from the burning of the Zulu house. She told the press that the perpetrators were "agents of the system," although she had not seen the incident herself. The ANC was reviling more and more of its township militants. It had no choice, yet to denounce them as stooges was merely to inflame the suspicions that already existed among the residents.

Sometime after noon, the residents' army began to disperse. By then I had already made my way to the hostel entrance with a British newspaper correspondent. We asked to go inside but the way was barred by a group of hostel dwellers, who conferred and pushed a spokesman forward. Joshua Ndaba, a short, agitated man in his early forties, asked us our business and said that we could not go inside. He denied that Inkatha members had been ferried into Kagiso. On the contrary, the trouble had been started by residents—or Xhosas, as he chose to describe them—creeping around the back of the hostel and plotting misdeeds against the inmates. In insisting on police neutrality, Joshua Ndaba used a curious expression. "The police," he said, "is not againsting to either side." The others watched him intently. They all wanted to remain here, he said, even if the Xhosa nation should attack them. "If they come to burn the hostel, there is nothing we can do but go back to Natal." Then, for a moment, Joshua Ndaba's party allegiance got the better of him "We are here to work," he said, "not for violence or sanctions or all the things that are out of order."

After another round of conferring, the ranks of men divided to let us through into a rectangular block surrounding a long courtyard with a brown patch of grass in the middle. Each entrance in the block led back into a concrete hall where the bright winter sunlight was obliterated after a few feet. Groups of men sat out with their backs to the walls, weapons in their laps and Lion lager bottles set down beside their fiberglass chairs. The comforting smell of *dagga* hung on the air but it could not contend with the reek of institutionalized migrant labor. When it came to South Africa's manpower requirements, very little had changed since Justino Gonçalves had spent his weekends in the Mozambican compounds of Crown Mines thirty years earlier. The men were bleary-eyed and suspicious. Having surveyed us for a minute, they rose unsteadily to their feet and retired indoors. In the middle of the grass area was a kennel made of twisted bedsprings and in it a lean, aged dog.

▲

I managed to stay in touch with a few people after leaving South Africa. In late 1990, Pane Moshounyane was planning to leave the South African Council of Churches after deepening political discord in the organization. He hoped to return to his family in Bloemfontein and scrape by on teaching. He wanted to be a writer. By the middle of

1992, Stephen was completing a degree in psychology at the University of Witwatersrand. He had not been called up. He said he had joined a small left-wing group with links to the Socialist Workers' Party in Britain; he sounded cheerful, although critical of the ANC for its drift, as he saw it, toward an enfeebling centrism. Louis Breydencamp had reservations too, but for different reasons. He was now an ANC member of two years' standing and admitted on the phone that the organization was "very confused." He also told me he'd received a set of call-up papers shortly after we met and had declined on the grounds that he could not be loyal to the ANC and the South African Defence Force. His statement arrived late and Louis was informed that if he did not appear at camp, he would be arrested. He went into hiding until he received notice of cancellation.

Edward had a phone number but the line was always disconnected and the only way to reach him was through the shebeen across the road, which had closed because of the general tension. I spoke to him several times. A year after I left South Africa he could confirm that the war had not come to Orlando. He implored me to send him "one hundred rand or just fifty"—a week's drinking or a plentiful supply of Deep Heat for his *sangoma*. I never had any success with the phone number for Zeek and Wide World, and I asked Edward if he had seen them. "That side, by Zola," Edward laughed, "it's another place."

5

MOZAMBIQUE

▲▲▲▲▲▲▲▲▲

There are, in addition, procurable for a consideration from the witch doctor, other charms which, when worn or otherwise exercised, are believed to make the owner invisible. . . . Other forms of medicine render him immune to bullets and arrows, whilst others again enable him to kill, invariably by the same means. There is one matter which I have overlooked in relation to native superstitions, and that is the complete absence of belief in any definite future state or condition, or any faith in the resurrection. They have, moreover, not the faintest conception of immortality. . . . Certainly no negro would believe that the body which he has seen laid in the ground, or, possibly, removed thence and deliberately scattered in the forest, could rise again, and, in its old aspect, or anything like it, put on incorruptibility.

> R.C.F. Maugham, *Zambézia: A General Description of the Valley of the Zambezi River, from Its Delta to the River Aroangwa, with Its History, Agriculture, Flora and Ethnography* (1910)

Whatever happens, whether we have to go on for ten or twenty years, fighting our way inch by inch to Lourenço Marques, or whether the Portuguese give up and move out within the next few weeks, our problems will not end with independence.

> Eduardo Mondlane, *The Struggle for Mozambique*

Τhe war in Mozambique began in the mid-1970s and lasted until the end of 1992. It reduced the country to a state of chaos, driving nearly a third of its inhabitants—roughly fifteen million at the present count—from their homes and putting many more at risk from hunger. It undermined subsistence farming, brought the distribution of local produce to a standstill and then hampered the delivery

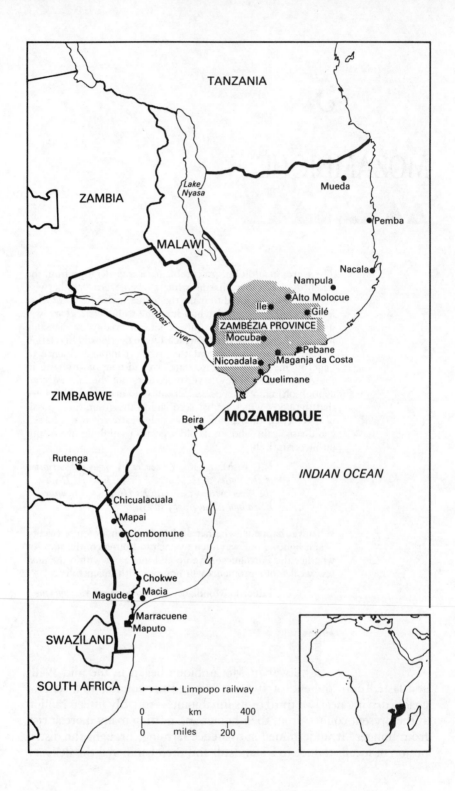

of relief supplies. The war turned all ordinary activities, even simple tasks, into herculean labors, requiring time and will power to achieve. It was also the most brutal conflict in southern Africa, with invisible fronts and strings of atrocities against civilians, the majority carried out by the rebel movement, Resistência Nacional Moçambicana (Renamo), who also took care to destroy anything the government built in the way of schools, clinics and other public facilities.

To a visitor, the effects of the conflict were clear enough. Mozambique contained large tracts of abandoned land; its provincial towns were crammed with hungry, homeless people. But the war itself was spectral and elusive. Journalists were constantly on the lookout for clues about the rebel movement's character and how it operated. If they went to the site of a recent attack, they behaved like insurance employees sent to verify a claim; if they found themselves in a place that had been trashed some time ago—Renamo was nothing if not thorough—they sifted through the debris like archaeologists. Slowly they tried to piece together a picture of Renamo's habits. But the country ran a thousand miles or more from north to south, with a cleft in its upper half, and rebel tactics differed from one place to the next. Reporters were always in danger of pursuing a lost cause, "an African shadow play," as the U.S. journalist William Finnegan called it.

Certain basic facts were beyond dispute. Mozambique won its independence from Portugal at the same time as Angola and the rest of Portuguese Africa. Frelimo—the Frente de Libertação de Moçambique—had been ten years in the bush before coming to power. By 1977 it was installed as the ruling party, pursuing similar goals to those of the MPLA in Angola. It had support from the Eastern bloc countries and was soon caught up in the escalating regional war against white minority rule. It was this broad context that gave succor to Renamo.

The ANC was a growing force beyond the borders of South Africa, and Mozambique's new president, Samora Machel, was willing to provide it with bases. He also offered sanctuaries to Robert Mugabe's Zimbabwean guerrillas, enabling them to move freely in and out of neighboring Rhodesia and to keep up the pressure on Ian Smith's government. As a quid pro quo, Rhodesia trained and supervised a group of disaffected Mozambicans to destabilize the new regime. In 1979 the Rhodesians handed the operation over to South Africa. From Pretoria's point of view, it was a useful means of chastising Frelimo for the support it gave to the ANC and for its anti-apartheid rhetoric. The offense was repaid with interest. By the end of the 1980s, long after Mozambique had ended its support for the opponents of apartheid, the rebels had made large parts of the country ungovernable and they were still getting aid from South Africa.

Mozambique and Angola had much in common: a history of Portuguese colonialism, which left them with little expertise to run their newly sovereign states; a large base of peasant agriculture; an early faith in scientific socialism; and a natural alliance with the Soviet bloc. Above all, both were prey to destructive rebel movements backed by Pretoria.

There were striking differences too. Moscow did not make a big military commitment in Mozambique and, above all, the Cubans did not field a large expeditionary force. In Washington during the 1980s, the State Department won its running battle against the pro-Renamo fringe: the rebels had vocal friends in Congress, including Senator Malcolm Wallop of Wyoming and Representative Dan Burton of Indiana, and also in the administration itself, where William Casey and Pat Buchanan had good access to the White House. As a result there was no grand showdown in Mozambique, only a terrible attrition that the government was powerless to stop. To begin with, both Frelimo and the MPLA had followed the model of economic mismanagement that the Soviet Union proposed to all its African clients. But Frelimo took up a new approach with greater alacrity. The Cold War, and the shadow it threw in southern Africa, had held both countries to policy positions that were hard to abandon without giving the impression that a broad range of moral issues was also being jettisoned. Only a gifted pragmatist like Samora Machel could steer away from collectivization and state monopolies while seeming to betray no ideological cause. He had seen the need to do so in the early 1980s, but already the war had stripped much of the substance from policy decisions in Maputo.

The early hopes of Frelimo and its active pursuit of a Marxist agenda are an important preamble to what happened later. In Mozambique a million people were sold into slavery during the nineteenth century and virtual slave labor persisted on colonial plantations until the 1960s. By 1961, when the Portuguese carried out a massacre in the northern town of Mueda, there was already a long history of anticolonial resistance in parts of the country. Mueda merely hastened the formation of Frelimo in 1962, the same year that Algeria won independence from the French. The movement was the product of an alliance between three anticolonial groups in Mozambique: one from the center and two from the northern areas. The scope for ethnic conflict among its members was restricted by the multiracial politics of the leadership, several of whom had been educated in Europe and the United States.

It was not simply by studying overseas that supporters of the liberation movement came to hold nonracial views. There were plenty of less privileged activists who understood the dangers of a politics based on race or region. One of these was Samora Machel, who assumed the leadership after a brief power struggle following Eduardo Mondlane's death in 1969. The two men were very different. Mondlane was an ethnographer and an intellectual who had studied in Portugal, South Africa and the United States. Machel was a nurse before he rose to prominence as a guerrilla commander. As the head of Frelimo, he was an authoritarian and a populist. The fluency of the transition and the continuity that underlay such different styles of leadership was a tribute to Frelimo's singlemindedness.

When the movement took up arms in 1964, there were 200,000 Portuguese in the country, and thousands of Asians and people of mixed descent. The African population was defined by several ethnic groups speaking many different dialects. For Frelimo, socialism was the only plausible unifying doctrine. It had rigorous objections to the idea of difference; it laid claim to universal principles and could propose a common genealogy for all forms of dispossession, however diverse. Finally, it could argue that ambitions for clan, race or creed were divisive and misleading. In Africa these arguments were persuasive. Colonized Africans, moreover, could be forgiven for thinking that the metropolitan powers of Europe, the imperial power of Ethiopia, and the settler minorities in Rhodesia and South Africa were delegates of a single monolithic system bent on extracting resources and cheap labor from the continent.

Any residual doubts among nationalists about the character and allegiance of Portuguese colonialism were dispelled after 1964 by NATO's provision of weapons to Lisbon. When helicopters landed Portuguese commando units in villages, when communities were strafed from the air, when patrol boats scoured the waterways for signs of guerrilla activity, Frelimo could state with confidence that the technology was provided to the Portuguese under the terms of NATO agreements. The overtures of China and the Soviet bloc were doubly welcome, for with the ideological opposition to the "free world" came armaments, training and money.

Mozambique became an independent African state in 1975, a year after the demise of the dictatorship in Portugal. Frelimo's constitution proclaimed equality of rights and duties, "irrespective of race, sex, ethnic origin, place of birth, religion, level of education, social position or occupation." Two years later Frelimo formed itself into a vanguard party with Marxist-Leninist principles, which it assumed would give discipline and substance to the peace, as they had to a decade of guerrilla war. Within a few years, however, much of rural Mozambique was restless and discontented. The peasant population had taken against the idea of communal villages and people's fields. With distribution already weakened, food production began to fail. By the end of the 1970s, the activities of Renamo, with Rhodesian officers in support, grew steadily more effective. As they did so, the cycles of cultivation in the hinterland were further disrupted. Before long it was hard to distinguish the ravages of war from the failures of the government's agrarian policy or from the drought that took hold of the central provinces. By 1983, when Frelimo began to revise its strategy for the rural areas, favoring small family production and moving away from the collectivist model, the war was already fanning out through the country.

I made three visits to Mozambique at the end of the 1980s and a fourth in 1991. Journalism thrived in this harrowed country, despite the constraints of one-party rule: there were many able Mozambican and expatriate journalists based in Maputo and, on the whole, visiting reporters were treated impeccably. To the outside world, on which it relied so largely, Frelimo was an open government. It believed that it had nothing to hide. There was consensus among the foreign press on the most striking point about Renamo: its barbarity. In Angola, one felt captive to the elaborate negligence of the Press Center, but in Mozambique, the capital itself was a more obvious hostage to circumstance. Maputo lay in the south, on the coast, far removed from the center of the country. In the adjoining provinces, the war zone shrank and expanded, according to Renamo's supplies and energy. Within five to thirty miles of the city limits the rebels made overland travel a high risk. Maputo had an atmosphere of siege and siege mentalities flourished: this was a city of rumor and, for those who lived there permanently, claustrophobia. It was packed with refugees from the countryside, socialists from the Western bloc who had come to offer their services to the revolution, and many other foreigners who had enlisted in the aid and development drive. Foreign aid was a sector in its own right; its most conspicuous effect was to create an artificial economy in Maputo, providing jobs and money to a limited number of Mozambicans.

There was nothing to stop a foreign journalist traveling to and from the capital by plane and no shortage of flights—a fleet of light aircraft was on hire to the aid agencies, allowing them to reach more remote parts of the country. It was also possible, with a little persistence, to travel by road and rail. Light planes were a good way to get about, but in this enigmatic country, where every hour spent on the ground outside the capital was a learning process, flying seemed wasteful. In fine weather, one gazed down at the endless, reticent bush under calm African skies until a little strip of parched grass or laterite would list into view above the cabin controls; in bad weather the plane fought its way through the very origin of rain and, after an hour or so, dropped abruptly into a dank universe of war and deprivation. There was something predatory about descending on a Mozambican calamity, inspecting crowds of emaciated children, being briefed by the local party official and hurrying back to the airstrip a few hours later.

Yet these excursions furnished valuable clues about what had happened in the hinterland during the war. Like all reporters, I tried to piece together a picture of civilian life from the scraps that were available—some, but not all, quite horrifying. I also tried to engage with the questions that troubled the conscience of Mozambique's intellectuals, and Frelimo's fellow travelers from the West, in the closing stages of the war: had rural discontent with the old Marxist-Leninist policies allowed Renamo a freer hand in the countryside? How far did the rebels profit from anger in rural communities that had seen their chiefs deposed by Frelimo and their lands run down because the revolution favored communal farming? If Mozambique was on its knees, what share of the blame fell to Frelimo?

The answers differ, but the questions are important in their own right. The collision in Mozambique between a self-confident ruling party and a rural culture with its own established order is a variant of the more general encounter in Africa between the modernizing state and the people it aspires to govern. Elections and Western-style democracy can only sketch out theoretical solutions to the clash between entrenched African institutions and new orthodoxies drawn from European political thought. When no practical solution can be found, both sides begin to take hostages: government disrupts the livelihoods of peasants and pastoralists, who in turn reject the legitimacy of their rulers. The first stop is alienation and the last stop, all too often, hunger. On the way, unlikely local solutions to despair and indignity are thrown up. However short-lived they appear to be, it is foolish, and simplistic, to dismiss them as mere superstition.

The best way from Women's Movement Square, where I was staying, to the Villa Algarve, was to keep to the avenues: straight down Avenida Vladimir I. Lenine, over the junctions with Kwame Nkrumah and Mao Tse Tung, and then left on to Ahmed Sekou Toure. I had passed the villa several times during my stay in

Maputo and it had aroused my interest. It lay off the avenue but it was difficult to miss. Twenty-or thirty ill-dressed people sat outside, keeping to the shade of the wall. It was a large building roofed with Roman tiles; its high walls contained a series of ceramics showing scenes from nineteenth-century European life. Access was through a wide brick arch inlaid with blue-and-yellow faience. Every evening the sun would linger above the arch and flood the windows at the front, the glass long gone. It was a well-chosen spot for a piece of colonial elegance, but now it was being used to billet the homeless, many of whom came from the countryside.

Mateus was a private in the government army staying in the villa; he spoke an intelligible blend of Portuguese and English, as well as several local languages. As I walked into the courtyard, he introduced himself and sat me down on an upturned can by one of the porches. He asked me for some money, which was spirited away by a young boy who returned after a few minutes carrying a bucket of cold beers. The keenest drinker was Mateus's wife, Catarina, a stout woman dressed in a yellow blouse and a homemade felt skirt. Catarina wore a *capulana* over her shoulder, with a print of Machel's successor, and the words *"Viva o Presidente Chissano."* It was said in Maputo that if you tied this *capulana* correctly around your waist, the president's face would appear three times—once in front, between the thighs, and twice behind, set solemnly on each buttock. A good dancer could make the President smile.

As a private serving in the ranks, Mateus earned 11,900 meticais a month. The metical traded on the parallel market at about seven hundred to the dollar. At least while he was in Maputo, he was guaranteed three meals a day at the barracks. Mozambique had joined the International Monetary Fund (IMF) and the World Bank in 1984. After three years of negotiations over a structural adjustment program, Frelimo announced its own recovery plan, which everybody knew by its acronym, PRE, at the beginning of 1987. It did so without the final approval of the World Bank and the IMF. The PRE was less austere than they would have liked, which was the reason for Frelimo's initiative; but PRE was structural adjustment in all but name: devaluation, higher rents and the removal of subsidies on a range of goods and foodstuffs. To the World Bank and the IMF it was an auspicious start and they endorsed it, but its benefits in Maputo were very dubious.

Soon the requirements of urban Mozambicans were edging beyond their means. Catarina had four children to feed and she calculated the family's basic corn consumption at thirty kilograms a month. The price of subsidized corn from a government outlet was 250 meticais per kilogram, but on the open market it was higher—one estimate put it at eight hundred meticais. Catarina was not from Maputo and on arriving in the capital had qualified for a number of benefits, many of which had since lapsed. Two of the children were suffering from worms, but the cost of a remedy was prohibitive. She had already spent one thousand meticais on medicine from the drug store and that had run out. Yet, like most of the people in Villa Algarve, Mateus and Catarina had a system.

Mateus handed his salary to Catarina, who then bought subsidized food and resold it for a profit. Rice, sugar and corn flour were still obtainable by quota at subsidized rates but the reduction of subsidies represented an opportunity for someone like Catarina, since fewer and fewer people could afford to purchase their full allocation. Catarina would use Mateus's salary to buy up unclaimed quotas. She would then set out for one of the open markets and sell at the going rate. She was trading on scarcity to a narrow band of people who could afford to buy. Her customers might be returnee workers from South Africa, buying for family and friends, and friends of friends; people with lowly but dependable jobs in the aid community and people who lived by their wits—theft and prostitution had begun to boom under the PRE—as well as the growing number of traders like herself. As canned beer and tobacco from South Africa came onto the market, Catarina tried her hand at these, but they were less lucrative, she reckoned, because foodstuffs were always in high demand.

Catarina was at a loss to say how much money she actually made. Her way of life simply kept the family ticking over. She would get up at five in the morning, leave the villa at six and hustle for flour, or rice, or sugar. She might make it out to Xipamanine market where all kinds of goods could be bartered. She would get back to the villa at 7:30 in the morning and cook for the children, leaving them in the care of her sister as she set off again, an hour later, for a market known as Museu, where she would trade until dark. The combie (minibus) back from Museu would bring her transportation costs for the day to at least six hundred meticais and she would probably have made a round of purchases to bring home to the family. Catarina admitted it was difficult to know how much money she might have in her pocket at the end of the day.

For many people in Maputo life was harder. Indeed a curious war was being waged against the poorer citizens. The rationing system that provided families in Maputo with about half their nutritional needs, in the form of beans, oil, sugar, rice and corn at subsidized prices, was known as the *Nova Sistema de Abastecimento*. The World Bank did not approve of this system. It agreed, however, that the *Nova Sistema* should be maintained, in order to soften the blow that would certainly be dealt to the poor by its fantastic experiment in Mozambique: a consumer-led recovery program in an underproductive country racked by war, drought and hunger. Before long, however, the World Bank had introduced the idea of a corn stamp to replace subsidies, and a study group was convened to work on the idea. The poor would receive stamps that they could then exchange for a corn quota. Frelimo was appalled; it had kept subsidies in place to avoid just this kind of absolute dependence. The study group remained in deliberation while prices for the basic foods in the *Nova Sistema* doubled.

The Bank had also reviewed the matter of cash benefits for the very poor. It talked this over with experts from the U.S. Agency for International Development and soon there were moves afoot to do away with cash handouts altogether and replace them with a food allocation. In all likelihood, this would be yellow corn from the U.S. grain surpluses and a proportion of it would be sold to the Mozambican government at the going rate. Frelimo would pay out of the funds made available by the World Bank and the IMF.

As the debate proceeded, the proportion of nutritional needs being met by the *Nova Sistema de Abastecimento* began to fall. For every rise in prices, there was a corresponding rise in crime and also in the experts' assessment of malnutrition, known as "growth faltering." A growth-faltering index was reached by computing the percentage of monitored children who failed to gain weight in the weeks between two consecutive weighings. Before the PRE, growth faltering among children in Maputo was running at around 7 percent. Eighteen months later, the figure had doubled.

Catarina had her head above the torrent of economic liberalism, but she was struggling. She was from Massinga, a district of Imhambane province, about four hundred kilometers north of Maputo. The insurgents were there in force. There had been shooting every day in her part of the district for a month or more before she finally left. When the insurgents seemed to be close, she and her relatives would leave their house and shelter in the bush, returning when it seemed safe to do so. One day she came back to the village to find everything gone: her chickens, her pots and pans, her grain, her flour and her meager furniture. Shortly afterward, her nephew and her grandmother were taken by the insurgents. She had no news of them here in Maputo, nor of the land she once worked. She gave her husband a glance of despair while he translated. When he reached the part about the empty house, she caught the gist of it and seized my arm, repeating, "*Naaa-da, naaa-da,*" ("nothing") and wrinkling her nose in anger, or humiliation.

After the war, Catarina was planning to return to Massinga. In

Maputo she had become a small-time merchant, with a resolve that the World Bank would surely have admired. Yet she was an unhappy woman. "I like to live according to my wishes," she said with her hand resting on the top of her head. "I like to eat things I don't have to buy with my own money." Markets and a cash economy meant as little to her as collectivization had. She still hoped for the freedom to work on family land, to feed herself and her children with what they had grown, to pound the surplus into liquor after a good harvest and praise the ancestors before the round of tilling and planting began again. Like tens of thousands of peasants crowded into Maputo, she cherished the thought of going home.

Mateus showed me round the Villa Algarve. Inside, it had been partitioned with sheet metal or cardboard into tiny rooms, eight or nine to a corridor, which were impeccably tidy. In the courtyard behind the building and the arches underneath were many more. Mateus reckoned that at least a hundred families lived in this warren and that something in the order of four hundred people came and went from the villa every week. There was one outside tap.

A slight man in a brown safari suit, carrying a volume of Lenin in Portuguese, followed us around the building without a word. It crossed my mind that he was there to keep an eye on things, but in the name of what? Surveillance was not what it once had been, as anyone who knew the somber history of the Villa Algarve could attest. During the war of liberation, this tasteful town house had belonged to the Portuguese secret police. It was used for detention, interrogation and murder. Once a place of despair, it now served as a transit point for people pinning their slender hopes on peace and homecoming.

Peeling and crumbling at the edge of the Indian Ocean, Maputo was a case of splendid isolation. For expatriates there was food and hot water; there were duty-free shops, tennis courts and embassy functions. Two rail links led out of the city; a road ran north and another cut down to Swaziland, but the war had made all these unsafe. Flying was the best way into Maputo and the best way out—a fact that only added to the city's rarefied atmosphere. Here, real information about the rest of the country was hard to come by. The alternative was a plethora of statistics, which were compiled by the government departments and the aid agencies, often working together. There were statistics on almost everything. First came the big ones for the "structural emergency," that is to say, for a massive food and cash appeal, which in most other countries would have been an abnormality, as the word "emergency" suggests, but which had become an annual feature in Mozambique. From one year to the next, the crisis was kept on the books of the aid agencies. Each new year a fresh set of figures was presented to the donors, among whom there were roughly twenty countries, besides the overseas charities and U.N. agencies.

These assessments had a basis in fact, since the number of dispossessed people who had flocked to government-held areas could be counted, but there was also a measure of inspired guesswork, for an appeal would have to estimate the number of people who might emerge from the bush and present themselves in any one of fifty government centers in the course of the year. The appeals also presupposed that anyone living in insurgent territory was suffering a shortage of food, although this was contested, off the record, by International Red Cross workers. An overall annual figure of people in need might be wide of the mark by a hundred thousand.

The government of Mozambique was one of the biggest recipients of aid in the world and came to regard it as a key sector of the economy. By the end of the 1980s foreign aid of one kind or another amounted to 75 percent of the country's gross domestic product. If the number of people in need was uncertain, it was safer to overestimate. Several hundred tons of extra grain, or a modest dollar surplus, would not go amiss. However, there was another factor in the calculation that could not be ignored. This was known as "donor fatigue": the reluctance of the international community to supply the same levels of emergency aid as they had the previous year. Trying to read the signs of donor fatigue correctly could prejudice the appeal. In 1988 a request was made for nearly 230,000 tons of food aid for free distribution. The donors pledged to provide almost all of this but only half of the request was actually received. It turned out to be sufficient for most of Mozambique's needs. In view of this, the government and the agencies decided the following year to subtract a few hundred thousand from the total of estimated beneficiaries—and then, the year after, to make almost the same request again, but by now there were a million displaced people in the province of Zambézia alone. No figures were available for the privations that may have resulted.

Behind the dramatic totals for hunger and displacement came a procession of lesser statistics that helped to build a more detailed, but not necessarily a truer, picture. It was easy to establish, for example, the number of tires (22,204) and the number of bicycles (21,003) produced in 1987; the growth rate in gross domestic product (GDP) in 1988 (5.5 percent); the number of pupils in primary schools (1,362,838). Or the proportion of the population reached in 1980 by the government's latrine program (43 percent); the number of women who had not been displaced in 1988 but were still at risk from war and hunger (2,757,818). Or finally the estimate for the total population of the country on August 1, 1989 (15,326,476—a bold commitment to accuracy in a country where huge tracts were inaccessible). The insurgency too could produce statistics: the Washington office of Renamo claimed that they controlled 85 percent of Mozambique, although they had yet to circulate a map showing precisely which parts these were.

In Mozambique the insurgents were referred to as armed bandits—*bandidos armados*—whence the acronym BAs. The Angolan government used the same term for UNITA; in Ethiopia the Amharas referred to the Eritrean guerrillas as *shifta*—brigands; Morocco called the Polisario "Algerian mercenaries"; South Africa described SWAPO and the ANC as terrorists. The language in which a government chose to vilify an armed adversary had above all to assert the legitimacy of the regime and to heap disdain on the pretender. Yet in much of Mozambique a general and deep suspicion of the *bandidos* made name calling superfluous.

The insurgents originally referred to themselves as the MNR—Mozambique National Resistance—the name given to them by the Rhodesians. From 1983 they preferred to be known as Renamo. *Bandidos*, Renamo, MNR, the BAs—ordinary people in Mozambique had a better name for them: the Matsangas, or just Matsanga. The name derived from the movement's first chief, André Matsangaíssa, whom the Central Intelligence Organization in Salisbury appointed to lead its collection of disaffected Mozambicans and angry Portuguese. Almost all the Portuguese left Mozambique around the time of independence; of these a good number went to Rhodesia and South Africa. Staunchly opposed to the new regime, they regarded Mozambique as unfinished business. They were grist to the CIO's mill. So were the people who were released or managed to escape from Frelimo's detention centers.

Matsangaíssa was one of these. He had served with Frelimo during the liberation struggle but had fallen out with his colleagues, and was accused of car theft. After his escape from a "reeducation" camp, the Rhodesians decided that Matsangaíssa should lead the MNR, and he spent the remainder of his brief life on operations intended to destroy the infrastructure of Mozambique. He was killed in 1979 near Gorongosa, in the center of the country. Outside of Renamo, and perhaps official Frelimo circles, the circumstances of his death are obscure, but any number of stories are woven around it. In one of these, it is said that Frelimo invited him to negotiations and killed him as he was arriving. In another, local witch doctors, or *curandeiros*, misled him about Frelimo's dispositions in Gorongosa. Matsangaíssa decided on an attack but met with a far bigger force than he expected. Apparently, the *curandeiros* had tired of the abuses that Commander André meted out to the local community.

The second story is interesting, for it suggests that in certain parts of Mozambique Renamo's fortunes were influenced by its relations with traditional figureheads. Frelimo had a profound distrust of religion; of the Catholic church, above all, but also of the acquiescence that piety of any kind entailed. So, for example, Samora Machel was said to have entered a mosque with his shoes on—hearsay denied by his defenders. In many of the rural areas, the *curandeiros* came under attack from Frelimo, not only because they were seen as purveyors of superstition, but because they were part of the system of political authority in the countryside with which a radical break was conceived. In the party's thinking there was a dangerous association between colonialism and tradition—it even made its way into the constitution, which promised the elimination of "colonial and traditional structures."

These attitudes had serious repercussions for Frelimo, and tended to favor Renamo; they led to the estrangement of rural communities— how deep one cannot know for certain, but in 1990 Frelimo was scouring the countryside for what it called "people of influence" to resume a role in local political life. These were the very people it had deposed or marginalized at the outset of the revolution, the guardians of "traditional structures"; it is a fair guess that in the intervening years they had come to resent the ruling party and everything it stood for. In the center of the country, and perhaps elsewhere, there was thus a base of disaffection on which Renamo was able to build, working closely with local chiefs, lineage heads, *curandeiros* and others who had seen their authority swept away as Frelimo set about constructing "the material and ideological base of a socialist society."

In the early 1980s, a French ethnographer called Christian Geffray, working in the north of Mozambique, began to sketch out an account of what had happened in the community he was studying. Geffray found that the people of Eráti district, in Nampula province, were delighted with Frelimo's victory, but puzzled when they were asked to work on "people's fields" and participate in the communal village plan. At length they decided to cooperate as a form of tribute to their liberators. Frelimo's idea was to rationalize the sprawling land holdings in the countryside and create efficient centers of production from which the surplus could be invested in infrastructure and amenities. Eighty percent of the population of Geffray's area were simply supposed to abandon their own family lands and perform collective labor for the state. The communal villages, according to the revolutionary poet Sergio Vieira, would be "the crucible of the new man."

To Geffray this was a dangerous misunderstanding. "It was as though the peasants and rural populations had no organization of their own," he wrote, "as if they had fallen from the sky and were simply waiting for Frelimo to come along and organize them." He pointed out that they had practiced their own forms of social and economic organization for centuries. In 1977 there were elections at the national and district levels. Frelimo, however, debarred certain groups from candidacy, among them all the local administrative chiefs. These men, known as *régulos*, had cooperated with the Portuguese by collecting taxes, rounding up labor and imposing colonial edicts on what could or could not be cultivated.

It was natural for Frelimo to identify the *régulos* with the old colonial order, but, equally, for the *régulos* to have bent with the wind of colonial intervention to protect their own status and their communities. Some had been guilty of gross collaboration and betrayal, but most of those had lost the respect of their constituencies. Frelimo was not satisfied; it forbade all *régulos* to enter the lists in Eráti, and also the clan chiefs—important figures in the "traditional structures." The hierarchies of local life were being challenged. When the time came for the people of Eráti to elect representatives, they voted massively in favor of their lineage heads, the next best thing to their clan chiefs. Frelimo's district administrator promptly annulled the result. There would be another vote, only this time dignitaries of any kind would be excluded. In a snub that was doubtless more apparent to the voters than the administrator, a rabble of village nobodies was elected. They forsook their duties after a matter of days.

Frelimo had in effect cast the keepers of order and stability from the community; for many of them the shame was so great that they left their lands and disappeared for long periods, leading semiclandestine lives. Meanwhile, the district of Eráti, along with most rural areas, was growing more isolated by the day. The war in Mozambique was concentrated five hundred miles away, yet its effect was soon felt, as goods had simply ceased to reach local traders. Cloth, gasoline, farm tools, pots and pans could, however, be obtained at the consumer cooperatives and the prices were reasonable. The people of Eráti were quick to grasp that it paid to be a member.

This was impossible without enrolling in a production cooperative, that is, a communal field or village. Geffray observed that local families were soon making strenuous efforts to ensure that one of these was developed on their own lands. The district administrator, of course, would want to found as many villages and people's fields as possible, to prove the "dynamism"—an important Frelimo word—of his stewardship. The families who vied for the site of a people's field or a communal village would, in turn, have to prove to him that they were worthy of the award. Those who succeeded found members promoted to important administrative posts, while other sectors of the population were denied access to the goods arriving in Eráti. In attempting to do away with the vestiges of feudalism, Frelimo had introduced a new system of privilege and denial.

Whether similar stories unfolded in other parts of Mozambique I do not know, but there is one more thing to say about Frelimo's relation to the rural areas that was clear even to a casual observer. Unlike the MPLA, Frelimo always took an ardent interest in rural development. It set up schools and clinics wherever it could and right up into the 1990s it was still building them. It believed passionately in literacy and the right to modern health care, and its early fascination with collectivism reflected these convictions. Having lived through severe hardship themselves, Frelimo assumed that the benefits of education and good health care would be ample compensation for the disadvantages of collectivization; but this was quite wrong.

Within a few years it was obvious that the production targets Frelimo had set after independence were not going to be met. Machel was an ideologue with a streak of pragmatism that kept the party on its toes. By 1983 the grand agrarian projects had failed and he pushed through a bid to support the small farming or family sector. But this came too late. The war on the other side of the border had been won; Rhodesia was Zimbabwe now and Zimbabwean guerrilla bases in Mozambique had been dismantled. Renamo's fate hung in the balance; there would be no more paymasters in Salisbury. Far from being left to fend for itself, however, the insurgency was adopted by South Africa on the eve of the Zimbabwe settlement. From that point on, the People's Republic of Mozambique descended into anarchy.

A "low-intensity" conflict in Mozambique suited Pretoria. The collapse of Portuguese colonialism meant an increase of ANC and SWAPO activity along a vast stretch of hostile borderland. Angola was a logistical drain on South Africa, but Mozambique was just across the border and destabilization was a simple question of training and supply from northern Transvaal. Matsangaíssa had been replaced by his deputy, Afonso Dhlakama, another graduate of the Frelimo reeducation camps. In 1980 Renamo was a fighting force of one thousand. Under the aegis of South Africa, this number began to increase. So did Renamo's area of operations, for units could now move with impunity across the common border with South Africa, opening fronts in the south. Malawi too began to serve as a rear base. Before long Renamo was operating in most of the country, especially the drought-prone central provinces, and Frelimo was unable to meet the challenge.

In 1984, four years after Pretoria inherited Renamo, Machel and the South African president, P. W. Botha, signed a nonaggression pact. There would be no ANC bases in Mozambique; in return, South Africa would wash its hands of Renamo. But a year and a half later, when Renamo's center at Gorongosa was overrun, captured documents showed clearly that Pretoria was still supporting the rebels. From then on, it became harder to know the extent of South Africa's involvement. The deeper Mozambique slid into ruin, the smaller the incentive to run a destabilization program in the country. Machel was killed in a plane crash in 1986—further evidence, to some, of South African subterfuge—and when Joaquim Chissano took his place, Pretoria's ambitions in Mozambique were all but realized. Frelimo had ceased to pose either an ideological or a logistical threat to South Africa. As a government it was ineffectual; it sheltered only a handful of anti-apartheid elements, its Marxism-Leninism was a thing of the past, its army was in pitiful shape, its people were desperate and it was begging for help. It only remained for South Africa to step in for a stake in its future as Mozambique became a tangle of foreign credit lines.

In Maputo, Renamo was thought of purely as an instrument of South African aggression with no real popular base. On the face of it, this was plausible. Even if the war dragged on long after Pretoria had officially reduced its support, this could be explained by the fact that elements of the South African military were still willing to help the rebels. Most probably they continued to do so even after de Klerk took office. Besides, Renamo had been so lovingly oiled by Pretoria at the outset that even when the clutch was disengaged the thing was sure to coast for some time. Nor was Pretoria the only backer; donations came from expropriated Portuguese in Portugal and South Africa. Ideologically, Renamo won approval from right-wing conservatives in the West; it also received money from extremist religious groups in the United States. One Renamo defector alleged that the rebels had been given one million Deutschmarks by the West German secret service during the 1980s.

In 1988, the U.S. State Department published a damning report on Renamo that announced that the movement could well be responsible for 100,000 civilian deaths. The object of this exercise was to preempt the Renamo lobby in Washington and ensure that the Reagan administration provided no aid. Robert Gersony's research pointed to what he called "extremely high levels of abuse"; Renamo was well organized and murderous; it put slave labor to work in the fields and raised taxes—often collected by the old *régulos*—and indulged in "systematic forced portering, beatings, rape, looting, burning of villages, abductions and mutilations." In other words it was orchestrating a terror in Mozambique. Yet the figure of 100,000 deaths was a mystery. If the 170 families questioned in the report, who had fled during a two-year period, could provide eyewitness accounts of 600 killings and there were over 200,000 refugee and displaced families in total, the number of deaths might well have been twice as high. Two years later the Mozambican government gave the overall figure as 550,000.

The Gersony report successfully scotched Renamo's hopes of U.S. funding, but it furnished no clues about the psychology of the movement. In Washington Renamo responded with an angry rebuttal. "Anyone who knows the theory of guerrilla warfare knows that guerrillas depend on the support of the people. . . . Frelimo and its Marxist allies have embarked on a systematic programme [of] pseudo-guerrilla operations and massacres to discredit Renamo politically in the international media and to alienate the populace from Renamo and destroy Renamo rural support base." The document suggested that Renamo found it hard to make a coherent case. Gersony had argued, on the basis of his research, that it had done no better in the bush. "The refugees," he observed, "report virtually no effort by Renamo to explain to the civilians the purpose of the insurgency, its proposed program or its aspirations."

▲

For most Mozambicans travel was an immense problem. Renamo had turned many of the roads into death traps, but in a country of more than 300,000 square miles, people were obliged to travel in order to look for markets or to get relatives to hospital, or simply to make their way to a place where there might be relief grain. Foreigners were strenuously discouraged by the Ministry of Information from traveling by road or rail. To protest that thousands did so was useless. The answer was invariably the same: "You are not Mozambican."

Renamo took a dim view of mechanical motion. Afonso Dhlakama buzzed around his bush headquarters on a little motorbike, but that was exceptional. The Matsangas used no armored carriers, no tanks, nothing of that kind. They went about their business on foot, regarding anything that worked by internal combustion as a fair target, no matter who or what was in it. Having no use for vehicles themselves, their work was primarily destructive. The roads and railways of Mozambique were Renamo's broadsheets. Here the rebels scrawled their objections to Frelimo in a profane vocabulary of sabotaged track, upturned railway carriages, burned-out pickups and crumpled cars, at a tremendous cost to the government and aid agencies, and to the many people who were forced to travel.

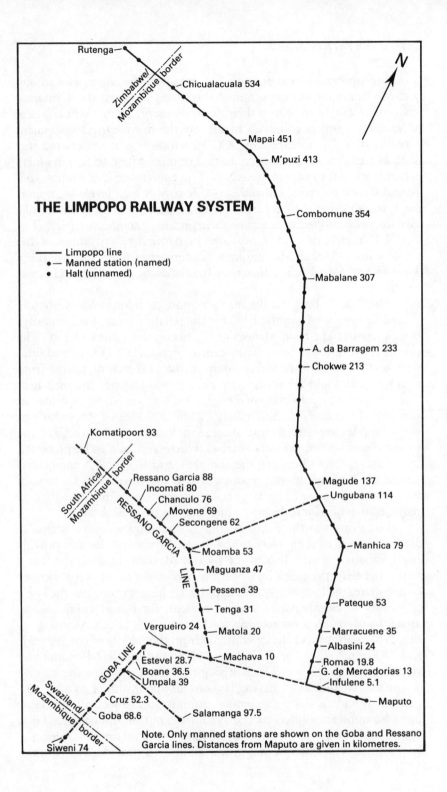

THE LIMPOPO RAILWAY SYSTEM

—— Limpopo line
●— Manned station (named)
● Halt (unnamed)

Rutenga—

Zimbabwe/
Mozambique border

—Chicualacuala 534

—Mapai 451

—M'puzi 413

—Combomune 354

—Mabalane 307

—A. da Barragem 233
—Chokwe 213

Komatipoort 93

South Africa/
Mozambique border

Ressano Garcia 88
Incomati 80
Chanculo 76
Movene 69
Secongene 62

RESSANO GARCIA

LINE

—Magude 137
—Ungubana 114

—Manhica 79

—Moamba 53
—Maguanza 47
—Pessene 39
—Tenga 31

Vergueiro 24
—Matola 20

GOBA LINE

Estevel 28.7
Boane 36.5
Umpala 39

—Machava 10

—Pateque 53

—Marracuene 35
—Albasini 24
—Romao 19.8
—G. de Mercadorias 13
—Infulene 5.1

Cruz 52.3
Goba 68.6

Swaziland/
Mozambique border

—Salamanga 97.5

—Maputo

Siweni 74

Note. Only manned stations are shown on the Goba and Ressano Garcia lines. Distances from Maputo are given in kilometres.

Transportation was an issue that involved the region as a whole, and Mozambique was important to the strategy of several neighboring states that sought to reduce their dependence on South Africa. There were nine member countries in the Southern African Development Coordination Conference (SADCC). Pretoria was at undeclared war with two of them and at liberty to raid or otherwise interfere in others when it wished to harass the ANC. The conference had a tough rhetorical stance on apartheid and was able to win high levels of support for transportation projects from foreign donors, especially those, like Britain, who wished to improve their profile in southern Africa. The SADCC members, and Zimbabwe in particular, saw three of the railway lines through Mozambique as alternatives to the long routes to Durban and Port Elizabeth, where freight costs were high and tariffs exorbitant.

The Nacala line was the northernmost corridor in Mozambique. There was money from the EEC for the rehabilitation of this railway, which led straight from Malawi to Nacala on the Indian Ocean. The north, however, was beset with security problems and the rehabilitation had made little headway, despite the presence of troops from SADCC states and a British mercenary force, Defence Systems Ltd. Another corridor consisting of a road, a railway and an oil pipeline cut through the center of the country, from the edge of Zimbabwe to Beira, and was mostly secure. A large multinational, Lonrho, ran the pipeline and several projects nearby, which were said to be protected by an arrangement between the company and Renamo. Nonetheless, thousands of Zimbabwean troops guarded the corridor and a kind of buffer had been created by large resettlement centers that brought this narrow strip of Mozambique to life, despite periodic attacks.

The third was the Limpopo line, a single-track railway of some 540 kilometers running close to the South African border and providing Zimbabwe with a link to the port of Maputo. In theory it was a better bet than the Beira line. With no major curves or steep inclines to negotiate, the locomotives could pull a far bigger train. But the line's proximity to South Africa was a problem, for it was vulnerable to attack by Renamo units moving freely across the South African border. Although it was fully operational from the middle of the 1950s, it had fallen into disrepair during the 1970s, and by 1982 Renamo had shut it down altogether. The British government was now the leading donor for rehabilitation, having laid out an initial sum of roughly $15 million. It had also made a nominal commitment to security by training Mozambican soldiers at the Nyanga camp in Zimbabwe. They would still need regular supplies of food and equipment, which the Republic of Mozambique might not be able to provide. A firm near

London had won a lucrative engineering contract, the soldiers trained in Zimbabwe would guard the line and the whole well-publicized procedure would do something to compensate for Britain's refusal to impose sanctions against South Africa.

For the Mozambican government the benefits of handing over the Limpopo line to an assortment of foreign donors led by Britain were obvious. The rehabilitation, which was under way by 1987, was not in the interests of South Africa: it stood to lose revenue from the passage of Zimbabwean freight through Maputo and thus had every incentive to see the project disrupted. Frelimo would be powerless to stop this, but the British commitment was sure to make Pretoria think matters over before it let Renamo loose on the line.

To get a trip on the railway from Maputo was difficult. The funding for the rehabilitation was made over to Mozambican Railways, who had contracted two companies for the work. Mott, Hay & Anderson were the British firm—it was normal for a donor country to repatriate a portion of its aid budget in this way. A competent business with an excellent record, Mott was responsible for repairs at the southern end of the line, from Maputo up, in conjunction with a department of Mozambican Railways. The second contract was awarded to National Railways of Zimbabwe (NRZ), who were to start at the Zimbabwean border and move down. In theory the two companies and their personnel would meet somewhere in the middle and celebrate the completion of the first phase of the project. However, progress from the southern end was slow. Mozambique was a difficult place to work in, and nearer the frontier with South Africa the fragile jurisdiction of the capital held little sway.

I made my way to Bulawayo, in Zimbabwe, at the beginning of winter in the hope that I could travel from there to the border and down into Mozambique on the Limpopo railway. Bulawayo was the headquarters for NRZ's operation in Mozambique; it was populated by Zimbabwean railway staff with a fiercely proprietorial attitude toward the line. For them, every meter of track they revitalized was a snub to Renamo, a jibe at Pretoria and a laugh at the expense of Mozambique, which they saw as a basket case.

The assistant general manager of NRZ cleared my visit to the line. Joe Strachan was a civil engineer in his mid-fifties who had left Scotland in 1971 to work for Rhodesia Railways. A year later the armed struggle became a serious military threat to minority rule. This thoughtful citizen of Aberdeen worked on the track in Rhodesia for the rest of the decade, taking the same risks as his staff, out at night repairing sabotage and running the guerrilla gauntlet. "We learned to repair a blow-up in half an hour," he remembered, "while the worst derailment—and we had some bad ones—used to take us twelve hours at the most to put right." Now he lived in an African democracy and defended its interests with a modicum of loyalty. He was an able character with a developed sense of duty, praising the Limpopo project to any journalist who cared to listen.

In his office, Strachan introduced me to his plant and renewals officer, with whom I was to travel. Joe Mayers was a stout man from Bulawayo whose eyes lay in his huge head like slashes of charcoal; he was Strachan's principal source of information about daily progress on the Limpopo line. He was a curious kind of racial hybrid known in Matabeleland as a Bulawayo Arab. Mayers had worked on the permanent way for twenty-eight years. It was his passion in life. He traveled regularly from Rutenga to the border station at Chicualacuala, where he would proceed south along the line in a self-propelled armored trolley, inspecting the track and offering encouragement to his repair teams, who worked throughout the year in difficult conditions.

We stopped over in Rutenga that night in a comfortable house by the sidings. Mayers had been joined by two other NRZ men, both from Bulawayo, and cut from the same coarse cloth as the plant and renewals officer. At supper, they received word by phone of an incident across the border. Renamo had attacked an armored car patrolling the dirt road that ran parallel with the railway. There were no deaths, but a Zimbabwean officer had been wounded in the stomach. Mayers stayed up late that night, talking to the others, drinking prodigal quantities of beer and gin. I woke around five next morning. He had already been up for over an hour, preparing his paperwork for the day. After breakfast we left by diesel trolley for Chicualacuala, with two Zimbabwean soldiers riding escort. Light drizzle was falling on the railway and a pair of impala were drinking from a watering hole near the frontier. Mayers took this to be a good sign. "If the animals are coming to the water, Renamo must have gone." The insurgents had been operating in a minor but irksome way inside Zimbabwe for a year now and the last twenty kilometers to the border had become unsafe.

Mayers spent the morning in Chicualacuala, at the old colonial station, organizing the army and the staff to leave at dawn the following day. His teams were already working eight kilometers south at Mapai, but he hoped to go another hundred kilometers to Combomune to assess the state of the track. The Zimbabweans had fulfilled their initial commitment to repair the northernmost sixty kilometers of the line two months earlier. Their contract had promptly been renewed and now they were pressing on with a target of twenty kilometers a month. As matters stood in Mozambique—and at the Maputo end of the project they were standing very still indeed—the Zimbabweans believed that if the donors and Mozambican Railways were serious about the railway, NRZ would have to carry on to within eighty kilometers of the coast.

Joe Strachan and the others called this "going for the prawns." Even before independence, Mozambique had exercised a deep attraction for Rhodesians, who had no access of their own to the sea. The drive for a rail link to the Mozambican coast was as strong in those days as it was now; so was the wish to avoid the costs of running freight through South Africa. Accordingly, the Rhodesians negotiated with the Portuguese, who began to extend the Limpopo railway from Lourenço Marques, as the capital was then known, toward the Rhodesian border. Sir Arthur Griffin, chairman of the board of Rhodesia Railways, had hoped to strike a bargain with South Africa for an alternative route, but after several meetings he reported back to his colleagues that he had been unable to wrest concessions from the Boers in return for the obvious advantages that a Rhodesian rail link to the Transvaal would have given them. The following year, 1955, the Limpopo line was ready and the first goods train left Bulawayo for Lourenço Marques.

Mayers was on the platform of Chicualacuala station before sunrise. Three armor-plated railcars, known as Cougars, sat on the track at the far end of the station. They were sinister gray-green contraptions, flanked with metal cages, which had done sterling service during the Rhodesian war. A pale electric light bathed the station but it was still dark and chilly. Mayers and his two colleagues stamped their feet on the ground; their breath hung in the air around them, mingling with the diesel fumes from the elderly railcars. Mayers was muttering already because the army escort was late. "Like lambs to slaughter," he said with a mixture of amusement and impatience. "How are you ever going to win a war if you have to wake up the army?" A gray dawn began to saturate the darkness. Within minutes a handful of soldiers had appeared from a camp behind the sidings and we were on our way.

The railcars were like large metal vats, surrounded by a steel grille. Each seated half a dozen people. There were no windows apart from a small aperture of reinforced glass for the driver. A gap between the roof and the rest of the car enabled the soldiers to survey the surrounding bush. From Chicualacuala the track was perfect for sixty kilometers and the bush had been cleared back. About fifteen kilometers from the station, the line ran under two parallel rows of pylons striding down to the Transvaal from the big hydroelectric station at Cahora Bassa, way to the north. It was here that Renamo was believed to cross to and from South Africa. Mayers's two colleagues from Bulawayo, Peter and John, claimed that at night the insurgents moved over the track like columns of ants. By day they kept an indolent watch on the railway, attacking it when they saw fit. Where the scrub began, so, in effect, did Renamo. Hour after hour, the track crews scrutinized the bush and it returned their gaze with hostile monotony.

After little more than an hour the going grew rickety. In places the wooden ties had rotted away until they were barely distinguishable from the rich topsoil of the Limpopo valley. High temperatures and sporadic rains made maintenance crucial and the line had been neglected for years now. For twenty kilometers or more the rails were like thread stretched over a shallow gully of mulch. Now and then they gave out a plaintive creaking as the three railcars lumbered over them. No work had been done on this section. Some of the two hundred men that Mayers had based in Mapai were working their way back up, but they would not be here for another fortnight at least.

The railcars drew to a halt at an encampment of Zimbabwean military. Mayers and the soldiers who were with us got down and whistled. Slowly the men emerged from the trees in twos and threes, with blankets and spare cuts of webbing drawn around their shoulders to keep out the cold. They looked frail and insubstantial, like spirits issuing from the soil in memory of an earlier war. For many years the guerrillas of the Zimbabwe African National Union (ZANU) had fought for independence on this very ground, hiding, moving, attacking, retreating, living from hand to mouth. Now, as a national army, the Zimbabweans were back, protecting their railway workers by arrangement with Frelimo. The soldiers came to life as sacks of meal and a package of meat were unloaded from the front trolley. The remains of the ambushed armored car, about which Mayers had heard in Rutenga, lay on a sandy rise to the right of the track.

Further down the line, at Mapai, shell fire had spooned out chunks of masonry and concrete from the buildings around the station. Again it was the old war, Ian Smith's war, that had left these marks—hot pursuit had pushed ZANU guerrillas right down here and occasionally further. Dozens of young Zimbabwean track workers in bright yellow outfits were working on the outskirts of the station, laying continuously welded rail. An aged crucible blazed white-hot over a join. The gangs threw molten metal into the grass, starting small fires that gradually cleared the vegetation back. We waited while they clamped down two sections of old rail and eased us over the groaning track. Mayers got down and spoke with the foreman. The Zimbabweans were all high-school graduates who had volunteered for the work.

We passed several settlements on the way down to Combomune. Children draped with bright cloth picked their way over the cold ground and gray cattle stood placidly in wooden pens under the trees. Now that units of the Zimbabwean army were moving up and down the line a brisk trade had begun to develop between the soldiers and the local people. In what Mayers believed was the biggest deal, a Zimbabwean officer had bought a Suzuki motorcycle in Mapai for four hundred kilograms of sugar. Not everyone liked the Zimbabwean army; it had a reputation for carrying out forced removals and was suspected of spreading HIV. But Renamo was at its most brutal in the south, simply because the south was the Frelimo heartland. The Zimbabweans may have seemed a better option. They brought defense and a return to some semblance of normal life.

The track beyond Mapai was semicharted territory for Mayers and the others. When we arrived in Combomune many people gathered around the railcars and Mayers strode about the platform giving instructions. It would not be long before the rehabilitation reached the town. We were running late by the time he had finished his business. The dusk was already gathering as the railcars were turned around and the inspection team began the journey home; we had only been two hours in Combomune, but while we were there Renamo had set fire to a block of ties twenty kilometers north of the station and crept away to observe us on our return. You could see the smoke rising from about a kilometer off. We took the stretch at speed, pounding over the smoldering track and on without incident. After nightfall, however, the Cougars began to fail and Mayers had to bring them back in a series of towing and shunting operations until the worst breakdown, two kilometers from the power lines, brought us to a halt. It was pitch dark under an overcast sky as John and Peter repaired the last of the crippled railcars by flashlight with the soldiers deployed on the ballast inclines.

"The new generation just watches the clock," said Mayers back in Chicualacuala after a few drinks. "They've washed their hands by lunchtime and they're ready to leave." He was joking, but it was obvious that he thought of himself and his two friends as the last of the real railwaymen—and that is how they were remembered. By early summer all three men had been killed on the permanent way.

▲

I visited Mozambique three years later in 1991. On the face of it, much had changed. Frelimo had drafted a new constitution and was planning to hold multiparty elections; four new parties were hawking their wares around Maputo and Beira. Direct negotiations had opened in Rome between the government and Renamo, but the insurgency was not confident of its chances in a democratic election. At the talks it played a spoiling game; in the countryside it stepped up its attacks wherever it could. The change in Mozambique was thus one of mood rather than substance. Frelimo was sincere enough in its wish for peace and a new democratic experiment, but war was still the real authority in the land.

Even President Chissano agreed that Renamo was no longer subsidized by the government of the new South Africa; Mandela was free, there was a constitutional settlement in the air. Yet the insurgents had arms in abundance, an effective, centralized command structure and no shortage of admirers south of the Limpopo, including people who were willing to enter Mozambique and bargain with Dhlakama about the security of the power lines that ran down from Cahora Bassa to the South African grid.

Tie by tie, the Limpopo railway was edging forward, but the political ballast of the project had shifted. South Africa was no longer an overtly hostile force in Mozambique. Indeed it was now an avuncular well-wisher with a myriad of business interests in Maputo and a concern for the future of its neighbor. Having invested millions of rand in the upgrading of Maputo port—a sign that it viewed the city as the natural seaboard outlet of the northern Transvaal—it was no longer keen to see the Limpopo project vandalized.

Extensive migrant labor to South Africa throughout the war had maintained informal ties between tens of thousands of Mozambicans and the apartheid state; it was nonetheless hard for Frelimo to accept that a fund of goodwill was now on offer from the country that had done it such harm. The people involved in the Limpopo project had always played down South Africa's role in the sabotage business and they were evidently confident that Renamo, on its own, would not prevent a full track rehabilitation. However, there was now a "third phase" where originally only two had been envisaged. Mott, Hay & Anderson, the company from London contracted to repair the southern end of the line, had rebuilt the concrete tie factory in Maputo but it was plagued by theft. Up to ninety tons of cement might disappear from the factory in a day. This had delayed progress. So had the lack of military escorts, for many of Frelimo's crack troops from Nyanga camp, the British training center in Zimbabwe, were now wandering around in rags looking for food. Like every foreign enterprise in Mozambique, NRZ—which had gone into debt to finance its initial work on the project—had seen its contract extended; so too had Mott.

I was eager to set eyes on the railway now that so much progress appeared to have been made. There was talk of a train going up from Maputo to Chokwe loaded with fines, a dusty grit used to raise the track before ballast was laid. But the train was not supposed to leave without an escort and for several days now the military had failed to arrive. Mozambican Railways advised me to wait for a light plane bound for Chokwe, where the engineers were based that month. I asked instead to travel by rail and Mott arranged to put me on the fines train one morning at dawn. If it didn't leave, there was a company truck setting out a few hours later. It too was meant to have an escort. It would go up the road toward Xai-Xai for seventy-five miles and then bear off to Chokwe.

The fines train did not materialize and so at around eight in the morning I was shown to an old but serviceable Leyland truck parked outside the station. It was loaded with welding kits. An elderly, bleary-eyed man in a woollen hat was perched on top with a bundle of sugar cane by his side. "That'll be your escort," said the representative from Mott, pointing up at him, "because I can tell you the army is not going to show." The old boy grinned and raised one hand to his hat. Fifteen minutes later, we drew out of the square and made for the road to Xai-Xai.

The driver's name was Matsinhe. He thought it comic that I should be traveling by road. "*Avião!*" he kept saying with a finger pointed up into the sky, in case I missed his drift. He stopped the truck in the gloomy suburb of G. M. Dimitrov on business of his own and then we were moving up to Marracuene in top gear at about forty miles an hour. Two soldiers tried to flag a lift but Matsinhe bore down on them, hooting and scowling, and drove them back onto the shoulder. We seemed to eat up the road to Marracuene and for the next few miles we were following the railway. Running beside us, the permanent way was a comforting sight, the profile of the dark rails riding up on the ballast and driving north, honorably, imperturbably, through a plain of desolation.

Beyond Marracuene the land began to open up. We passed a child flying a rag kite by a cemetery wall splashed with bougainvillea and after that, scarcely a soul. For some time we ran along the Incomati River, past the incinerated shell of a health clinic and on up the edge of the valley. Slowly the road began to deteriorate until it brought us down to a crawl. Matsinhe banged the base of his palm on the chipped steering wheel and swept the horizon with his free hand: "Very dangerous," he shouted above the roar of the engine. "*Muito, muito bandidos.*" I looked around at the old man perched on the welding kits. He was working his way through a segment of crisp white cane.

Matsinhe's spirits began to drop from now on, and mine with them, although there was some relief to be had from the trickle of other vehicles traveling in both directions. There were wrecks in the culverts too, burned and riddled, but they looked old. After an hour we came to an army base, passing through a roadblock manned by a group of disheveled soldiers. Matsinhe took them on the move, waving through the open window, laughing, fast-talking, all the while edging stealthily forward in first. Once we were clear he shook his head from side to side and moved up quickly through the gears. The surface had improved and the road was fringed with fertile but untended plots, beyond the reach of their owners now, like vessels cut loose from their moorings by the war and left to drift.

Matsinhe slowed down for the next roadblock—six hungry soldiers around a rusted oil drum from which a red flag on a stick protruded. A bit of string lay across the road and one of them hoisted it in front of us. Matsinhe negotiated on the move again, but as he pushed at the string, easing, edging, fobbing off the soldiers with his patter, the tail of the truck caught on the oil drum and pulled it over. A youngster in a forage hat yelled at him to stop. Matsinhe nudged on. The soldier leveled his weapon and screamed. He came flailing forward, shouting, until he reached the cab. He tried to open the door and brandish the gun at the same time, fulminating. Matsinhe wedged a piece of wood under the handbrake, left the engine running and got down from the cab. The youngster took him by the collar and dragged him away. His comrades stood back as he drew an automatic and prepared to whip Matsinhe with the butt. Matsinhe was smiling and making his excuses. He waved his hands here and there until at length the other soldiers surrounded the young man, catching at his arm, but he continued to yell. Matsinhe stepped up to the oil drum with a dignified air and set it back on its base. He retrieved the flag and placed it deferentially in the nozzle. He took a pace back, surveyed it for two seconds and stepped forward again to adjust it. Then he skipped toward the truck, smiling and waving. He was already at the wheel when the youngster broke loose and ran to the cab, staring up at him with tired, vengeful eyes.

Matsinhe knocked the wood from under the handbrake. After a few seconds he began to curse. One hundred yards down the road he spat out of the window with furious contempt and slammed his hands down on the steering wheel. He turned and swore at our elderly escort through the back window of the cab and then he looked at me. "Eh!" he shouted, "avião, avião!"

We passed a wall inscribed with a Frelimo slogan: "Long live the alliance of workers and peasants." By way of response, a few minutes further on, a wrecked car and an upturned bus lay by the side of the road under the scorched branches of a cashew. Two pickups overtook us at frenetic speed, and once they were out of sight there was no more traffic for half an hour. Matsinhe's anger had given way to a nervous attention. "Bad, bad, bad," he said, gesturing around the landscape, "Matsanga." Yet there was nothing more in the way of wreckage, just a bare road flanked by a line of telegraph poles with the wires cut.

Ten more minutes and he was a happy man. He beamed and patted me on the shoulder. We had entered a long stretch of guarded road. From now on, there was a commando perched on the narrow crossbeam of every third telegraph pole, scanning the land to our west. These were some of the best trained soldiers Frelimo had to offer, and they were a welcome sight, squatting at the top of the poles like birds of good omen.

By the time we reached Macia, the commandos had thinned away and the poles were bare again. There was one more checkpoint, run by a surly policeman and a young inquisitor whom Matsinhe dispatched with ease. From here on, most of the culverts contained wrecks; shaded paths, like the back alleys of a threatening city, led off from the road into the fields, and Matsinhe was steeped in anxiety again. He revived at the sight of a newly ambushed British Petroleum tanker with a soldier standing by its side. A mile beyond, there were three more soldiers sitting on the shoulder as a haulage crew with a mobile crane recovered a pickup. Suspended from the pulley by its tail end, the car turned slowly in the air while the crew stopped work to watch us pass. Renamo had made its mark on this part of the country. Thousands of dollars' worth of damage littered the road. The troops on long-term duty between Maputo and Chokwe were not a reassuring sight and a man like Matsinhe had much to fear from both sides in this conflict. So too did the people of the province. It was unsafe to travel and impossible to farm.

"The people," said an old party slogan on a wall in Chokwe, "are the builders of their own destiny." Mozambique was full of similar graffiti, part prayer, part decoration, some of them quite specific. "Comrades, let us change the meaning of VALUE!" or "Let us build a state apparatus in the service of the edification of socialism." Now they looked like atavistic scratchings, reminders of a culture whose odd enthusiasms and alien transpositions had failed to take root. It had flourished briefly but intensely. The inscriptions it had left behind often suggested a certain refinement—a preference for "The Eighteenth Brumaire" over the complete works of Kim Il Sung, but now these little texts showed a chaste disregard for the social chaos spreading around them.

There were tens of thousands of displaced people in the district flooding the modest town to capacity, and the track engineers lived in two railway carriages—a restaurant car and a sleeper—in a siding near the aid stores. It was a good place to observe the state of things in Chokwe, for every morning a dozen very thin children would deploy through the archway and start to pilfer from the grain-stuffed wagons between the two rows of warehouses. Each boy had a stick and a plastic bag. He would slip the stick between the wooden slats of the wagon, puncture a sack of corn, then jiggle rapidly, eliciting a pale yellow cataract of emergency food aid from the bottom of the vehicle, beneath which an open bag was held. This incensed the watchmen, who carried sticks of their own and loped around in pursuit of the gang. The children were delighted by the chase, for they were as bored as the watchmen were sluggish, but there was an element of risk in the game, since capture was always possible and resulted in a beating.

If the children were part of the disorder, they were also a great improvement on the passive, downtrodden icons of televised African emergencies. Not that Chokwe was a hive of self-esteem. A large shantytown had spread along its northern outskirts and most of the inhabitants were very poor. But there were good vegetables in the market, grown within the security zone, and there was a firewood racket run by the railway staff and soldiers, who would strip the forests further north and return with whole truckloads. Musty bundles of flared trousers, platform shoes and wide-collared shirts, sent to Mozambique by charitable persons in the West, were on sale in the square beside the market.

I shared the railway carriages with five men: Ismael Momina, a young and rather fragile Mozambican bridge technician; Ray, a hulk of a track inspector from Bulawayo who had worked for the NRZ with Joe Mayers; Carlos, an engineer from Venezuela, roughly half Ray's size; and John Ryan, another thick-set engineer, who had lately given up his job as supervisor of the line from Waterford to Limerick Junction, County Cork. The fifth was Joe Strachan.

Strachan bade me welcome and fetched some cans of Lion lager from the fridge of the restaurant car. Mozambique was awash with beer from South Africa. "Aye," said Strachan, "it's Lion country now." We turned gingerly to the subject of Joe Mayers's death. He told me that Mayers and the others had been speeding home in a Cougar after a major track inspection when they were derailed. They had all been killed. The track had been washed away by heavy rain but the stupidity of it was that this had happened north of Chicualacuala, in the relative safety of Zimbabwe. Ray said he thought Renamo had got wind of the inspection and had planned an ambush, hence the hurry. Everyone had his own embellishments but, in any case, the fact that Mayers and his colleagues had made it back over the Zimbabwean border added to the poignancy of their deaths.

Joe Strachan had changed sides since our last meeting, leaving the NRZ and signing up with Mott as chief bridge engineer. "I'm not as young as I was," he explained, "and I've no hard currency savings." He was planning for his retirement, after a grand career across the border. He had a bluff pessimism about Mozambique. "I'll tell you," he said, "there'll never be peace here." To him, the conflict had become an uncontrollable cycle of banditry. The sides no longer mattered; hunger was the only real concern and policy was a makeshift thing determined by whoever carried a weapon. "Oh aye," he said about South Africa, "those buggers have a lot to answer for, but you see, it was a mess here from the moment the Portuguese left, and even before."

Strachan had survived fourteen years of war in Rhodesia without a scratch. No sooner had he moved to Maputo, however, than he was shot through the thigh on his way to the Limpopo line by helicopter. It still needled him to think about it. "Some miserable little bugger," he said, "some drunken *bandido* from Christ knows where must have heard the helicopter, stuck his weapon out of the bush and taken a pot shot." Strachan was rushed to South Africa for surgery but there was no point trying to remove the bullet; it was lodged way up in his midriff. A year or more on now, he had made a good recovery.

There was no security in Mozambique, Ismael complained, which was why these things happened. Strachan seemed to think the army as much of a liability as Renamo. After all, who fired at his helicopter? Someone with a gun, someone who was bored, hungry, resentful, as any soldier would be after a year in this inhospitable place. Carlos recalled a journey back to Maputo with the Nyanga crack troops. It was dusk some way out of Magude when the soldiers opened fire from their armored wagon and the passengers hit the floor, suspecting a Renamo attack. The target was meat, however. They had spotted a trio of cattle and emptied their guns. "They stopped the train," said Carlos, "they ran down to the cattle and carried them back on their heads, four to a cow. Then they lifted them over the edge of the wagon and used their bayonets to divide the meat."

The time had come, everyone agreed, for the Nyanga troops to go on "refreshers." By now they were more trouble than they were worth and the engineers were better off working the track without escorts. Even with South Africa's newfound magnanimity, this was a risk, because Renamo still attacked the railway. Whether escorts made much difference was debatable. A year earlier Renamo had attacked a supply train between Chokwe and Magude. An impromptu escort had been present but two of the soldiers and a track worker were killed.

In all the sleeping compartments there were black-and-white photos of the old Lourenço Marques screwed to the walls above the couchettes. Sleep in a motionless railway carriage is almost impossible. The body waits with sacrificial patience for the signal to succumb: a brisk jolt forward, a screech of wheels, and then the sedative, rocking motion that will spread oblivion across five hundred miles or more. But the hours dragged on in the stifling little town. I tried to imagine it as a curt change in the rhythm of a night express, a blur of buildings slumbering in peace as they receded behind the guard's van—a kind of Market Harborough. But there was no guard's van and definitely no locomotive. In Mozambique rail transportation was a thing of the past and a dream of the future.

The next morning Strachan planned to go down with the work train to Kilometer 186—locations on the track were designated in this way—but it failed to leave Chokwe on time. We drove the twenty-five kilometers or so in a Land Rover, cutting down off the road after Leonde and making our way through the bush along a network of dirt tracks that led to the railway. Rows of gray cement ties had been laid out ready for work and on one side of the line was a small clearing where a bulldozer had leveled the ground. Renamo was active twenty kilometers south but they could move up the line if the urge took them, so machinery could not be left overnight. Bringing a bulldozer down on the work train and loading it on at the end of the day cost valuable time. From Renamo's point of view, this was all to the good.

The threat to the physical plant, like the threat to human life, imposed precautions on the project. The insurgents had presence down to a fine art. All they had to do was cling to the bush like some obscure species, emerging now and then to shed blood or tamper with a stretch of track. Yet the railway seemed to braid a strange goodness into the ground, or so I fancied. In spite of stories to the contrary, I was sure that no real harm could come to anybody here. For the next few days, until my return to Maputo, I moved up and down the line without a care in the world. It was clear too that the further the rehabilitation crept out of Chokwe, the more confidence it gave to Mozambicans living along the corridor.

The morning got under way with the arrival of the works train. After an hour or so, people began to emerge from nearby villages, settling down to watch for the day as the gangs heaved new ties into position, wrenched up the old ones and hauled the quivering sections of rail into place. Gradually the blue sky above the railway filled with a symphonic tinkling and thudding. Carlos, John and Joe Strachan were sorting out some concrete decks for a bridge repair a little up the track. Ismael was resolving, or perhaps compounding, a dispute between a foreman and two workers over the chant to be sung as they keyed up a stretch of rail with their crowbars. Ray, meanwhile, was everywhere. Whistling and cursing, he stormed about in a white cloth hat, adjusting ties with a thrust of the arm and nudging with his boot at the singing steel as the teams brought up the rails. He was much admired by an audience of bystanders, mainly women, who stretched out in the dust, playing with their children or knotting one another's hair.

Ray, however, was not the only attraction. They were there for the discarded wooden ties, which could be used, or sold, to build or burn. Half a kilometer of wooden ties might be torn up in a good day's track laying and they were highly prized. At first, Mott and Mozambican Railways had decided to run them down to Maputo, sell them and put the proceeds back into the project. When news of this plan reached the army, its habitual stupor gave way to a passionate enthusiasm for escort duty. The detachments were even oversubscribed. In due course, a well-guarded train set off for Maputo, several of its cars groaning with wooden ties. It took a couple of days to reach the capital and when it did the ties were gone. The train had made every plausible stop along the way and the soldiers had sold the ties straight off the cars.

Then the track gangs decided to cut themselves in. A little mafia developed, lining up the best ties for a select group of women, who soon began appearing by the track dressed for the Kings Road, circa 1967, in floral skirts and tunics with velvet cuffs, all from the mountains of Western castoffs that were selling steadily in the Chokwe market. The arrangements had since become more random. As the works train prepared to pull out at the end of the day, dozens of women simply rose to their feet and set off to bag the finest ties. They worked in groups, two lifting the quarry onto the head of a third, who would then make off toward the nearest settlement, a mile away, with her tremendous burden reared above her.

When we got back to Chokwe, Strachan was happy and so was Ray. Kilometer 186 was looking good. Ismael had found a piece of dried fish and ordered the cooks in the restaurant car to prepare it. Carlos, dressed in a turquoise T-shirt, spotless white shorts, white socks and sneakers, wanted to head for Kloob, one of the nightspots that now graced Chokwe, and mingle with the girls.

Kloob occupied one corner of a large complex, probably conceived as a shopping center, around which ran a covered walkway with crumbling cement pillars. From the car it looked as though the floor of this scruffy colonnade was strewn with empty sacks, but as we pulled up, three pairs of eyes appeared above the wrinkled piles, blinked in the headlights and disappeared again. Then I could see that the whole complex was full of sleeping people. From the entrance to Kloob down as far as the corner, it was packed with displaced peasants, or those who felt too threatened to sleep on the edge of town. Loud music issued from Kloob, which was empty apart from a few soldiers and some well-dressed women at a table near the wall. The soldiers were demanding drinks on the house.

At the back of the room was a dance floor and behind that a plywood cabin with a dudish disc jockey inside, wrapped like an eel around a tape deck. Gradually Kloob began to fill and Carlos asked one of the women for a dance. Carlos was small and his partner was a solid Shangaan lady, nearly a foot taller. As he took her in his arms for the first slow number of the evening, the other dancers fell back slightly to give the couple space. They moved off together in perfect unison. Occasionally she smiled down at him. Now and then, Carlos craned his head around her stately profile, like an artist carrying a massive sculpture to its plinth. Yet they were the most graceful pair on the floor. Ismael looked on with approval but his face fell when Carlos escorted her back to her own table.

Two young peasant girls in torn clothes came in and took the floor, dancing wildly to a fast disco beat. One of them fell over, the other helped her up and they ran out of the club to their pallets in the colonnade. A few minutes later we left for our couchettes.

Joe Strachan and Ray were riding on the footplate of the blackened loco; the driver was hooting furiously. The train was full of fines—the last of them until the new load came up—and men, about two hundred, in overalls and hard hats, plus the earth-mover, cement ties, bags of cement, fishplates and a small water tanker, maybe fifteen cars in all. Today a bridge would go up across the depression near Kilometer 186.

From Chokwe down as far as the site, much of the track was Phase Two standard, all retied with minimal ballast and sectioned rail. The engineers had set the speed limit for all traffic on this stretch at forty kilometers an hour. At about thirty the loco began romping and seething on the rails. The driver hooted and forged on, somewhat faster now, and on reaching fifty, hooted yet again. Great blasts of defiance shook the dazed countryside. At sixty, several thousand tons of iron and steel began to waft like chiffon half an inch above the flanges. Ray and Strachan were shouting and edging their way up the outside of the loco. Ray yelled in at the driver through the broken window of the cab. The driver grinned back and gave another monstrous blast on the whistle. Hanging on to the side of the loco with one hand, Ray raised the other as if to strike him and slowly the speed decreased.

At the bridge Ismael was waving. He had left Chokwe earlier by road, with a thirteen-ton crane, to lift the concrete decks into place over the culvert. Most of the men went down the line to lay new track, but thirty or forty stayed by the bridge. By ten o'clock the permanent way was buzzing with activity. Gangs of men emptied bags of cement, others hacked back the undergrowth by the bridge, others knocked out the metal clips from the ties and removed the old rails. For an hour the earth-mover was roaring up and down between the cement gang and a water hole at the edge of the bush. It sank its jaw deep into the water, raised it in a flurry of brown spray, turned abruptly and slavered its way back toward the men, who waited with their shovels poised above the gray heaps of dust. The elderly Soviet crane coughed into life and the site began to fill with fumes. Once the rails were off, the old wood-and-concrete structure was knocked away with sledgehammers, leaving six piers between the abutments.

The heat of the sun was cut by the veil of carbons rising from the crane. Slowly but inexorably the decks began to fall into place. Each weighed five tons and required a dozen men to guide it as it swayed from the pulley, another dozen by the piers to ease it down and a gang of men with crowbars to nudge it into alignment. John Ryan darted between the abutments with a level, raced around the piers, leaped onto the decks as they hung in midair, and bellowed in brogue at the men, who performed his obscure bidding by instinct. A celebration of power was under way, in which everyone shared equally, broker and contributor, supervisor and supervised. The sixth sense of the collective took wing, bolts of genius lit up the fog of Stakhanovite filth billowing out of the crane, feats of strength squared the lamentable circle of deficiencies. The bridge was nearing completion.

The final deck was suspended from the crane when the work force came to a standstill as two of its number started to smash the sharp ends of their crowbars into the remains of a stone floor below the piers; first one, with great force, then the other, twisting the end into the broken pavement. A shout went up and a crowd of workers leaped off the bridge to gather around. The two men smashed at the ground again and, as they raised their arms high, the pavement gave a sinister tremor. One of the slabs heaved upward and split to reveal a scaly green back. The crowbar drove down again and a jet of blood splashed across the withered grass. The men wrestled on, one pushing down with his entire weight and the other jabbing furiously. Three adjacent slabs began to rise and crumble.

The cement gang rushed forward to tear up the pavement as the crowbars fell again through a cloud of dry earth and now one of the men was heaving a giant lizard into the air. Speared through the middle of its body, it writhed and spat, lashing at the weapon with its tail. A gloved hand grabbed at it, then another, until one of the workers wrenched it off the crowbar and beat it to death against the platform of the archaic crane. A cheer of delight went up, followed by the hoarse whisper of negotiation, for this was a trophy. There was enough meat on it to feast a tie team. The two champions of the hunt ran back down the train and slung the carcass into a car as John Ryan summoned the others to the rescue of the groaning pulley.

By four the bridge was complete and the men shoveled the last of the precious fines off the wagons, turning white from head to foot as the dust rose about them. When there was none left to pack around the ties on either side of the bridge, the earth-mover jerked into action again, digging mounds of soil out of the ground and bringing them up to the track. The rails were fastened back and Strachan ordered the loco onto the bridge to see how the structure sat. The men were pleased. The driver pulled back and the train prepared to leave for Chokwe.

A few hours later, as we were finishing our meal, Matsinhe came into the restaurant cat. He was in high, almost manic spirits, laughing and a little drunk. He had just brought up another load of welding kits from Maputo in the Leyland truck and had stopped at Macia junction, where he noticed one of his tires was down. Three cars passed him while he changed the wheel, and half an hour later he found them burning ten miles up the road.

Carlos and Ismael took me to another club, a gloomy place with about thirty tables. There was a ninja video in German on the monitor, then an awful war film set in Vietnam. A myriad of bright eyes shone in the darkness beyond the windows of the club, where groups of children gathered to watch. We drank South African beer and then made our way out. There was a young soldier in the doorway, paralytic, begging for another drink. He had been trained at Nyanga but had lost the distinctive beret. Instead a blue synthetic feather boa hung from his neck, one end knotted in a festive tangle around his rifle. He swayed under the lintel of the club door and cursed our lack of generosity.

We were woken later that night by the sound of tanks moving about and mortar rounds landing at the edge of town. Then the fighting seemed to degenerate into crazy bursts of small-arms fire somewhere to the south. I let up the blind of the marooned *wagon-lit* and stared out at the sidings. The sky was clear but the moon had dropped out of sight, leaving a belt of faint yellow light behind the town. In the entrance to the warehouse the guards were fast asleep.

Not a lot could be done until the fresh supply of fines arrived from Maputo. Five days had elapsed and there was still no sign of it. The work force embarked on another bridge repair but the energy seemed to have drained out of them. By midafternoon the bridge was only halfway up. There were fewer men on the site today, as a lot of them had registered sick, which was the same as taking a rest. The last shift had been a triumph; everyone had been happy; the workers had seen exactly what they were capable of and it had so impressed them that they were sitting out the next round.

They might well enjoy a sublime sense of common purpose with the supervisors while everyone toiled together, like monks rebuilding an immense cloister, but their conditions of work were deplorable, and when they retired to meditate on the successes of the day this cannot have failed to strike them. Their wages were better than the army's, but Strachan reckoned a month's pay was worth about sixty loaves of bread. He called it a disgrace.

In theory, the work force did not have to buy bread, since they were fed by Mozambican Railways, at three times the cost of engaging their labor, but the food supply was unreliable, because it was the responsibility of the army, which naturally set some of it aside for its own use. One answer would have been to see that the army was properly fed. The Canadians donated ration packs to Mozambique for troops on the Limpopo corridor, and if the engineers had supervised the delivery they might have reached their destination. As it was, the army supplied the army, which is why few of the soldiers in this murderous, fever-ridden, hostile posting had ever known the pleasure of a vitamin-enriched chocolate biscuit from Vancouver.

Right now, Ismael confessed as we sat by the line near Leonde, there was a serious shortage of corn in the camp and the men did not like to work if they had no porridge. "I think the army keep it," said Ismael, twirling his sunglasses. But he was working on it, he assured me. So were the camp cooks, who had started bartering a portion of their dried fish for grain. You could smell the fish on the open market in Chokwe, stacked beside cans of pork and beef hash issued by the World Food Program and bags of sugar donated by the government of Finland.

"That's it," said Strachan at about 2:30, "there's not any more we can do without the fines." The teams packed up and clambered onto the train. Two hundred yards away, on the road, a recovery truck was crawling into Leonde, towing one of the cars that had passed Matsinhe at Macia junction, but it hardly looked worth the effort.

▲

The railway promised to bring security and a chance to trade, not only on a local scale, but regionally, since it was likely that the new South Africa would dwarf its neighbors as much as apartheid had squeezed them in the past. It was a "development" project and development was synonymous with the modern state that Frelimo so desperately desired. The language of Marxism-Leninism had failed to articulate it and now the party's hopes were pinned on aid.

With negotiations going on in Italy, the time had also come for Renamo to find a modern political gloss that would give it authority. It was seeking advice on this, but it still lacked an agenda, a platform of international support and a solid base inside the country. Frelimo's entente with the West and the aid agencies had done much to reduce the rebels' options. The alliance had cast Renamo as a brutal and backward force, a characterization that was self-fulfilling. Fifteen years of ostracism had compounded the movement's sullenness and incoherence. Frelimo was suing for peace in a language of which the rebels had only a smattering. In the meantime they fell back on their own idioms. Government propaganda depicted mutilation by the rebels as a simple case of barbarity, but this was misleading. Barbaric it certainly was but it also served as a form of political expression, which made it far more chilling. Indeed, when it was done with the just measure of zeal, there was nothing more horrible.

Rodrigues Laïce was in the Maputo Central Hospital, recovering from an encounter with Renamo in Ndlavela, a small settlement outside the capital. Rodrigues had been living there for several years, working in a metal furniture concern until he was laid off and took to fishing in the local reservoir to feed his family. He was willing enough to tell his story; eager in fact, for he did so more than once, and each time he was able to relate it in finer detail, as though to say exactly what had happened was a kind of relief.

One evening, about ten days previously, Rodrigues had returned from the reservoir to hear gunfire in Ndlavela. He hid in his house with his wife, Olinda, and their two children, but the family was discovered by a group of insurgents, who bound the couple and beat them with sticks. After a time, they asked Olinda and Rodrigues whether they knew why there were being beaten. "We do not know at all," said Rodrigues. "Please tell us."

The rebels were looking for members of the government militia, whose whereabouts the couple did not know. They were also looking for local stores in Ndlavela where they could get food and a few bottles of *tontonto*, the local liquor. Rodrigues explained that the main supplier of *tontonto* had just died; it was no longer so easy to find. Still bound, the couple were led out of the house on the beginning of a long trek. There were twelve or thirteen insurgents, said Rodrigues, but at this stage, he and his wife were the only captives. The group walked out of Ndlavela and met a militia member coming the other way. They asked if he was armed, he replied that he was not and they shot him dead. Then, after some discussion, the group headed back toward the village.

Rodrigues and Olinda led Renamo to the house of a widow. They found her drunk, asked her where she got the liquor and beat her to show they were in earnest. She brought them to another house, belonging to an old man. Olinda and Rodrigues, still bound, were taken along. The old man had finished every drop in the house. The men tied him up and debated what to do. One authoritative figure in the group suggested beating him to death with a corn pestle and this was agreed. Afterward, the group moved on, taking the pestle with them, to the local market site. Everything was closed. They entered several other houses, picking up whatever goods and food they found and gathering a few more people. In one house, they discovered three liters of *tontonto* and some boiled chicken. Their disposition improved, to the relief of Olinda and Rodrigues.

The insurgents searched the village again and surprised four more residents in their houses, one of whom had an aluminum army issue plate on his cooker, which was tantamount to membership of the government militia. So, Rodrigues said, they ordered him to lie on the floor and beat him to death with the pestle. The last house they entered belonged to an elderly couple who were well provided; they cleaned it out and took the couple with them.

Olinda and Rodrigues were now untied and all the captives were given goods to carry, as the group set off into the bush. "Carrying, carrying," said Rodrigues, "that is how we left Ndlavela." The old couple found it hard to keep up and at length the husband collapsed. He seemed to have a defect in one leg, leprosy perhaps. Renamo beat him to the ground, severed the leg below the knee with a machete and left him.

"I was carrying groundnuts and corn, about thirty kilograms," said Rodrigues. "I could change the position of the load, from my head to one shoulder, then to the other, then back to my head and in this way I was able to continue until we came to a big canhoeiro tree." Rodrigues thought they had been walking for three hours. Here they stopped while the rebels cut off the lips and noses of the two oldest women, who were no more use for carrying, and prepared to let them go. During the mutilation, Rodrigues, Olinda and the others were made to clap their hands in time, while the rebels disparaged the government by singing anti-Renamo songs, which were often broadcast on state radio. The leader of the group, a man called Santane, ordered the women to go to President Chissano and explain that what they had suffered was not the work of bandits, but of Renamo: Resistência Nacional Moçambicana. There was a body by the tree, Rodrigues recalled, about a week old.

The remainder of the group were led on another forced march of about four hours that ended at a small Renamo camp. There were several guerrillas, as well as young girls sorting cashew nuts. Two youngsters on the trek from Ndlavela, both girls, were taken away, leaving Olinda and Rodrigues and three others, who were told to prepare for mutilation. "Some very young ones came with a small knife and we were put in a line," said Rodrigues. "They did not even tie us up. They said, 'Kneel and if you cry out, we will kill you.' " Then, one by one, their ears and noses were slashed. Santane told them to gather the severed parts and cook them. When they took this dish to Chissano, they were to be careful to explain that it was a gift not from the bandits, but from Renamo.

The group was released and fled into the bush. Exhausted, they made their way to a village and from there they were taken to the hospital. Olinda had been discharged the day before. Rodrigues had one ear missing; the other was stitched back on, but it looked unlikely to heal. The right nostril of his nose was attached by a mass of stitches. He said he was lucky. The children, after all, were unscathed and Santane's group had taken no great interest in Olinda. He had a *machamba*, a plot of land, and he thought he would be working it again before the month was out, although the family would now have to look for somewhere else to stay after dark.

▲

Xavier was my Ministry of Information minder in Zambézia province. We flew up there together from Maputo. He was a slight man in his twenties from Cabo Delgado, to the north, who liked to tell how as a child he had believed that Frelimo was a monster—not a band of monsters, but a single enormous beast whose wire head blazed with St. Elmo's fire, as it stalked the land, consuming all before it. This is what he learned at the Portuguese school (his father was an *assimilado*), heard on the radio and saw on Portuguese propaganda posters. His grandparents were arrested as Frelimo sympathizers during the liberation war. They used to listen to Frelimo's broadcasts from Tanzania. One day Xavier met a group of guerrillas outside Pemba. His fears were allayed, and from that day until the end of the war, he ran little errands for them. He remembered with amusement how on Independence Day the Portuguese flag had been lowered and stamped into the ground. Within three years, the friendship between the townspeople of Pemba and their liberators had turned sour, he said, but there was no point telling me why, since I couldn't write about it without getting him into trouble.

Xavier was a very clever man indeed, subtle, attentive, skeptical but driven on by curiosity. Every evening during our week in Zambézia, he would mull over the day's events and piece together elements that suggested things he had not already thought about. At night he liked to visit Lion country, returning late, to sleep with his body entirely covered by a blanket, skillfully pegged at the toes and the back of the head. It took patience to coax him from this sanctuary at six or seven in the morning, not only because of his earlier exertions, but because Xavier's day loomed ahead like a dark track through solemn country, where the misery of his compatriots stretched away to the horizon. He had to gird himself for this, weighing up the likely proportion of pain and profit that lay in store. For Xavier, a day in which nothing had been learned was a waste of effort.

We hired a driver, a Portuguese, whose ancient truck seemed to have no suspension, to take us from Quelimane to Nicoadala. We made the journey, fifty kilometers maybe, in a little over two hours. The white man was a settler who had decided not to return to Lisbon at independence. He regaled us with stories about the superstition of the natives. Xavier asked polite questions, encouraging him to make a fool of himself and laughing volubly as soon as he did, until at length the poor man held his peace.

Sections of the road to Nicoadala were bad, but in essence this was a secure corridor from Quelimane. At Nicoadala there was a feeding center and a series of settlements where people lived in grim conditions. We had agreed to avoid these, however, and carry on to a little village called Micajuna. We had been going for about an hour when the sky blackened and a wind drove in from the northwest, pitching the trees into blurred agitation. The rain beat on the side of the truck and, by the time we reached Nicoadala, everyone in the area was under cover.

We had to stop here to pay our respects to the local Frelimo administrative structures. In a narrow shed that belonged to the party, we waited for the rain to abate but there was little sign of this. It was remarkable how much smaller the displaced population in the area seemed by comparison with 1988. Something very important had happened in Zambézia. Xavier and I had a change of heart, deciding after all to walk across to one of the resettlement camps and meet some of the refugees. When the weather cleared, we would go on up to Mica-juna. A young Frelimo official in khaki trousers and a frayed polyester blazer introduced us to a group of elders. Soon thirty men were congregated near the truck, waiting to know what on earth we wanted with them. We put a few casual questions and they raised their arms slowly, shielding their heads from the rain and answering in low murmurs. Xavier became irritated with the Frelimo official and claimed that he was telling them what to say.

"We are journalists," said Xavier haughtily. "When we want to talk to Frelimo, we will talk to Frelimo, but just now we would prefer to talk to the *povo.*" A few minutes later we were squatting under a thatched roof with three men from Namacurra. It was about as private as you could get in a refugee settlement.

Namacurra was a day's walk from Nicoadala but Filipe, Thomaz and João had lived through four years of harassment from Renamo before leaving for the safety of the settlements. In the early days of independence, their small community had been left largely to itself. Frelimo did not force them into collective farming, but it did send party brigades to "mobilize" in their area, telling them that they would have to contribute money to a people's shop and produce a vehicle once the shop got started. The brigade members were from Maputo. They delegated an Asian to head the project for the shop and the party offices in Quelimane gave him a special authorization to collect the levy; five or ten thousand meticais from each family, perhaps more—a lot of money in 1978. One day he took off to Quelimane with all the funds and never returned. After that the brigades abandoned the idea of the people's shop and left the area alone. "We lived in peace for several years," said Thomaz. "We worked our land and we kept some savings inside our houses."

It was obvious that the three men had been prosperous farmers before the war, which was one of the reasons Renamo came to Namacurra: the land was good and there was food to be had. The other was that Frelimo had built a prison camp near their fields. By 1983, they said, the center held about two thousand detainees. In the same year Frelimo began deporting thousands of people from the cities. The idea was to reduce the number of urban unemployed from the cities and set them to work in the fields. It was not long before all kinds of people, some of them employed, were being dumped in camps in the middle of the countryside for a range of obscure offenses against the state, or their local vigilance committees. Thomaz and João had heard of Operation Production; they said that they were always trying to keep abreast of news in the country, but they were confident that the center at Namacurra was for common criminals. They fraternized with the guards and inmates, selling them a local liquor known as *kachaso*. I learned later that the Operation Production deportees were sent much further north.

Mozambicans were always happier referring to a specific misfortune not by its name but by the generic word "situation." This applied to hunger, violence, disease and above all to the state of the war itself. Propriety required that even this anodyne term be qualified, so that four thousand people stranded in a refugee camp without food for a fortnight, or a major Renamo offense over a third of the country would be described as "a small situation" or even a "very small situation." By 1984, the three men from Namacurra agreed, there was undoubtedly a small situation in Zambézia. Renamo had begun to swarm over the province and bands of insurgents were gradually appearing around their farmlands.

When Renamo launched its first attack against the prison camp, rather than putting everyone to death, the rebels simply came in and took the livestock. According to Filipe, there were no deaths at all; the other two agreed. "They behaved as herdsmen would, only they had guns," Thomaz added. The inhabitants of Namacurra were frightened and considered leaving but, at that stage, Frelimo forbade them to do so. Thereafter, the three men and their families would stay overnight away from their plots in places they considered safe, returning periodically to work the land.

Before long they had their own direct dealings with Renamo. The rebels came onto the land and demanded food. Filipe remembered their courteous form of address: "Papa, can you give us rice, please? Papa, we are hungry, please give us that piece of fish." As for chickens, they would help themselves without asking. "The ones we came to know were not a difficulty for us," said Thomaz, "but we could not live in evenness or tranquility because there were too many new groups that kept coming. Really we began to run out of things for ourselves."

It was penury rather than terror that wore away at Namacurra. Renamo simply bled the people dry. The inhabitants knew that there was emergency food available in Nicoadala but they did not dare to leave because Frelimo now defined Namacurra as an area of bandit activity and anyone who emerged from it was liable to be seen as a collaborator. This was a serious problem throughout Mozambique. "If you tried to leave," said João, "the chances were that you would be killed outright by the army." The men remembered a very small situation in 1987 when four of their friends set out on foot for Nicoadala. They had been picked up by a military convoy and, two days later, a group of fishermen had found their bodies by the river.

Namacurra was a no-man's-land and its inhabitants were stranded.

Filipe said that if the army managed to mount an operation against Renamo, the insurgents would carry out reprisals against the local population. The men recalled two public executions in which peasants were put to death by bayonet. The army often killed, they thought, but it did so discreetly, in the blank intimacy of the bush.

Filipe, Thomaz, João and their families lived in this precarious world until 1988 when Frelimo offered an amnesty to insurgents who were prepared to give themselves up. At that point thousands of peasants decided that the coast was clear and flocked to government-held areas in search of food. Filipe, Thomaz and João had been in Nicoadala for three years now. Each member of their families received five kilograms of corn and a liter of beans a month, and each household was entitled to a monthly liter of oil. They were also able to find intermittent work in the fields of Nicoadala. João had earned five hundred meticais the previous week harvesting manioc for a local landowner. Filipe and Thomaz cut wood, which they sold to an entrepreneur for anything between five hundred and one thousand meticais a bundle. The trade was thinning with the wood, however, for there were now twenty people cutting in the same area and the brush was almost bare.

Filipe and Thomaz both had two wives. Each wife had received a *machamba* from the government. This was another vital means of survival, but it was available only to a handful of displaced people. Frelimo's policy of finding plots for the displaced also raised interesting problems for the future of all peasants in Mozambique, if the war should ever end. Many beneficiaries of the policy retained claims to the old *machambas* they had been forced to abandon. In Zambézia and at least two other provinces with which I was familiar, the war had brought with it the possibility of prodigious land accumulation, since influential families would one day be able to assert control over their ancestral fields while seeking titles to the plots they had been allocated under the resettlement program. Even if they were enforceable, the most carefully drafted laws would do little to ease the strains that this might cause.

In most of Africa, the rout of socialism was greeted with improbable hopes but in Mozambique, at least, a certain sobriety was in order, if only because the new state of affairs presaged the kind of rural conflict that Marxists would once have described as a primitive phase of development. In this case it threatened to continue long after the cities of Mozambique were safely under the wing of "world markets."

We left the three men from Namacurra with cigarettes and money. Thomaz was rocking his two-year-old son on his knee and folded the meticais in under the elastic of the boy's shorts without waking him. It was no longer raining quite so hard as we set off for Micajuna. Whatever the complexities of the land issue, the change in Nicoadala was astonishing. There were now fewer than 100,000 displaced people by Frelimo's count, which could only mean that large numbers of refugees were drifting back to their own lands.

It was less than ten minutes' drive to Micajuna. The settlement was just off the road. A large truck stood in a parking area at its edge. Beneath the trailer fifteen or twenty people were squatting, kneeling or sitting, sculpted into this dark rectangle of shelter. Two children curved upward and sideways at the wheels, insinuating their way under the remains of the mud guards and flowing along the curve of the tires like cats. Nothing moved in this strange relief except for the eyes of the children and the odd trickle of rain from the leaky trailer, glistening down a cheekbone or a bare thigh.

We had come to see Manuel António, a kind of prophet, who had been working in Zambézia for nearly two years and had set up a headquarters in the settlement, but there was no sign of him. The sky was slate gray and the rain continued to fall. The driver was unhappy and refused to turn off the engine as Xavier and I got down, walked by the truck and in under the dripping trees. It was a deeply lugubrious place. There were no women and everywhere the prophet's disciples were sheltering under the eaves of the thatched huts or standing in groups around the trunks of the cashews. Most of them were carrying machetes, knives or spears and looked us over with a mixture of suspicion and hope. Perhaps we had news, or money.

Xavier explained our purpose to a senior disciple, who replied that Manuel António was in Quelimane on business. He had promised to return the day before with food but had not done so. "Look at us," the man told Xavier, "we are waiting; we are hungry." He thought that we should try again the next day. We hurried away, ducking under the sodden leaves like supplicants hastening from a dank church. Some of the disciples followed us, begging, then demanding, tobacco and cash. The driver was sitting at the wheel of his truck with the engine running.

Manuel António had come to the attention of the world in 1989, roughly twenty years after he died of measles, or perhaps malaria. There was nothing unusual about a death of this kind in Mozambique; what distinguished Manual António from a million others was that he had risen from the grave. Some said the resurrection had occurred seven days after his death, others that it had happened more recently. It had been followed by a long sojourn with wild beasts and spirits on a mountain in Nampula province, at the end of which Manuel António had received divine instruction to go down to the plain and perform Christ's work in Mozambique.

The task in hand was a holy war against Renamo and the crucial battleground would be Zambézia, one of the most fertile and bitterly contested areas of the country. Renamo was already a serious threat by 1984. In 1986 the movement fought tenaciously for control of this rambling province in an attempt to split Mozambique in two. The plan failed but Frelimo's hold on Zambézia was tenuous. After the amnesty, the army devised an informal policy of its own, without the sanction of Maputo. Forced removals were the order of the day, just as they had been under the Portuguese. The idea was to deny Renamo a base for food production, but the effect was merely to add to the overcrowding in the provincial and district capitals, where great columns of peasants were arriving on foot. The towns creaked under the influx of displaced people, while the hinterland lay fallow or burned. It was a "situation" by any standards, and without peace, in which Renamo had no interest, or a proper military capacity to deal with the rebels, there was little the government could do.

Manuel António was the miracle worker that Frelimo had been waiting for, although it had not expected salvation from such an eccentric quarter. Military expertise and equipment from the Eastern bloc, special forces trained by foreign officers, a contingent of British mercenaries, thousands of soldiers from neighboring states and a massive foreign aid program that should have allowed the government to extend its relief effort deep into the rural areas—all these had failed to achieve what Manuel António managed in a matter of months by raising a peasant army of about fifteen thousand men and going in pursuit of the rebels.

Early in 1990 Manuel António and his followers liberated the northern edge of the province. From there they moved south toward the coast. Renamo fell back, to the general astonishment of the government and the agencies. To begin with, people were herded into government-held centers. By the end of the year the prophet had flushed the insurgents out of an area of land between Ile, Maganja and Mocuba, known as the Death Triangle, where Renamo had wreaked unquantifiable havoc since the middle of the 1980s. More than half of Zambézia was free for the first time in years, and slowly but surely the district capitals were now starting to empty as thousands of peasants returned to the land. It was the result of this process that we had seen in Nicoadala. Frelimo must have looked on with puzzled satisfaction. Had Manuel António emerged from his seclusion a decade earlier, they would have driven him straight back into the bush, for he was a paragon of *obscurantismo*. Now, they hailed this resurrected prophet as a "person of influence" and his army as a "traditional militia" whose efforts were making a serious contribution to peace in the country. But then they had no choice.

Manuel António had a preparation called *naparama*, or *barama*, with which he immunized recruits against enemy bullets. The contents were a secret but the potion was probably made from the ashes of a local shrub. It was administered by making a number of small cuts around the collar and chest with a razor. The potion was then rubbed into the wounds. Sometimes, at the end of the recruiting ceremony, a *curandeiro* would slash at the new Naparamas with a machete. If their bodies remained unscathed, the vaccine had taken. It was said that when Manuel António himself came to a settlement to recruit new Naparamas, his lieutenants would dig a grave and bury him in it. He would address the crowd from under the earth and then rise up, exhorting them to play a part in God's work.

For a decade the people of Zambézia had been powerless in the face of the war. When Manuel António raised his obscure voice, he spoke in terms that were perfectly clear to his listeners: the government and the aid agencies could do little for the people, the army almost nothing; if they wanted peace, they would have to fight for it themselves; if they wanted to go back to their *machambas*, they would have to drive Renamo out by faith and courage, putting their trust in the efficacy of the vaccine and the use of traditional weapons—knives, machetes, spears. The word of God, which Manuel António brought down from the mountain, forbade the use of firearms. This prohibition struck a welcome note with the inhabitants of Zambézia, for whom the gun was a symbol of everything that had gone awry in their lives. By 1990, however, the Naparamas were coordinating their operations with army units and for all intents and purposes they were a Frelimo militia.

As we set off for Quelimane, I asked Xavier what he thought our chances really were of running into Manuel António. He had already made three visits to Zambézia with journalists who wanted to meet the prophet, he told me, but none had been successful. I asked him what he thought of Manuel António. "I don't know," he said. "I don't believe in this thing, but it has changed the whole province."

The following day we cast around Quelimane for Manuel António and found no trace of him. We left once more for Micajuna under black skies in a Volkswagen combie painted with palm trees and beach scenes. The daily rental was too expensive and we walked from Nicoadala, leaving the two young owners with an armful of meticais. Xavier told them we would find a way to get back to Quelimane. The sun came out as we arrived at the settlement. Manuel António's men were in better humor. They assured us that the prophet would be arriving in the afternoon. However, he would not be stopping; he was liable to press on for Mocuba. If we wanted to find him, we should go back to Quelimane at once, to another of his premises near the church of Sagrada Familia. In passing, a disciple mentioned to Xavier that he and his colleagues had still not eaten. We left tobacco and dried fruit, hurrying back down the road into Nicoadala on foot to see if we could find room in a car to Quelimane.

At the feeding center an American doctor was ferrying a group of lepers to the central hospital. There was room in the back of the Land Cruiser; we wedged ourselves between his patients, with the strange aroma of their sickness flooding the back of the car like the smell of warm grain. We seemed to fly along the road to Quelimane. It was early afternoon when we asked to be let down near the church.

Sagrada Familia was like many provincial Catholic churches in Mozambique—built in the 1960s, I supposed, with a tardy nod in the direction of modernism. Surrounded by poverty as they invariably were, these buildings looked like leisure centers whose finance committees had drawn the line just as the swimming pool was about to be dug. A network of tracks ran between clusters of huts and dirty children were playing in the mud. In other cultures this would have been an unsavory place, but in Mozambique it was a haven of peace and prosperity. Manuel António's house was long and narrow; ten disciples sat around the porch using their traditional weapons to crack open hairy gray coconuts and drain the juice. We were told to sit down; the prophet was coming. We squatted on the porch waiting for the man who had changed the face of Zambégia province.

Half an hour went by and the door opened behind us. A young woman with dress straps lolling off her shoulders stepped out to survey the scene. Xavier watched her with gloomy interest until she went back inside. "Naparama inspiration," he said when she had shut the door. Shortly after that we heard the festive din of an approaching truck. Muddy children stood up from their labors in the puddles and tottered out into the path of the vehicle, scattering as it drew to a halt opposite the yard. It was loaded with sacks of grain, covered in a torn tarpaulin. Stacked on these, and bound with synthetic rope, were a hundred cases of South African lager. At the top of the heap sat the prophet and a group of followers. I had never seen his photograph but I spotted him at once, a small, inconspicuous man in battle fatigues and a military beret with a wooden cross fastened to its front. His hands were clasped firmly around a box of Pink Harmony china teaware, which he was eager to prevent from falling off the truck in the general confusion. Eventually he clambered down and jogged past us, wielding a black plastic briefcase. On his way into the house, he collected the young woman, who had reemerged on the porch, and the door shut firmly behind them.

"Listen," said the prophet indignantly when we were ushered inside, "the government of Mozambique will not help us. Why not? Ever since I came to this province nothing is left of the bandits. We are responsible for that, but we need help, we need money, it is not possible to do this thing without resources."

Xavier translated as fast as he could, but Manuel António was agitated; he spoke quickly and repeated himself often. He said there was not much time; he had to get on the road to Mocuba to take food to his people and beer to his shop, which was how he raised money for his work. He paused and fished inside the briefcase, bringing out a wallet from which he removed an ID card, which he handed to us. He waited until we had checked it and then pointed at his chest so that we were sure to make no mistake about who this was. The hut was filling up with smoke from the back and there was a great deal of activity behind us. He was obliged to hold several conversations at once; everyone was making demands, asking questions, checking instructions. The girl stood behind him chewing something. She looked about nineteen. Under the glaze of indolence her eyes were attentive, even nervous. The prophet himself had an innocent and gentle face. His skin was clear and a sparse beard covered his jaw and chin. There was a gap between his front teeth; his eyes were wide apart and shaped like almonds.

"I was reborn," said Manuel António casually. "I stayed six months in the mountain. I am the son of Jesus Christ." He bent down and gazed intently at his red sneakers. "I didn't come down from the mountain to end the war," he went on, "I came down to live my life and to see how matters really are. What I saw was that Renamo has many sins in this world. I don't kill anybody, I don't act like a soldier. I capture Renamo and hand them to Frelimo; this is a simple thing. . . . Besides all this," he added briskly, "I heal the sick."

We asked if *naparama* was still effective. Manuel António chided us. No doubt we had heard that five hundred Naparamas had been massacred in Mulevala, making a mockery of the vaccine; but it was not true—they were Renamo people posing as Naparamas.

"You journalists," he said, "you mustn't play with *naparama*; you must stop asking foolish questions. I can turn into any animal and deal with you if I have to. Your work is to tell Renamo that wherever they go, they are sure to suffer."

He stood up and zipped his briefcase shut. Xavier asked him where he was working and when we might see the ceremony, but he shrugged off the questions, muttering something to the girl, who gathered up a bag and followed him out of the house toward the truck. A tall man put out his arm and tried to stop him as he climbed aboard. A brief argument ensued, during which the prophet and the girl slid deeper into the recess of the cab, while their driver started the engine. It was clear that the angry man owned the truck. He was shouting for payment. He turned in anger to Xavier and said that the Naparamas owed him 300,000 meticais; he could not let them use his truck any longer. Some of the disciples remonstrated with him while Manuel António sat with his head between his hands. The owner was still shouting as the Son of Jesus Christ and his Magdalene set out for Micajuna.

▲

"I am pleased to inform you," said Loborino Alamane, "that the majority of displaced people have now returned to their place of origin. This was facilitated by the party and government structures here in Pebane. It did not make sense to keep the people in the city after Naparama and Frelimo had liberated the district." Mr. Alamane studied a notebook made in the People's Republic of China, the cover decorated with a large butterfly. "By now, 152,114 people have returned," he went on. "The people you still find here are the hesitaters. In terms of food, we are supplying them, and also the people who have gone back, for they have nothing. They will receive emergency supplies for eighteen months. Excuse me if I ask you to repeat your questions; I am suffering from an ear infection."

Mr. Alamane coordinated the emergency in Pebane, 150 kilometers up the coast from Quelimane. Xavier and I had traveled north in a light plane with two workers for the British agency ActionAid, and we were now in a place where the effects of Manuel António's work were abundantly clear. Over 100,000 souls were back on the land. We had no questions; the little man with the gap in his teeth had brought this about.

To keep the people fed, with grain going out to the whole district, was Alamane's responsibility. But the provider, and the organization with influence up here, was ActionAid. It cost about U.S. $4 million to run an emergency over five months for 150,000 people and required about nine thousand tons of grain. The process was complex. The agency would raise the cash through an appeal. Then it would have to find a supplier—this could be anybody, but aid organizations tended to use the same German company with a British subsidiary. This subsidiary had links with a South African company whose agent in Zimbabwe had a subagent in Maputo. The subagent could draw up a shipping contract with a Mozambican state company, which in turn would subcontract the work to a company in Mombasa. This company plied the east coast of the continent with a variety of cargo, but aid provided it with a dependable core of work that took its vessels regularly to ports in Mozambique, Eritrea and Sudan.

For three days, while we were in Pebane, the company's old boat lay anchored beyond the bar and a lighter shuttled back and forth from the dock. The stevedores brought the grain down the gangway and across to a waiting truck, like a column of ants carrying sugar. From there it went to the warehouse, where a crowd was gathered, protesting that the previous consignment was rotten. "Look," they shouted at Xavier, as we walked by, "the last grain has rotted away in there and the Structures"—local government and party officials—"won't let us have it!"

Yet Pebane was a calm place now; with the fever of overcrowding past, the town slept the deep sleep of recovery. There was nothing doing here, apart from South African beer and Zimbabwean grain— and a strange courtship rite that took place on Friday and Saturday nights at the top of the main street, as dozens of young people milled around the exterior of a big shebeen. Renamo had tried to take Pebane a few years back and the government had mustered a prompt response. War damage was evident, but there was disagreement on whether this was from aerial bombardment or naval guns. However hard I put my mind to it, I was unable to imagine the Mozambican navy.

The afternoon of our arrival, we drove to the accommodation center to see if Loborino Alamane was telling the truth. As soon as we set foot in the center, it was beyond doubt. Like tourists in a cinder block Ephesus, we found ourselves standing in an empty city of mud and concrete, a relic, and we were awestruck. Here, for once, silence and desertion had lost their usual connotation; they were simply evidence of the liberation that had crept across the province. The center was nothing, just a collection of empty huts between a sandy track and a row of palm trees, yet, had we been pilgrims, this would have been the end of our journey and the moment to offer up thanks. The palms broke up the sunlight, scattering it across the gray dust tracks between the empty huts. There were two or three hours before dusk, but it felt like early morning.

From one end of the complex an official came to meet us and announced that there were now only forty-seven people here, in a place that had once held thousands. Some had come in recently from pockets of Renamo territory, others were sick or afraid—"the hesitaters," Mr. Alamane had called them. There was an old lady who had lived with Renamo for about two years and was no longer sure what to do. Her name was Mahala. She came from Mocuba but she was reluctant to go back; there might be no one left now with whom she was intimate. "It is true," she said, "things were easy for me with Matsanga. I wasn't beaten or abused because I am old already." Her *machamba* in Mocuba, she said, was prodigal. She claimed that a square meter of that rich, ancestral earth would yield her a sackful of manioc.

A young couple with a child was staying on at the center. João was in his twenties, Lourdice in her teens; they had met as captives of Renamo. Their baby had been born before Naparama had driven the insurgents out. Lourdice would not speak. She paced around in a desultory way, bouncing the child on her arms. She had no *capulana* to tie him to her back and nothing to cover her breasts. Her head was shaven. In captivity, they had lived at the mercy of a young Renamo leader called Mutati—a *nom de guerre* meaning sorghum. Mutati made his captives live around the edges of his base, picking cashews, growing manioc, cooking and keeping vigil for the fighters. If the captives' harvests were plentiful, they were allowed to keep back a proportion; if not, they lost everything. João used to dam the river for *nkopo*, a local fish, and he would have to surrender a portion of his catch. He had been abducted with six friends. During his time with Renamo, no one had been killed, he said, but when he and Lourdice had taken up together, Mutati and his friends were angry. They beat him for sleeping with her. One day, he said, they tried to persuade her to go with them but she refused. They persisted and he intervened. Mutati beat him badly and Lourdice was taken away to another part of the base.

After two cashew harvests, Naparama came. João saw them; he told us they were "like Frelimos," only they carried spears and sometimes animal tails: "They came during the day, we were in our houses. There was fighting and we ran away. Afterward they came looking for people in the bush and they found us. They said, 'We are Frelimos, you are the *povo*. If you want to go to a safe place we'll take you there.' We walked for three days with the Naparamas. They were many, so many I am afraid to count. I recognized one of the Structures from my village. He had become a Naparama. He was carrying a spear."

João and Lourdice went back to his village at the end of 1990. They spent Christmas there; they planted and he fished. João had intended to take the vaccine but the local Catholic priest had discouraged him. The church did not like Manuel António. It would rather see the peasants starve and suffer than walk with a man who called himself the Son of Christ and who had, in truth, performed a miracle in Mozambique. One day, while João was fishing, his leg was savaged by a crocodile, which was why he had come back to the center. He was lucky to be alive, for he should have died from loss of blood, but his days of farming and fishing were over.

That night we ate with the two ActionAid people and talked until late. Joaquim Segurado, the director, was in especially good spirits, but a kind of euphoria had seized them both and even the circumspect Xavier was a happy man. Our companions were both former Frelimo supporters, of Portuguese origin, who had done ethnographic field-work in the north during the liberation war. Josi Negrão had been in jail under the Portuguese, as had his father before him; perhaps it was an old communist family. Negrão was a gifted anthropologist, re-searching a policy document on the condition of peasant women to present to the government and the donors. His data, he said, suggested that the collectivization of land was a crucial part of the catastrophe in Mozambique. In much of Zambézia the prosperous peasants worked three *machambas*, rotating every six years to complete what was roughly a twenty-year cycle. The communal village system had begun between 1976 and 1978, Negrão reminded us, and the real surge in Renamo activity had followed approximately six years later: the time it took for a single plot of land to become exhausted and for collectivization to bite, making it hard for peasants to move on to their next *machamba*. This account played down South Africa's involvement in the conflict, and was consistent with the new thinking, which emphasized the in-ternal causes of the havoc in the rural areas.

The Tanzanian captain of the vessel anchored off the sound had presented the ActionAid staff with a case of Kenyan beer. Xavier drank to Manuel António's health; he thought of the prophet as a ludicrous man, a charlatan, but it was clear that he also saw his coun-try as a theater of anomaly in which a comic figure might be called on to play the hero's part. When Segurado and Negrão had gone to bed, I told Xavier about Rodrigues Laïce, the injured man I had met in Maputo Central Hospital, and asked how it was possible for Renamo to operate in such a way. Xavier said he had spent many years asking himself that very question.

"This," he said, "is my conclusion: they make this mutilation to show that the government is nothing. Where is your president now? Where is Frelimo? Tell them to come and help you. Such is the meaning." He said that Renamo's real strength lay among the Ndau people in the center of the country—Dhlakama, the leader of Renamo, was Ndau—where the narrowness of the constituency made atrocity permissible against other groups. "But you will sometimes notice," he went on, "that it is a foolish thing for Renamo to do. It can work against their interest. For example, to do it now, when the peace may come soon, is foolish. If the war ends, this one, Laïce, and his wife, they will not vote for the Matsangas, that is certain. And so you must ask yourself: who is doing it? Is it possible that someone wants to bring down the name of Renamo by coming with these things? I can say no more about this. It is a puzzle and we may not know the answer. In Mozambique you must write only what you saw. Here, war is like a terrible accident. It must be as if you were driving in an ambulance toward that accident. You must write what you saw when you arrived, but do not ask why."

Majiga lay an hour's drive inland from the town of Pebane, beyond a place known as Malinde. It was a small village and, like all such villages before the war, family lands extended for miles around. To get to Majiga you drove through a massive palm plantation, after which the land leveled off and the sandy soil of the coast grew darker. Majiga itself was a crossroads; someone suggested that the very name was the local word for crossroads. It was a sad sight, with a cluster of huts on one side of the road and a school on the other. Renamo had destroyed the school; it was simply a shell, but there was a young teacher lining children up for a hundred-meter dash on the football field beside it. A bigger building behind the school was used for classes. The pathos of Majiga was deceptive, for what really mattered in a place like this was the quality of the land and the size of the harvest. If it seemed to be a little desolate, that was because most people were at work on their *machambas*.

Negrão had business with the women of Majiga and when he was finished he left us there, promising to return with the car before dusk. We paid our respects to the members of the local administrative structures: the first secretary of the party, the head of production and trade, and the head of vigilance, and then we began a tour of the *machambas* escorted by the clerk of the Majiga tribunal, Nuro Abdul Karimo, a delicate man in his forties, who walked with some discomfort in a pair of plastic ladies' sandals with raised heels.

Nuro had grown up in Majiga under Portuguese rule, when a colonial agent for the big sugar plantation nearby used to recruit villagers for planting and harvesting. The work was compulsory until 1968; the peasants were paid 180 escudos a month. Each able-bodied member of the village was also obliged to do seven days' work a year for the administration—mostly menial jobs, such as cooking and cleaning. Nuro remembered his father, a sailor by profession, had once failed to report for this work and had been beaten with the *palmatória*, a wooden bat that was used on the palms of the hands.

There was no Frelimo presence here during the liberation war but the movement came to Majiga after independence, bearing tidings of Sergio Vieira's New Man and ushering in a period of confusion. By the middle of the 1980s the inhabitants of Majiga numbered about twelve thousand but many fled when Renamo came in 1987. "They remained for nearly three years," said Nuro, "and although their base was some distance from here, they used the people to grow and work for them, as the Portuguese had done before. I myself had fled. Majiga lost many people during that time, but we do not know if they were all killed." Renamo's policy of abduction had left many young children without parents.

We had arrived at a handsome-looking *machamba* with young manioc growing in half an acre of rich soil flanked by cashew trees. I asked whose it was and we went in search of the owners, at another plot further up the road. Chabane was a sly man, not more than thirty-five, with a full beard and evasive eyes. I had hoped to speak to his wife, but she was among the women who had vanished after their meeting with Negrão was done. Chabane was suspicious when we asked after his wife. He gestured off up the road. His mood did not improve when we asked to talk with him instead.

"On that very day of the bandits' attack we ran from the war," Chabane explained. "They came and took all my clothes from the house. My wife and I, we ran to Malinde, and this is where we stayed, Malinde, and Pebane, for six harvests. I knew that if I came back here, I would find my *machamba* but my house would be burned, and I was correct." Chabane was building a new hut behind the plot, and the wooden structure was bound together with dried grass. He had yet to mat the walls with palm leaves. "For the moment," he said, "we are staying up by the school."

Chabane and his wife had been back for six months now. They had found everything overgrown and had spent a month and a half weeding their best *machambas*. Since then they had gathered one harvest of beans. Chabane expected to pull the manioc in August. He looked at us with a concealed suspicion. It did not do to let strangers know too much about how matters stood with the yield, particularly if you were doing well, for it could seem like ostentation and anyone might take against you for it. Chabane was almost certainly doing well.

He conceded that he had been afraid to return. Despite the efforts of the Naparamas, he could see no reason why Renamo might not come back. He told us that, for this reason, the inhabitants of Majiga had performed a ceremony on their return home, but when asked what it was, he laughed and shook his head. This he was not prepared to say. We pressed him and after much anguish, he said, "We drank root medicine and our feet were slapped with leaves from a tree called *npurunha*. Then it was safe." He glanced darkly at the clerk of the tribunal.

Chabane was still receiving emergency corn, and would for several months to come, but no one in Pebane liked corn. They were manioc eaters and living off corn as they had for so long was an ordeal. Chabane saw us off his property with a surly eye.

"It was hard," said Nuro, on our way back toward the school, "this is a fact. For us to come back here and not be in fear that the bandits might return required some special effort and"—alluding to the ceremony—"the necessary arrangements." Yet it was done; the return had been effected and now, by Nuro's count, the citizens of Majiga numbered 803.

"You see," said the clerk of the tribunal, when we were seated inside the rectangular hut near the football field, "there is more than what Chabane has said to you. The Naparamas were the ones who helped us with this matter. The Naparamas advised us how to improve the situation here. After they had freed Majiga, and we had come back, they told us to expect a sign. They said that before five days had gone by, a man would fall on the ground in Majiga and then we would know how to proceed."

We were joined in the hut by Comrade Francisco, the party secretary. We now asked both men to tell us more precisely what happened in Majiga from the moment that the Naparamas freed the district of Pebane.

"We were in Malinde," the clerk began, "and we were told by the army not to come back here; it was full of bandits. There were many engagements, very many, between the army and Renamo during those three years, but it was impossible to drive the bandits away." For about two months in 1988 Majiga was held by a commando unit that came up from Quelimane, but once they left, Renamo returned. The following year the villagers heard news that the Naparamas were operating in Gilé. They sent word that they needed them to come and organize a Naparama force in Malinde. Manuel António's second-in-command came, a man they called Nambila. There were two groups of Naparamas who had arranged to meet at Ratata, not far from Majiga. Both had carried out successful operations. Nambila's group arrived with many children he had gathered on the way, and the other group had captured a Renamo officer whose name was Rassia. (The clerk of the tribunal spelled this name in the dust with his finger.)

Nambila arrived first at Ratata and sent word to Pebane that he needed a truck to bring the children to the town because they were exhausted. Nambila left Ratata, and later the other group followed. "Two trucks full of people entered Pebane. The people were sick and hungry. The Naparamas were with them. They were many; we could not count them all.

"We think that Renamo fled Majiga when they heard news of all the Naparamas gathered in Ratata. Also they knew that Rassia had been captured. This is why they fled. The bandits fear the vaccine and they know their bullets cannot touch the Naparamas. Sometimes they fall into the ground as they leave the barrel. Sometimes they pass straight through the body of a warrior without doing harm, just as they might pass through oil without changing its flavor."

Nambila told them all to go back to Majiga, but they were afraid. "He told us, 'Look what we have done, we Naparamas, in Gilé, in Alto Molocuè and Mocubela. Do you doubt it? The bandits are finished in this whole place.' He gathered our young men of Majiga and administered the vaccine, so that now we would have our own Naparama force. Then he told us again that we must go home. He would come within the week and visit us, to see that all was well. We left in trucks and we came here to find our old *machambas* thick with weeds, our houses burned or neglected. We began work on the fields and built temporary shelters. We started to repair our homes, all the time waiting for Nambila. Then, one day, as he said he would, he came with his own Naparamas, on his way to Mocubela.

"He stayed with us here for two days and on the second day he worked with us to make this village of Majiga safe for the people. Nambila traveled with an oracle, whose name is Maria. Perhaps we should not be telling you this but anyhow you will know it one way or another. Maria is a whiskey bottle with three sides—you call it Grants—but the label had been taken off. This bottle is filled with water and in this water is a root, and the lid is on tight. Nambila kneeled on the ground and stood the oracle on her head, holding her with his two hands. He asked her many questions, which we could not hear because his voice was very soft. Each time he released Maria, she could not stand alone. She fell. And so he picked her up and whispered again, and she fell, and it went on in this way until the time came that he whispered to her and let her go and she was standing upright on the ground, by herself. 'So,' said Nambila to the people now that he had finished, 'this is not a difficult business.' And he informed us that we must wait for a man to fall to the ground. This man would say many things and we must follow his instructions. After that, no harm would befall Majiga."

Three days after Nambila left, the clerk recalled, a young man called Garamane Ossifo came back to Majiga and took up residence in his mother's house, beyond the school. Comrade Francisco added that he had been conscripted in the 1980s. He was an ordinary young man, well known in the village, who had spent three years in the army and returned to work on his wife's *machamba*. He was now twenty-five.

"Well, at six o'clock, just after dark on that same day," the clerk continued, "Garamane Ossifo fell down. It was close to his mother's house. She and the relatives came running to find us. We called together all the local Structures and we went to her house. Garamane Ossifo was possessed; he was singing many things about the war that we did not understand, because they were spirit songs. Then he rose to his feet and ran around the village in all directions. He ran at great speed and sometimes we could not keep up. Besides, we were surprised. Even we, the Structures, had never seen him doing such a thing, although we know this village well.

"He told us he was looking for something and he would not stop until he found a place in the village that had changed. When we asked him how—changed in what way—he could not say, and so he went on, running, running, until he came to a tree and stopped. 'Here,' said the spirit that had entered Garamane, 'this place is different.' And searching on the ground beside the tree he found an old container of water. He shook the container and the spirit said, 'The water that should be in here has changed. There is false water in this thing and it has brought harm to the village. This must be disposed of.' Garamane Ossifo handed the container to the Structures and once he had done so, the spirit left him. He lay down and slept right there by the tree. We carried him, still sleeping, to his mother's house and he slept through the night until the middle of the following day.

"The next day at the same time, just after dark, the spirit came to Garamane and he fell down a second time. Now we were in fear. The spirit spoke about the war and we could hear it clearly. It was angry. 'This place is in bloodshed,' it said. 'You have to wash and cleanse this place. You must make ceremonies for that purpose and for the orphans who have lost their parents.'

"We fetched an old man who knew the history of the place and he came with a *curandeiro*, the son of the old *régulo*, and together they prepared a large pot of herbs over a fire. Everyone in the village, including the Structures, had to wash in this remedy, carry a stick from the fire to their own house and use it to start a new cooking fire.

"Every day, for many months now, we have kept the same fires alight. As long as one fire is started from the ashes of the fire before, the whole fire leads back to the day we took the sticks from beneath the *curandeiro*'s pot and in this way we remain safe. The *curandeiro* brushed our feet with bunches of leaves, as Chabane was telling you, and some of us were given a special tea to drink. Then we performed a dance known as *twaha*, with six drummers, four male cantors and many dancers. Meanwhile clean food was prepared for the orphans. There was no manioc and so we used emergency corn, which is disagreeable for us, but it was done. The orphans ate freely and what remained was shared among the rest. We danced *twaha* until five o'clock next morning while our children slept beside the *curandeiro*'s fire."

Xavier and I went back to Majiga the next day, to go over the story once again with Comrade Francisco and the clerk of the tribunal. I also had hopes of meeting Garamane Ossifo. We traveled with Negrão and Segurado, who dropped us on their way to a village further inland.

"Garamane's place is a long way from here," Nuro informed us. "You will not walk it in less than three hours. He has moved to the *machamba* of his second wife and anyway we hear he has a sickness at the moment." Comrade Francisco sent a boy to the house of Garamane's first wife, to find out whether he was too ill to talk to us. When the boy returned, the party secretary announced that Garamane Ossifo would almost certainly be indisposed. He was suffering from a bad case of diarrhea.

We picked over the details of the account we had heard the day before. In the afternoon we spoke with the band of Naparamas posted at the western entrance to Majiga. They said that there were three companies of ninety men each in the area. Most of them wore shorts, like a Scout brigade, and two of them sported bright red forage hats. All the men had traditional weapons. Their version of things differed only in one respect from that of the party secretary and the clerk of the tribunal, for they said that Manuel António had been present at the time of their recruitment. "There was a rally," said the leader of the ragged group, "after which we were chosen, and very soon we went on an operation further west, to attack a Renamo base. We were successful, we captured the base and moved on; two days later we attacked and overran a second base. Then we took a third. In all we were 320. All the time we were running in attack, through the tall grass." Another youngster said that they could see Renamo when they came close to a base but as they entered, the bandits vanished, carrying whatever they could, although at the second base, the Naparamas had taken prisoners and captured weapons, which were handed over to the army. I asked to look inside their small headquarters but this was refused. When I asked them about the contents of the vaccine, they laughed. Then we heard the ActionAid car approaching the village.

On the journey back, Negrão and Segurado told us they had heard reports that Renamo had captured a group of Naparamas. Alert to the instructive detail, Renamo had impaled the commander on his spear and put the rest to death with their own weapons, leaving the bodies on the edge of the settlement so that people could judge the efficacy of the prophet's vaccine for themselves.

As we reached the edge of the palm plantation we saw that the truck from the port was standing just off the road. A crowd of people, about three hundred, had gathered under the colonnade of tall trunks to receive the grain we had seen unloaded in the port. They were in jubilant spirits and struck a range of mocking postures for the Action-Aid cameras. Segurado's photos would be valuable evidence that the food was being properly distributed.

▲

Xavier remained in Maputo on our return, but I traveled up to Zambézia once more, in the company of two journalists and a television director, to seek out Manuel António. We had also to visit some settlements inland by means of a light plane. After flying to the beleaguered town of Dere to record the pitiful "situation" of its inhabitants, and flying out again, we were making our way back to another airstrip on the outskirts of a liberated settlement when we found an injured Naparama laid out on a pallet a hundred yards from the plane. He had bullet wounds in both arms and both legs and needed treatment in Quelimane. It was abundantly clear that the vaccine had begun to lose its potency and that the demise of the movement was already a reality.

Although it was said that Renamo had developed a powerful magic that rendered the prophet's militia helpless, it was still possible to blame a warrior's death in combat on his failure to abide by the prohibitions to which all Naparamas were subject. It was forbidden, of course, for Naparamas to have anything to do with women during their menstruation, but there were many proscriptions besides, which varied from place to place. It was said that a Naparama could not eat the burned rice that stuck to the bottom of the pot. Nor could he eat from a ladle that had been overturned when it was dipped into the soup. In Nicoadala, the bereaved sister of a Naparama told us he had died because he had stood in the shade during an attack. A Naparama, she insisted, must stay in the sun while he is fighting.

In Mocuba, the prophet allowed the television director to film a little rally in town, but he was reluctant to perform any kind of mobilizing ceremony. It was as though he had offended Frelimo in some way, for he was adamant that nothing would happen without permission from the authorities in Mocuba. That night he came to see us in the hotel and sat in silence at the dinner table, drinking orange juice. He refused to eat anything at first but agreed eventually to take some bread. The video camera was set on the table and the prophet put his eye to the viewfinder as the pictures of the rally were played back to him. At first he seemed startled and his face went gray, but then he began to smile. He could see himself speaking and the people of Mocuba listening scrupulously. The tinny cheers of *"Viva Manuel António!"* issued from the playback speaker. He was still smiling when the tape was stopped, but his features, so animated as a rule, were drawn with fatigue. He sat back in his chair and closed his eyes. A few minutes later he ordered his assistants away to Mogonda, on the outskirts of town, to prepare the grave. He would perform the ceremony in the morning.

As his confidence returned, Manuel António inquired whether we were not trying to make a fool of him. "You don't believe in Manuel António," he said. "You cannot," and he pointed to the video camera: "You invented this." We sat in disgrace beneath the cold truth of this remark. The filmmaker passed the fruit bowl and Manuel António peeled an orange. "The airplane too," he said, when he had finished eating. "You know everything. Everything, everything. And if I tell you that I have invented a new weapon against Renamo, a spear that can hit him when it is thrown from thirty kilometers, you will not believe me." He broke into an ingenuous laugh. "Still," he said, "we're only spirits. Here we all are, waiting to die."

The grave in Mogonda was no more than three feet deep and the people in the settlement had already begun to congregate around it. Manuel António was wearing the beret with the wooden cross, white shorts and a Bayside Cheetahs T-shirt, inscribed with the name of the previous owner: Leslie. His girl was there in a faded blue drop-shoulder dress and yellow flip-flops; so were his followers, some in dowdy military regalia, others in shorts and T-shirts. They had captured a young man whom they believed to be a member of Renamo. They stood him before the crowd and interrogated him. He responded in a high-pitched voice, full of terror. They checked the texture of the skin on his shoulder for calluses, which would suggest he had borne arms with the rebels, and led him away. A Naparama lit a fire a few yards from the grave.

Then, abruptly, the ceremony had begun. Manuel António was wielding a rifle and scampering into the bush behind a band of Naparamas. He pursued them with one hand on his beret, and the other holding the weapon. He stopped and fired into the air, ran again, stopped, fired and ran. Then he tripped over and disappeared from view in the tall grass. Soon the men were jogging back, their spears held in front of them, and a circle was formed around the grave, Naparamas on one side and the population of Mogonda on the other. Manuel António approached the grave and led the whole assembly in jubilant song.

When the time came to enact his resurrection, he moved to the grave and knelt beside it. His adjutant began keening in a low voice and now the prophet sang as well. The two voices rose to a warbling plain song, then a drone, gaining and fading, and gaining once more, like the sound of angry bees, until it fell away. A folded blanket was placed in the grave and Manuel António lay in the fold while his men shoveled the earth back over him and the people of Mogonda watched without a murmur. The rhythmic cutting of the shovels and the crackle of the fire by the graveside were now the only sounds. When the grave was full, it was covered with a rush mat and the adjutant squatted down at one end, near the head of the buried man. He craned over with his ear to the mat, to hear the muffled words that had begun to issue from the ground, and transmitted them to the audience: "He is saying Naparama isn't beaten; he's down here in the grave." The adjutant leaned over and listened again. "He is doing the same work as Jesus Christ. He agrees to be buried to stop the bloodshed of the Mozambican people." Once again he lowered his head: "He is saying that the war should stop."

Manuel António said many things from the grave, but I did not understand them all. After six or seven minutes, the mat was removed and the earth began to shift. He was helped from the ground by his assistants and, as he approached the fire, the *povo* began singing mobilization songs. Manuel António removed a stick from the fire, knocked out the flame on the ground, grasped the smoldering end in one hand for a few seconds and extinguished the last of it on his legs and feet. At the back of the circle his girl looked on, the vigilant hazel eyes peering out behind a mask of indifference.

The Naparamas walked ecstatically along the edge of the crowd, raising the song toward the sky as the little man in the Bayside Cheetahs top worked his way through the brands in the fire. When he was done, his legs and hands were blackened and the song was rising higher still, as he clapped and chanted with the crowd, leading them at length to the closing antiphonal cheer.

"*Viva Frelimo!*": "VIVA!"
"*Viva Frelimo!*": "VIVA!"
"*Viva Manuel António!*": "VEEEEVA!"

"*Manuel António!*": "VIVA!"
"*Abaixo* [down with] *Renamo!*": "*ABA-A-IXO!*"
"*Abaixo os bandidos!*": "*ABA-A-IXO!*"
"*Viva o povo Moçambicano!*": "VEEEEEEVA!"

Then the Naparamas piled in the back of a red pickup. Manuel António and the girl jumped in the front and they were gone.

▲

To find a solution in Zambézia, Manuel António had simply ducked beneath the pretensions of the modern nation state. For a while in Maputo I remained under his spell, or rather, the spell of his spectacular success in returning people to their land. To emerge from this unsettling condition, the weight of recent acquaintance had to be shaken off, and in Maputo I soon came back to the realities of the aid community and the government departments.

Naparama was not a problem for Marxists, of whom there were many in Mozambique. They argued that Manuel António's success was the result of popular despair and the failure of the postcolonial state; that the prophet's triumph was the very yardstick of that failure. The only consolation was the thought that Frelimo had at last managed to tap the resources of rural tradition. For its part, Naparama had won a reappraisal of the old ways, earning respectable definitions for itself in the process. It was a "jacqueries," a "peasants' revolt," a "reassertion of traditional values." Terms like these circumscribed it, as they must, but they also signaled a new tolerance on the part of Mozambique's intelligentsia. As regimes collapsed in the Eastern bloc, religious belief, long hostile to the state, had reemerged as an overtly political force—a point that was often made in Maputo when the subject of Naparama came up, but the comparison was not accurate. The state in Mozambique had withered away long before the Naparamas swept through Zambézia. Moreover the adversary was a guerrilla movement whose fighters drew on a very similar cosmology. At first the vaccine had been too much for them, but gradually their own *curandeiros* were getting the measure of it. Naparama's time was up but the beliefs that informed it were no doubt more durable.

At the Maputo office of Mott, Hay & Anderson, the mood was ebullient. Now that a ceasefire had finally come in Angola, the staff had high hopes of a contract for the rehabilitation of the Benguela railway. Strachan was taking a rest in the capital. He and Carlos would return to the track the following week. Carlos told me that things in Chokwe were much the same. The nightlife was still going strong. He said he had been in a club during a mortar attack. The clientele had dashed for the door and left without paying, but as Carlos beat a retreat, the proprietor had stopped him on his way past the rattling tables and demanded that he pay for everybody's drinks. The fines train had arrived two days after my departure, so now all the bridges on that section were finished.

▲

A fortnight after I left Mozambique, news came through of a massacre in Nampula. The original report said that a thousand people had died in the area of Lalaua during a month of Renamo occupation, but this figure was revised to forty-nine in the weeks that followed. According to a later report, released when the facts had become a little clearer, the Naparamas were singled out for special savagery. But, as Xavier would have said, there were no ambulances at the scene of the accident. Sometime later the talks between Renamo and the government resumed in Rome. At the end of 1991, a few weeks before Christmas, another report emerged from Zambézia, but the veracity of this one was not in doubt. It was issued by the Mozambique News Agency and announced the death of Manuel António, "the leader of a Mozambican peasant militia, who claimed supernatural powers." The facts of the case were plain:

> Mr. António met his death on 5 December when he was leading a Barama group defending the headquarters of a co-conut plantation in the coastal town of Macuse from Renamo attack. Nine other members of the militia died, and Barama sources say that twenty-five Renamo members were also killed in battle. Mr. António's body was taken to the provincial capital, Quelimane. It was riddled with bullet holes and bayonet wounds—sad testimony to the failure of the Barama rituals, which are supposed to confer invulnerability.

The report suggested that the prophet's death could well be a "fatal blow" to the movement. By October 1992, when Renamo and the government signed a peace agreement, the Naparamas were dispersing. As for Manuel António, he had died once already and so it was less of an occasion for him. As he had said that night at dinner, "We're only spirits. Here we all are, waiting to die."

A week after the prophet's death, a meeting of the World Bank's Consultative Group on Mozambique ended in Paris with the donors promising to fulfill all Mozambique's external financing requirements for the following year. The sum in question was just over a billion

U.S. dollars. "Unless a solution to the ongoing conflict is found soon," the Consultative Group observed, "the economic recovery will remain fragile." The group's enthusiasm was reserved for Frelimo's privatization of large state companies. It praised Frelimo for "redefining the role of government to one of strategic macroeconomic management, while enhancing private-sector initiative in economic production." The hinterland of Mozambique seemed as remote from the donors' tables as the spirit of the prophet from his second body, which was brought back for burial to Nicoadala.

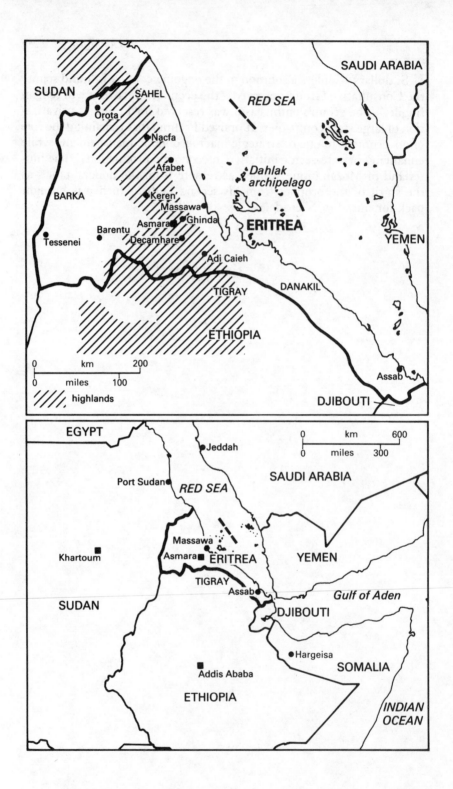

6

ERITREA

▲▲▲▲▲

> In the burning element of War, ordinary natures appear to become heavier.
>
> Clausewitz, *On War*

> "Do you think our guest house a little impoverished?"
> Lady Julia denied it.
> "Let me tell you," Genete continued, "that sadly this is an Eritrean palace. One day we will enter our holy and much desired city of Asmara. There, evening prayer will be called from the Eritrean mosque, and benedictions from the Cathedral. And you will see better things then."
>
> Thomas Keneally, *Towards Asmara*

In Cold War archaeology, Eritrea is the site of the last great military confrontation between Soviet imperialism and an African army. Its hills and plains are strewn with buckled, rusting Soviet armor; outside the capital, Asmara, there is a graveyard for Russian tanks and armored vehicles destroyed during the closing stages of the war. The most decisive battle was fought in 1988, as the struggle for control of Cuito Cuanavale was reaching its height in southern Angola. In Eritrea, the Soviet client was the loser and the Eritreans, who had been fighting for independence from Ethiopia since 1961, were on their way to victory. It was the end of a long, harsh, and extraordinary story.

Until the middle of the nineteenth century, Abyssinia was a complex of rival potentates of different ethnicity. It was in the *habash*, or northern highlands, that the centralizing impulse gave rise to a military

261

kingdom that extended its power over most of what is now known as Ethiopia. The peoples of the *habash* were predominantly Christian and claimed imperial authority from a succession of states dating back to the ancient kingdom of Axum in present-day Tigray. The two largest ethnic groups in the highlands were the Tigray people and the Amhara. The Amhara laid the foundations for the state of Ethiopia at the end of the nineteenth century. The central figure around whom the new imperium took shape was the Shoan king, and emperor of Abyssinia, Menelik II. Under his rule, the borders of the Amharic state of Shoa were pushed forward and consolidated in a crude process of military subjugation.

During the same period, Eritrea too came under a new form of domination. In 1890 it was colonized by the Italians, who then sought to enlarge their acquisitions in the Horn by moving inland to Abyssinia. In 1896 they were checked by the imperial army of Menelik II at the battle of Adowa. The treaty that Menelik later signed with Italy formalized Eritrea's status as an Italian colony. It remained under Italian jurisdiction until 1941, when the defeat of Mussolini's army in East Africa led to a transfer of power to the British. Nationalists long maintained that Italian colonialism gave Eritrea a distinct identity, annulling any claims derived from precolonial Abyssinian history. Ethiopian rulers and scholars, however, argued that it was a historic part of Abyssinia. Many of Eritrea's inhabitants speak Tigrinya, the language of neighboring Tigray. Moreover, in the 1870s they had fought for Menelik's predecessor, the Tigrayan emperor, Yohannes IV, against the Italians and Egyptians, in what was later interpreted as a show of Abyssinian unity against foreign incursion. Seventy years on, Eritrea's arguments for independence were seen by the Ethiopian court as so much casuistry. Yet there were marked differences between the small coastal colony, after half a century of Italian rule, and the feudal mass of Abyssinia, which had successfully resisted European domination until 1935.

Although the Fascist armies met with strong Ethiopian resistance, their fortunes were only reversed when Italy declared war on France and Britain in 1940, whereupon a large armed force, with troops from the colonies, entered the field from Kenya and Sudan in support of the Ethiopian patriots. By May of the following year, Italy was defeated and the war in Ethiopia was over. The colonial regiments fighting with the Allies had performed with distinction, including a Nigerian brigade and fifteen Indian battalions deployed for the assault on Keren, which the Italians abandoned after fifty-three days of intermittent fighting, some of it intense and terrible. Surrounded by high peaks, the town had seemed almost impregnable.

The British administered Eritrea for eleven years, during which they dismantled and sold much of the industrial plant installed by the Italians—a severe blow to the wealth of a potentially independent Eritrea. But after 1945, the views of the Attlee government on the colonial question brought certain advantages to the population. Education was extended and freedom of the press encouraged; political associations and trade unions flourished in Asmara. It was in this propitious climate that Eritrea's most eloquent champion emerged. Wolde-ab Wolde Mariam had established his reputation as a teacher, writing and designing the first classroom textbook in Tigrinya. An energetic figure in his thirties at the time of the British takeover, he was also the director of a newspaper, the *Eritrean Weekly News*, published in Tigrinya. In a regular column he called on the inhabitants of the colony to play an active part in their own future. Under the British, Eritrea's future was far from clear, but Wolde-ab was an advocate of independence. Eritreans maintained that his column was avidly discussed throughout the colony, not only by the paper's readers but by less educated people, to whom it was read aloud by literate friends and relatives. Before federation, Wolde-ab had also formed a political party to campaign for an independent Eritrea.

Haile Selassie had good reason to oppose such an idea. The prewar boundaries of the empire had not included Eritrea, but Ethiopia wanted a coastline. In 1947 the four Great Powers sent a commission to the territory. After an inconclusive partition plan, the matter went before the United Nations, which dispatched a commission of its own, instructing it not merely to ascertain the wishes of the Eritreans but to weigh these against the emperor's claims, "including in particular Ethiopia's legitimate need for adequate access to the sea."

In the meantime Haile Selassie set his own processes in motion. The first was to bolster the pro-union party in Eritrea, bringing it under the effective control of Addis. The second was to enlist the support of the Ethiopian Orthodox Church, with its loyal congregations in the Eritrean highlands. The patriarch denied communion or any rite to devotees who were known to favor independence. Finally, the enthusiasm of the nationalists would have to be dampened. In 1949, not long before the U.N. commission was due to arrive in Asmara, a bomb exploded at Wolde-ab's feet as he stepped from a car outside his house. He recovered after three months in the hospital and went back to his work, but the tide was not running with his cause.

In December of the following year, the U.N. resolved to place Eritrea under the sovereignty of the Ethiopian crown, in a federal arrangement that would allow the territory its own assembly and judiciary; 1952 was the date envisaged for British withdrawal. There had been no real process of consultation beyond the ad hoc soundings of the commission. The Soviet Union strenuously opposed the idea. To give the territory to the emperor, whose allegiance was clear, would consolidate Western influence in the Horn. "The General Assembly," said the Soviet representative, "cannot tolerate a deal by the colonial powers at the expense of the population of Eritrea. . . . In the circumstances, the only solution to the problem of the future of Eritrea is to grant independence."

Two years later, with the federation due to come into effect, Eisenhower's secretary of state, John Foster Dulles, explained the position to the U.N. Security Council. "From the point of view of justice," he declared, "the opinions of the Eritrean people must receive consideration. Nevertheless the strategic interest of the United States in the Red Sea basin, and considerations of security and world peace, make it necessary that the country has to be linked with our ally, Ethiopia." Within a few years Haile Selassie had moved against the opponents of the unionist party. Further attempts on Wolde-ab's life led him to seek refuge in Cairo. The emperor suppressed the official languages of Tigrinya and Arabic, and authorized the use of force to break up strikes and political protests. In 1962, the federation was dissolved and Eritrea was incorporated into the empire. Under intense pressure, the Eritrean parliament ratified the decision in November, but already a small group of nationalists had taken up arms against Ethiopian rule.

▲

Haile Selassie ruled Ethiopia, and held the military line against its newly annexed province, for a further thirteen years. He was a founding figure in the Organization of African Unity, a stubborn opponent of apartheid and a supporter of Namibian decolonization—in the early 1960s he had supplied the ticket for Jacob Kuhangua to fly to New York and petition the United Nations. Despite his independent turn of mind, he relied increasingly on help from Washington to maintain himself on the throne and to prosecute the war in Eritrea. At home the emperor was revered but not entirely loved, and in time he was seen as a reactionary leader whose policies had failed to democratize Ethiopia. At the end of his reign it was still a feudal empire. And it was in the grip of a severe famine. In 1973–1974 a quarter of a million people perished for lack of grain while the little man, whose name meant "Power of the Trinity," fed meat to the cats in his menagerie.

A military coup deposed Haile Selassie in 1974. The new leadership in Addis Ababa was known as the Dergue—a word revived from the ancient Ge'ez language, meaning "committee of equals." Once installed, the Dergue was riven by disputes. One of the main sources of contention was whether or not Ethiopia should enter the Soviet sphere of influence. In time, as Moscow held out the promise of tangible benefits, the pro-Soviet line prevailed.

This was a source of anxiety to the United States. In the last ten years of the emperor's reign, Ethiopia had qualified for roughly half of Washington's military assistance to sub-Saharan Africa. Despite the coup in Ethiopia, and the drift toward Moscow, the U.S. did not choke off its aid at once. The Horn was an area of keen superpower rivalry, on the threshold of the Middle East. For as long as neighboring Somalia remained in the Soviet camp, the best approach to Addis Ababa was a waiting game.

In 1977 the Dergue began drumming U.S. personnel out of Ethiopia and a team of Soviet advisers was on standby to replace them. A campaign of repression against rival revolutionary groups, mostly in Addis Ababa, began in the same year, leaving thousands dead. In Ogaden, the Dergue faced a grave military threat from resident Somali clansmen who claimed this triangle of territory in southeast Ethiopia as a part of Somalia. As revolutionary Ethiopia slid into disarray, Mohamed Siad Barre, the socialist president of Somalia, saw an opportunity to incorporate Ogaden and duly sent his own national army into Ethiopia in support of the Ogaden Somalis.

By the end of 1977 the Dergue was sounding the retreat from Ogaden; it was in this state of crisis that the Soviet Union stepped in with support. A large airlift of Cuban troops, some redeployed from Angola, and the arrival of tanks and aircraft from the Warsaw Pact countries saved the day for the Dergue. Within a matter of months, Ethiopia had regained control of the Ogaden. One of the most distinguished Cuban commanders in the field was Arnaldo Ochoa Sánchez, who would be decorated on his return to Havana and go on to command the Cubans in Angola.

In the throes of defeat, Siad Barre reversed his own allegiance entirely. Just as the Dergue had evicted the United States, so Siad Barre rid Somalia of its Soviet advisers and, almost overnight, became a born-again beneficiary of Western patronage. During the rest of his presidency, he received some $600 million in U.S. military aid, which he used to enforce a new but no less ruinous form of totalitarian rule in Somalia. After almost twenty years of tyranny, his country simply fell apart. Picking its way through the pieces, and collecting weapons paid for by U.S. military assistance, was part of the brief for Operation Restore Hope at the end of 1992.

The heaviest fighting in Ogaden was short-lived. Further north on the coastal margin of the Ethiopian empire, the Eritreans had also taken advantage of the turmoil in Ethiopia to launch a successful offensive. By the time that the Cubans were drafted into Ogaden, the Eritrean guerrillas were on the verge of military success. But the reversal of superpower alliances in the region was, for them, the greatest catastrophe since federation. Once Ethiopia's control of Ogaden was secure, the regime in Addis Ababa and its new benefactors in the Soviet bloc turned their minds, and their armor, to Eritrea. A ferocious drive against the rebels pushed them back into the hills and consigned them to another fourteen years of war. Eritrea was the marathon runner of African liberation, pulled out of a life-and-death race just a few yards from the finish and ordered back to the start. The first run had pushed the Eritreans to the edge of exhaustion; the second would force them through the pain barrier.

Over the next decade, the rebel stronghold in the north of the territory was the object of regular campaigns planned by seasoned Ethiopian commanders and Soviet bloc advisers with large conscript armies, mechanized divisions, and a well-equipped air force at their disposal. At the center of the Ethiopian war effort stood the diminutive lieutenant colonel who had shot his way to the head of the committee that supplanted Haile Selassie. Mengistu Haile Mariam—the name meant "Power of the Virgin"—was a Marxist-Leninist by alliance, if not conviction. Like his predecessor, he would not concede an inch on the issue of Ethiopian integrity; independence for Eritrea, with its access to the coast, was inconceivable. Under Mengistu, Ethiopia was no less of an empire and for most of his years in office, the main currents of African political thought moved in his favor. The breakup of any African country—all of them defined by colonial boundaries—was anathema on the continent, for it would open the way to a thousand ethnic separatisms, and the fragile nation states of Africa, it was said, would run to sand.

It was an irony, and a cruel one, that the Eritreans took much the same view. They were willing to fight for a multi-ethnic state based on the old colonial map—the territory had belonged to Italy for half a century—but maintained that it was Ethiopia, not they, who were in breach of African (and international) principle by having annexed Eritrea against its will. The resemblance to the conflict in Western Sahara was very striking, but most African heads of state rallied to Polisario while denying that Eritrea was an issue. Perhaps as a result, the conflict in Eritrea was far more devastating. Dropped by the United Nations after 1952 and ignored by the OAU, Eritrea had no protection against the worst excesses of Cold War enmity.

Had a war of thirty years' duration, costing perhaps three quarters of a million lives, been waged purely as a matter of principle, both the Eritreans and the Ethiopians would have much to answer for. But Eritrea was more than a question of scruple. By abolishing Eritrean institutions, raising punitive taxes and banning the two most widespread languages in the territory, annexation struck at the very heart of national aspiration. It was a test of endurance by a people who could not live under occupation. Once resistance had begun, the strains became much harsher, but when the first dramatic superpower shift had been registered—and withstood—there was no going back.

Mengistu's famine hit Ethiopia and Eritrea alike at the end of 1984. He had pulled more and more peasants from the land to fight the wars of empire. The men pressed into service left their own land in a state of neglect and, as they marched, preyed on the resources of others like a swarm of locusts. When these were scarce, the army requisitioned international food aid. Withering drought and blistering bombardment did the rest.

After the worst of Ethiopia's ordeal, the hunger lingered on. In Eritrea, Mengistu managed to conscript it to his cause. By the end of the 1980s, when I first traveled with the liberation movement in the north of Eritrea, the famine was still in evidence. In the rebel feeding centers, there were women and children whose state was as pitiful as any imprinted on the conscience of the West a year and a half earlier. I began to argue with my guide. It took more than one kind of intransigence to turn a child into a withered elder dying in its mother's lap, and the Eritrean struggle struck me then as a petty nationalism that had played its part in the famine. I think now that this was wrong. It was history, and the vagaries of international politics, that led people to die of hunger in Eritrea. The Eritreans had made many sacrifices under Ethiopian rule—first the Trinity and then the Virgin—and their position on the right to self-determination was not negotiable.

I went back to Eritrea in 1990 to find the situation changed: the rear bases of the movement had emptied out and the fronts were dug around the capital, Asmara. The fighters always spoke lyrically of this city as a gem set in a crown of hills. From the trenches on the new southern front, in 1990, you could see an edge of Asmara in the far distance once the mist had lifted. It looked much like any city in the distance and I thought then that I might never see it at closer range.

In May of the following year I was in Mozambique when I heard of Mengistu's sudden flight from Addis Ababa. Shortly afterward, Asmara fell. In the months that followed, the news from the city was encouraging. Good news from Africa is a rare and irresistible thing, but it pays to hurry to the source. Before the end of the year, I was on my way to Eritrea, not by rocky tracks below the Sudanese border, but by plane from Addis Ababa direct to Asmara.

In May 1991 the Eritrean People's Liberation Front entered the city of Asmara. The army of Ethiopia, which had occupied Eritrea for thirty years, was routed. The Ethiopians had dug fortifications to the south of the city. Here, in the hills around the village of Afalba, six Ethiopian divisions and an elite commando unit known as Spartakiat were destroyed in combat. As the Eritreans advanced on the capital, thousands of Ethiopian soldiers simply gave themselves up. A large contingent fled north to Keren but their retreat was cut and many died on the road.

Asmara had been surrounded for over a year, but the Eritreans wished to take it with a minimum of damage and so they waited, disposed along two fronts, to the south and the east, until the moment was right. Delirium broke out in Asmara as the Liberation Front arrived. The townspeople climbed onto the tanks and trucks to embrace the fighters. They told them how the Ethiopian army had threatened to burn the city to the ground as it left. They tore down the symbols of Ethiopian occupation and brought out food and drink for the rebel battalions.

There was almost no destruction in Asmara. When the garrison surrendered, the Eritreans took several grounded fighter aircraft and a quantity of heavy armor. Cordialities were exchanged between the new rulers in Addis Ababa and the victors in Asmara, who were invited, but declined, to take part in discussions on the future of Ethiopia. Instead they announced that a referendum would be held on the status of Eritrea within two years. It would be a formality; their territory was in effect an independent state.

Tens of thousands of Ethiopians, most of them soldiers or administrators, were evicted from Eritrea and the celebrations in Asmara began. Families were reunited after five, ten, fifteen years, sometimes longer. The celebrations continued until they threatened to get out of hand. Before long, the citizens of Asmara were too tired to get up in the morning, to work or cook or go about their business. There were deaths and injuries from festive gunfire and the city was at a standstill. In the end, the EPLF put a halt to it by fixing on a date four months distant for a formal celebration.

In the meantime, those divisions that had not entered Asmara were allowed to visit in rotation, staying for a few days and then returning to their posts elsewhere in the territory. The units based permanently in Asmara were regarded as the lucky ones. They were billeted in the old American communications base at Kagnew. During the day they would visit relatives or pass among the tables in cafés on the wide main street, which was colonnaded with tall palms. You could tell the fighters right away, not from any vanity of bearing, nor from their dress, but by their fascination for the ice cream tubs or the way they hovered by the espresso machines. These were people who had spent a decade in a wilderness of rock and desert.

The citizens of Asmara remained in a state of sublime shock from which they would not emerge before the collective rite of welcome and mourning had been performed in September. Until then, security was not an issue. By the end of the year not a single weapon was to be seen on the streets of Asmara.

▲

During the war the EPLF, the Eritrean People's Liberation Front, welcomed aid workers, dignitaries and journalists, anybody who might serve their purpose, directly or indirectly. I went first in 1987, a year before the movement took the garrison at Afabet and embarked on the campaign that liberated Asmara. "The field," as they called it, could only be reached through the Republic of Sudan, which gave the Eritreans sanctuaries near the border and offices in Khartoum. There were planes or buses to Port Sudan, after which the Front took over, ferrying its charges south along the Red Sea coast, through the old slaving port of Suakin and over the Ethiopian border. The journey from Port Sudan was made in Land Cruisers over dry riverbeds. Anywhere between nine and fourteen hours to the base area inside Eritrea was regarded as good time. In our case—we were five, including the driver—it took nearly thirty. We left during the rains and reached the northern bank of the Baraka, usually a dry course, when the river was in spate. The Land Cruiser was driven onto a large Soviet truck, which crossed the flood without mishap. The rest of the journey was made on empty riverbeds between high, bare mountains.

We were negotiating a dry river course when a fighter halfway up the slope at a bend in the way began to gesture at us. She was too far off to make herself heard and fired three warning shots in the air. Rounding the corner we were confronted by a wall of brown water, three feet high, thrashing toward us. A sapling was torn out of the ground, tossed along for a few yards and sucked under. Then a boulder, the size of a cushion, rose gaily into the air. The driver reversed at high speed in search of a suitable incline; we abandoned the car and scrambled up the rocks to watch the torrent pass. The water rose until the back of the car was full; on the way we had come were two white clefts on the surface of the flood, where an acacia and a taller tree remained standing. Beyond them the water gathered momentum as it thrust into the bend. It was a piece of dreadful profligacy in a land so prone to drought. This water ran off the Red Sea Hills and sank into the deserts of Sudan. On the edge of the catchment there were aid projects for a small group of Beni Amer tribesmen who could no longer survive as nomads, but inside Eritrea, where people lived with their eyes raised in search of rain or in fear of air raids, the water ran uselessly off the side of the mountains.

Much of rebel-held Eritrea was parched by the sun and cratered by air-to-ground weapons: detonation bombs, cluster bombs, phosphorus and a Soviet variety of napalm. Two fronts ran diagonally across the territory and, north of these, the movement had full control on the ground. It was largely worthless mountain and arid plain, a uniform color by day, when it was saturated with intense light, and at sunset a range of blues and livid reds. Tens of thousands of people lived and worked in this hostile terrain, a place for saints and martyrs, where endeavor should have sunk without trace. Any patch of earth from which a blade of grass could be coaxed was under cultivation. As the fronts dropped down to the southwest, the mountains fell away into a fertile floodplain. The rebels controlled little of this but what they had was given over to agricultural projects. Here they were spared the cruelty of the drought but were at greater risk from the Ethiopian air force.

From the movement's rear base to the front line was a further 150 kilometers over grueling track and half a day's climb to the trenches. Through a slit the enemy lines were visible, two hundred meters away over a bone-strewn gully. The place was known as Den Den. Another two miles along the trenches, at a salient, we gazed down at a column of Soviet trucks moving through the valley. This place felt more like the edge of some remote and unacknowledged world than a military front: it was a precipice at which the domain of the rebels came to an abrupt halt. Beyond this point only aspiration could make its way, through a country sealed off by the largest army in Africa.

Fesseha Ghebrehiwet worked for Protocol, a filter through which visitors passed once inside the territory. He had a beard and stood about five foot eight. He read through my documents and looked me over with keen indifference, announcing that he would probably accompany me south when the time came. At the moment I was a problem; I had been traveling for two months and the London office of the EPLF had not confirmed my arrival. Fesseha and one of his colleagues in Protocol declared that they would have to "carry out a check" and that until this was done, I was confined to the rear base.

The Eritreans referred to this craggy, uncompromising place as Orota: a complex of departmental offices, lodgings and food distribution centers, with a large school and an even larger hospital, spread out over several square miles. Here too the Front had its own modest means of production, enabling it to make plastic sandals, sanitary napkins and simple drugs: penicillin, chloroquine, aspirin. There was a spaghetti factory and a bakery. Some of the plant had been dismantled by the EPLF in the south and brought up to Orota by truck, some had been donated by aid agencies. The production units were powered by generator, as were the operating theaters in the hospital area—shipping containers where remarkable surgery was performed with outdated equipment. A mountain valley or a steep gorge, where air attack was impossible, made good sites for most of these amenities, but others were simply built underground. The generators were started up at night, when the mountains became more sociable and the inhabitants seemed to stir into activity. So much of life in Orota was lived with exemplary patience in shadow or darkness by people who came from a highland capital with wide roads, tiled roofs and café terraces filled with light.

Fesseha Ghebrehiwet grew up in Asmara but had moved to Addis Ababa to study accounting. Shortly afterward, he enrolled in the Front. He had lived here for nine years. He had been wounded twice in action but not seriously. One of the most familiar sounds in Orota was the rattle of aluminum crutches being laid down on stone. They were heaped like scrap along the side of any crowd that had gathered to hear music or speeches. It was striking to see how many members of the Front were disabled and, of these, how many were youngsters. In this sense, Fesseha was fortunate. Almost all members, regardless of status or gender, had seen combat before they took up paramilitary or administrative work.

The isolation of the EPLF was complete. Just as they were separated from the rest of Africa by the habitat into which they had been forced, so too they were cut off from the fraternity of liberation and the two most important international bodies that gave it help, the United Nations and the OAU. Fesseha greeted the mention of other movements on the continent with a cold reserve. He would ask probing questions about them and then withhold any judgment of his own, although on other topics he spoke with candor. The resolutions of the EPLF's Second Congress, which had just been held inside the territory, expressed solidarity only with the "peoples" of South Africa and Namibia, not with their guiding organizations.

"We have nothing to say to them," Fesseha declared, "and they have nothing to offer us. For many years we approached them but they have rejected us. This is because of games in Africa. We are at war with their allies, the Soviets, and it is from Moscow that they receive their orders to leave us alone. Let them take whatever orders they like. The EPLF has never taken orders. From whom should we take them?"

On our journey south to Nacfa, which was held by the Eritreans, ill-concealed animosity soon developed. I was a guest in the walled garden of rebel territory, from which it was impossible to step away and elicit a second opinion, as you might in another country. When Fesseha announced that the EPLF had special units operating south of the two fixed fronts, I did not believe him. When he said that the movement received almost no support from the outside, beyond remittances from wealthy exiles, I was skeptical. When he proclaimed the familiar phrase, "Victory is certain," I felt the EPLF would never take control of the territory from a military regime that was equipped by Moscow, oiled by Israel and led the progressive camp in Africa.

Fesseha responded with cautious hostility. He took guarded offense at the suggestion that in Eritrea the EPLF must bear as much responsibility as the government of Ethiopia for the famine of 1984–1985. After all, it had preferred its nationalist agenda to the passage of emergency food aid—the EPLF was disrupting the relief effort in 1987—and scarcely differed in this respect from UNITA, or any insurgency one cared to name. From that point on, our journey became an unending argument. The wilderness of Fesseha's persecuted kin was little more than a backdrop to our disagreement. We strode through feeding centers where people lay in a state of terrible malnutrition, yet we never really saw them. Fesseha would proffer them as evidence of Ethiopia's reckless conduct while I would trade them back as confirmation that the Eritrean struggle was an extravagance in a region plagued by drought and famine.

At the Nacfa front we regained our composure. It was not the trenches that sapped my stamina for argument but the spectacle of ruin in the town itself, which the EPLF had liberated in 1977 during their first push to Asmara. After an auspicious start, the offensive had been checked at the port of Massawa, when the Soviet Union came to Mengistu's aid at the end of the year. It was the worst setback the EPLF would ever suffer and marked the beginning of their retreat into the far north. By 1978, they had fallen back in disarray to Nacfa and dug in to withstand a massive Soviet-Ethiopian counterthrust that should have wiped them out for good. They had held it ever since, and it had been pounded by air and artillery until it was no more than the name of a strategic position. Everything was leveled apart from the mosque. We stopped over in Nacfa on our way to and from the trenches, sleeping in a well-appointed bunker. We walked in the rubble of the town the following morning. In the ruins of the market square a colonnade of jacarandas was in full bloom; a light wind stirred their leaves. Occasionally an EPLF jeep rattled through the dirt intersections that divided the ruins. From a small garden below the square came the sound of a hoe in stony soil; the fighters grew onion and tomatoes to supplement their diet of grain. This and the repetitive clap of artillery fire were the only sounds. On our return from the trenches later that day, we walked over to the mosque and up the winding stair of the damaged minaret, emerging at the top to sit in silence for a few minutes, Fesseha's gaze fixed throughout on the south, before descending to the car and heading back toward the rear base.

Fesseha was single and eager to disparage the idea of partnership, although there were many couples in the Front. When asked why he was not a husband and father, he would smile at the indiscretion. "Maybe," he said once, "when we have won our independence." These choices could not have been easy; plenty of people in the field had children, which gave a continuity to their lives and, indeed, to the cause, but bringing up a family in such conditions was hard. Fesseha seemed to have adopted an attitude of thorough austerity, in keeping with his circumstances, as though it were easier to live and work here with no mitigations until the war was won. He laughed and told me, "I am married to the Front." He was born in 1952, the year of the ill-starred federation that precipitated Eritrea into conflict, and thus too late to remember European colonialism. But his knowledge of the history was confident. Despite half a century of Italian rule, Fesseha's generation still saw their struggle in its epic dimension as a war of resistance against an expansionist African empire.

▲

Dr. Berhana Haile seemed to be made of eggshell. A gust of wind, one felt, might drag her out of her plastic sandals and sweep her into the nearest thornbush. She wore faded jeans and a check shirt. Her hair was matted, her features fine and her hands small. It was as though she had been set apart for some purpose other than life on earth. Fesseha, who had a similar physical frailty, no less deceptive, had taken us through the lowlands on our way back from Nacfa. We ran into Dr. Berhana by chance, having finished our work for the day, as we waited until dusk to travel.

Berhana's life was exemplary, not merely in its virtue, but in its coincidence with an important period of campaigning in Eritrea at the end of the 1970s. Berhana, like Fesseha, was regarded as a fighter, but while he had borne arms for several years, she had not. She was a barefoot doctor and later a field surgeon. At that time there were said to be about ninety thousand "fighters" in the field, of whom a third at any one time may have actually been soldiers.

Berhana was born in the southern highlands of Eritrea, below Asmara, two years before the federation came into effect. She was a Tigrinya speaker from a Christian family. She had an older brother, almost twenty years her senior, whom she accompanied at the age of six when he left for Addis Ababa to enlist in Haile Selassie's air force. Her parents remained in the south. She never said what became of her brother, but the air force was a prestigious vocation and, with military aid from the West, the Ethiopians became some of the best pilots in Africa. Berhana was successful at school and completed her secondary studies in 1969, going on to train as a nurse. News from her relatives was infrequent.

The main armed opposition in Eritrea, of which she was aware, had not come from her own community, but from the Muslim chiefs of the lowlands bordering Sudan. They had canvassed support for their cause in the Arab world and joined Wolde-ab in Cairo, where he had been broadcasting to Eritrea with the approval of Gamal Abdel Nasser. In 1960 they had formed the Eritrean Liberation Front and a year later turned to armed struggle. The ELF was an inchoate movement dominated by Islamic leaders, often conservative, who resented the influence of Christian Ethiopia. Eritrea itself consisted of Christians and Muslims in roughly equal proportions. The Christians were concentrated in the highlands; their cultural and linguistic links with the Tigrayans in Ethiopia proper meant that they were viewed with suspicion by the ELF. As a nationalist, Wolde-ab welcomed the arrival of his compatriots in Cairo, but his background was Christian, which tended to isolate him from the ELF leadership and the pan-Arab milieu in which it thrived abroad. Inside Eritrea, there were few signs of popular confidence in the leadership, which seemed more concerned with its foreign contacts. Within a few years it was firmly established in Cairo, under Nasser's auspices. Approval and a measure of support came from the Algerian FLN, Cuba and the Soviet Union. The Baathist regimes of Syria and Iraq were also interested in the movement's fortunes.

To Berhana and many young people in Addis during the 1960s, Cuba and Algeria were models of successful resistance to oppression. Berhana viewed Haile Selassie largely as an instrument of Western policy in the Horn. The emperor's pursuit of Ethiopian integrity did not endear his Western allies to the Eritreans. As the ELF expanded, repression increased. In the mid-1960s, Israel began training a special counterinsurgency unit near Asmara known as Force 101. It consisted of Eritreans and Ethiopians, and many of its operations were supervised by Israeli officers. In 1962, a period of brutal repression began in the Muslim lowlands. At the end of the year, about three hundred villages had been razed, six hundred civilians massacred and sixty thousand head of livestock slaughtered. Twenty-five thousand lowlanders fled to Sudan and a policy of forced relocation was imposed on those who remained.

In 1971 Berhana left her nursing school in Addis with a special qualification in anatomy and physiology and took a job at the Haile Selassie I Hospital where she was assigned to a children's ward. Another violent onslaught against civilians in Eritrea gave rise to a mood of mistrust between Amharas and Eritreans in Addis, moderated only by general dissatisfaction with the policies of Haile Selassie. Berhana was often in the company of young Amharas as critical as she was of the war in Eritrea. "Students in Addis and many of my friends," she said, "argued that the problem in Eritrea was not a question of national rights, or even a colonial question, but a direct result of Haile Selassie's policies. They thought that if the government was overthrown and a progressive regime put in its place, the Eritrean question would disappear automatically. This is what Marxism taught."

Within the Eritrean movement, meanwhile, there were signs of strife. The ELF was still failing to distinguish itself as a democratic force. Its members moved in baronial style from village to village, raising taxes and confiscating livestock as a contribution to the war effort, for which the people had little to show. In 1971 the ELF carried out a massacre in a Christian village that refused to pay. By now, a new faction with very different attitudes to the conflict was challenging the ELF. The Eritrean People's Liberation Front criticized the ELF for its dependence on foreign support, its internal rivalries and lack of strategy. Above all, they claimed, it had no will to develop and educate the "broad masses," the ordinary inhabitants of Eritrea on whom any guerrilla movement would have to rely. In 1972 a fratricidal conflict broke out between the two Fronts, and only ended a month after Haile Selassie was deposed in Addis Ababa.

Berhana greeted the revolution in Ethiopia with relief. Surely now the Eritrean question would wither away. The Ethiopian famine of 1973–1974 had discredited the old order entirely: not just the emperor but the archaic style of government and social organization with which he was associated. The new regime was known as the Provisional Military Administrative Council, or the Dergue. Berhana and her friends took comfort from the fact that this group of progressive officers was headed by an Eritrean. But within two months Lieutenant

General Aman Andom, who had urged negotiation with the Eritrean fronts, had died in a factional shootout. The rise of Lieutenant Colonel Mengistu Haile Mariam had begun. Henceforth any death inside the Dergue was a new lease of political life for Mengistu, who became head of state at the beginning of 1977 and dispatched the last of his rivals before the year was out. By then Berhana had left Addis and enrolled in the EPLF.

"With Aman's death, and the reports of fresh fighting in Eritrea, there was a persecution of Eritreans in Addis, which is one of the reasons we wanted to leave," Berhana explained. "The other was that students and nurses were supposed to go out to the rural areas of Ethiopia and work in an education and health drive. I was assigned to Harar, in Ogaden, and I decided I could not serve the Ethiopian government. Some of my friends in Addis had gone already to the field and so by now, I believe, I was being watched. I went to the airport with three other nurses from my hospital, Eritreans, and we flew to Asmara. After that, you know, the Dergue started to kill. How many people died in Addis? Nobody knows."

In Asmara Berhana found the stories of renewed fighting she had heard back in Addis to be true. The two Eritrean Fronts had made peace early in 1975 and embarked on a joint effort to liberate the territory. In February they launched an attack on Asmara but failed to take it. Four days of reprisals by the Ethiopian garrison followed and the atmosphere in Asmara on Berhana's arrival was tense. She decided to leave for the field as soon as possible. It was rumored that the ELF and the EPLF were planning a big offensive.

"In Asmara," she said, "we formed a group, myself and some friends, and we were led out of the city by three EPLF. It took us eight days to reach the northern area of Sahel and by this time we were 115. It was here that I received military training, for six months, in light combat weapons and hand grenades and then I was transferred to a hospital, not far away." In 1977, a few months before the movement made its big push, Berhana was transferred again, this time to a front on the outskirts of Nacfa, which was still held by the Ethiopians. She was part of a mobile surgical team, eleven altogether. She remained there for six months. "We were repairing chest and soft-tissue injuries, sometimes through the night. The fighting was very hard and we had some losses, even in the field clinic during surgery." Then, in March, Nacfa fell and the Ethiopian defense of Eritrea began to crumble. The ELF liberated Tessenei in the lowlands, then Mendefera, Adiquala and Agordat. The EPLF took Afabet, Decamhare and, after three days of hard fighting in July, the garrison of Keren, which the Allies had captured with such difficulty from Mussolini during the Second

World War. By December Asmara was encircled and the guerrillas were inside the coastal town of Massawa. There was a good chance that they would now win redress for the cynicism of the Western powers and the United Nations by taking Asmara and renegotiating Eritrea's status with the Dergue.

Berhana moved from Afabet to Keren in July. There had been heavy casualties at Keren and she remained in the town until the civilian hospital was functioning efficiently. "We found a lot of drugs and supplies in the stores at Keren," she said, "and we set up something very good. It was possible to treat people for common ailments. Malaria, simple infections and even pneumonia. I stayed in Keren for four months, and here I was really becoming more than a nurse. There was secondary surgery to do now, mostly to remove shrapnel, and I was performing some of these operations myself, under supervision. Then, in November, we were moved south. Our fighters had opened two fronts on the road from Asmara to Massawa and I was working between them. The fighting was very hard and we lost a lot of material. The shelling, though, was the worst and we took many casualties. It was here that I did my first real surgery.

"Well, you know, we had our big disappointment when we withdrew from Massawa in 1978, and we made our front at Nacfa. In those days the big central hospital was not in Orota. We had it in the Sahel district, right up until 1981. But in the end we relocated this as well. Since then, I have spent some of my time in Orota but I have traveled and worked in all our liberated areas, often for as long as a year at a time. In the lowlands I was in charge of a mobile surgery unit and also I was training nurses to work in places after we left; some I could even train up to surgery. In 1984, I was in the northeast and the following year in Barentu. I was in Nacfa in 1985 and 1986. I have been in all our liberated areas since the withdrawal. I came several times to work in Nacfa when the Dergue launched new offensives. In general I can say it has gone smoothly. I think the war will soon be over"—she glanced across at Fesseha—"and as for what I am doing now, I don't know if we are ready to discuss this yet."

Fesseha raised a hand by way of interruption.

"She has been working behind the enemy lines," he said. Then, turning to Berhana, he added, "He doesn't believe our forces can be there."

She looked quite astonished. They spoke in Tigrinya, after which her eyes ran down the length of my body and came to rest on my bag.

"You seem to take many things with you when you travel," she said, pointing at it with a brittle hand.

▲

Massawa had been a disaster. Dr. Berhana had passed over it lightly, but the reality was cruel. For thirteen years, under Haile Selassie, the Eritreans had been faced with a powerful pro-Western alliance, which remained in place after the revolution. They had weathered the storm, however, and in 1977 they were poised for victory, when the Dergue was rescued by the Soviet and Cuban intervention in Ogaden. The guerrillas were camped on the edge of Massawa when the first shells from Soviet vessels off the coast began falling on their positions; within seven months they had been forced to abandon almost every town they had taken.

At the end of 1979, Mengistu could enjoy a sense of relative well-being, derived from the knowledge that from henceforth the isolation of the EPLF would only increase. The U.N. had washed its hands of Eritrea, and since its inception—in which Haile Selassie played such an important part—the OAU had not been prepared to consider it. The Cairo Declaration of 1964 on the inviolability of colonial boundaries was deemed irrelevant in the case of Eritrea: it was already the fourteenth province of Ethiopia and the principle could not be applied with hindsight. Mengistu was a beneficiary of the fraternal Soviet Union spirit in Africa. On their visits to the OAU headquarters in Addis, the main liberation movements would pay him their respects by condemning the Eritrean cause as an infantile disorder. In this, the ANC would be the most compliant, and Polisario, whose own case was strikingly similar, the most reluctant. Only Samora Machel broke the rules by providing the EPLF with facilities in Maputo. The difficulties of the EPLF were compounded by the crushing defeat inflicted on the ELF, which had decided to stay and fight as the Ethiopian armies moved up through Eritrea. The remnants broke up into factions, most of them opposed to the EPLF. There was little support from the outside now, beyond intermittent funding from the Arab states, and even this was compromised by the Marxist discourse of the EPLF. Saudi support now went to the remains of the ELF, in an attempt to build a conservative Eritrean nationalism indebted to Riyadh. The first priority was war not against the Dergue but against the EPLF. It was a desultory affair, however, with no resemblance to the strife of the early 1970s. For the EPLF there was only a trickle of arms and money from disparate sources; in effect, they were on their own.

It was difficult to find an Eritrean document that referred to the retreat from Massawa, although there was no shortage of documents on almost every other subject. In an unpublished typescript of a report that went before the EPLF's Second Congress a few months before I arrived, the retreat of 1978 was referred to as a "strategic withdrawal" and described in general terms as "a task that demanded heavy sacrifice, fortitude and perseverance." A terse summary said simply, "The objectives of the strategic withdrawal were achieved." Above it an interlinear addition had been added in handwriting: "Thanks to the heroism and steadfastness of the people and the Eritrean People's Liberation Army."

The EPLF drafted, rewrote and stored a prodigious amount of text, from medical records on the nomads who came for treatment in Orota to long disquisitions on the phases of the struggle. They were vehement believers in the word. The enthusiasm with which they went about transmitting it was remarkable in view of how many languages were spoken in the territory. In the end the little print works they had installed in the mountains at Orota settled on five languages, including English and Arabic.

Inside the unkempt propaganda offices stood a line of old typewriters, mostly with Amharic script, and duplicators. There was also an Italian offset machine in a large bunker across the way. Over one wall of the offices was a slogan: "Increasing efforts of the Department of Information and Propaganda to reach the receptive ears of the masses have given fruit." In addition to reports from the various departments and resolutions from the Second Congress, the Front produced a weekly bulletin of monitored international broadcasts, a fortnightly news sheet (*Events*) in Arabic and Tigrinya, and a quarterly cultural Xerox (*Reflections*), whose latest issue carried an abridged essay by Tolstoy on folk tales. Adult-literacy and schoolbooks were produced along with versions of *Othello*, *Eugene Onegin* or *Oliver Twist*, rendered in Tigrinya. Yet the most fastidious and delicate of their productions were the minute prescription slips printed in Arabic and Tigrinya for cough syrup, zinc ointment and ear drops. As I stepped outside, the old editor in charge of the offices quoted one of the maxims of the movement: "Learn to read," he said, "before you carry a gun."

On our way back to the guest house in the dark, we passed a stony outcrop that flickered with a strange blue light, as though the ground were awash with burning paraffin. We discovered a large crowd of civilians squatting in the rubble before an old monitor rigged up to a video machine, set out on the rock. They were watching a love scene from a Soviet serialization of *Anna Karenina*. A woman fighter with a cloth wrapped around her head stood by the monitor and barked a Tigrinya translation through a megaphone. The blue light crept along the faces of the audience, rapt, intrigued—at the front sat a couple of elderly herdsmen in robes with their crooks propped on their shoulders.

We were in the territory of the National Guidance Department, and when we repaired to the video library nearby, we found row upon row of taped material, including several compilations of World Cup football matches and three copies of *The Battle of Algiers*. There was a tape of *Under Fire*, a Hollywood production about American newsmen in Nicaragua and a favorite with the people, who thought well of Western journalists as a result. Video copies of *The Front Page*, which might have set the record straight, were sadly absent from the National Guidance library. It did, however, contain detailed war footage shot by EPLF cameramen. Rousing battle scenes and hideous images of bomb victims had their propaganda value, but beneath it all lay that same concern for documentary record.

The eerie light was still playing on the rubble as we passed by the open air screening of *Anna Karenina*. I suggested to Fesseha that we stay and watch the end, but he was not keen.

"I have seen it before," he said with evident contempt. "I do not even know why we must show these heavy Soviet films, except that we are always short of something or other."

To drive the EPLF back into the hills, Mengistu relied on the use of a large Soviet arsenal, with Eastern bloc advisers fielded alongside. Libya had loaned out troop transports to the Dergue, while armed units from South Yemen, once an ally of the Eritreans, were also deployed. This odd and formidable alliance would alter during the 1980s, but the core of massive Soviet provision would remain. Haile Selassie had severed relations with Israel during the October War, but in 1976 the Dergue resumed them informally for two years, and again at the end of the 1980s, when Israel set about improving Mengistu's aerial munitions in return for the acquisition of Ethiopia's Jews, the Falashas. The Israelis upgraded Soviet rockets and supplied the Dergue with cluster bombs, probably obtained from Chile. The pilots in Ethiopia were skilled and the officers were able; this eclectic range of weaponry did much to compensate for the reluctant ranks of peasants who made up the Dergue's army.

In 1982 Mengistu decided to settle matters in Eritrea once and for all. His first thought was to effect a cultural cleansing of the fourteenth province. He called the campaign "The Multifaceted Operation to Solve the Conflict in Eritrea." Mengistu's conception of culture was narrow in the application, however, and within weeks of his arrival in Asmara, the operation had turned into a remorseless drive to wipe out the EPLF, which was now the only plausible threat to the Dergue in Eritrea. The planned economic rejuvenation of the territory was secondary to Red Star, as the military campaign was known. The EPLF were quick to see this. Having survived the initial saturation bombing, they made ready to withstand the advance of more than 100,000 troops in four coordinated commands.

Red Star was a failure, despite the quality of the Ethiopian officers. In this and subsequent campaigns in Eritrea, Ethiopia's Second Revolutionary Army depended on heavy aerial bombardment, which the EPLF was learning to survive, and ground assaults in difficult terrain by demoralized, expendable conscripts. The EPLF, by contrast, were highly motivated, and sparing of their own fighters. As Red Star got under way, the EPLF drove Mebrek Command—the word means thunder—from the western lowlands in a matter of days. It took two weeks for Mebrek to regroup, during which time the entire campaign was thrown off balance. Even so, in the mountains, the Ethiopians had made progress and were on the point of overrunning Nacfa. After a lacerating bombardment, waves of infantry were sent to their deaths under fire from the EPLF's high positions. With the Eritrean defense on the point of collapse, however, the opportunity was lost by the Ethiopian chief of staff, when he decided to hold back and offer Mengistu's old division, the 3rd Infantry, the honor of taking the town. This won vital time for the guerrillas. By the end of their counterthrust, eleven thousand Ethiopian lives had been lost on the Nacfa front. Among the dead was the commander of the 3rd Infantry Division.

The figure for the campaign as a whole was undoubtedly far higher. Early in 1983 the Ethiopians estimated that nearly 100,000 government troops, and fewer than 10,000 guerrillas, had been killed or wounded in Eritrea since 1975. Whatever the sufferings of the nationalists, the lot of the ill-trained armies dying for Mengistu was far harsher. But it was the ordinary inhabitants of Eritrea who suffered the worst fate. The same sinister audit proclaimed over 250,000 civilians dead as a result of the war; 400,000, meanwhile, were languishing in Sudan.

Mengistu left Asmara and returned to Addis unannounced. Talks were opened with the EPLF in East Germany but both sides were uncompromising. A new offensive in 1983 broke through the EPLF lines but failed to consolidate. The guerrilla dispositions remained unchanged, although it was now no longer accurate to describe them in this way, for they were fixed fronts and the forces holding them were engaged in conventional combat. It was only in the south and center of the territory, in their mysterious work "behind enemy lines," that the EPLF still relied on guerrilla tactics.

The conventional character of the war spared Eritrea some of the hardships that Ethiopia suffered as the famine gathered momentum.

Unlike imperial levies of the past, Mengistu's army in Eritrea was fairly well provisioned and relied less on the herds and granaries of the territory. However, the Ethiopian army was now 300,000 strong; a high proportion of these men would normally have worked the land.

If Eritrea escaped lightly, this was only in the most relative sense. There were many Eritrean deaths by starvation in that critical period of 1984–1985, for continued fighting imposed drastic limitations on commerce among a population that had always made up its grain shortages by trading over the borders into Sudan and Tigray. Large areas of the north and west were laid waste by bombing and the rising tide of refugees meant that much of the cultivable land was now going to waste. Restrictions on civilian movement also denied valuable pasture to livestock owners. Hundreds of thousands of people were crammed together in dangerous inactivity.

The fighting continued during the famine with further campaigns on a formidable scale. In 1984 the EPLF went on the offensive in the lowlands. In January they overran Tessenei and Aligidir. Within two months they had redeployed large quantities of captured armor in the northeast and driven the Wekaw command—the word means crush— from its positions near the coast in a series of engagements that suggested theirs was now a fighting force as structured as any national army in the Horn, and more adept at conventional warfare. The EPLF hung on to this part of the territory for the remainder of the war, but Tessenei and the big garrison of Barentu, which it took the following year, were recaptured in a massive Dergue offensive in 1985. Thereafter, the fighting diminished, and Mengistu replenished his army, which was soon nearly half a million strong. The EPLF had been pushed out of its positions in the west and had chosen not to engage. Instead it had withdrawn from Barentu and Tessenei with a further quantity of armor, ammunition and medical supplies, and reviewed the situation.

As early as 1985, it should have been obvious that even with the withdrawal from the lowlands, the EPLF was undefeatable. I understood this only dimly, however, and imagined that even if it were true, this invincibility was in its way a misfortune, for it did not mean that they would win, only that they would live on in the hills, contributing to the instability of the region with little to show for their efforts. Nor was there a resolute superpower to ensure that they were well supplied. In Africa, the Eritrean struggle was often likened to that of UNITA, but the comparison was misleading. UNITA fought its battles with, and often on behalf of, South Africa. From 1986 to 1991, it received generous military aid from the United States. Dr. Savimbi could woo eminent conservatives in Washington with his anticommunist posturing, his fatigues—which proxy crusaders of all persuasions find attractive—and the matching ivory handles of his cane and pistol. The Eritreans lacked that kind of glamour.

"Tell me," said Fesseha, whose questions were often rhetorical, "if we had support from America and a big army fighting next to ours, would we still be in the mountains? So why is UNITA not winning, even with two armies and all this money? We find it strange. But one good thing we hear about Savimbi: he is most of the time in the field."

The EPLF argued that the nationalist movement in Eritrea had suffered at the hands of expatriate leaders with agendas of their own. The worst offender, in their eyes, was their former foreign affairs chief, Osman Salih Sabbe, an influential fund-raiser in the Gulf, who was eventually expelled. The Front did not like deals being struck without proper consultation. Their leaders were almost always in the territory, which is what they respected about Savimbi. The UNITA bases, however, were decked with photographs of the leader, and his nostrums were chalked on the walls, while in Eritrea the only cult was that of the people.

Fesseha denied that the EPLF was Marxist, yet its early pamphlets were classics of revolutionary discourse. "In Africa," said one of their productions in the late 1970s, "imperialism is hatching new political conspiracies and undertaking military offensives to establish puppet movements and weaken and crush the ever-intensifying struggles of the peoples of South Africa, Namibia, Zimbabwe and Western Sahara, which are scoring great victories over the forces of colonialism, oppression and reaction." As an appeal to African liberation movements, it was largely useless; their reliance either on Moscow or the OAU would soon rule out the formal expression of sympathies.

Despite Fesseha's protestations, the EPLF had once been enthusiastically Marxist. The National Democratic Program, adopted at its First Congress in 1977, announced that it would "confiscate all land in the hands of the aggressor Ethiopian regime, the imperialists, Zionists and Eritrean lackeys and put it in the service of the Eritrean masses." It would keep the Dergue's system of nationalized farms and introduce cooperative agriculture, while seeking to "organize, politicize and arm the peasants with a clear revolutionary outlook." This kind of talk merely confirmed Washington's opposition to Eritrean independence; the Saudis too took the Front at its word. Yet it is likely that the EPLF were revising their opinions as early as 1983. Certainly they made no effort to interfere with itinerant trade, and by the Second Congress, in 1987, all nationalization plans had been dropped, along with the Manichaean rhetoric. Their formal ties were now with the socialist and social-democratic parties of the West, including the British Labour

Party, which had promised support for a referendum in Eritrea and, once in office, a policy that struck at "the roots of the agony."

We were in a settlement a few hours' drive from the rear base when we heard the results of the British general election on the radio. Our hosts were preparing food, but as the news of Margaret Thatcher's comfortable victory was announced, breakfast came to a standstill and a dozen people huddled around the set. The Eritreans admired "Tacher" for her stubbornness and thought well of her record as a critic of Soviet policy, but they were wary of her indifference to what they called "injustices," of which their own was high on the list.

A century earlier the Liberals had championed the Boers against Britain's annexation of the Transvaal but, on assuming office, Gladstone had changed his mind. If opposition pledges were trifling things, how much more so when Britain was a third party? The defeat of their declared champion alarmed the Eritreans less than the margin of victory for the Iron Lady, which they took in a broader sense to indicate the widening gulf between North and South. Fesseha was especially downcast. He had three kinds of smile, one signifying genuine amusement, another—the Protocol smile—that meant "inquire no further" and a third that masked anger or dismay. It was this last that he wore now, leaning forward to switch off the radio.

One of the results of the Second Congress was a change in the EPLF leadership. The new general secretary was a military man in his forties whose family had played a prominent role in the nationalist movement. A few days before I left Eritrea, Fesseha took me to meet him. We drove for half an hour from our quarters onto a hillside road that dropped slowly down to a dry riverbed. At the narrowest point lay a group of camouflaged dwellings. Anchored by the heat of the afternoon a donkey stood with its eyes half shut while two goats tussled at a denuded shrub growing on a ledge of rock. The headquarters of the General Secretariat were indistinguishable from any other set of buildings in the wilderness. We waited in a room with stone walls, a desk, an old sofa and some chairs, until Isayas Afeworki stepped from an adjoining room. He talked at length while a secretary from the Political Bureau took notes on the proceedings, his pen moving so slowly across the page that I thought: "He won't keep up. The archive is compromised forever now."

Mr. Isayas spoke good English with a faint slur caused by a swelling inside his lower lip, the result of using snuff, with which the Front made do instead of cigarettes. In what he had to say there was nothing remarkable and it was not dressed up for external consumption. Indeed, he seemed concerned at every turn to address his people, as though they were listening from the rocks, when he might have used the occasion to transmit some message beyond the confines of the Nacfa front and the Baraka River. Yet his very doggedness, his stubborn fluency in the idiom of struggle, was convincing. He kept his hands held forward, the palms open but inclined, giving everything he said a faint inflection of reproach. Now and then they would wipe the air, remonstrating with a legion of flies.

In good time, Mr. Isayas turned to the subject of the referendum. Only this, he said, could end the war. The people of Eritrea must be asked whether they desired regional autonomy within Ethiopia, some form of federation with their neighbor or full independence. No imposed solution would work; Ethiopia and a complicit international order had sought to impose federation. It had been a failure; so had annexation. Solutions that did not correspond to the wishes of the Eritrean population would be short-lived. He brought the interview to a close and wished us a safe journey. Perhaps the EPLF's inability to turn its grievances into a presentable case was a virtue. It had long ago learned to doubt that salvation could come from any foreign quarter. The man from the Political Bureau was still writing, even as he rose to his feet while his leader left the room.

Several Beni Amer families were gathered outside the underground hospital in Orota. Their camels were tethered by a stand of acacia. I had been attending an operation in one of the sterilized containers, where the EPLF surgeons were repairing a burst eardrum. It was late when I emerged, but there was enough light to see that some of these people were attached to drips, with bags suspended from the trees. It was clear too that their relatives knew how to monitor the flow of the rehydration solution that was being administered to the weakest members of the group. They had made their way to the hospital in search of help, having been without food for over a week. A tall youngster with matted hair was turning a bag of solution in his hands, trying to judge by the light of the stars how much was left. Fesseha stepped over and offered his flashlight. Beneath the trees lay a woman with a ring through her nose, her body covered in a blanket and her eyes fixed on the container of clear fluid, shot through with light.

There were nine ethnic groups in Eritrea; the Beni Amer were among the most refractory. The entrenched habits of nomadism gave them a strong indisposition to government of any kind. Yet they had made their peace with the EPLF, coming to rely on them for shelter from air raids and as a source of medical treatment as well as grain—ample recompense for the proselytizing ways of the Front, which opened a dossier on each family who came for treatment, took the children off to literacy classes and discouraged female circumcision.

"You see," said Fesseha, "we have interests in common. They can have nothing from the Ethiopians but fire from the air—that is how they call it—and hunger. From us, well, we give them what they need while this war continues."

The Land Cruiser was leaving for Sudan before dawn. I imagined that, like all visitors, I was a reminder to Fesseha of an ordinary life beyond this dreary place. For a few days, perhaps, I was diverting enough and then quite the reverse. Moreover, there was the question of what, if anything, I would manage to publish after all his hard work. As we walked to the Protocol guest house, we heard the sound of an airliner high above us and looked up to see it inching its way across the fine net of stars.

"In fact this plane is now in Eritrean air space," Fesseha observed. "Probably it comes from Nairobi and maybe it is going to Jeddah. The stewardesses are serving cocktails, beer, whiskey—anything you want—and the passengers are relaxing. Even the slightest thing about our lives down here, they do not need to know it. They have opened their magazines and pulled down the trays from the seats in front. They are waiting for the drinks."

We climbed the steps of the guest house and sat for a while on the lip of the stone veranda, gazing into the sky until the plane had disappeared. Fesseha's shoulders were hunched; his head drooped and we remained without speaking.

"What are they reading?" I asked at length.

"The *Economist*," he replied without conviction. "And they are drinking Johnnie Walker. Born 1820, still going strong."

▲

In 1988, at the height of the fighting in southern Angola, an unconfirmed report came through from the Horn that the EPLF had captured the Ethiopian garrison of Afabet. Shortly afterward, independent accounts were broadcast by the BBC, including one by Basil Davidson, whom the EPLF took down to Afabet. He compared it to the fall of Dien Bien Phu. The main command had been shattered, but as the rest of the Second Revolutionary Army regrouped a state of emergency was declared in Eritrea and a period of atrocity against civilians followed. In Ethiopia, the situation had grown bleaker for Mengistu, who now faced a multitude of armed uprisings. The Tigray People's Liberation Front and the armed alliance of which it was the core had full control of Tigray and was pressing south. Mengistu had foiled an attempted coup within the army but more than forty officers had been liquidated in the process, which augured badly for his last stand, whenever it came. As far as Eritrea was concerned, Afabet was a moment of decisive change, but developments were slow and it was not until the beginning of 1990 that the EPLF inflicted another heavy defeat, this time in Massawa.

For anyone wishing to see the gains made by the EPLF after 1990, entry was still through Sudan, but there was now a handsome charge for all visitors, including aid workers, who were obliged to hire a Toyota and driver from an Eritrean businessman in Khartoum at a fee of $200 or $250 a day. Nobody doubted that there was revenue in this for the EPLF, which was also levying a fee for processing permits and "voluntary contributions" for nights spent in bunkers, guest houses and the like. The Front was now run as a business as well as a liberation movement. The dramatic increase in the amount of territory it held was stretching every resource to the limit and the search for hard currency was on. In Khartoum, a group of Eritrean entrepreneurs who backed the EPLF were offering shares at U.S. $1,000 each in their consortium, the Nacfa Corporation—"import-export"—with the lure of substantial profits after the war. Much had changed since the days when the Front had sought to "deepen the class content of the people's struggle." Yet even if the terms had gone out of fashion, national unity had been built on the EPLF's concern for the "broad masses."

In November 1990, I was again among Eritreans when an event of some significance in Britain was reported on the World Service. On the balcony of the guest house at Port Sudan I stood with the radio pressed against my ear as the newsreader announced the resignation of Margaret Thatcher. It was received by the Eritreans indoors with little more than polite interest, for events in Westminster and even in the Gulf, where Desert Storm was gathering, were no longer so significant. Three years ago the Eritreans had treated radio news from distant capitals like a complex of riddles that, if properly interpreted, would shed light on their own obscure fortunes. Now, poised for control of their country, they no longer listened so attentively to the crackling oracle. Their own judgments were far more important.

There was confusion at the guest house over the rental car system, which had just been introduced. Several Eritreans seemed opposed to it, although this may have been a show of courtesy. In England the EPLF office had advised me to find my own way to Port Sudan and work out an arrangement, probably a Protocol car, for the journey to Orota and beyond. After two days in Port Sudan I reached Orota with a generous Australian aid worker, but the new chief at Protocol turned me back to Port Sudan two hours later with instructions not to appear again until I had a vehicle from the business in Khartoum. In good English, with an American accent, he said it was "a whole new ball game now." When I gazed at the rocks on either side of the guest house, unchanged since my first stay there, I did not believe him. In Port Sudan I remained for six days until a tall man in a baseball hat arrived at the guest house and said we would leave the next morning, when curfew was lifted.

Tesfai was in his mid-fifties, and lived in Khartoum. This was his first run into Eritrea for the car company. He spoke very little English but I could understand his Italian. He had been a driver for most of his life and had owned a taxi for a few years in Asmara. When the Ethiopians requisitioned it, he left. He appeared to enjoy the open road, or rather, the network of tracks going south, for there was no road to speak of. "Khartoum," he said, pidginizing for my benefit, "*troppe macchine!*" While the absence of roads here in the east was acceptable, in the capital it was not. "Khartoum," he said again, "*non c'è strada. Incredibile!*" Then on reflection, "Sudan, *non c'è niente.*"

Tesfai decided to break our journey near the course of the Baraka, more than a hundred kilometers from the border. Here the livestock looked terrible. There had been drought in Eritrea for almost two years. Aid workers in Khartoum told stories of a sharp rise in the numbers of Beni Amer coming out of Eritrea to relief camps in Sudan. They had been doing so for five years but, until recently, had given air raids as the reason for their arrival. Now they were saying that there was no water. Their herds were depleted and some of their elders had failed to survive the journey. Around the Baraka the lower limbs of the thorn acacias had been browsed bare, leaving the goats no choice but to scramble up the trunks and right through the matted tops, on which they now perched with their legs spread for balance, pecking at the cover like monstrous birds. We heard differing opinions about the rainfall inside Eritrea. Some held that not a drop of rain had fallen for twelve months, others that there had been small rains in April. In the *kola,* or lowland, crop failure was reported to be total. The Baraka was fed by two rivers that cut through the lowlands and, with fair rains, it would have been in spate from July to September. This year there had been three or four sporadic floods at the end of August, nothing more. Now, in December, the land rippled feverishly beneath a blank, asphyxiating light.

Fesseha Ghebrehiwet stopped the car on the way out of Orota and disappeared for a few minutes to say goodbye to his wife and child. Without his beard he looked older than he was, but the penitential air had gone. His face was that of a happy man, fuller than I would have thought. There was also a scar on the edge of the chin, where a bullet had entered, passing out behind the jawbone with no serious damage done.

"She is a fighter," he said of his wife. "Only now she is having to be a mother." Her name was Tsehai, which means sun. They had called their child Yohannes.

We fixed on an itinerary that would take us first to Afabet and then to a refugee settlement called Filfil, but at the last minute we reversed the order and headed straight for the camp.

Filfil lay in a mountain gorge, almost safe against air strikes. More than two hundred families were quartered here. At the neck of the gorge they had dammed the tiny stream, diverting it into miniature terraces where Swiss chard and tomatoes grew, but for grain and a proper water supply Filfil depended on the EPLF's aid operation. Their relief effort, and that of the Tigrayans, which I never saw, were said by aid workers to be the best in Africa. To Mengistu, starvation was an instrument of class struggle and national integrity; he was opposed to food aid reaching civilians in rebel areas. Both movements had to run their own convoys through the Sudan; to minimize the risk of bombing, most of the hauling was done at night, when the stony tracks of northern Eritrea became very busy. After the famine of the mid-1980s the fleet of trucks in Eritrea was greatly expanded by the foreign aid agencies. Distribution was always methodical and had even extended behind the Ethiopian lines, where lists of the needy were prepared by village heads and presented to rebel relief officers who arranged for deliveries by camel or donkey. Here in the base areas, grain and water could be transported directly to distribution points, but drought and the expansion of the liberated areas meant that larger quantities were now needed.

Filfil consisted mostly of refugees from Semha district, on the eastern escarpment, which bore the brunt of the Ethiopians' fury after the fall of Afabet. We took coffee with a group of men and women who told us that the Ethiopians had simply trained their artillery on the villages and fields of Semha and pounded them for the best part of a month. At the outset there had been military grounds for the bombardment, since EPLF units had been in the vicinity, but in the end it was just an act of malice. One middle-aged refugee, his shirt decorated with a little green man swinging a golf club, explained that he had come up north when the EPLF had offered to evacuate the area. He had been working his land at the time. The shelling was so intense that he could not go back to the village and tell his wife he was leaving. Over the next few days several groups of people left, but many stayed behind to bring in the harvest.

Further up the gorge was a school building, where two women and a man, all of them Tigre speakers, were sitting. They came from Sheib. Kadija Yassin was thirty-five. She was nine months' pregnant when she ran from the outskirts of her village on the day the Ethiopian army came in. She lost her child on the way. Hawa Haseb, two years older, fled at the same time and hid for a month before reaching Filfil.

"Everybody who could," said Hawa, "was fleeing, some directly to the mountains, others going into the plain to hide in the scrub, but these ones that hid were taken and machine-gunned." The man, Mahmoud Adem, had been on his way to Sheib when he heard gunfire. He ran away and soon found himself among a large group of people heading toward Afabet. Much of the ridge was under bombardment. He passed two burning villages on the way. "There was war in Degha and Dimnet," he said. "We stopped at the place where we were and watched as Degha burned. We saw fire to the right of the mosque, and to the left, and we continued walking." In Sheib the Ethiopian army had summoned the inhabitants, men, women and children, to a meeting in the shade of a tree. A few minutes later a formation of tanks closed on the gathering and crushed them to death, about eighty residents in all. The remainder, upward of three hundred, were shot. The soldiers picked through the bodies, removing gold rings from the noses of the women, after which the dead were plowed into the ground with a bulldozer.

"That time, you remember, was before the drought," Fesseha explained. "When the rains came, they washed the earth away and so, later, we saw how many had been killed."

On the way out of Filfil at dusk we crossed the trucks bringing water. A group of children ran behind, laughing and brandishing sticks. The trucks waited, delayed by a yearling camel with its hindquarters in the track and its graceful neck stretched to crop a shrub from the rock wall.

The absence of artillery fire in Nacfa, indeed the total silence that now lay on the ruins, drove home the extent of the change in Eritrea. We arrived at night and the headlights of the car lit up the ghostly lineaments of the place. When Tesfai cut the engine, we sat in the stillness for a few moments before opening the doors. Everything had moved on, the front had swung away to the center of the country; I knew this, but it took the silence to make it palpable. In the morning we walked through the town and stood beside the minaret. Two young herdsmen sat on a rubble wall while their goats tugged at the fallen masonry. As we prepared to leave, an old man appeared and Tesfai approached him with narrowed eyes until at last, a few inches from his face, he greeted him with a laugh of recognition. At the time of the federation they had both worked for the same boss, an Italian entrepreneur. Tesfai had driven the Mercedes; the other, I think, had been the gardener.

We left Nacfa and drove south. After a time the old front was visible, first the Eritrean lines and then the Ethiopian. They seemed to merge at Den Den, where we had watched the Ethiopians flit like wraiths in their trenches three years earlier. As we began to descend, a widening valley pushed them apart once more.

In December 1987, the EPLF had broken through the Ethiopian lines at Nacfa after heavy fighting and, in March the following year, had pursued the best part of a mechanized division toward Afabet. Just north of the garrison the valley contracted into a narrow pass. To block it, the Eritreans had only to destroy one large vehicle with artillery fire, and that is precisely what was done.

We reached the pass a few hours later. The approach resembled an outlandish sculpture park in which millions of roubles' worth of metal had been welded into a single vast exhibit commemorating the end of Soviet pretension in Africa. For the first fifty yards or so I tried to list the identifiable remains of tanks, armored cars, trucks and mounted artillery, but quickly lost count. The whole sinister tailback stretched much further and fused into the craggy terrain; ruin grounded on ruin.

"Just a few shells onto the first vehicles, to cut the pass," Fesseha said, "that was all. Then they were finished. And, you know, EPLF did not destroy so much of this. We wanted to keep it ourselves, of course, but when the Ethiopian air support arrived, they saw there was nothing they could do. They went away and came again and then they bombed it, which is how you find it now."

The EPLF entered Afabet within forty-eight hours. They claimed that their casualties were low, about one for every ten or more Ethiopians, of whom there were at least fifteen thousand, in the course of the operation. A further six thousand Ethiopians were taken prisoner. Fesseha believed that the garrison commander at Afabet escaped on the road to Keren. "Tsegaye is the name of this man," Fesseha recalled. "He left by camel, with a column of civilian hostages."

The sun was still bright but the moon was up in the blue sky over Afabet as we entered the town, made up almost entirely of single-story buildings separated by ample ground. There was a shabby main street, distinct from the rest, with a mosque on one side, the minaret destroyed and under reconstruction. A mist of uneasiness clung to the township, which was almost deserted. After a few moments a European came out to greet us, an intense aid worker whom I had met on

the plane from Amsterdam to Khartoum. In a state of curious elation
he announced that Afabet had been bombed that morning. Fesseha
nodded sagely. The change of plan that took us to Filfil had been
judicious.

At 7 A.M. a pair of MiGs had swooped over the town dropping
two detonation bombs and a cluster bomb, without much material
damage, although there had been several injuries, all of them civilian.
We looked at the list drawn up by the EPLF official who had joined us
by the car. There were six injuries in all, with names, ages and types
of wound. To make an inventory of this kind was, at first sight, a
flimsy riposte to Ethiopia's control of the skies. Over the years, however, it had kept the indecency of mere numbers at bay.

I pressed to leave, but another raid on the same day was unlikely.
The sun was dropping and the inky shadow of the western ridges had
begun to spill across the valley. A steady flow of townspeople, with
goats, donkeys, camels, appeared from the base of the surrounding
hills and made for the town, where they would spend the night in
safety. In the morning they would leave for the hills again. It was safer
this way, now that the air attacks were regular. Those on the list of
casualties would have had good reason for staying in Afabet and de-
fying the established rhythm of the place, which breathed out at first
light and in again at dusk.

It was dark as we climbed down from the highland toward Massawa, and it became much warmer. Tesfai had a tape of Sudanese
Muzak, all of it played on a synthesizer. "Oh Boy," "Kung Fu Fighting" and "Rock Me, Baby" went around and around until Fesseha
inspected my own tapes and began to play them. He and Tesfai greatly
enjoyed a recording of "Nkosi sikelel' i Africa" though it did nothing
to improve their low opinion of the ANC. Augusto, my Angolan
minder, had attributed all the ANC's shortcomings to an unhealthy
interest in hymn singing. *"La lutte, vous savez, ce n'est pas l'église! Pas
dimanche! Il faut distinguer quand même."*

In the plain a few hundred yards of thick mud took us half an hour
to cross. After another four hours we joined a metaled road, traveling
at speed for the first time since leaving Orota. Then we were moving
in a gully between two rows of riddled, broken buildings on the outskirts of Massawa. Here and there a streetlight flickered or a vehicle
turned at a junction, bathing a ruined block of apartments with yellow
light. It was so extraordinary to be in a real town that the damage in
Massawa was lost on me.

Hotel Luna was almost deserted. There was a counter at reception with a Bayer Aspirin clock behind it and a big, elderly mirror

bearing the legend *"Liquori—aperitivi."* An antique Gaggia espresso machine stood on the bar at the right of the entranceway. I had the most unnerving sensation of stepping back half a century into a newsreel about the Allied invasion of Sicily. When the proprietor appeared, he gave us a room in the annex. There was no water, but the lights worked and an overhead fan, tugging away at its last fastening on the ceiling, kept the mosquitoes from settling.

"I am sure," Fesseha said, as he lay down, "you never thought you would sleep on a bed in a hotel in Eritrea. If you like, I can order breakfast and tomorrow we will drive out to the beach, with our towels and a picnic."

Massawa consisted of four sections. The first was a rambling shantytown on the mainland that was joined by a long causeway to the island of Tualet, the city's residential section. Another, smaller causeway linked Tualet to a second island, which contained the port facility. Finally, to the north, above the shanties, a stubby peninsula protruded into the Red Sea; this had been used by the Ethiopians as a naval base. Tualet had seen the worst of the fighting. The roads had been churned up and the old buildings in the Italian colonial style were ravaged. Here, near the ruined church of Saint Michael, we met a young EPLF video cameraman.

Ftsum Ghebrai was tinkering under the hood of a Fiat 500. Fesseha engaged him in conversation, during which it emerged that he had been seconded to a large force of infantry taking part in the capture of Massawa. With his help, I was able to trace the outlines of the battle. The units to which he was attached had approached Massawa from the north and had walked for nine hours before their first engagement with Ethiopian troops, positioned well behind the town, which had lasted for a further three. It must have been dark, and impossible to film. He had then traveled for six more hours until his units encountered a second line of defenses. This time they fought for six hours. From where we were sitting you could see the place where the third and final confrontation had occurred. Ghebrai pointed across the bay toward the naval base on the jutting mainland.

Beyond the water was a sparse stand of trees, eucalyptus perhaps; Ghebrai's colleagues had fought for eighteen hours in that coppice, and an hour or so after first light he had begun to film. By the time the EPLF broke through, the ground was strewn with Ethiopian casualties. It was useless to ask how many men and women the EPLF had lost. Ghebrai simply refused to answer, moving his hand over his head twice in quick succession, smiling as though the question were a trick. He had extraordinary footage, he said, of an Ethiopian tank being destroyed. Ghebrai shot two hours of tape in all. "In fact," he said, "I taped our entry into Massawa."

The main force of the EPLF, meanwhile, had come from the west, where they had cut the road between Asmara and Massawa. It must have been a bitter fight. Within eighteen hours of their advance, several thousand Ethiopian troops, three senior officers and a mass of armor had been "put out of action." Half of the victorious Eritrean force, numbering thousands, pushed east toward Massawa. A thousand or more Ethiopian troops retreated ahead of them under the command of a Brigadier General Teshome, who pulled back through the shantytowns and over the causeway to Tualet.

When the Eritreans arrived at the other end of the causeway they halted. To bombard Teshome into surrender would have meant inflicting heavy casualties on the Eritrean population in Tualet. The EPLF was not keen to jeopardize its support in the town, already tenuous after twelve years of isolation from the movement. Instead, the three officers captured on the road were instructed to write to Teshome, explaining the hopelessness of his position. They were sent down the causeway under a white flag to present the letter. Teshome was given twelve hours to think it over.

Fesseha told me that Addis had been in radio contact with Teshome and ordered him not to surrender. Reinforcements would arrive by sea. To maximize the civilian cost of any bombardment, Teshome now closed off all exits from Tualet. As the brigadier general's grace period ticked away, Ghebrai's units consolidated their hold on the naval base and another small EPLF force set out by boat—possibly from the base itself; this part of the story was always withheld—in order to land at the back of the island. Perhaps the EPLF hoped to take Tualet without using any artillery. When the twelve hours were up, however, the EPLF put aside their misgivings and began a fierce bombardment. It was unclear how long it took to overrun the town—a matter of hours—but by the time the main EPLF force had crossed the causeway and the others had landed at the back of the island, Teshome had disappeared.

The Melotti villa lay at the eastern edge of Tualet. It was the size of a hotel, set in rambling grounds with a drive down to the front porch. At the back of the villa lay a vast, empty swimming pool, set in a paved terrace under vaulted white arches, with one end running out into an unkempt garden. Beyond that, like a bright band of pewter, lay the sea. A gust of wind blew in off the water and a thin clump of bougainvillea swayed in the brilliant sunlight. The wall by the front entrance bore a shrapnel scar and there was a crater in the garden. We went around to the main door and entered the hallway. It was cool inside and the silence was broken only by the sound of slippered feet shuffling somewhere in the depths of an enormous kitchen.

Lule Tewolde Medhin had a small face and dark eyes. Her hair was drawn away from her forehead, plaited in tight lines across her scalp and gathered at the back of her head. She wore a blue-and-white check dress with buttons at the front—a servant's dress. We sat at a table next to one of the arches surrounding the shaded section of the pool. Lule poured unsweetened tea from a china teapot into china cups with saucers. I had never seen Fesseha drink anything but dark, sweetened tea from a glass. He and Lule spoke briefly in Tigrinya and we were introduced with more formality.

The Melottis had made their fortune from liquor. The business was started before the Second World War, but was expropriated by the regime in Addis during the 1970s. Signor Melotti was dead but his distillery, now owned by Ethiopia's toiling masses, had continued until recently to produce a plausible gin and a good local *raki*. Lule Tewolde Medhin was sixty; she was both cook and general helper to Signora Melotti. Lule had worked there since 1982. Though the signora now lived in Monaco, she still came to Eritrea for a few months every year. She would fly to Asmara, collect Lule and drive to the villa in Massawa. This time, however, her stay had coincided with the rebel assault. The front ran across the road to Asmara; Signora Melotti and her staff were stranded in the villa.

For Lule the battle of Massawa began with the noise of distant fighting to the west. As it drew closer, the inhabitants of Massawa began to look for refuge. Once Teshome had sealed off the island, the villa was the only place that seemed safe. Soon there were hundreds of impoverished townsfolk—Massawa had not prospered during Ethiopian rule—asking for shelter in the immense cellar that ran under the house. Signora Melotti took them in. When the cellar was full, people crowded together under the vaulted roof of the terrace, scores of them, lying and sitting around the pool. They came with whatever food they could muster. Signora Melotti, meanwhile, set about finding more. Lule thought that there were about two thousand people in the house in all.

Despite the twelve-hour grace period, there must have been intermittent shelling from both sides—the standoff at the causeway did not preclude fighting elsewhere. Lule spent her time in the enormous kitchen over vats of pasta, porridge and lentils, while Signora Melotti supervised. When the shelling resumed, the two women would heave the pans off the heat and bolt for the cellar. There were also Ethiopian troops on the Melotti property. They had tanks in the grounds at the front and an observation post with a mounted machine gun on the roof of the building. Signora Melotti was opposed to this and said as much to Teshome when he arrived at the villa. It was now a civilian refuge, she told him; he should remove his men, otherwise it would come under attack by the EPLF.

Teshome had more urgent matters to attend to. He requisitioned one of Signora Melotti's boats and ordered it to be prepared at once. With some reluctance another of Signora Melotti's workers, a man by the name of Gherezgehier, made it ready. It was hauled into the water and a party of soldiers boarded while Teshome looked on. The motor was already running when Gherezgehier, who thought his duties were done, was ordered aboard at gunpoint. The boat disappeared and Teshome apologized to the signora for posting so many soldiers on the property. Shortly afterward, he left but the soldiers remained.

Lule could not recall when Teshome had paid his visit, but if he needed a boat, the EPLF had probably overrun the naval base. Nor could she remember when the shell exploded by the pool. The burst, she said, injured "fourteen or fifteen" people. For the first time I noticed that the white plaster on the terrace wall was disfigured by shrapnel. Still vivid in Lule's memory, however, was the sight of Signora Melotti tearing up her sheets in order to dress the wounded.

Signora Melotti and Lule remained in the cellar for most of the night before the EPLF entered Massawa. The following morning Lule was greeted by a party of young EPLF fighters who came inside the house. One of the first things they asked her was whether she knew the people sitting around the table on the patio, just beyond the dining room. She went with them to find four dead men slumped in chairs. She raised her hands to her face and turned away. Yes, she told the fighters, the three in uniform had helped push the boat down into the water. About the fourth, who was in plainclothes, she was less sure. She did not remember having seen him before. Everyone at the table— and Lule's description evoked the end of a long, unpleasant game—had bullet wounds to the head. Fesseha believed they had committed suicide. There was nothing back in Addis for vanquished generals, he said, and death might well have been a better option than retreat.

As for Teshome, he had wanted the boat taken to another part of Tualet for a quick getaway, in the event of defeat. The EPLF believed he had still been hoping for reinforcements and had sent a party out to the military base in the Dahlak archipelago, forty miles off the coast, to prepare his colleagues for a rapid counteroffensive. The reinforcements never arrived. Teshome was seen once more on the Melotti property. He had stripped all signs of rank from his uniform. His body was found later near the leisure club for workers at the port facility.

The club was a building with tall windows, bereft, since the battle, of any glass whatever. It now looked like an enormous bandstand. Death by suicide was the EPLF's summary verdict. The battle of Massawa had cast Teshome as a callous figure, but his last hours, wandering through Massawa, must have been desperate. A few days later, the Eritreans evacuated Signora Melotti, taking her up to Orota by car and into Sudan.

Before we left, Lule showed us around the inside of the villa. At the top of one of the staircases a tiled corridor with white plaster walls led past a succession of rooms. Several were locked and the fine latticework on at least two of the wooden doors was smashed. One door was missing altogether. Lule attributed this damage to the Ethiopian conscripts at the villa. The approach of the EPLF filled them with panic, she said; they had tried to tear down the doors with the idea of using them as rafts. She laughed, trailing a finger down one of the wrecked panels.

Fesseha told Tesfai to drive out of town half a mile or so and stopped him by a large tree, walled around with corrugated iron in the manner of a latrine. "You should see this," he said, helping me through a gap in the metal, but remaining on the other side himself. Around the trunk were piles of wooden ammunition boxes filled with human remains. The lids had been prised from several and some of the skeletons inspected. I asked Fesseha how many there were and he replied that no one had counted. I found that each box contained a dozen. Most of the bones were draped with scraps of Ethiopian uniform. The skin was like parchment. There were over thirty boxes, stacked on top of one another and side by side. Fesseha asked if I would have thought it possible to arrange so many bodies around a tree with such discretion.

Two EPLF doctors at the hospital in Massawa had already examined the remains and believed that some were at least ten years old, others less than a year. There were bullet holes in most of the skulls and spines. These people had probably been executed at close range. "The cartilage around the chest," said one of the doctors, "suggests that they are men of middle age. Between thirty-five and forty, probably officers. Perhaps they tried to mutiny; perhaps they were punished when offensives failed."

The other medic, who was now running the hospital, was Dr. Berhana. She agreed with her colleague. "It is possible," she said, "that the Dergue kept them to show to other officers, as a warning. We cannot tell." Berhana remembered our meeting three years earlier and my skepticism at the time about EPLF actions behind enemy lines. "I can tell you now," she said, "what I was doing when we first met. I was behind the lines in Barka. We had three brigades operating close to Asmara and a team of twenty-five medical staff to care for them. I was part of a caravan service, bringing wounded people back to Barka. The journey took about six days by camel from Asmara to the lowlands. The camels would be loaded up with provisions and then we would go back again. Like a railway." She had done this dangerous work for a year and then settled down to run the hospital in Barka. Two months after the fall of Massawa, she had been brought here and appointed medical director.

From Massawa we headed south and up into the highlands again, looping below Asmara to reach the little town of Adi Caieh by a steep pass, which the Eritreans had cut into the escarpment in a matter of weeks. A disconcerting road to travel at night, on slippery draughts of sand, with the relief trucks coming the other way, it was nonetheless a magnificent achievement and would provide the movement with a supply route from the coast until the war ended. Asmara was almost encircled and it was only a question of time before it fell.

Rainfall in the southern highlands had not been good and although from now on we were making our way to the front, it was sometimes hard to take an interest in military matters when the drought was apparent everywhere. Over a single year in the south the price of sorghum had increased threefold while it cost nothing to buy goats. Cows were selling at half and sometimes a third of the normal price and going straight to slaughter with scarcely any meat on them. As a rule, cattle owners kept reserve grazing for the dry season but this had been used up six months ago and the emaciated remnants of the herds stood motionless on pastures of brown shingle.

Before moving up to the front, we stayed for two days in Adi Caieh. It was a place of great clemency, in spite of the drought, for it still basked in the dreamlike reality of liberation and, besides, Eritrean relief convoys could now reach the area with ample grain and water. People would survive, even if their livelihoods were ruined. The occupation had been harsh here, as elsewhere. The imam of Adi Caieh told us that in 1975 the Ethiopians had come up from the lowlands and desecrated the mosque. They entered and killed a number of people inside, dragging others out and shooting them in the street. "The mosque door was broken," he said, "and there was blood in the place of prayer." He decided to close the mosque for three years.

We found the imam and the Coptic priest together, in an office on the ground floor of the town hall. Both remarked on the increase in their congregations since liberation. Like Frelimo in the early days, the Workers' Party of Ethiopia discouraged religion and a dim view was taken of any family that baptized its children. The Christian women of Adi Caieh used to steal out to the villages and have their newborn sons and daughters baptized in secret, to avoid incurring penalties at the hands of the party, to which many were forced to belong in order to qualify for food aid. The imam and the Coptic priest agreed that the persecution during the time of Haile Selassie and immediately afterward had been directed chiefly against Muslims in the area, whereas local Christian males tended to be taken by the Israelis for Force 101. "It was a way of trying to stir up conflict between Muslims and Christians," said the old priest, smiling across at Mr. Mahmud Mohamed, who nodded his assent and added that under Mengistu the savagery in Eritrea was indiscriminate. Both clerics, severe and elderly gentlemen, were as meek as lambs in the presence of the EPLF: the Front imposed no restrictions on worship.

It would have been foolish to try. The old rifts in the movement had less to do with religious zeal than with broad cultural differences between Muslims and Christians, yet, in the end, even these had little bearing on the political divisions that brought about the strife between the ELF and the EPLF. There were plenty of Muslims in the EPLF at the end of the 1970s and much of the Front's success lay in its secular attitudes, which prevailed over other definitions of community. Nonetheless, the EPLF could see the potential dangers of religion, above all if it were suppressed. Whether the two communities would coexist in the future, without the unifying force of Ethiopian occupation, was hard to know. For the moment, there was a common objective and, in Adi Caieh, the freedom to pray in the church or the mosque without recrimination.

A young woman with a white head shawl arrived at the town hall on business just as we were about to leave. Saba Fesahai was not a native of Adi Caieh, but four years earlier she had been arrested near Quatit, just to the west, and brought here with her child by the Ethiopians. An EPLF operation near Quatit had led to several Ethiopian casualties and the authorities were angry, rounding up people at random. Saba was accused of cooperating with EPLF fighters, which she denied. She and another detainee walked for several hours under guard until they joined a column of prisoners making its way to Adi Caieh under heavy escort. Four of them were executed during the journey, because their captors could not wait to reach town to press the charge of collaboration. Saba's child, Ruth, was less than a year old at the time and she carried her on her back to Adi Caieh.

Mother and child were locked up and a young policeman, an Eritrean, interrogated Saba over several days. "We have tangible evidence of your misdeeds," he told her. "You have informed the *shifta* where we put our land mines. You are having some affairs, some sexual intercourse, with *shifta* people and during our revolutionary anniversary you were hiding them in your house and giving them ambush strategies. It is because of you that we were hit hard in Quatit."

Saba replied that these were rumors spread by people who did not like her. After ten months in prison her case was decided. She had a cousin in the Workers' Party of Ethiopia who went to Asmara and begged a cousin of his own, a security man, to see that she was transferred. There were so many prisoners in Asmara that the sentence might never be carried out. Saba was taken to Asmara shortly afterward, only to discover that the cousin's cousin, who arranged the transfer, had been replaced. This was a blow, for if she were to survive the first few weeks, she would need an ally.

Matters took another turn for the worse when she found that her interrogator in Asmara was an Ethiopian. She was questioned in a room with a couple of toys in one corner, for Ruth, who was now nearly two. "If you confess," said the interrogator, "the government will show you mercy." "How can I confess to what I have never done?" she replied. The interrogator had a whip and for the next six days he beat her every day, in front of the child. Saba held out, denying the charges. "Do what you like," she said, "I have nothing to tell you." The following week the interrogator was replaced. Saba was questioned in the same cell, with the same toys in the corner for Ruth, who was supposed to divert herself while her mother was suspended from the ceiling and beaten for an hour, after which a group of men ducked her head in a bucket of "foul water." Saba, who had been cleaning her teeth with a twig during her story, now lowered her head shawl and began to plait a loose strand of hair.

"I told them nothing," she said, "not even about the man who was arrested with me in Quatit. I know him, he's a peasant, that's all. If you start by giving a little information, it leads on to more, and then you can get into serious trouble. That was my position."

Saba was imprisoned in Asmara for eighteen months. She prevailed on her captors to allow her mother to come and collect Ruth when she was almost three, whereupon she was transferred to another prison. In 1989 a peace initiative by Jimmy Carter led to the release of thousands of prisoners from Ethiopian jails, many of them common criminals, but Saba was among them. She spent a fortnight with a relative in Asmara and made her way down to Adi Caieh, where her mother was renting a house and looking after Ruth. Saba installed herself and began brewing *siwa*, a local beer, for a living. "Then, six months later, Adi Caieh was liberated and the past was behind us," she said.

Saba put up her shawl and we walked down to her house to sample the *siwa*. On the way, Fesseha plied her with questions, to which she replied with a laugh or a tug of the shawl.

Ruth was there with Saba's mother, an infirm old lady who sat in a patch of light by the door to keep warm. The child was restless, but she got up on Fesseha's knee and played with his ear while we drank the milky, bitter *siwa* from beakers made out of plastic bleach containers. Fesseha asked how long it was since Saba had seen her husband. Not since her detention and even before, she told him. He was a fighter and had been when they married; he was up in Ghinda now, she had heard, waiting for the final marching orders on Asmara. The Ethiopians had been correct about her loyalty to the EPLF.

It was midafternoon; the sky was pale blue with a gray moon rising over the mountains. Fesseha and I made our way to the *latteria* and drank sweet tea. At dusk we were to embark with Tesfai for the Decamhare front, two stages by car to the main command, an overnight stay, and half a day's walk through the hills. In the *latteria* the prices were announced on a sheet of yellow foolscap covered with torn cellophane. At the bottom, in Amharic, was a request that patrons kindly refrain from polishing their boots on the premises.

We arrived at the command around one in the morning. It was an old Italian farmstead with rambling outbuildings. Loud music issued from one of the downstairs rooms of the main house and through the windows we could see a few couples dancing in a bare room. The night was clear and chilly. There was sleeping space in one of the outbuildings across the yard, a kind of shed, where Fesseha left me, going off to enjoy what remained of the party. The floor was cold and uncomfortable and there were rats. I was already awake when the rest of the farmstead rose at six to boisterous artillery fire and the truculent cry of a rooster, strutting in front of the sheds. The yard began to fill with bleary-eyed men, stumbling from the main building with sandals in one hand and guns in the other. Once again I had the sensation of having fallen through the cracks into an earlier war, not in East Africa, but in Italy, as though the men in the yard were partisans and this was some Umbrian village in the autumn of 1944.

We set out toward the Decamhare front in a small column, accompanied by an American photographer in his twenties, who had traveled down behind us from Massawa with his minder and a pair of fighters. As we left the battery petered out—it was Eritrean fire, designed to impress visitors and wake the units on this drowsy Sunday. After an hour of steep climbing, we found ourselves on a plateau, where we continued until we arrived at the foot of another, much steeper climb. The front lay several miles to the southeast of Decamhare, itself about twenty-five miles from Asmara. The EPLF had positions high above the village of Afalba, occupied by the Ethiopians and visible from the Eritrean trenches.

Up at this height there were cattle herders, a young boy and a little girl, who had driven their own cows across exposed ground within range of Ethiopian guns in a desperate search for grazing, but there was almost none, and now they sat behind cover while their poor beasts stooped among the hot rocks. It was characteristic of the Ethiopian command that they had ordered an infantry assault on these trenches, which were virtually unassailable. It could not have been long ago. The ground beyond was scattered with the bodies of Ethiopian conscripts, bringing a plague of flies and an unbearable smell to the trenches, which the fighters lived with day after day. The American's minder covered his mouth and nose with his cotton scarf. Inside the trenches, which were roofed with timbers and sandbags, as they had been at Nacfa, we drank water with the section commander and two young members of the Front, both women. In this thankless place there was a feeling of restless optimism. The Eritreans knew they were near the end of the war and it showed in their manner. Further north along the front they had artillery positions within range of Asmara airport. Since the capture of Massawa, they expected orders to move on the capital at any time.

The two women were in their early twenties. Tiblets had left Keren to join the movement when she was fifteen, without telling her parents. However committed to the nationalist cause, parents were always afraid when their children took up with the Front. Fesseha added, "They would not have resisted but I think she was not willing to see them upset." Tiblets had been too young to go straight into combat and had been enrolled in school at Orota for several years before training as a barefoot doctor. Here she was the company medic. She had a suturing kit and the bare minimum of medicine to dispense: malaria pills, antibiotics and painkillers. A lot of the injuries occurred while the positions were being fortified. There was always digging at night as the trenches got deeper and new consignments of timber were laid. This was dangerous work. Stones and timbers fell on the soldiers' feet, hands became trapped, pickaxe wounds were common.

The other woman, Nebiat, was from the south. Her eldest brother had already joined when she made contact with the EPLF in a nearby village and walked up with them to the rear bases. Nebiat was put up

for military training at the age of sixteen and served in the infantry at
the Nacfa front until 1984. During the capture of Afabet she was
wounded by a hand grenade, but returned to service after a month.
Later, in 1989, she was shot through the arm in the fighting around the
town, and required two months to recover in Orota. She had been
wounded yet again a few months back, here above Afalba, in the
constant skirmishing for salients and strategic trench lines as the front
was established. "That battle won us these very lines," said Nebiat
with justifiable pride. The two women were like twins, a healer and a
soldier, and had become close friends, to the point that their gestures
and bearing were nearly identical. I found this likeness disconcerting.

We asked what they would do after the war. Tiblets wanted to
continue working in medicine, "as a laboratory technician, if possible."
Nebiat enjoyed soldiering. "The state will need an army," she said,
and the commander, a quiet man with long, straggling hair, murmured
assent.

We passed the cattle on the way back and stopped below the
trenches at a tank position, where the American took some photographs. There were aircraft overhead: MiGs at a height of several
thousand feet, silvery dots, easily confused with the particles on one's
retina, and an Antonov; we stayed under cover until they were gone.

For Mengistu, the drought was an ally and he sought to compound its effects by starving the *shifta*. Reaching Afabet, on our way
back to Orota, we heard that a food distribution point across the valley
had been bombed the day before. There had been several injuries and
two deaths. A large quantity of grain had been burned and a water
tank destroyed. After the liberation of Massawa, 25,000 tons of grain
had been bombed in the port. Six months later, as the World Food
Program was busy trying to negotiate grain deliveries by sea to Massawa for distribution by both sides, the Ethiopians felt within their
rights to agree in principle while continuing to bomb the port.

The drought posed an unpleasant dilemma for the EPLF. Now
that it had Asmara and Keren under siege, the situation of Eritrean
citizens in the enclave formed by the two was very grave. Under
Ethiopian occupation, the inhabitants of the capital would have to wait
their turn for grain, since an army of 120,000 or more took priority.
Until the World Food Program could come to an arrangement at Massawa, Asmara relied on airlifts of food, quite inadequate to the needs
of the population, but a small mercy nonetheless. The relief flights put
down on a runway that was also used by the government's MiGs to fly
several sorties daily. It was now within range of EPLF artillery. To
refrain from shelling it was to jeopardize the lives of Eritreans in the

liberated territories, who lived under the constant threat of bombardment; to shell it was to deny the civilians under siege their meager
allocations of food. At present an unsatisfactory compromise obtained.
The EPLF did not shell the airport when relief planes were coming in,
unloading and leaving. Ethiopian military aircraft, however, took advantage of the airlift, landing or departing with impunity while relief
planes were on the ground. During my last few days in Eritrea, there
were rumors that the first WFP shipment would dock at Massawa
shortly. The Front would now feel justified in shelling the airport
freely, for if it were shut down, grain would still reach the enclave by
road.

Afabet was quiet when we arrived. The town itself had not been
bombed since our earlier visit, on the way south. We slept soundly in
small huts but were woken at seven by a pair of MiGs skimming the
town; the anti-aircraft batteries, the only military target in Afabet,
stammered into action.

We stooped in the trembling doorways of the huts until we heard
the evil popping of a cluster bomb in the next valley. It occurred to me
that to live with this kind of terror day after day, as Eritreans had,
required a dramatic moral adjustment, a redefinition of things that was
only possible by virtue of its being imposed. The seamless skies of
Eritrea were no better than the low vaults of a prison cell into which
the warders might choose to stride at any time with some perfunctory
cruelty in mind.

We reached Orota late the following night. I said goodbye to
Fesseha and a handful of acquaintances and prepared to leave at day-
break.

"We will see you in Asmara," Fesseha announced, "if you ever
come again." He would be there with his wife, Tsehai, and their son,
Yohannes. He asked me for a subscription to the *Economist*.

"But where shall I send it?"

"Through our offices in Port Sudan, and when we have taken
Asmara, I will just arrange so it is redirected."

▲

Even by the end of 1991, the cheapest route from London to
Eritrea, which had superseded Namibia as Africa's newest nation, was
through Moscow. Aeroflot still ran a weekly service to its abandoned
satrapy and connecting flights from Addis to Asmara had been resumed. In Moscow, a morbid anxiety prevailed—far worse, it was
said, than the unenviable certainties of the past; Moscow itself was
hackled with frost and swept by a gale of desolate venality. Everything

from the brash dolls on the Arbat to the very soul of the city seemed to be negotiable. It was in these circumstances that Mr. Andrei Sharaev found himself appointed, as resident specialist on the Horn, to the Africa Institute, a department of the Academy of Science of the U.S.S.R. I had jotted his name on the back of an EPLF propaganda pamphlet, and, as I sat in the silent vestibule of the institute waiting to see him, I browsed through it. On the last few pages, the Eritreans had transcribed the speeches made by the Soviet delegations to the U.N. General Assembly in 1950 when the federation was proposed. Forty-one years later, the text that the Ukraine delegation had delivered was by far the most striking. "The delegation of the Ukrainian Soviet Socialist Republic," it read, "a country where national oppression and its causes have long been abolished and where no national discrimination is possible, urges that independence should be granted to Eritrea immediately."

Mr. Sharaev was a shambling, scholarly man in his fifties, morose, but with sparkling eyes and a soft, ironical mouth. He apologized for being unable to present a card; it was his second day at the institute and the Soviet Union would shortly cease to exist. "Nobody knows who anybody is now," he said in a flat voice. "As a matter of fact, until my card is printed, even I cannot be sure who I am."

The corridors of the building, once a prestigious place where Soviet policy in Africa was debated, had a neglected, ignominious air. As we made our way along them, Sharaev told me he had come in specially for our appointment. Nowadays few members of the institute put in more than one or two appearances a week. The office we entered had seven desks piled with aging papers. Its walls were hung with monochrome maps. Sharaev looked it over with a disconsolate eye, uncertain where we should sit.

"So," he said, when we were settled, "you are going to Ethiopia and now we may converse. This is our purpose." He told me he had spent many years as the Amharic translator at the Soviet embassy in Addis. Later, he had translated at high-level meetings in Moscow between Mengistu and President Gorbachev. Then he referred me to his forthcoming article on Ethiopia in the institute *Yearbook*. We struggled to sort out a correct rendering of the title into English. "Totalitarianism Is Dead," we agreed, "Long Live Totalitarianism!" At once, Sharaev's disposition took a turn for the better.

The gist of the article was that the new Ethiopia had not acceded to democracy with the overthrow of Mengistu. No one doubted that he had to go, but a Tigrayan elite at the head of a transitional government in Addis was not the answer. The Amharas would never accept it. Ethiopia, said Mr. Sharaev, had no political culture and could not, therefore, accommodate the demands of the more than forty groupings now attempting to share power. "What we see at present," he said, "is the euphoria of freedom. Every tribe, every ethnicity is rising. It is like so many mushrooms after the good rain." A multiparty system, he said, would mean chaos and violence. "The tribes on the whole are primitive. Ethiopia will break open." The old African empire was in jeopardy now.

"Mengistu," Sharaev continued, "struggled all of his life for unity. It was an *idée fixe* for him. He was not a pure Amhara, but a half-caste; even so, he was in the old imperial line. Unity was everything. But, if I may go again to my article, now the new regime is in control there is a throwing away of all that was good in Mengistu. There is fanaticism against unity, against the party—all people who were party members must now go to register at a local police station once a week, others are detained. It is totalitarianism, is it not? The Tigrayans say that Mengistu's regime was fascist. In my article I say that we are now seeing a false de-Nazification. Everyone in the party is barred from a job. In Mengistu's time there were one and a half million unemployed in Addis. Now there are three million."

Even if the figures were correct, it was a curious way of looking at them. After all, the capital was filled with demobilized soldiers, conscripts without food or a livelihood, and returning prisoners of war. The idea of the north, Eritrea above all, filled Mr. Sharaev with foreboding.

"If the new president of Ethiopia is a realist and a patriot," he said, "he cannot permit Eritrean separation. At this stage in Ethiopia's development, good relations with Eritrea must be based on the premise of autonomous administration. Eritrea cannot be an internationally recognized state. How can it survive without Ethiopia? There are still millions of hectares of good land in Ethiopia; in the mountains of Eritrea nearly all the soil is gone. The wooden plow has killed farming over the last thousand years. For Ethiopia too it is impossible to live without the coast. I don't like Eritrean separatism. It's new trouble."

But what could Addis Ababa possibly do, I asked, if Eritrea was set on independence? Sharaev turned and looked out of the window, craning so that his eyeline rose above a patch of melting frost on the lower part of the pane.

"Precisely," he said. Then, looking down at his watch without, it seemed to me, the slightest interest in the time, he began, "The revolution was a tragedy. At the beginning it was antifeudal, antibourgeois. It was for the people and for democracy, but it went wrong. I had many good friends who died in the Terror. But to say that nothing about the revolution was good, this is dangerous." As he spoke it was not entirely clear which period of history, or which country, he had in mind.

"What about the international glory of Ethiopia?" he asked. "Kosygin came, Castro came. Or medicine and schooling? Or infrastructure? On the tenth anniversary of the revolution, in that year alone, Mengistu built twenty factories. He was an active man, always for unity. Do you know he had most of Stalin's works translated into Amharic? I have a full collection, including texts that you cannot find in Russian now." Sharaev dipped into his inside pocket for a pen and began to write his name and address for me. "If you are going to Eritrea," he said, "you have a chance to see some interesting things and I would like to hear, one day. Also I would like to know why they do not send delegations to the Soviet Union. Everywhere else yes, but not here. They will need us, I think, and we will need them. Joint ventures, new markets." The last few words sat uncomfortably with Sharaev, it was obvious from the way he spoke. He handed me his address and composed himself for a second stab at the lingua franca of the new world order. "Africa," he said without conviction, "is a good market."

We walked down the stairs, Sharaev leading the way. "You know," he said, "I opposed a military solution in Ethiopia and in Moscow I advised to cut military expenditure." He stopped five steps from the bottom of the staircase and tapped my arm. "It was in 1989," he went on. "We all agreed. So, for the last eighteen months of the war, Mengistu was supplied only by North Korea and Israel. Yes, and some outstanding orders from the defunct government of East Germany."

Sharaev and his colleagues had scarcely been quick off the mark: 1984 conceivably, even 1985, but 1989 was too late by the better part of half a million lives. And it was a year after Afabet, where Mengistu's defeat had become a certainty. The kindly, donnish Sharaev had advocated Ethiopian unity to within an inch of the bitter end. Now the Soviet Union was crumbling around him. At the door of the institute we shook hands. It was like being seen off by a solicitous teacher at the start of the school holidays. "Drink only bottled water," he urged. "With meat, please be sure it is cooked a long time. The big danger is the salads. I advise anybody to avoid them."

▲

From the air, Eritrea looked parched and guarded. The sky was clear but the land below threw up a wall of angry thermals around Asmara. The head of Protocol, the small man with the American accent who had sent me back from Orota the year before, was waiting on the tarmac to receive a delegation. He recognized me and put a welcoming Protocol arm around my shoulder. Then, without further ceremony, he warned against changing money on the street. "It might be a trap," he said, "and then you could have a problem. Really." He smiled and pointed to immigration. In the terminal, passports were inspected and a piece of paper inserted bearing a triangular stamp: "Provisional Government of Eritrea." I discovered that there were two tiers in the new exchange system. Eritreans could change hard currency for birr at the street rates in Addis while non-nationals changed at the artificial Ethiopian rate, donating over the odds to the Front's lean treasury—an acceptable compromise.

The taxi driver took me to the Amba Soira hotel, where most visitors stayed. In the lobby a familiar voice called my name, in full, remembered from the forms I had filled in for Protocol. Fesseha Ghebrehiwet was dressed in a jacket and tie, and told me he had just shown in a delegation from one of the Gulf states. He asked if his new appearance suited him. "My son, Yohannes, reached Asmara before you," he said, "and he is not yet three. Why are you so slow?"

He explained that I was more or less on my own; he was only in the hotel because Protocol had temporary offices behind reception. "We will help you to rent a car," he said, "then you may go anywhere in the city, see anything, report what you like. If you need us to help you with appointments or to accompany you, we are here. I hope you will accept dinner at my house, perhaps the day after tomorrow." Our encounter left me with an odd feeling of loss. Constraints, injunctions, arguments, passive acquiescence in the journey—in short, "the program"—this was the very stuff on which I had depended in Eritrea. At the heart of it all was the minder. Without that central relationship, things would take on a formlessness that a more inquisitive spirit might have welcomed. Notwithstanding our early difficulties, Fesseha was one of the guides I had come to cherish most. The fact that he had been too agile for me, and often elusive, was less important than the cumulative weight of his presence during two difficult journeys. Here in Asmara, for the first time, there was a leisurely air about him, bordering on fatigue, as though he were only now feeling the effects of a long period without sleep.

That evening I wandered through Asmara, calling in at the bars and shops, aimlessly intrigued. I was summoned into a small dive by the proprietor and given a glass of Asmara cognac, a Melotti product, on the house. The owners had remained in Asmara through the occupation, running the business on a tight margin, although this had been whittled away by Ethiopian army clients requisitioning bottles at will. Two drunks entered and complained about the mark-up of fifty cents on all drinks, imposed by the EPLF. They were advised to seek out another establishment that did not enforce it. A scuffle broke out and they were evicted. One of them fell hopelessly to the pavement. The Eleven O'Clock Bar, as it was dubbed after the Front's insistence on licensing hours, had the authentic, difficult ring of peacetime in a place that had known nothing but conflict for a generation.

Many of the shops and bars had posters in the windows showing the three founding figures of the national struggle, Idris Awate, Idris Mohamed Adem and Wolde-ab Wolde Mariam. As in the field, so in Asmara, I saw no pictures of Isayas. The shops were sparsely stocked with clothes, shoes, cassettes and bolts of cloth. A stationer's at one end of the main street sold pens and exercise paper, envelopes and even a handful of books: *The Backroom Boys* by Noam Chomsky, *The Penguin Book of Christmas Carols*, *Ritorno a Peyton Place* and the *Teach Yourself* guide to camping—an understandable source of mirth to browsing fighters. The movie theater was showing an old Italian comedy, *Two Nights with Cleopatra*, billed as "the bawdiest, craziest romp in the history of cinema." From the cafés and bars issued the smell of freshly ground coffee and the hum of conversation. Lured by the click of billiard balls into a pleasant establishment beside the town hall, I found one of the Front's former delegates in London stooping over the baize. His name was Amdemicael Kahsai. He had been a pilot in the Ethiopian air force before joining the EPLF, after which he had been posted abroad. He was now the mayor of Asmara. I stood at the back of the billiard room and watched the game.

The next day I moved to a cheaper hotel and went with Fesseha to pick up a rental car, a Fiat 124, which we drove to the town hall. Amdemicael was seated behind a large desk with a pile of notes to one side.

"In this town, the most beautiful town in the world," he announced, "the problems are set before me like chocolates. I am not sure which to pick." Like all Eritreans who were back in Asmara after a long absence, he was shocked at the state of it. Ethiopian maintenance struck the Front as very shoddy. In fact Asmara was an elegant place with good roads and amenities. Had they seen Maputo or Luanda, they would have thought themselves lucky.

Even so, there were serious difficulties. In twenty years the population had doubled to over 400,000 and Amdemicael estimated seventeen thousand homeless in the town, without counting members of the Front who might need housing in the next few years. For the moment, the fighters were billeted by the provisional government, a modified version of the Front. The old departments, plus the municipality of Asmara, almost a department in itself, were now constituted as a form of cabinet, which had superseded the EPLF Political Bureau and Central Committee as the decision-making body. The provisional government was turning many of the Front's battalions into rehabilitation teams, working to rebuild the ruins of the country outside Asmara. A few weeks hence a form of community service would come into effect for those who had never fought. They too would work on national reconstruction projects, again mostly in the countryside and smaller towns, thus easing, or rather, deferring, the population problem in the capital. All property nationalized in 1975 would be returned to its original owners and a commission had been set up to investigate outright expropriations that had occurred when people were known to have relatives in the Front. There was also the question of property awarded by the Dergue to Eritreans who had cooperated with the regime. "While the Dergue owned all property," Amdemicael observed, "there was no incentive to build, but with property rights restored we expect that slowly this may change, but we will not be able to begin without capital investment."

Before the war Asmara had been a prosperous city, with tanneries, textile factories, potteries and, of course, the Melotti brewery. There was a cement mill, a salt-processing plant, a glass factory; the city baked its own bread, produced its own pasta, manufactured its own cigarettes and matches. When the EPLF arrived, hardly any of the factories, roughly forty in all, were working to capacity. Since then about ten had become fully operational and others were working one shift out of three. The brewery also came back into production a few days after my arrival; in four days 750,000 bottles of beer had left the gates. Because these firms had been nationalized under Mengistu, the provisional government had now to pay the workers' wages. Where the original owners had not been compensated for their business by the Dergue, they would be entitled to reclaim them. Those for which the Dergue had paid were now the property of the provisional government, which was planning to sell them, wholly or in part, into private ownership. The Front was also paying civil servants' salaries, although there were fewer of these now that the cumbersome Ethiopian administration had been purged. As for the majority of people in Asmara, who depended on small trade for a livelihood, their situation was still serious. They had been choked by constraints on movement during the last days of the siege and, even now, as they began to recover, there was very little cash in circulation. To add to these difficulties, the sewage system was breaking down and there was not enough fresh water reaching the city through the old pipeline.

"You see," said Amdemicael at length, "why we are not sure where to begin."

One week in liberated Eritrea was enough to establish beyond reasonable doubt what had always been accepted in theory: death by drought was a political, not a natural phenomenon. It was merely that over the last fifteen years in the Horn few occasions had arisen to test the hypothesis. Now, in Eritrea, months after the end of the war, the drought persisted, yet few adults appeared to be dying and the infant mortality figures were improving. Asmara, besieged and bitterly hungry in the closing stages of the war, had the air of a city coming back to life, preparing to face a new set of difficulties. In the territory as a whole, the free passage of relief meant effective food distribution. In addition, the private investors of the Nacfa Corporation had intervened in the rising price of teff, Eritrea's preferred grain, by purchasing 1,500 quintals in Ethiopia and flooding the market. The price fell by two thirds and the corporation made a profit.

One of the central debates, in the agricultural department and among most members of the Front, was what kind of cultivation would scale down the country's dependency on aid. Single-ox plowing had worn away at the land wherever it was practiced. Thousands of hectares were now irrecoverable. Sharaev had been correct about that but had omitted to mention the effects of the bombing, which had contributed greatly to the destruction of useful land. In Sahel district the eroded topsoil lay like a secondary range of reddish hills and there was talk of moving it with a fleet of graders to areas where it could be used, but the real challenge now was to accept that rain-fed farming had no credible future. Irrigation was thus the key, but the Front lacked the necessary capital for a comprehensive system. Tesfai Ghermazien had been the EPLF representative in Washington and was now in charge of agriculture. He had offices in a row of bungalows a mile or more from the center of Asmara. He was a large, imposing man with a somber countenance that belied his many enthusiasms. He contended that Eritrea would need five or six major reservoirs to establish food security. The expertise and the manpower were available nationally, which only left the problem of money. "The capital resources we simply don't have," he said. "In the United States it would cost roughly $300 million for the kind of dam we envisage, from the feasibility study through to completion. It would be marginally cheaper for us, because we can cover the labor costs and some of the materials, but it is still beyond our means. So we have to look for loans, which is a dangerous thing, as you know. We have watched as the rest of Africa was ruined by debts. I can say it was the one advantage of a thirty-year war. Our liberation has come very late and we hope we have learned from the mistakes of others. It means we will be considering offers very carefully, that is all." He liked to talk about Oklahoma and was fascinated by the absolute change it had undergone from a dustbowl into a viable farming state.

"Two thirds of the state, in the east, is green throughout the year," he said, "and the rest is part of the high-production wheat belt. Basically, the transformation was made possible by building three hundred artificial lakes. Ourselves, we do not think that all of our land can be rehabilitated but I am sure that we can keep the fertile areas alive if we can make at least some of these dams."

For the time being, the Front maintained that there would be no public ownership whatever in agriculture. The state would intervene, as it did in the United States and Europe, with incentives and artificial pricing through some form of marketing board. What was still undecided was the kind of produce to grow in the lowlands, although the tendency was now to think in terms of cash-crop production. Aligidir, in the lowlands, had one of the biggest cotton plantations in the region, developed by the Italians, which the Front had once spoken of turning into a vast grain project. Now, however, it doubted the wisdom of a conversion, believing that cash crops might make a better contribution to overall food security in Eritrea. Cotton, after all, would support the textile factories in Asmara, which had once enjoyed lucrative contracts with Italy. On the slopes of the semihighland, coffee could be grown. Carnations, peppers and tomatoes, which had been flown to Italy on a weekly charter, might once again be grown for export. Eritrea would never produce enough grain for self-sufficiency, and teff, in particular, would always be in demand. The Eritreans had begun to believe that their best policy was to become a dependable community of buyers, supporting the Ethiopian grain market even as they made provision for vulnerable subsistence farmers and pastoralists of their own.

This, however, presupposed stability in the affairs of Eritrea's neighbors at a time when Ethiopia was far from settled and a clan war of extraordinary violence had broken out in Somalia. As for Eritrea itself, there was still skirmishing near the Sudanese border. A mujahidin faction of the ELF, funded by the ruling party in Sudan, had embarked on a small but holy war against the provisional government of Eritrea. It had been confronted and scattered, regrouping in bases at the frontier. It posed no serious military threat, but its very existence implied difficulties at the margins of this new nation whose center appeared so strong. And to the south, in Danakil, there was the delicate question of the Eritrean Afars. Pastoralists with a marked tradition of independence, the Afars ranged across Ethiopia, Eritrea, Djibouti and Somalia. In the past they had suffered at the hands of the

Ethiopian government. Livestock and grazing losses through drought, massacre and government cultivation of Afar pasture had quickened a longstanding sense of grievance. In Djibouti, a demand had been made for an Afar territory. The difficulty of winning any allegiance to the Eritrean state from this group was obvious. The sense of the nation that the front had in mind was simply not available to the Afars.

One point in the National Democratic Program of 1977 had survived the dramatic shifts in the Front's thinking: the idea that nomads should be settled. For plenty of Beni Amer and Afar youngsters, the EPLF offered an escape route to the modern world, but the elders were less keen. Years of war and drought might mean that they welcomed settlement, but there was no guarantee of this, or that a past of shared adversity would become a future of common advantage. The Eritreans were pedantic about the trappings of nationality and its fledgling institutions, such as health care and schooling. To argue that nomads might wish to remain at the mercy of their ways, mitigated by their growing success as smugglers, was to incur the charge of romanticism—a variation on the theme of *obscurantismo*—besides which, public welfare projects were a basic expression of state authority.

In the late afternoon, I drove a mile or so from the center of town to a set of sheds at the back of a warehouse, where the World Food Program had set up offices. They were run by a wild young American called Jerry, who had led the food convoys from Massawa right up until the closing stages of the war. The Eritreans spoke well of him, which was a compliment in view of their reticence about the United Nations. After the fall of Asmara Jerry had been the only officer in liberated Eritrea, but now other staff had begun to arrive. Recently, he had been joined in the sheds by a special representative to Eritrea, a jovial but hard-headed man whose stature in the organization reflected the importance it now attached to the territory. His job was to estimate the emergency food requirement in Eritrea and then to see that it was met. Thereafter he was to look at the country's long-term rehabilitation needs. He hinted that he would be in Asmara for at least eighteen months, time enough to assist with the formalities of the referendum and set the seal of approval on independence. "The U.N. is becoming a more updated system," he observed, "more responsive to the needs of a changing world." A U.N. interagency mission, on a tour of the Horn, had arrived in Asmara and there would be a reception at Amba Soira the following night.

"Are you not impressed," Fesseha asked when I met him later that evening at the hotel, "that the U.N. has appointed a special representative to Eritrea forty-one years after federation? We are quite surprised. Don't you think it is rather sudden?" I raised the likely role of the U.N. in the referendum process.

"It does not matter," he said haughtily, "whether they endorse our referendum or not. Anyway we will proceed. But if they would like to help, we will not object." Such terseness was common enough. The EPLF still saw the U.N. as the parlor room in which the "colonialist swindle" over Eritrea had been hatched. Resolution 678 on Saddam's annexation of Kuwait had done little to improve the U.N.'s image in Eritrean eyes. Given their own history, they thought the righteous anger meretricious.

Later at Fesseha's house we sat drinking and talking. I asked what he would do now the war was over. He told me he would remain in Protocol, but he would no longer be escorting journalists, only delegations. A Department of Information would look after the press. He confessed to a feeling of relief. "It was not so interesting," he said. "For the journalists, okay; but for us, always the same places, the same explanations, the same risks." All members of the Front, he added, would continue to perform their duties until the referendum. "And then?" I inquired. He was not sure; perhaps he would like to run a hotel by the sea.

I had brought a present for his little boy, Yohannes, an English reading primer with color pictures and large text: apple, dog, moon. Fesseha took him on his knee and spoke the alien words into his ear, turning the pages, as the child slapped each picture hard with both hands in cursory approval, keeping his gaze fixed on me all the while. Looking at the boy's eyes, I was overcome by the memory of his father as a bearded celibate, sitting on the steps of the guest house in Orota more than four years ago, with his head bowed. The good fortune that had fallen to this family was very great.

Yohannes's mother, Tsehai, brought in an enamel dish of water, soap and a towel, followed by a bowl of lentils and a flat tray of *injera*—proper *injera* made from teff, not wheat. She placed the towel on a side-table beside a black-and-white photograph of her family, with an elderly man at the center of the group. We ate in silence and when we had finished, I remarked how the figure in the photo reminded me of Wolde-ab, a trivial association brought on by the faded quality of the print, the buttoned suit that the old man wore and the evocation of a prewar past with its poignant faith in civility and due process.

"Do you know," said Fesseha after we had worked our way through Tsehai's relatives in the photo, "that Wolde-ab is staying in the Amba Soira?" The Amba Soira was the hotel I had been taken to on arrival in Asmara.

"Of course," I said. "My first night here I had the room next to his. He knocked on my door and asked for shampoo."

"You think I am joking?" said Fesseha with an innocent grin.

"But Wolde-ab is dead," I said.

"Did I ever tell you?" Fesseha asked, shaking his head from side to side. "Who told you so?" It had not even occurred to me to ask. His name was so firmly associated with the first stirrings of the movement that he had taken on a mythic quality in my mind and I had assumed he was dead. I could not recall ever before having invented someone's death, but even now, I was unsure whether to take Fesseha at his word.

"He must be a hundred," I said.

"Not at all," he replied. "He is eighty and some years. You can go and talk to him. Amba Soira, room 112."

The following morning I asked the woman at reception in the Amba Soira to call up to room 112.

"His daughter says he is resting," she told me, replacing the old Bakelite phone by the switchboard. "The best time is to try this evening."

"Is he well?" I asked.

"He is okay," she said, "but he is very old."

In the lobby of the hotel a heated discussion was under way among a group of Eritreans, who called me over and sat me beside them. A tall man in glasses was dressing down an older, bald man in a mixture of Tigrinya and Italian. He stopped briefly to acknowledge my arrival and resumed his argument. It concerned Italy's decision, someone explained, to set up an informal mission in Asmara. Daniel Yohannes, who had served as the EPLF representative in Belgium, held that after years of indifference to the Eritrean case, Italy's behavior now was shameless. The bald man, who had settled in Italy and was here on a brief visit, felt obliged to disagree. Daniel was arrogant, clever, mocking.

When he was done, he turned on me with eagerness. "Excuse me," he said, "I wish to tell you the moral of all this. It is not that Italy is worse than others, but that all we have done here in Eritrea, we have done it for ourselves. From the Middle East we have had help, this is certain; even from governments. In Europe and the United States, we have many friends—individuals and organizations. But in the final analysis we were alone. We were not recognized in the West or Africa. They called it the forgotten war and this is true. Please allow me to tell you a most interesting story. In 1985 the Belgian aid agency Solidarité Socialiste organized a colloquium in Brussels on the liberation struggles in Africa. They sent invitations to Polisario, ANC, SWAPO and ourselves. But the Ethiopian embassy heard of this and they complained to Solidarité that the EPLF is not a liberation movement. We are 'antipeople bandits' and we cannot speak at such a colliquium.

"Solidarité is attached to the Belgian socialist party and they were so surprised, you know, that they referred this matter at once to the Political Bureau of the party. Now the Dergue informed SWAPO and Polisario and the ANC that they must refuse to come if the EPLF is speaking. But Solidarité had already purchased air tickets for the others. They called me and said this: 'We are very embarrassed, but we have sent the tickets and they are refusing to come because of you.' The Political Bureau told Solidarité to make a separate meeting on Eritrea. When they came to me with this suggestion, I refused absolutely. They said, 'Naturally, we have always supported the Eritrean struggle, but you know it is delicate in Africa, because of the OAU and the fraternity of these other movements.' I told them, 'Surely, you are free to do what you like? You must invite everybody and if people refuse to come, that is their business.' So they went back to the Political Bureau and they said, 'The Eritreans are right: we can invite whomever we like.' New invitations were sent, but the three movements refused. On the day of the colloquium, only one liberation movement was represented: EPLF. I spoke to three thousand people. They were asking, 'Where are the others? Why are they not here?' The chair was obliged to explain that the others had refused."

Daniel finished his tea and rose to leave, but he could not resist another salvo. "Never kneel down," he said, "and never refuse an invitation. We have been fortunate. Look at Polisario. They were going to have their independence now, through the United Nations and OAU, but King Hassan is objecting and now the U.N. is changing its mind. They try to forget Polisario like they were forgetting us. Today if they come to Eritrea, it is only to recognize a *fait accompli*: our victory. I tell you, it is a serious problem for liberation struggles who depend too much on others. That is why I say we are fortunate. Nobody has come to our rescue, nobody has said, 'Do this or do that.' The rest I think you know. Mengistu was finished when the Cold War ended. So we must also admit that we are 100 percent beneficiaries of the new world disorder." He chuckled and shook my hand. "You are staying in Asmara. Perhaps tomorrow we will have another interesting discussion."

That evening I attended a reception at the Amba Soira for the U.N. mission. There were thirty or forty people, an equal number of Eritreans and foreigners. To begin with, the two groups mixed. Then, as the occasion wore on, they began to separate. I found myself listening to an English member of the mission who remarked that they had all been profoundly impressed by the diligence and organization of the EPLF and had no doubt that these were the people to set Eritrea back on its feet. "They are a delight to work with," he observed. "All the structures are already in place in the form of departments and the will for reconstruction is overwhelming." He called it a haven of sanity. Beside the tension in Ethiopia, the deepening despair of Sudan and the clan wars that had destroyed Somalia, Eritrea was a welcome prospect for the aid community, whose praises bordered on flattery.

"My only reservation," the Englishman continued, "is their pride. Beyond a certain point they are unwilling to discuss things. You get the impression that if you don't agree, you should pack your bags and leave. That attitude, I'm afraid, will need moderating if Eritrea is to get the most out of the international community." The most, in this case, meant U.N. support for the referendum that the EPLF planned to hold within eighteen months on the status of the territory.

I left the gathering, walked over to the desk in the lobby and put in a call to room 112. The receptionist spoke a few words of Tigrinya and replaced the phone.

"He will see you now," she said. I handed my bag across the counter and walked upstairs. At the door of room 112, I knocked and, after a lengthy silence, a woman in olive fatigues let me in to a narrow front room and retreated to the main part of the suite. A moment later a frail man in a thick tweed suit and carpet slippers appeared in the doorway; after shaking my hand he crossed slowly to an armchair, lapsing into it with some difficulty. We sat in silence until Wolde-ab Wolde Mariam extended his trembling hand across the table and shook mine once again.

"Welcome to Eritrea," he said at length. I introduced myself and the old man nodded graciously, his eyes lowered with a peculiar discretion. It was as though I had come and gone across the continent with a vague question in mind and finally I had arrived at the place—not a bare, luminous plain, a packed football stadium or a refugee settlement, but a room in an undistinguished hotel—where it might be asked. But if I had ever formulated it, it eluded me now.

"Forgive me," I said. "I was delighted to know that you were in Asmara."

"I too am delighted," said Wolde-ab, touching the rim of his thick glasses. "We are both delighted." He had come three months earlier, he explained, for the celebrations.

"They have chosen a house for me in Asmara, but it is lacking some furniture. When it is ready and all my belongings have arrived from overseas I will move." I asked where they would come from and Wolde-ab looked up distractedly.

"Yes," he said, after a moment, "they are in transit from New Jersey." I inquired how he found Asmara; he leaned across and asked me to repeat the question, to which he replied with a laugh.

"Very fine," he said, "very pleasant. It is thirty-four years since I have seen the city. Yes, thirty-four." He drew in a series of short breaths and lay back in the armchair.

For an hour the old man spoke about his life, struggling sometimes for the names and places, and always to transpose the dates from the Ethiopian to the Gregorian calendar. There were many things of which I had no inkling. It had taken seven attempts on his life for the Ethiopians to dislodge him from Eritrea in 1954. Before the federation there were two more bombs, but neither went off, and two attempts to shoot him down. When, for the sake of his family, he moved to the Pensione Milano, strychnine was put in one of the meals for which he sent down; he recovered in the hospital. He was at the *pensione* for fourteen months, running his nationalist weekly in Tigrinya, without setting a foot out of doors. In 1952 he fought on—a question now not of preventing but of revoking the federation, and founded the Eritrean Workers' Party with that ambition in mind. Ten days later he was shot again. He spent five months in the hospital struggling for his life. The bullet had entered his back and left by his throat.

In 1954, almost recovered, he set out for Cairo, where his nationalist broadcasts into Eritrea began, but in 1956 they were suppressed. When Haile Selassie offered to mediate on Nasser's behalf during the Suez crisis, it had been on condition that Wolde-ab be silenced. Inside Eritrea an urban-based movement known as the Groups of Seven began distributing tracts, often in his name. A Christian in a pan-Arabist and largely Muslim world, Wolde-ab began to founder, but the arrival of Idris Awate and Idris Mohamed Adem gave new strength to the nationalist base in Cairo that he had set up single-handed. Together the three men scoured the Arab world for support—Saudi Arabia, Iraq, Syria, Jordan, Kuwait, Lebanon, the Emirates. Wolde-ab saw the ELF into existence, but was soon watching from the margins as it began to break apart. In 1965 he broadcast a series of unity appeals from Damascus that held off the division for a while longer. In Aden in 1970 he began to define the terms of a new, more democratic movement. He was a founding member of the EPLF and, when the old Front declared war on it, he met with the ELF in Khartoum in an attempt to reconcile the two groups. The military wing of the EPLF turned on him for acting without proper authority. In 1977, after a further failure to end the strife, he resigned and returned to Cairo.

"I remained silent," he said. "After that my main activity was to correspond with Eritreans abroad. In America, Italy, France, anywhere, offering encouragement, reminding them that one day we must win our Eritrea. I was not so young of course." Breathless, he rocked forward, clasping his mottled hands around one knee.

"That's it," he declared with a scrupulous inclination of the head, as if the public life that he had slowly ushered into the room might have something of its own to add. But in the long pause that followed, the obscurity of Wolde-ab's commitment was plain, its heroic absence from the community of African political culture where it might have won renown. Wolde-ab leaned back in his chair, smiling.

It occurred to me to ask what the Eritrean nation was. As he searched for a reply, he seemed to falter. "It is land," he said eventually, "and a people. And besides these two, there is language, and the capacity to read and write it." In this sense, Wolde-ab's Tigrinya primer was just as important as the *Eritrean Weekly News.* "The identity of a nation is its language," he went on. "Through language we feel sure we exist—in the true sense of existence." He nodded to himself. "And now that we are free, we find we are a nation of nine languages. But we do not suppress the others as the Ethiopians did. And of course there is the map of Eritrea, which we inherited from the Italians. This is some of it." He seemed to drift for a while and then explained, unprompted, that he had moved to New Jersey in 1982 to live with one of his daughters and his son-in-law, an American doctor.

"I was there when I heard of the fall of Asmara," he said. "My mind was empty. There was nothing. I was without a sense of joy or surprise. Feelingless. Only little by little I realized I was alive. And now I am going to stay. I cannot leave Eritrea again." Once more he was following his own train of thought and remarked quite suddenly, "When I was in the hospital in 1953, after I was shot, the Workers' Party put my name up against eight other candidates for the municipality of Asmara. I was elected and the result was annulled with a stroke of the pen. The Ethiopians said, 'Ah, yes, but Wolde-ab's candidature is irregular.' " He chuckled.

I had acquired one of the posters of Wolde-ab that the National Guidance Department had issued for the celebrations. It showed an elderly, unshaven man with a handkerchief in his jacket pocket and a small microphone pinned to his lapel; he was in midspeech, his left hand raised as though shielding his eyes, slightly glassy with the onset of cataract, from strong sunlight. Above it was a legend in Tigrinya, repeated in Arabic at the base. When I told him I had the poster, he seemed unaware that there was such a thing. It was in the bag I had left at the reception desk and I went downstairs to retrieve it. On my return, Wolde-ab seemed very tired. I unfurled it on the table in front of him and he studied it carefully.

"What's this?" he asked, running a shaky hand over the Tigrinya characters. Behind the glasses his eyes were full of tears. "Wolde-ab," he translated, "Father of the Nation."

The following morning I drove out to Decamhare. There was a new man working for Protocol who called himself John. He had suggested a visit to the old Ethiopian lines. It was a good idea from his point of view, since he had a sister in Decamhare who had just given birth. On the way, we put ten liters in the Fiat, using John's Protocol coupons, and stopped once more to pick up his cousin, a shy young girl who sat in the back without speaking. The weather was good. A dry wind honed the sky deep blue and brushed the heat of the late morning off the road. In Decamhare, John's mother took us inside to see the new child and drink coffee. After an hour, John and I set off for Afalba.

At the edge of the village the land rose abruptly on either side of the road, which was cut at ninety degrees by the Ethiopian lines. Before the EPLF moved south toward Assab to draw Ethiopian resources away from the defense of Asmara—and they claimed to have drawn off the best part of five divisions, flown out by transports over six weeks—there had been sixty thousand troops along this front. We left the car and, under escort from a growing band of children, climbed up toward a group of houses. For a time we stopped and talked with an elderly mother and daughter living in a bare but comfortable house with two rooms. The daughter's name was Gemga; she was sixty-five. We had interrupted her during the preparation of *injera*, which she made from her wheat allocation. She had found a way to improve the taste by leaving half the wheat to germinate before she ground it. The pair were entirely dependent on food brought through by the EPLF. The mother was pale and nearly blind, but it was old age rather than sickness that had begun to overcome her. Large numbers of Ethiopian soldiers had been in Afalba for a year before the liberation and so, on the day the fighting began, a Sunday, Gemga assumed that the shooting was just practice. Then it grew more intense and continued into the afternoon. "The Ethiopians knocked on our door," she said, "but we hid. Then our own fighters came. We saw them and we could not believe it. They took us that night to a shelter in the rocks. Next morning it began again, for many hours. Then we saw the EPLF tanks moving into the village. After that, I do not know. We heard that Decamhare had fallen and they were moving forward to Asmara. All that time, my mother was praying, and we were thinking of her son, my brother, who was in the field."

There was a commotion below the house as we left. An exasperated man in a robe had just lost a cow on a land mine. He wanted to butcher it immediately and was sending a group of children off in search of a donkey so that he could bring the meat down from the hill. They were crowding around him shouting, jumping off the rocks by the side of the road and skipping back again as he issued instructions. Further down into Afalba, the first groups of people were returning from the market in Decamhare. John led me up the steep gradient on the opposite side of the road. We climbed for five minutes until we could see a ridge to our right where the battle had been fiercest. The fighters called it "Autobus." John described the assault by the EPLF infantry and its synchronization with the entry of the mechanized units along the road into Afalba. The sky above Autobus was furrowed with sparse cloud. We stood for a time gazing across at the place; I thought of Tiblets and Nebiat, the similarity of their gestures and the cramped cover of sandbagged timbers under which we had sat.

On the climb through the rocks John and I had passed the remains of two Ethiopian soldiers below a clump of aloes. As we turned to go back, a group of goats skipped nimbly up the rise and cropped the new grass growing in the bleached khaki rags. A dozen more followed behind, driven by a grizzled and toothless goatherd in white pantaloons and a T-shirt bearing a print of San Francisco Bay. He greeted us and, after a short conversation with John, took over the description of the battle, gesturing with his crook, bringing the fighters down from the ridges while the tanks rumbled up the road. When this was finished, he raised the crook once more in the direction of Autobus and then swept it over the ground in a low, scything motion. Hundreds of Ethiopians had fallen there, he said. He squinted at the cloud over the ridge and urged us to set out for the battlefield now. "That way," John translated, "he says you will never forget the victory we have made." We begged to differ, turning instead to the subject of his goats and their manifest good health. The old man said that although the drought was still severe, there was far more browsing now that the war was over. They could crop their way from here to Autobus and back. He knew roughly where the land mines were and claimed that his animals were learning too. He drove them to the top of the rise, clicking and shouting. Before disappearing around the first bend in the track, he turned and gazed down at us, raising one hand in the air.

On the way back from Afalba John drove while I brooded. I could not believe that my susceptibility to myth was such that I had made the eighth attempt on poor Wolde-ab's life. Yet the lapse had a meaning, or so I thought as we headed up to Decamhare through this new state in the making, based on aspirations that had failed in much of Africa, not least the Horn. Ethiopia, Somalia, Sudan: these were not nations in the sense that Eritrea intended; perhaps they never had been. Wolde-ab might still be alive but just across the borders of his country, the ideas he stood for had withered beyond recognition. Eritrea was alone in its moment of hope, just as it had been in its long years of misery.

A few miles out of Decamhare, we passed lines of people coming the other way on foot. Many were women, driving donkeys with sacks of grain over their backs, but there were children too, with bunches of vegetables and small packets of teff. They zigzagged behind the adults and tried to hitch one another on to the animals. In the town we parked by the mosque. The market would soon close but there were still plenty of traders and even more customers. A small sum would buy a week's supply of teff for a family of five or six; for wealthier people, with salaries from the provisional government or jobs in Asmara, there were fruits and vegetables in abundance. One stall in particular was piled high with capsicums and tomatoes. Bunches of ripe bananas hung from iron staves above the counter. A woman in a red head scarf cut a slice from a massive pumpkin and weighed it for a customer. We bought musty green oranges, wrinkled chile and purple onions to take to John's relatives. In one section of the market there were women with wide panniers of grain and pulses spread out on lengths of cloth. A large crowd was gathered and the vendors were so busy pouring out measures that the air was charged with pale, sweet dust.

EPILOGUE

▲▲▲▲▲▲

In 1992, the provisional government of Eritrea began to register voters. An official in London related with a smile how the first person to show up at the new registration office in Asmara was the incorrigible Wolde-ab. Before the end of the year, Boutros Boutros-Ghali, secretary-general of the U.N., was in the region. During his visit to Addis Ababa there were violent demonstrations against the idea of the Eritrean referendum. Many Ethiopians still regarded Eritrea as the fourteenth province of their own country. Independence was inevitable, however, and the referendum was held at the end of April 1993. The result showed overwhelming support for the existence of a new state in Africa.

It is harder now to grasp the strength of opposition to Eritrean nationalism, not simply in Ethiopia but among African leaders and intellectuals who saw a separate nation state in Eritrea as a threat to the notion of inviolable boundaries and thus to the basis of national sovereignty throughout the continent. Yet Ethiopia's profligate defense of its shape on the map did little credit to the doctrine of integrity at any price.

As for Eritrea, it was in many ways a model of successful liberation, proven in a lengthy trial by fire. The leadership was tough-minded and resourceful; it managed skillfully to leaven the daily fare of coercion with a steady dose of benefits, keeping civilians fed, watered and, whenever possible, protected from the travails of war and drought; it fought using the pen, the medical prescription and the seedpod as much as it did using the gun—and it achieved its goal.

It is an indication of the rapid pace of change in Africa that such a model now has almost no application on the continent. Crucially, the gun speaks only for those who use it. The familiar symbol of the

Kalashnikov crossed with the hoe—a symbol used by more than one liberation movement—no longer stands for self-defence and the right to the fruits of the earth, but for the greatest conflict of interest on the continent: almost all the wars in Africa, over the last three decades of this century, have disrupted food production.

Yet the gun has not gone away; neither have hunger and displacement. In the Western Sahara conflict, a prolonged ceasefire has brought no change to the condition of the refugees on the Tindouf plain: a military impasse has been replaced by a diplomatic stalemate, in which the possibility of a return to arms by Polisario cannot be ruled out. Elsewhere, matters are worse. In Liberia, many guerrilla soldiers have not yet reached the age at which a child in New York would be permitted by responsible parents to go once round the block on a bicycle. Some of the weapons that reduced Somalia to a physical and political ruin are still in caches, in case influential people should fail to see eye-to-eye about a new dispensation. At the start of 1993 the humanitarian crisis in Sudan was so extreme—3.5 million already displaced by war, of whom half were now said to be starving—that the government in Khartoum was shamed into allowing aid workers greater access to the south of the country. Within weeks, United Nations workers were under threat from a southern rebel faction.

Angola faced one of the worst situations on the continent. In May the Clinton administration recognized the elected government, after more than fifteen years; U.N. forces on the ground had been calling for much greater efforts by world leaders to end the fighting which erupted after Savimbi's refusal to abide by the election results. It was no longer appropriate to call this a breakdown in the peace process: Angola was back at war. UNITA took the city of Huambo at the beginning of March, after prolonged and bloody fighting. The government's military hospital was overrun and, according to eyewitnesses who fled the city, the patients were put to death. Large numbers of refugees, some of them UNITA supporters, began moving toward government-held areas, and the coastal town of Benguela braced itself for a new intake of shocked, hungry, dispossessed civilians.

With the approach of the southern winter, it was as though the country had known no other season for thirty years. UNITA had lost several of its most able senior officers but it appeared to have no shortage of arms. It would require discipline and, for soldiers on both sides, an uncommon courage to give up the way of the gun. In the meantime, the rest of Africa read the return to war as a bad omen. At the start of 1993 there were few people with encouraging words about the future of a continent where peace seemed so elusive.

As the government and rebels of Angola prepared to meet in

Ivory Coast for negotiations, South Africa lost one of its best guarantors of a peaceful settlement. The black nationalist Chris Hani was shot to death outside his home in a newly integrated suburb of Johannesburg on April 10th by a Polish exile extremist, one of many white men, marginal or estranged in their own cultures, who have drifted to South Africa for want of a better place to nurse their grievances. Chris Hani had been the hero of the ANC's armed wing and had led it for a time in Angola. In December 1991, nearly two years after Mandela's release, Hani was elected secretary-general of the South African Communist Party. A principled man pitted for years against a ruthless adversary, he too had been ruthless. But it was precisely this that earned him the respect of the township youth. For them the language of reconciliation meant little—it was so much talk in the absence of firm guarantees—even when it came from Mandela. But they paid closer attention to the president of the ANC when Hani endorsed him.

Mr. Janus Jacob Waluz, a man with a handgun and connections with the far right in South Africa, took out Mandela's interpreter in the townships and, like all assassins, contrived a shortcut to fame. In the aftermath, Mandela looked old. He had already lost a wife to one version of South African tragedy, which conflated violence and ambition with the struggle for human rights; another now decreed that he should lose an able son. Chief Buthelezi offered his condolences. So did President de Klerk. When Mandela relayed them to a crowd in Soweto, he was jeered. For Edward, my acquaintance in Orlando, Hani's name had always had the force of a magical utterance; to speak it was to draw down some invisible protection, the r of the first name rolled crisply in front of the lengthened vowel, with the surname following as a prophetic gust of breath. Edward's neighbors were relatives of Hani's, a mother and two schoolgirls; I never established what their kinship with him was. But the tens of thousands who mourned in the streets of South Africa on the day of Hani's funeral were all family in a self-evident sense.

As the date for South Africa's first nonracial elections looked set to move forward, the schedule for elections in Mozambique was delayed. Since the peace in October 1992, numerous international commissions and monitors appearing in the country had realized the complexity of the task they faced in bringing people home, drawing up a voters' roll and trying to ensure that everyone in government and Renamo areas received adequate food. The U.N. estimated that humanitarian aid alone for 1993–94—which included the provision of essential services and emergency relief—would come to just over $700 million. The peace was fragile but appeared to be holding, even if

Angola had set a discouraging precedent. The U.N.'s military observers in Angola had not been equipped as a potential fighting force; in Mozambique it was proposed that more than four thousand armed troops be drafted in to help keep order. The U.N. was prepared to throw far more resources into the settlement in Mozambique than it had in Angola. Elections would probably take place in mid-1994.

There was no reason to suppose that the experiment with modern multiparty democracy would suit Mozambique—the project had already run into trouble in Angola, Kenya, Zambia, Zaire and Nigeria, among others—or that the profound suspicion with which many rural communities viewed the idea of central government would abate. The city and what remained of the countryside were quite distinct places, within which lesser differences were also beginning to appear as some of the political parties, which sprang up under the new constitution, were unable to conceal their regional bias. In the 1960s and 1970s it had been hard to conceive of liberation as anything other than a unifying socialist project: now the only available model seemed to be political pluralism along western lines. In much the same way as the anti-bullet vaccine had been applied to the Naparamas by Manuel António, an essence of multiparty democracy could be rubbed into the wounds that already existed in Mozambique's body politic, but it would take more than this to immunize the country against poverty and violence.

Toward the end of 1992, Penny Hango showed me into her offices in Windhoek. She was doing research into marketing and pricing at the Ministry of Agriculture, Water and Rural Development. She had a decent salary, accommodation of her own and a say in the agrarian policies of the new Namibia. Many years back, in Leipzig, she had chafed at the idea of studying agriculture; now she regarded it as a privilege to be tackling the problems of sustainable farming in peacetime. The first rains of 1993 had been prolific, she said. But Ovamboland was so dry that much of the rain had run off, carrying topsoil with it. Then in April came the small rains. The earth was already primed; it yielded and drank like a dark sponge. The prospects for the millet harvest were good. Penny had travelled thousands of miles from home but she had never severed her links with the past. Her firstborn son, Tuyeni, now had a younger brother. She had called him Tuyoleni, which means "Let us rejoice." UNITA bands were raiding across the Angolan border, Penny said. They were taking cattle and robbing the odd grocery store, but for the moment it was containable.

NOTES

ACRONYMS AND ORGANIZATIONS

GLOSSARY

INDEX

NOTES

INTRODUCTION

16 *"small wars"* . . . : An expression used by some English newspaper editors for debatable stories on their foreign pages. See, for example, David Kynaston, *The Financial Times: A Centenary History* (London: Viking, 1988), pp. 420–21. At the end of the 1970s, "small wars" played a large part in discussions about the role and content of the newspaper. In the 1980s, *The Financial Times* underwent a number of significant changes but managed admirably to keep Africa in the news, and many "small wars" with it.

16 *. . . the continent's debt repayments were roughly double what it received in emergency aid:* Paul Vallely, *Bad Samaritans: First World Ethics and Third World Debt* (London: Hodder & Stoughton, 1990), p. 85.

16 *The cuts made by indebted African regimes . . . :* See Richard Jolly, "The Human Dimensions of International Debt," in Wells and Hewitt (editors), *Growing Out of Debt* (London: Overseas Development Institute, 1989), p. 52.

17 *. . . it was obvious that history had miscarried fearfully:* It was Amilcar Cabral, the anticolonial leader in the Portuguese territories of Guinea-Bissau and Cape Verde, who described "armed struggle" as "an act of fertilizing history": Amilcar Cabral, *Unité et lutte I: l'arme de la théorie* (Paris: François Maspero, 1975), p. 334.

19 *"Anybody can imagine war . . ."*: Martha Gellhorn, *The Face of War* (London: Sphere Books, 1967).

1. ANGOLA

Some of the background material for this chapter is drawn from G. J. Bender, *Angola Under the Portuguese: The Myth and the Reality* (London: Heinemann, 1978); Basil Davidson, *In the Eye of the Storm: Angola's People* (London: Longman, 1972); John Marcum, *The Angolan Revolution (1950–1962) vol. 1: The Anatomy of an Explosion* (Cambridge, Mass.: MIT Press, 1969); Marcum, *The Angolan Revolution (1962–1976) vol. 2: Exile Politics and Guerrilla Warfare,* ibid., 1978; John Stockwell, *In Search of Enemies: A CIA Story* (New York: W. W. Norton, 1978).

For material about Savimbi, see Fred Bridgland, *Jonas Savimbi: A Key to Africa* (London: Mainstream Publishing, 1986). This book is a defense of UNITA and might usefully be read in conjunction with William Minter, *Operation Timber: Pages from the Savimbi Dossier* (Trenton, NJ: Africa World Press, 1988). *Operation Timber* is a compilation and analysis of documents, including several letters written by Savimbi, that show the extent of his collaboration with the colonial authorities and influential settlers before independence. Savimbi has denounced the letters as forgeries. For further examples of Savimbi's prolific correspondence, see Augusta Conchiglia, *UNITA: Myth and Reality* (London: European Campaign Against South African Aggression on Mozambique and Angola/UK, 1990).

For material on the South African campaigns in Angola, see Helmoed-Römer Heitman, *War in Angola: The Final South African Phase* (Gibraltar: Ashanti Publishing, 1990). See also Fred Bridgland, *The War for Africa* (Gibraltar: Ashanti Publishing, 1990). Both books were prepared in cooperation with the South African Defence Force. Fidel Castro gave the Cuban version of Cuito Cuanavale at the beginning of his speech to the Council of State approving the sentences handed down to Division General Arnaldo Ochoa Sánchez, head of the Cuban Military Mission in Angola, and others, in July 1989. It is published in *Case 1/1989: End of the Cuban Connection* (Havana: José Martí Publishing House, 1989). A more succinct account is given by Stephen Ellis and Tsepo Sechaba in *Comrades against Apartheid: The ANC and the South African Communist Party in Exile* (London and Bloomington, Ind.: James Currey, 1992), pp. 184–87.

For a fictional account of exile Angolan life in Zambia and of conditions in Jamba, see Sousa Jamba's novel *Patriots* (London: Viking, 1990).

For an impartial record of abuses during the conflict, see *Angola: Violations of the Laws of War by Both Sides* (London, Washington and New York: Africa Watch, 1989). The Africa Watch researcher, Jemera Rone, failed to obtain a visa from the People's Republic of Angola; the report is based on interviews with refugees in Zaïre and Zambia.

26 *During his travels . . . :* Joaquim John Monteiro, *Angola and the River Congo* (London: Macmillan, 1875).
26 *. . . in numbers that were only guessed at . . . :* UNICEF, for example, estimated the number of deaths among infants and under-fives from 1980 to 1986, as a result of war and destabilization, at 214,000, adding that "no exactitude can be claimed for these estimates"; see *Children on the Front Line: The Impact of Apartheid, Destabilization and Warfare on Children in Southern and South Africa* (New York and Geneva: UNICEF, 1987). In 1992 the Angolan government claimed that half a million people had died in the course of the entire war (London: *Angola News*, April 1992).
27 *"He who has striven . . .":* This and other quotations from Neto's verse are translations by Marga Holness, *Sacred Hope: Poems by Agostinho Neto* (London: Journeyman/UNESCO, 1988). See also *Poems from Angola* (London: Heinemann, 1979), selected and translated by Michael Wolfers.

29 *They were detained in ANC camps . . . :* On dissent within the ANC in Angola and the rebellion in 1984 at Quatro camp, see the detailed account by Ellis and Sechaba, *Comrades against Apartheid,* pp. 128–36. See also Thandeka Gqubele, "Young Lions Lie Buried in the Frontline States," *Weekly Mail,* Johannesburg, 18–24 May 1990. The dissidents believed that they should be deployed in "the country they were recruited to fight" rather than Angola. They were disarmed and detained by ANC authorities, after which, "dissidents alleged . . . that they were starved, that many died of scurvy and anaemia, that electric shock torture and excessive physical labour were used as punishment" and that "some mutineers were beaten to death and others were shot."

29 confusão: See Ryszard Kapuściński, *Another Day of Life* (London: Pan, 1987), for a more elegant explanation of *confusão.*

29 candonga *and the war effort:* On trial in Havana in 1989, Division General Arnaldo Ochoa Sánchez, who headed the Cuban military mission to Angola from the end of 1987, admitted to illegal barter and money changing during the war. In his defense he argued that he needed funds to construct airstrips. At the time of the South African buildup in the southeast this was imperative if the Cuban air force was to be deployed to maximum effect for the defense of Cuito Cuanavale. Ochoa claimed that the mission to Angola had earlier requested money for an airstrip from Havana but that this was not forthcoming. "And I just decided, 'Look, I'm not going to go looking for something else, so sell some things and we will build the airport anyway' " (*Case 1/1989: End of the Cuban Connection*).

34 *Che Guevara:* For a synopsis of Che's role in the independence struggle and the subsequent Cuban commitment in 1975, see Gabriel García Márquez. "Operation Carlota," London, *New Left Review,* no. 101–2, 1977. The dispatch of troops to Angola, says Márquez, "was not a simple expedition by professional soldiers, but a genuine people's war." Márquez argues that the Cubans were coming to the rescue of a people "with a magical dread of aeroplanes" who were "convinced that bullets could not pierce white skins."

43 *"When she gets her artificial limb . . .":* also recorded in the television documentary *Chain of Tears* by Toni Strasburg, Birmingham, Central Television, 1988.

44 *"We are really stretched here . . .":* also *Chain of Tears.*

47 *In September the Portuguese fell on Hanoi II . . . :* Details of this raid are added to Katila's story from Don Barnett's eyewitness account. *With the Guerrillas in Angola,* a pamphlet published by the Liberation Support Movement, Richmond, British Columbia, 1970.

53 *Jamba:* as distinct from the actual town of Jamba, over three hundred miles west in the province of Huila.

2. NAMIBIA

Some of the background material for this chapter is drawn from Peter Katjavivi, *A History of Resistance in Namibia* (Paris, London and Addis Ababa:

UNESCO/James Currey/OAU, 1989); Dennis Herbstein and John Evenson, *The Devils Are among Us: The War for Namibia* (London and New Jersey: Zed Books, 1989); John Ya Otto, *Battlefront Namibia: An Autobiography* (London: Heinemann, 1981); and Richard Moorsom,*Transforming a Wasted Land* (London: Catholic Institute for International Relations, 1990).

86 *. . .the SWAPO leadership was harsh on its rank and file . . .* : See *Africa Confidential*, London, vol. 29, no. 5, December 1988: "Many SWAPO cadres . . . are disturbed at the prospect of SWAPO taking power in its present form. The reason is simply that the leadership has behaved with incompetence and brutality towards its own cadres." *Africa Confidential* maintained that there were "perhaps many hundreds" of SWAPO detainees in Angola. During the Namibian election campaign in 1989, representatives of many detainees who were not from Ovamboland joined the United Democratic Front, which came in third at the polls. The matter was thoroughly aired during the campaign. Bience Gawanas, a barrister and SWAPO member accused of spying for South Africa and detained in Angola for five months, remained in the organization. In 1990 she was working at a law center in Windhoek. "I got the impression that they [SWAPO] knew they had made a mistake," she said in the course of an interview. "The fact that I'm sitting here, at home: in that sense SWAPO has not disappointed my expectations."

88 *Commonwealth:* Formerly known as the British Commonwealth. A voluntary association of fifty independent states, including Britain and most of its former dependencies. The organization emerged in its present form with Britain's withdrawal from India in 1947 and Nehru's decision that India should remain within it. Namibia was the most recent state to become a member.

91 *During the war, security forces had laid explosives . . . :* St. Mary's suffered several attacks by security forces. See the linocut by the Kwanyama artist John Muafangejo, *The Anglican Seminary Blown Up,* 1983. The text in the picture reads, "The seminary blown up by bombing by Master No body. This building was destroyed by un known people on Thursday 18-6-1981 at 1 a.m. It is near the border of Namibia and Angola. This destruction is the 3rd of St Mary's building those were same about like that one. (1) House of archdeacon in 1975 (2) House of Priest, Engineering for lite house and carpentry work shop in 1979. The Eighth Bishop Rt. J. H. Kauluma was preaching in saddness together with his Archdeacon Revd. P. H. Shilongo for the destroyed houses of Odibo mission. . . ."

92 *Ja Ioivo concealed the tape in a copy of* Gulliver's Travels . . . : But according to Katjavivi, *A History of Resistance,* it was *Treasure Island.*

92 *. . . the U.N.'s Fourth Committee . . . :* The Special Committee on the Situation with regard to the Implementation of the Declaration on the Granting of Independence to Colonial Countries and Peoples, nowadays referred to as the Committee of 24 or the Special Committee on Decolonization. The declaration was contained in General Assembly Resolution 1514

(XV), adopted in 1960, and the committee was established the following year. It played an important role in the independence of the Portuguese African colonies (1975), Zimbabwe (1980) and Namibia (1990). Since it was established, over fifty colonial territories have won their independence.

93 *He told the Fourth Committee . . . :* Kuhangua appeared more than once before the committee. Details of his remarks can be found in General Assembly documents A/C.4/SR.1564 (November 1965), 1602 (6 October 1966) and 1603 (7 October 1966).

96 *AG:* An Administrator General's Proclamation. Thousands were held under the AG9, promulgated in 1977, which allowed detention without charge for an unlimited period. In 1986 the right of access to a lawyer after thirty days was established.

3. WESTERN SAHARA

Some of the background material for this chapter is drawn from John Damis, *Conflict in Northwest Africa: The Western Sahara Dispute* (Stanford, Calif.: Hoover Institution Press, 1983); Tony Hodges, *Western Sahara: The Roots of a Desert War* (Westport, Conn.: Lawrence Hill, 1983); Minority Rights Group Report no. 40, *The Western Saharans*, London, 1984, and the MRG Update, London, 1991, both by Tony Hodges; John Mercer, *Spanish Sahara* (London: George Allen and Unwin, 1976); Richard Lawless and Laila Monahan, eds., *War and Refugees: The Western Sahara Conflict* (London and New York: Pinter Publishers, 1987).

105 *After 1975 Algeria was Polisario's only dependable ally.:* Support from Libya was inconsistent and, in 1984, Morocco concluded a treaty with Qaddafi at Oujda. Cuban assistance for Polisario arrived in 1976, in the form of a medical team. For allegations of Cuban military involvement, see Bridgland, *The War for Africa*, p. 19. Bridgland claims that General Arnaldo Ochoa Sánchez took part in the combat. "In 1979 he commanded a Cuban unit fighting with Polisario Front guerrillas in their successful campaign against Mauritania." Polisario denies any Cuban military assistance. The guerrillas stopped raiding into Mauritania at the end of 1978 and lifted the ceasefire only once, in July 1979, to attack a Mauritanian post inside Western Sahara. By August, Mauritania had relinquished its claim on the territory.

113 *. . . the name meant "water of the twin springs" . . . :* Lloyd Cabot Briggs, *Tribes of the Sahara* (Cambridge, Mass.: Harvard University Press, 1960). By extension: "water of the eyes."

113 *He had settled for a time in Tindouf . . . :* This account of Ma el-Ainin is derived from Hodges, *Western Sahara*, pp. 55–60.

114 *"I have seen you completely." Smara, The Forbidden City; Being the Journal of Michel Vieuchange while Travelling among the Independent Tribes of South Morocco and Rio de Oro* (London: Methuen, 1933), p. 215.

114 . . . *Ma el-Ainin's declaration proved that every people . . .* : If it occurred to
Moroccan nationalists that Ma el-Ainin had seen the sultan less as a
political authority than as the defender of western Islam in what the
sheikh construed as a holy war, this distinction was easily overcome by
arguing that the Commander of Islam *was* the sole political authority. See
the discussion by George Joffé, "The International Court of Justice and
the Western Sahara Dispute," in Lawless and Monahan, *War and Refugees*.

117. *"the Rude Ruler of Morocco"*: "Good riddance," London, *The Sun*, 18 July
1987.

118 *In 1981 Washington extended $33 million . . .* : For more information on
arms deliveries to Morocco see David Seddon, "Morocco at war," in
Lawless and Monahan, *War and Refugees*.

118 . . . *UNITA commandos received . . . some of the weapons . . .* : See Bridgland, *The War for Africa*, p. 14: "Morocco also gave Savimbi arms which
dropped off the back of trucks delivered by the United States for King
Hassan's war against the Polisario Front in the former Spanish Sahara."
See also Ellis and Sechaba, *Comrades against Apartheid*, p. 110. Ellis and
Sechaba suggest that weaponry provided by Morocco to UNITA came
from Saudi Arabia.

119 . . . *Riyadh provided anything between $500 million and $1 billion a year:*
Damis, *Conflict in Northwest Africa*, p. 122.

133 *He described a vicious antitribalism in Tindouf.*: Omar Hadrami's story is
taken from an interview he gave to *Jeune Afrique*, no. 1503, November
1989.

134 *El Ouali had been for integration . . .* : On El-Ouali's early views, see
Hodges, *Western Sahara*, pp. 158–59: "In Rabat El-Ouali formed a loosely
structured collective of Sahrawi students. At first they did not specifi-
cally advocate the establishment of an independent Western Saharan
state. . . . Indeed . . . they worked hard in 1971–72 to lobby support
from the Moroccan opposition parties that were the standard bearers of
the Greater Morocco cause." On El-Ouali and Qaddafi, see Hodges,
Western Sahara, p. 162: "El-Ouali, who first visited Libya sometime in
1972 or early in 1973 . . . later remarked that 'we came to Libya barefoot,
we left armed.' And Qaddafi himself remarked in 1976 that, when the
Polisario guerrilla campaign began in 1973, 'The Libyan Arab Republic
fulfilled its Arab national duty by furnishing arms to the front and setting
up an office for it in Tripoli.' "

135 . . . *a mission force . . .* : in accordance with U.N. Security Council Resolution 690, April 1991. The team is known as MINURSO: Mission for
the Referendum in Western Sahara.

136 *In June 1991, the king released a batch of detained Sahrawis . . .* : "About 300
Sahrawi civilian prisoners," according to Hodges, MRG Update, 1991.
Many detained Sahrawis remain unaccounted for, however. On human
rights abuses by Morocco in Western Sahara, see *Morocco: A Pattern of
Political Imprisonment, Disappearances and Torture* (London: Amnesty In-

ternational, March 1991), pp. 40–41: "In November 1987 over 300 people in El-Ayoun were arrested just before a visit by the King. But the largest number of arrests, numbering many hundreds, took place in the years immediately after Morocco took possession of the territory. . . . Eighty-eight of these cases were investigated by Amnesty International groups and have been raised countless times with Moroccan authorities without receiving any substantive reply."

136 *By the end of 1991, the peace process was in deep trouble.*: A detailed account of the collapse of the U.N. effort can be found in a staff report by George A. Pickart to Senator Claiborne Pell, Chairman of the Committee on Foreign Relations, U.S. Senate, in January 1992. The report argues that "MINURSO finds itself attempting to carry out its duties, but without the necessary political backing of the U.N. and without the full cooperation of Morocco"; that the "obstructionist posture" of Morocco has led to the delay of vital supplies to the MINURSO team and that the mission has been compromised by financial irregularities: U.S. $58 million was said by the U.N. deputy special representative to have been spent in only four months, while the MINURSO command maintained that the figure was "grossly inaccurate."

4. SOUTH AFRICA

Much of this section is informed by material from the press, in particular *The Financial Times*, *The Guardian* and *The Independent*, London, and *The Weekly Mail*, Johannesburg. Also *SouthScan: A Bulletin of Southern African Affairs*, London. There is a large and readily available literature on South Africa, to which recent, notable additions include Nomavenda Mathiane, *Beyond the Headlines: Truths of Soweto Life* (Johannesburg: Southern Book Publishers, 1990); Rian Malan, *My Traitor's Heart* (London: The Bodley Head, 1990); Allister Sparks, *The Mind of South Africa: The Story of the Rise and Fall of Apartheid* (London: Heinemann, 1990); Sebastian Mallaby, *After Apartheid* (London: Faber and Faber, 1992); and Noel Mostert, *Frontiers: The Epic of South Africa's Creation and the Tragedy of the Xhosa People* (London: Jonathan Cape, 1992). *Time Longer than Rope: The Black Man's Struggle for Freedom in South Africa* by Edward Roux (Madison: University of Wisconsin Press, 1978), remains one of the best introductions to South African history. The first edition was published in 1948, and the second in 1961, five years before the author's death.

144 *His case had been written up in the* Weekly Mail: Thandeka Gqubule, "Nights of Gunfire in Angola, by a Man Who Said 'No' to It," *Weekly Mail*, 22–28 September 1989.

147 . . . *about the time of the South African assaults on the Tumpo Triangle* . . . : A lengthy account of Operation Hooper, consisting of the first two assaults on the Tumpo Triangle, and Operation Packer, which involved the third, is given by Heitman, *War in Angola*, pp. 245–380.

150 . . . *the outrage of the British concentration camps* . . . : See Thomas Pakenham, *The Boer War* (London: Weidenfeld and Nicolson, 1979), Chapter
39, "When Is a War Not a War?" Pakenham quotes Emily Hobhouse
after her visit to Bloemfontein camp in April 1901: "I began to compare
a parish I had known at home of 2,000 people where a funeral was an
event—and usually of an old person. Here some twenty to twenty-five
people were carried away daily . . . it was a death rate such as had never
been known except in the times of the Great Plagues . . . the whole talk
was of death—who died yesterday, who lay dying today, who would be
dead tomorrow." See also Brian Roberts, *Those Bloody Women: Three Her-
oines of the Boer War* (London: John Murray, 1991), especially Chapter 10,
"A Camp in the Transvaal."

160 . . . *armored cars sold to Morocco by Pretoria* . . . : A version of the French
AML-90 manufactured in South Africa. See Victoria Brittain, *Hidden
Lives, Hidden Deaths* (London: Faber and Faber, 1988), p. 41.

160 *During the 1980s the security apparatus* . . . : During the 1980s the State
Security Council, a combination of Chief of Staff Intelligence (the South
African Defence Force) and the South African Police, played the dominant role in affairs of state. The SSC was a cabinet committee with a
secretariat consisting mostly of SADF members. Its predominance during these years led to an entrenched security culture in South Africa that
remained in place after President de Klerk's reforms in 1990. By 1992 the
president could depend only on the loyalty of National Intelligence staff,
who constituted less than a quarter of the SSC secretariat. If de Klerk had
ever wished to embark on a purge of the security forces, this would have
been a formidable obstacle. See, for instance, Shaun Johnson, "Beware
Night of the Generals," *Johannesburg Star*, 25 August 1992. According to
Colonel Gert Cornelius Hugo, who resigned his intelligence post in 1991,
all heads of SADF units received a "top secret signal from Pretoria"
shortly after Mandela's release the previous year. "The hidden message—
but it was absolutely clear—was that we had to make contingency plans
for a total military take-over. . . . My officer commanding, for example,
envisaged martial law."

163 *In its fascination with murder and disorder* . . . : On publication in South
Africa, *My Traitor's Heart* by Rian Malan, subtitled *Blood and Dreams: A
South African Explores the Madness in His Country, His Tribe and Himself*, sold
over ten thousand copies and went on to become a stock item in paper-
back.

163 *The promise of an end to the sports boycott* . . . : And, for Afrikaners, a return
to international rugby above all. "The pursuit of inflated leather by thirty
sweating endomorphs should not by rights have much to do with anything. But to think so is profoundly to misjudge the place of rugby in the
white South African, and particularly Afrikaner, psyche": Drew Forrest,
"Why the Wallabies Must Win," *Weekly Mail*, 21–27 August 1992. When
the New Zealand All Blacks toured South Africa, two months after the
Boipatong massacre in June 1992, the ANC requested a minute's silence

before the final game at Ellis Park, to commemorate those who had died in the township violence. The request was ignored; instead the crowd burst into a rendering of the Afrikaner national anthem, "Die Stem," which praises "the creak of the ox wagon" and readiness to lay down one's life for the Afrikaner nation. The South African team, the Springboks, lost 27–24.

166 . . . *it was clear that she would later have to stand trial herself.*: Winnie Mandela was brought to trial the following year. In May 1991 the Rand Supreme Court found her guilty of kidnapping and being an accessory to the assault of four of the youths abducted from the manse. In July she was given leave to appeal her conviction—and the six-year sentence that went with it. In June 1993, the South African appeals court reduced Mrs. Mandela's sentence to a fine of fifteen thousand rand (approximately five thousand dollars) and a suspended prison term of two years. Her reaction was described as "ecstatic." Nelson Mandela also expressed relief at the outcome of the appeal.

172 *A reliable newspaper . . . :* Philippa Garson, "How the Trojan Horse Drove into 'Vietnam,' " *Weekly Mail*, 18–24 May 1990.

174 *Pane's family was already on the Coetzee farm by then:* Details have been added to Pane Moshounyane's story from a short manuscript of his own.

181 *There was some truth in this . . . :* For detailed allegations of police collusion with Inkatha, see *The Killings in South Africa: The Role of the Security Forces and the Response of the State* (London, Washington and New York: Africa Watch, January 1991). The report is based on affidavits gathered by local human rights groups and some forty eyewitness testimonies.

182 . . . *as their predecessors had destabilized the postcolonial governments of Angola and Mozambique.*: "Destabilization" was the cornerstone of P. W. Botha's "total strategy." Formulated at the end of the 1970s, the "total strategy" presupposed a "total onslaught" against South Africa by "communism," since the ANC, SWAPO, the MPLA and Frelimo received support from the Eastern bloc. The State Security Council took charge of the total strategy, deploying death squads in South Africa and neighboring states. UNITA and Renamo were instruments of the much broader military destabilization in Angola and Mozambique. See Phyllis Johnson and David Martin, eds., *Destructive Engagement: Southern Africa at War* (Harare: Zimbabwe Publishing House, 1986).

5. MOZAMBIQUE

Background material for this section is derived from Allen and Barbara Isaacman, *Mozambique: From Colonialism to Revolution 1900–1982* (Boulder, Colo.: Westview, 1983); Joseph Hanlon, *Mozambique: The Revolution under Fire* (London: Zed Books, 1984); Eduardo Mondlane, *The Struggle for Mozambique* (Harmondsworth: Penguin Books, 1969); Karl Maier with Kemal Mustafa and Alex Vines, *Conspicuous Destruction: War, Famine and the Reform Process in Mozambique* (New York, Washington, Los Angeles and London: Africa

Watch, 1992); William Finnegan, *A Complicated War: The Harrowing of Mozambique* (Berkeley and Oxford: University of California Press, 1992); also from journals and newspapers, in particular *AIM Information Bulletin*, subsequently *Mozambiquefile*, Maputo, published by the Agência de Informação de Moçambique; *The Independent* and *The Guardian*, London, and *The Weekly Mail*, Johannesburg.

For the encounter between traditional belief systems and modern political struggle in the region, see David Lan's play *Desire* (London: Faber and Faber, 1990) and, by the same author, *Guns and Rain: Guerrillas and Spirit Mediums in Zimbabwe* (Harare: Zimbabwe Publishing House, 1985). For background to Zambézia province, see Leroy Vail and Landeg White, *Capitalism and Colonialism in Mozambique: A Study of Quelimane District* (London: Heinemann, 1980). R. C. F. Maugham, *Zambézia: A General Description* was published in 1910 by John Murray.

For investigative research into Renamo, its *modus operandi* and its sources of funding, see Alex Vines, *Renamo: Terrorism in Mozambique* (York: Centre for Southern African Studies/James Currey, 1991) and Anders Nilsson, *Unmasking the Bandits: The True Face of the MNR* (London: European Campaign against South African Aggression on Mozambique and Angola/UK, 1990). Published material in the United States and Britain in defense of Renamo is rare and often fanciful. See, for example, Jillian Becker, "Graveyard Mozambique," London, *Salisbury Review*, December 1987, and David Hoile, *Mozambique: A Nation in Crisis* (London: Claridge Press, 1989).

197 *As a quid pro quo, Rhodesia trained and supervised* . . . : The independence of Mozambique and Angola marked a decisive shift in the regional power balance and spelled the end of minority rule in Rhodesia. For the war in Zimbabwe and the implications of Frelimo's success, see Paul Hotz's novel *Muzukuru* (Johannesburg: Ravan Press, 1990): "Samora Machel gave Zanla bases up and down the length of the border, all 1,100 kilometres of it. The border areas were ideal for guerrillas. . . . Ya, to those who thought carefully about these things, after the Mozambique coup Rhodesia began to look quite vulnerable, very vulnerable indeed."

202 *Mozambique had joined the International Monetary Fund (IMF) and the World Bank in 1984.*: For a detailed discussion of the role of the international lending agencies, see Joseph Hanlon,"What Kind of Economy?" Part III, *Mozambique: Who Calls the Shots?* (London: James Currey, 1991).

203 *For many people in Maputo life was harder.*: This discussion of the effects of World Bank and IMF policies is based on interviews in 1991 with Kerry Sylvester, a nutritionist at the Mozambican Ministry of Health, and Iain Levine of UNICEF; also Hanlon,"The Road to Structural Adjustment," *Mozambique: Who Calls the Shots?*

206 *Trying to read the signs of donor fatigue* . . . : But see Hanlon, *Mozambique: Who Calls the Shots?*, p. 62, for another interpretation of cutbacks in Mozambique's appeal: "Some sources cited donor weariness, but others saw it as pressure on Mozambique to make further concessions to Renamo in the sporadic peace talks." This idea was fraught with dangers,

however, since it implied that Frelimo's humanitarian aid receipts were contributing greatly to its political and defense posture—that there might, in other words, be no real difference between Frelimo and the regime in Ethiopia, for whom aid was clearly a disincentive to negotiate with armed rebel movements.

206 *... a procession of lesser statistics ... :* these can be found in *Figures: Mozambique* (Maputo: Bureau of Public Information, 1990) and *The Situation of Children and Women in Mozambique* (Maputo, Ministry of Co-operation/UNICEF, 1990).

207 *They were grist to the CIO's mill.:* See discussion at length by Ken Flower, *Serving Secretly: An Intelligence Chief on Record, Rhodesia into Zimbabwe, 1964–1981* (London: John Murray, 1987).

207 *... local witch doctors, or* curandeiros, *misled him ... :* This story is told by Hanlon, *Mozambique: The Revolution Under Fire*, p. 229, and repeated by Anders Nilsson, *Unmasking the Bandits.*

208 *"the material and ideological base of a socialist society.":* The Constitution that came into force at independence named "the building of people's democracy and the material and ideological base of a socialist society" as one of five fundamental objectives to which the republic was pledged.

208 *... a French ethnographer called Christian Geffray ... :* Geffray began his field work in Mozambique in 1983, under the auspices of the Mondlane University in Maputo and with the cooperation of the government. His two years in Eráti satisfied him that there was a direct link between Frelimo's villagization policies and the growth of support for Renamo. He argued, on the basis of another stay in Eráti at the end of the 1980s, that Renamo had managed to build a popular base on the disaffection caused by Frelimo. He believed, however, that the local population "mistook" the character of Renamo, which was not a political organization and could never bring tangible improvements to their lives. His book, *La cause des armes au Mozambique* (Paris: Khartala), was published in 1990. In Maputo it aroused keen interest. It could not be dismissed, like most works of journalism by foreign writers, as another superficial gloss on the country, but it was by no means uncritical of Frelimo. Polemic and blame were absent, however. Instead, the book asked its readers to consider what institutions of modern civil society could be introduced in a rural community such as Eráti, whose own were well established, without the kind of upheaval that Geffray described. By the time of publication, this question had begun to preoccupy all but the most entrenched elements of the Mozambican and expatriate intelligentsia.

210 *Far from being left to fend for itself ... :* See remarks by Ken Flower of the Rhodesian (and then Zimbabwean) CIO in Maier with Vines and Mustafa for Africa Watch, *Conspicuous Destruction*, p. 26: "It had to be clear [to the MNR] that there were to be no further links with Zimbabwe. But I knew from previous approaches that the South Africans could be interested. So the members of the resistance were told that there was an alternative. . . . We made the arrangements . . . to effect a transfer to the

South Africans." By 1982 the insurgency had incorporated Africa Livre, another minor armed grouping, and the South Africans were putting pressure on Malawi to accept insurgent bases on its border with Mozambique.

210 *"low-intensity" conflict:* a fashionable term during the 1980s for the kind of wars prosecuted by superpowers, global or regional, in underdeveloped countries. Typically, a low-intensity conflict involved a minimal commitment of combat personnel and a preference for surrogate forces on the ground: insurgencies or trained counterinsurgency units working with advisers. Equally typically, such conflicts took civilian communities as legitimate targets. "Depending on where one is and what role one plays, a 'low-intensity conflict' may seem extremely intense": William E. Odom, *On Internal War: American and Soviet Approaches to Third World Clients and Insurgents* (Durham, N.C., and London: Duke University Press, 1992).

211 *Machel was killed in a plane crash in 1986:* The case against South Africa is made eloquently by Iain Christie in the introduction to *Machel of Mozambique* (Harare: Zimbabwe Publishing House, 1988).

211 *. . . a damning report on Renamo . . . :* Robert Gersony, *Mozambique Refugee Accounts of Principally Conflict-Related Experiences in Mozambique* (U.S. Department of State, Washington, D.C.: 1988).

214 *There were nine member countries in the Southern African Development Coordination Conference:* SADCC first convened in Tanzania in 1979. During the 1990s, its outstanding success was in raising funds for regional development projects. It was a vociferous opponent of apartheid South Africa, which had destroyed much of the infrastructure in member states. After 1990, the independence of Namibia—which became a member—and political changes in South Africa foreshadowed a wider and less oppositional role for the organization. In 1992, it recast itself as the Southern African Development Community.

214 *. . . said to be protected by an arrangement between the company and Renamo.:* The following year, 1989, Renamo announced it would refrain from attacks on the Nacala line, further north, and this too was rumored to be the result of a deal with Lonrho (LONdon-RHOdesia). See Finnegan, *A Complicated War*, p. 311. Finnegan also refers to Lonrho's "links to Defence Systems Limited, the British firm charged with protecting the [Nacala] railway." It seems likely that DSL was paid indirectly by Lonrho through the Mozambican state tea company, EMOCHÀ. Lonrho has also fielded a private defense team of its own on the Beira corridor. Its stake in Mozambican agriculture and mining, and thus in a profitable peace, is high; Tiny Rowland, the Managing Director of Lonrho, used his own jet to fly Afonso Dhlakama to Rome for the last stages of the peace talks in August 1992.

220 *Even President Chissano agreed that Renamo was no longer subsidized by the government of the new South Africa . . . :* Allegations of SADF deliveries to Renamo persisted, however. See Chris McGreal,"Pretoria Gave Arms to Renamo Last Year," *The Independent*, London, 24 February 1992. The source for the story was the U.S. Defense Intelligence Agency.

220 *Having invested millions of rand in the upgrading of Maputo port . . . : Mozam-bique Country Profile 1990–91* (London: Economist Intelligence Unit). The money (roughly £1.3 million sterling) went into port management and handling facilities. At the time of the report, South Africa had expressed interest in contributing further funds to a plan for major rehabilitation work, drawn up by a South African consulting firm.

223 . . . *"The Eighteenth Brumaire":* "The Eighteenth Brumaire of Louis Bo-naparte" by Karl Marx, written in 1852 and widely acknowledged to be one of the most readable texts in the canon.

232 . . . *each time [Rodrigues Laïce] was able to relate it in finer detail . . . :* There were also interesting differences. See Maier with Mustafa and Vines for Africa Watch, *Conspicuous Destruction*, pp. 47–48.

235 . . . *a little village called Micajuna.:* the name given by the Naparamas to the village. Discrepancies in various maps of Zambézia are compounded by the fact that fleeing communities often name their new point of set-tlement after the place they have left. The Micajuna that Xavier and I entered, on the outskirts of Nicoadala, did not correspond to either of the locations we identified on maps of the province.

250 . . . *a man they called Nambila.:* a different name to the one by which Manuel António's second-in-command had been identified in other parts of the province.

255 *Manuel António was wielding a rifle . . . :* And later remarked that, while Naparamas were not supposed to bear firearms, he was entitled to famil-iarize them with combat conditions by shooting into the air as they ran ahead of him.

256 *"He is saying Naparama isn't beaten . . .":* Also recorded by Adrian Pennink and Karl Maier, *The World This Week*, Channel Four Television, London, July 1991.

258 *"Mr. António met his death . . . :"* Agência de Informação de Moçambique, 7 December 1991.

6. Eritrea

Background material for this chapter is drawn from the following books: René Lefort, *Ethiopia: An Heretical Revolution?* (London: Zed Books, 1983); Anthony Mockler, *Haile Selassie's War* (Oxford: Oxford University Press, 1984); James Firebrace and Stuart Holland, *Eritrea: Never Kneel Down* (Not-tingham: Spokesman, 1984); Amrit Wilson, *The Challenge Road: Women and the Eritrean Revolution* (London: Earthscan, 1991); Dawit Wolde Giorgis, *Red Tears* (Trenton, N.J.: Red Sea Press, 1989); Roy Pateman, *Eritrea: Even the Stones are Burning* (Trenton, N.J.: Red Sea Press, 1990); and Bereket Habte Selassie, *Conflict and Intervention in the Horn of Africa* (New York: Monthly Review Press, 1990).

For a sympathetic approach to the Ethiopian revolution, see Fred Hal-liday and Maxine Molyneux, *The Ethiopian Revolution* (London: Verso, 1981); for a defense of Ethiopia's conduct during the famine of 1984–1985, see Germaine Greer, "Ethiopia between the Lines," *The Listener*, London, 24 October 1985, and "Resettlement, Ethiopia, 1985," in *The Mad Woman's Underclothes: Essays and Occasional Writings* (London: Pan Books, 1986).

But the most remarkable recent book on Ethiopia and Eritrea is *Evil Days: 30 Years of War and Famine in Ethiopia* by Alex de Waal for Africa Watch (New York, Los Angeles, London and Washington, 1991). This chapter makes extensive use of Africa Watch findings, in particular Chapter 2, "Scorched Earth in Eritrea," and Chapter 7, "Total War in Eritrea." From the mid-1970s to the early 1980s, *The Financial Times*, London, published frequently on Eritrea. Reports by Dan Connell have since appeared elsewhere, including *The Independent*, London. In France, Jean-Louis Péninou reported extensively during the late 1970s for *Libération* and others, and in Italy, Stefano Poggia continues to write on the subject. Many of the clippings are available from the EPLF's archives and this chapter is informed by reports from all three journalists.

262 *The colonial regiments fighting with the Allies had performed with distinction* . . . : But see Mockler, *Haile Selassie's War*, p. 324, on the disappointing performance of South African troops: "[Ethiopian] Irregulars judged the South Africans to be 'poor soldiers,' 'unwilling to close,' and 'had a very poor opinion of them.' The men of the Natal Mounted Rifles sold their boots to the Ethiopians and the crews of the South African armoured cars mowed down whole herds of oryx with their machine guns."

263 *The British . . . dismantled and sold much of the industrial plant* . . . : See James Firebrace, "The British Responsibility Towards Eritrea and the Moral Responsibility of the International Community," in *Eritrea: The Way Forward* (London, United Nations Association/UK, 1986): "£86 million worth of equipment was removed from Eritrea by the British. . . . This involved the dismantling of important port facilities at Massawa and Assab, as well as of a cement factory, a potash factory, a salt processing plant, and the removal of a lot of railway equipment." Sylvia Pankhurst toured Eritrea shortly before federation. In Massawa she counted around seventy-five installations destroyed by the British. "All these fine buildings and installations which had been erected in the heyday of Mussolini's Empire had been ruthlessly demolished and sold for what could be obtained for the scrap metal and the woodwork of the doors and window frames." Her companion, Mohammed Omar Khadi, remarked that it was a disgrace to British civilization. "His words affected me painfully, like blows, so just they were in my opinion. I was grieved and downhearted." E. S. Pankhurst, *Eritrea on the Eve*, Woodford Green, "New Times and Ethiopian Times," *Books*, 1952, pp.14–15.

264 *"The General Assembly," said the Soviet representative* . . . : Soviet defense of draft resolution A/1570, Fifth Plenary Session of the U.N. General Assembly, 1950.

264 *"From the point of view of justice . . ."*: Dulles's remarks were addressed to a session of the U.N. Security Council and are quoted by Abdul Rahman Mohamed Babu in "Eritrea: Its Present is the Remote Future of Others," in *Eritrea: The Way Forward*.

270   *. . . the largest army in Africa.*: The only other contender was South Africa, with half a million under arms (*The Military Balance 1989–90* [London, International Institute for Strategic Studies, 1989]), but this included Namibia's army of occupation, the South West Africa Territory Force. De Waal for Africa Watch, *Evil Days*, p. 291, estimates the size of the Ethiopian army at 450,000 in 1991. Wolde Giorgis, *Red Tears*, p. 70, adds a "paramilitary force of nearly 500,000 militiamen." In September 1991, EPLF General Secretary Isayas Aferwerki put the size of the EPLF fighting force at "almost 100,000," but this should probably be taken to include many thousands of EPLF members who were not bearing arms. The most commonly repeated figure, among Eritreans, for the numbers of EPLF and ELF killed in combat is 50,000. It is not clear whether this accounts for casualties in the fighting between the two movements during the early 1970s.

274   *Eritrea itself consisted of Christians and Muslims in roughly equal proportions.*: This was the EPLF official line, devised perhaps to play down any idea of religious difference. It is disputed by Wolde Giorgis, *Red Tears*, p. 73, who estimated 350,000 Muslims only in a population of two million. This did not necessarily include the hundreds of thousands of Eritrean refugees in Sudan and expatriates in the Gulf, many of them from the lowlands and therefore likely to be Muslims. EPLF estimates for the size of the population as a whole were of course much higher.

278   *In this, the ANC would be the most compliant . . . :* Although the vice president of the Permanent People's Tribunal, which concluded in favor of Eritrean self-determination in 1980, was South African activist Ruth First. Two years later she was killed by a letter bomb in Mozambique.

280   *The Israelis upgraded Soviet rockets and supplied the Dergue with cluster bombs, probably obtained from Chile:* See de Waal for Africa Watch, *Evil Days*, pp. 374–75: "Israeli officials at different times admitted to having supplied small arms, non-lethal military technology and training in counter-insurgency, and at other times denied giving any assistance. However, a confidential congressional staff memo leaked to *Washington Jewish Week* confirmed that in late 1989 about 100 cluster bombs were supplied, which the Ethiopian air force was particularly eager to have." That they came through the firm of Industrias Cardoen in Chile, which was also supplying military technology to Iraq until the invasion of Kuwait, is a view held by many, including Sabhat Efram, the EPLF's chief of General Military Staff at the time.

281   *Red Star was a failure . . . :* The account that follows is derived from an interview in 1990 with Sabhat Efram, and also from Wolde Giorgis, *Red Tears*, pp. 107–10.

281   *The Ethiopians estimated that nearly 100,000 government troops . . . had been killed or wounded in Eritrea since 1975.*: Wolde Giorgis, *Red Tears*, p. 113.

283   *"In Africa imperialism is hatching new political conspiracies . . .":* "The National Question in Eritrea," *EPLF Memorandum*, 1978.

284   *"the roots of the agony.":* Former Labour Party leader Neil Kinnock in a preface to Firebrace and Holland, *Eritrea: Never Kneel Down*, p. 10.

303 *The drought posed an unpleasant dilemma for the EPLF.*: See de Waal for Africa Watch, *Evil Days*, pp. 287–88.

318 *. . . the Groups of Seven . . .*: Also known as *Harakat Atahrir al Eritrya*, or the Eritrean Liberation Movement, organized in clandestine cells of seven members. During the 1960s the movement sought to establish an armed wing but the ELF was already active in Eritrea and scotched the idea. Wolde-ab remarked that, although invited to do so, he felt unable to play a leading role in the ELM because of its "communist" inclination.

ACRONYMS AND ORGANIZATIONS

This list is intended as a guide to the principal organizations and movements mentioned in the text.

ANGOLA

MPLA: Movimento Popular de Libertação de Angola (Popular Movement for the Liberation of Angola). Formed in 1956, the MPLA enjoyed widespread support in Luanda and among the Mbundu people. Its "armed struggle" was launched in 1961. Its first president was Mario de Andrade, who stepped down in 1962 in favor of Agostinho Neto. With support from the Soviet bloc—and subsequently Cuba—the MPLA led Angola to independence in 1975, when Neto was installed as the country's president. The MPLA constituted itself as a workers' party two years later. Neto died in 1979 and was replaced by his minister of planning, José Eduardo dos Santos, who headed the government through the worst period of the war and prepared the country for elections in September 1992.

FAPLA: Forças Armadas Popular para Libertação de Angola (Popular Armed Forces for the Liberation of Angola). Title conferred on the MPLA military in 1974. After independence, the Angolan national army. FAPLA was a highly influential component of the MPLA–Workers' Party. The peace agreement of 1991 entailed the dismantling of FAPLA and the formation of a new national army with personnel from FAPLA and UNITA's force, known as FALA.

UPNA: União das Populaçoes do Norte de Angola (Union of Peoples of Northern Angola). Formed in 1956, with a strong Bakongo base in the northwest and an ethnic agenda; led by Holden Roberto, Eduardo Pinnock and Manuel Nekaka. At the end of the 1950s it became the UPA.

UPA: União das Populaçoes de Angola (Union of Angolan Peoples). Under the leadership of Holden Roberto, UPA remained a Bakongo formation; its policy was one of unqualified hostility to the MPLA, whence the massacre of the MPLA column by UPA followers in 1961.

FNLA: Frente Nacional de Libertação de Angola (National Front for the Liberation of Angola). The next incarnation of the UPA, formed in 1962 under Holden Roberto and incorporating the Partido Democratico de Angola. Roberto scored an early success with the Organization of African Unity when it recognized his Revolutionary Government in Exile (GRAE). In the run-up to independence the FNLA received support from China and the United States but lost the battle with the MPLA for Luanda. By 1976 it was no longer a military force of any standing. Roberto put his name forward for presidential elections in 1992. The FNLA came in fourth in the legislative elections.

UNITA: União Nacional para a Independência Total de Angola (National Union for the Total Independence of Angola). Formed in 1966 by Jonas Savimbi, two years after he left the FNLA. UNITA was at first a small force confined to activity within the country. In the run-up to independence UNITA received covert aid from the United States but failed to impinge on the scene. After independence an alliance with South Africa and backing from the United States sustained UNITA until Savimbi signed a peace accord with the MPLA in 1991. UNITA came in second in the legislative elections and Savimbi lost the first round of the presidential elections by a sufficiently narrow margin to warrant a run-off, although by then, UNITA had already returned to the gun.

Namibia

OPC: Ovamboland People's Congress. Formed in the Cape in 1957 by expatriate Namibians, including Herman (Andimba) Toivo ja Toivo and Jacob Kuhangua, with close links to the African National Congress. The OPC was a nationalist caucus that believed that support for its ideas would come from African workers inside Namibia.

OPO: Ovamboland People's Organization. Founded in Windhoek in 1959 by Sam Nujoma and Jacob Kuhangua, it canvassed support in the fishing and mining industries. The forerunner of SWAPO.

SWAPO: South West Africa People's Organization. Formed in 1960, effectively banned after 1963, although it remained a legal organization. In 1966 it turned to armed struggle; two years later twenty of its leaders were sentenced to life imprisonment under the Terrorism Act. SWAPO of Namibia, as it became known, fought from bases in Zambia and, after 1975, Angola. It won elections in Namibia in 1989, ushering in the country's independence in 1990, and its leader, Sam Nujoma, became the first Namibian president.

WESTERN SAHARA

Harakat Tahrir: "independence organization," also known as the Muslim Party. Harakat Tahrir was formed at the end of the 1960s under the leadership of a Sahrawi teacher, Mohamed Bassiri, to agitate for decolonization. The organization drew its support from the towns. It was suppressed in 1970; Bassiri was detained and disappeared.

Polisario Front: Frente Popular para la Liberación de Saguia al Hamra y Río de Oro (Popular Front for the Liberation of Saguia el Hamra and Río de Oro). Formed in 1973 under the leadership of El Ouali Mustapha Sayed as an armed front against Spanish rule in the Western Sahara. When Spain ceded its colony to Morocco and Mauritania, Polisario continued fighting, with support from Algeria. El Ouali died in 1979 and was replaced by Mohamed Abdelaziz. Polisario proclaimed the occupied territory of Western Sahara to be a state—the Saharan Arab Democratic Republic—in 1976 and took a seat at the Organization of African Unity in 1983. In 1988 Morocco accepted the principle of a referendum and in 1991 the United Nations Security Council adopted the draft for a peace plan. By the end of 1992, with the referendum in jeopardy, Polisario was appealing to the international community to throw its weight behind the plan.

SOUTH AFRICA

ANC: African National Congress. Formed in 1912 as the South African Native National Congress, mainly composed of chiefs and educated black South African men. The ANC was radicalized soon after its formation by a struggle over land rights in 1913. In 1952, with the South African Indian Congress, it launched a passive defiance campaign against apartheid. In 1955 it took part in the Freedom Congress and adopted the Freedom Charter. It was outlawed in 1960 and in 1961 a number of its members opted for armed struggle. Their organization, Umkhonto weSizwe (Spear of the Nation), later became the "armed wing" of the ANC, operating from bases in the Frontline States. The ANC was unbanned in 1990. Since the mid-1920s it has retained close links with the Communist Party, several of whose members also serve on the ANC's National Executive. Nelson Mandela is the ANC president and Cyril Ramaphosa is secretary-general.

Inkatha: Zulu word for a woven coil placed on the head to support a heavy weight: by extension, that which bears up the Zulu nation. A defunct Zulu "cultural" organization revived by Chief Mangosuthu Buthelezi in 1975 and which has since become an instrument of Zulu political expression. Buthelezi was an ally of the ANC, on the "homelands" issue above all, until the end of the 1970s. By 1980 he had rejected armed struggle and sanctions. The war between the UDF/ANC and Inkatha began in the mid-1980s. In 1990 Buthelezi founded the Inkatha Freedom Party and claimed a membership of between one and two million. In July 1991 the "Inkathagate" scandal broke with proof of significant government funding for Inkatha rallies and for the pro-Inkatha trade union. Late in 1992 Buthelezi threatened a kwaZulu "secession" from South Africa and spoke of a "Yugoslavian" option for the country.

National Party. A "purified" party led by D. F. Malan that broke off in 1934 from the original National Party after it had fused with the South Africa Party. The National Party took power in 1948, introduced apartheid and won the referendum in 1960 that ended the Union. Under Verwoerd and then Vorster, it consolidated Afrikaner privilege and extended the sway of apartheid; under P. W. Botha, it witnessed a transfer of power from civilian institutions to the security apparatus. It fell in reluctantly behind F. W. de Klerk's reforms in 1990 and went on to campaign for their endorsement in a whites-only referendum two years later.

NUSAS: National Union of South African Students. The main English-speaking student organization.

PAC: The Pan-Africanist Congress. Formed in 1958 as a breakaway movement from the ANC. Its founders, led by Robert Sobukwe, argued that the land of South Africa belonged to "the African people," whereas the Freedom Charter, adopted two years earlier by the ANC, held that "all national groups" should have equal rights and that South Africa "belongs to all who live in it." Today the PAC is a small but influential force. Its motto is "One settler, one bullet." Its president is Clarence Makwetu.

SACP: South African Communist Party. Originally the Communist Party of South Africa, formed in 1921 to mobilize for a whites-only workers' state. In 1924 links with the ANC were formed through Josiah Gumede, who was elected CPSA president general three years later. The party was banned in 1950, restructured in 1953, becoming the SACP, and legalized in 1990. Throughout this period it held loyally to the doctrines of Marxism-Leninism and argued for a nonracial unitary South Africa. In April 1993, its secretary-general, Chris Hani, was murdered by a white extremist. Hani was replaced by his deputy, Charles Ngakula.

UDF: United Democratic Front. Formed in 1983 inside South Africa, a broad front for dozens of organizations, banned and legal, in support of the Freedom Charter, under the presidency of Archie Gumede, descendant of Josiah. The UDF carried its followers through the "unrest" of the mid-1980s; its aggressive campaigning in Natal incurred the wrath of Inkatha.

MOZAMBIQUE

Frelimo: Frente de Libertação de Moçambique (Front for the Liberation of Mozambique). Formed in 1962 and led by Eduardo Mondlane, it began the armed struggle against the Portuguese in 1964 and held its Second Congress in liberated territory inside Mozambique four years later. Mondlane was assassinated in 1969 and replaced by Samora Machel. Frelimo proclaimed independence in 1975 with Machel as the first president. It constituted itself as a workers' party two years later. Machel died in 1986 and was succeeded by the minister of foreign affairs, Joachim Alberto Chissano. Frelimo formally abandoned Marxism-Leninism at its Fifth Congress in 1989 and brought a new Constitution into effect at the end of 1990, guaranteeing private property, endorsing a multiparty system and universal suffrage. In 1992 it signed a peace accord with Renamo in Rome, and Britain offered to amalgamate the two military forces.

Renamo: Resistência Nacional Moçambicana (Mozambique National Resistance). Originally known as the MNR (Mozambique National Resistance), it took shape under the aegis of Rhodesian intelligence and dates its armed struggle against Frelimo from 1977. Its first leader, Andre Matsangaíssa, was killed in 1979, and succeeded by Afonso Dhlakama. After 1980 the movement was supported by South Africa. Large numbers of Renamo recruits were from the Ndau areas of central Mozambique. For over a decade, the movement made Frelimo's rule untenable in much of the country.

ETHIOPIA AND ERITREA

PMAC or Dergue: Provisional Military Administrative Council. The ruling military clique in Ethiopia, constituted after the overthrow of Haile Selassie in 1974. Dergue is an ancient Ge'ez word meaning "committee of equals." In 1987 a new constitution put a nominal end to the PMAC, but until the fall of Mengistu four years later, Ethiopia's rulers were still widely referred to as "the Dergue"—a term of contempt.

WPE: Workers' Party of Ethiopia. Inaugurated in 1984, a democratic centralist structure, whose own central committee was an expanded version of the Dergue's. At the outset, the majority of WPE members were military. Analogous to the Communist Party in the Soviet Union, the WPE brought many advantages to its members. While the EPLF disapproved of the WPE, card-carrying Eritreans were nonetheless able to help many families in difficulty during the war.

EPLF: Eritrean People's Liberation Front. Formed in 1970 as a democratic alternative to the ELF. By the mid-1970s it was the dominant front in Eritrea and, in 1977, in alliance with elements of the ELF, fought an arduous campaign that nearly resulted in military victory. It was driven back from the coastal town of Massawa in 1978 when the Soviet Union came to the rescue of the Dergue. The EPLF regrouped in the north, where it remained for a decade. In 1987, at its Second (Unity) Congress, its general secretary, Ramadan Nur, was replaced by Isayas Afeworki and it revised most of its Marxist-Leninist positions. In 1988 it began a steady push south and entered Asmara in May 1991, announcing that a referendum on independence would take place in 1993.

ELF: Eritrean Liberation Front. In formation by 1960, it opposed federation with Ethiopia and launched its first armed attack a year later. Inside Eritrea it was dominated by Muslim warlords. Within a few years, under the leadership of Idris Mohamed Adem, it had begun to fracture and in 1969 three groups split away to form the EPLF. The ELF lived on in various fragmentary forms, raising funds in the Gulf, but clashes between the ELF and the EPLF during the early 1970s left the latter in firm control of the field by 1975. In 1987 the EPLF held its Second Congress, known as the Unity Congress, because it concluded an alliance with a significant faction of the ELF, known as ELF-CL (Central Leadership).

TPLF: Tigray People's Liberation Front. A guerrilla army formed in Tigray in 1975, initially in opposition to Tigrayan overlords. The TPLF, in marked distinction to the Front in neighboring Eritrea, sought "autonomy" and self-determination *within* the boundaries of Ethiopia. By the end of the 1980s the TPLF was the major military force to oppose Mengistu in Ethiopia proper. After a period of hostility, the TPLF and the EPLF enjoyed close military cooperation, which hastened Mengistu's eventual downfall. In 1989 the TPLF spearheaded a broad anti-Mengistu alliance known as the Ethiopian People's Revolutionary Democratic Front.

EPRDF: Ethiopian People's Revolutionary Democratic Front. Formed in January 1989; an alliance of two armed movements, the TPLF and the Ethiopian People's Democratic Movement. Shortly afterward, other groupings joined the alliance and by 1989 the TPLF/EPRDF controlled most of Tigray. The EPRDF entered Addis Ababa on May 28, 1991, and took control of Ethiopia. The first head of the new transitional government was Meles Zenawi, a Tigrayan.

OTHER ORGANIZATIONS AND MOVEMENTS

OAU: Organization of African Unity. Established in 1963 in Addis Ababa "to promote unity and solidarity" among African states, after several earlier attempts to found an inter-African organization had failed. In its charter, the OAU pledged itself to defend the sovereignty, territorial integrity and independence of African states and "to eradicate all forms of colonialism from Africa." In 1964 the Assembly of Heads of State in Cairo returned to the issue of territorial integrity with a declaration acknowledging the "tangible reality" of colonial boundaries and pledging all member states to "respect the frontiers existing at the moment when they acceded to independence." A Coordinating Committee for the Liberation Movements of Africa—known as the African Liberation Committee—was set up in 1963 to provide financial and military aid to nationalist movements. Polisario, SWAPO and the ANC were the most recent beneficiaries of its dwindling funds. The headquarters of the OAU is in Addis Ababa. It consists of an annual Assembly of Heads of State, a Council of Ministers and a Secretariat. The secretary-general is elected for a four-year term by the Assembly of Heads of State. The OAU's initial membership of thirty-two countries has risen; the Saharan Arab Democratic Republic became the fifty-first member in 1983, prompting Morocco to leave the organization. Namibia joined on independence in 1990.

FLN: Front de Libération Nationale (Algeria). Formed in 1954 and assumed power in Algeria in 1962 after a conflict with the colonial power, France, estimated to have cost a million lives. The FLN went on to become the ruling party in Algeria, under three successive presidents. In 1991, planned elections were canceled after the threat of a fundamentalist victory at the polls. For thirty years, the FLN offered diplomatic facilities to many national liberation movements, and guerrilla training for much of this time. The FLN was held in high esteem in Africa, despite its waning popularity at home.

ZANU: Zimbabwe African National Union. Founded in 1963, one of the two main parties to fight for the independence of Zimbabwe. After 1975, under the leadership of Robert Mugabe, it operated from bases in Mozambique as part of the Patriotic Front, an alliance with Joshua Nkomo's Zimbabwe African People's Union. ZANU's army was known as ZANLA: Zimbabwe African National Liberation Army. ZANU became the ruling party of Zimbabwe after independence in 1980 with Robert Mugabe as prime minister. Mugabe provided several thousand Zimbabwean troops to support Frelimo in Mozambique during the 1980s and used his influence to hasten the Mozambican peace accords signed in 1992.

GLOSSARY

Angola, Mozambique

assimilado: under Portuguese rule, an "assimilated" African; *assimilados* received an education after renouncing their "uncivilized" background

barama: or *naparama:* the name of the vaccine that rendered Manuel António's followers bullet proof. Once vaccinated, they became known as *Baramas.*

capulana: a length of cloth, usually cotton, often brightly colored, normally tied at the waist or at the back to carry children

candonga: the general term for all transactions, great or small, in Angola's informal sector. By extension, "corruption."

canhoeiro: a tall deciduous tree yielding a fruit used to make liquor

curandeiro: a traditional healer with powers of divination

kachaso: local brew

machamba: a plot of cultivable land

mestiço: someone of mixed race

musseques: urban shantytowns mostly inhabited by black Angolans

naparama: see *barama*

obscurantismo: obscurantism

o povo: the people

régulo: a local chief in Mozambique with obligations to the Portuguese under colonial administration

tontonto: local brew

twaha: a cultural dance performed in parts of Mozambique

Western Sahara

haboub: dust storm

shadoof: a water pump with a lateral beam and counterweight

Namibia, South Africa

dagga: marijuana
impipi: informer
muti: magic
nyanga (inyanga): a herbalist
panga: a machete: a broad-bladed implement used for cutting crops or under-
    growth
sangoma: a traditional healer with powers of divination
toyi-toyi: a militant dance associated with followers of the ANC
tsotsi: a township thug
volk: Afrikaner term for "the people"

Eritrea

habash: highland
injera: a sour bread made from teff or aid grain
shifta: brigand or bandit
siwa (sewa): a liquor made from grain and yeast
teff (tef): Eragrostis abyssinica, a staple crop in Ethiopia and Eritrea

INDEX